Helga Köhnen
Deutsch-englisches Glossar der Jugendhilfe
German-English Glossary of Youth Services

Helga Köhnen

Deutsch-englisches Glossar der Jugendhilfe

Ein vergleichendes Handbuch

German-English Glossary of Youth Services

A Comparative Handbook

Juventa Verlag Weinheim und München 1992

Die Autorin
Helga Köhnen, Jg. 1939, M.A., Dipl.-Übers., ist Leiterin des Sprachendienstes
des IJAB e.V.. Schwerpunkte ihrer Arbeit sind vergleichende Untersuchungen und die Erstellung von Fachterminologien im Bereich der Jugendhilfe.
Sie ist Autorin des ersten „Deutsch-englischen Glossars der Jugendhilfe"
(IJAB, 1973) und Mitautorin des „Glossars der Jugendarbeit, Deutsch-Französisch" (Neuwied 1979).

Die Deutsche Bibliothek — CIP-Einheitsaufnahme

Köhnen, Helga:
Deutsch-englisches Glossar der Jugendhilfe : ein
vergleichendes Handbuch — German-English glossary of youth
services / Helga Köhnen. — Weinheim ; München : Juventa
Verlag 1992
    ISBN 3-7799-0475-6
NE: HST

© 1992 Juventa Verlag Weinheim und München
Umschlaggestaltung: Atelier Warminski, 6470 Büdingen 8
Printed in Germany

ISBN 3-7799-0475-6

Eine Veröffentlichung des
Internationalen Jugendaustausch-
und Besucherdienstes
der Bundesrepublik Deutschland (IJAB) e.V.

A Publication of the
International Youth Exchange
and Visitors' Service
of the Federal Republic of Germany (IJAB)

Vorwort

Über 15.000 britische und deutsche Jugendliche nehmen seit mehr als zwanzig Jahren jährlich an öffentlich geförderten bi- und multilateralen Austauschprogrammen teil. Für die Bundesrepublik Deutschland ist der deutsch-britische Jugendaustausch der größte nach dem deutsch-französischen.

Dies bedarf der fachkundigen Begleitung und Koordination der zuständigen Fachkräfte der Jugendarbeit und des Jugendaustausches. Vielfach ergibt sich die Notwendigkeit der genauen Übertragung von Fachbegriffen in die Sprache des Partners. Selten ist dann die wörtliche Übersetzung von Nutzen. Ein spezialisiertes deutsch-englisches Wörterbuch ist deshalb für die Praxis unentbehrlich. Es hilft, einen Fachbegriff in den nationalen Kontext des Partnerlandes einzuordnen. Es macht so die Diskussion straffer, Zusammenkünfte effektiver und erleichtert schon die Vorbereitung.

Ich begrüße diese Arbeit als einen Beitrag zum besseren gegenseitigen Verständnis zwischen unseren beiden Ländern auf dem Gebiet der Jugendhilfe und wünsche ihr eine weite Verbreitung.

Dr. Angela Merkel
Bundesministerin für Frauen und Jugend

Foreword

For more than twenty years over 15,000 young Britons and Germans have been taking part annually in bilateral and multilateral exchange programmes supported from public funds. Only our youth exchanges with France can boast more participants.

Programmes of this kind require professional guidance and coordination. In order to ensure proper communication, specialist terms must be accurately rendered in the language of the exchange partner. Literal translation is rarely adequate. Thus, a specialised German-English dictionary is indispensable to those concerned with the implementation of youth exchanges. It will help to place a technical term in the national context of the partner country. Adequate terminology will make discussions more concise, meetings more efficient and the preparation of exchange programmes less difficult.

I welcome the Glossary as a means of promoting better understanding amongst those involved in youth work and youth welfare services in our two countries, and I would be delighted if this publication were to achieve a wide circulation.

Dr. Angela Merkel
Federal Minister for Women and Youth

Inhalt

Teil I Übersichten

Teil II Glossar

Teil III Handbuch

Anhang

Table of Contents

Einführung

Das „Deutsch-englische Glossar der Jugendhilfe" ist ein zweisprachiges Handbuch, in dem die deutschen Begriffe nicht nur übersetzt, sondern — wenn erforderlich — auch inhaltlich den englischen gegenübergestellt werden.

Es ist für die Zwecke der internationalen Jugendarbeit konzipiert und orientiert sich an den Bedürfnissen der Teilnehmer von Fachprogrammen im Bereich der Jugendhilfe. Das Glossar soll deutschen und britischen Jugendleitern, Fachkräften der Jugendarbeit, Übersetzern und Dolmetschern helfen, bei Begegnungen, Konferenzen und Seminaren des deutsch-britischen Jugendaustausches zu einer terminologisch präzisen und inhaltlich richtigen Kommunikation zu gelangen. Ferner kann es allen, die sich über die Jugendhilfe in Deutschland und Großbritannien orientieren wollen, als nützliche Informationsquelle dienen.

Die Dreiteilung des Glossars und vergleichenden Handbuchs soll dem Benutzer den Einstieg erleichtern. Die beiden, dem lexikographischen Teil II (Glossar) vorangestellten Übersichten im Teil I ermöglichen es dem Benutzer, die zahlreichen Einzelinformationen des Teils III (Handbuch) in einen Gesamtkontext zu stellen. Ein schnelles Nachschlagen von Fachbegriffen der Jugendhilfe gestattet der Glossar-Teil, der Querverweise auf den Handbuch-Teil enthält. Dieser umfaßt in alphabetischer Reihenfolge ca. 100 Schlüsselbegriffe der Jugendhilfe mit zum Verständnis des Begriffs und seines britischen Gegenstücks erforderlichen Erläuterungen. Hinzu treten einige wenige Stichwörter aus anderen Bereichen, die Hintergrundinformationen anbieten. Die langjährige Praxis des Internationalen Jugendaustausch- und Besucherdienstes der Bundesrepublik Deutschland (IJAB) e.V. hat gezeigt, daß z. B. ein gewisses Verständnis von Staatsaufbau, Verwaltung und Bildungswesen gewährleistet sein muß, um die Strukturen der Jugendhilfe und des *youth service* besser überblicken zu können.

Eine schematische Darstellung des deutschen und englischen Bildungswesens (einschl. Wales), eine Zusammenstellung der für die Jugendarbeit relevanten Altersgrenzen sowie das Literaturverzeichnis runden das Werk ab.

Die Konzeption für das Glossar hat der Sprachendienst des IJAB entwickelt. Von hier aus wurden auch die Abstimmung der vom IJAB verfaßten Texte für das Handbuch mit den jeweils zuständigen Ministerien und Fachstellen im In- und Ausland, die Übersetzungen sowie die redaktionellen Arbeiten vorgenommen.

Eine Redaktionsgruppe, bestehend aus deutschen und britischen Fachkräften der Jugend- und Sozialarbeit, erarbeitete unter der Leitung der Verfasserin einen Teil der Textentwürfe sowohl für die deutsche als auch die britische Seite und überprüfte die Übersetzungen.

Der Redaktionsgruppe gehörten an Desmond McGlynn, MBE (Chairman, Joint Steering Group, Youth Exchange Centre, London), Christine Jenkins

Introduction

The "German-English Glossary of Youth Services" is a bilingual dictionary of special terms providing not only translations but also definitions where necessary.

It is designed for international youth work purposes. The Glossary is based on the needs of those participating in exchange programmes organised in the field of youth work and youth welfare services in Germany and the United Kingdom.

The subdivision of the Glossary into three parts is designed to facilitate orientation. The two surveys of Part I, preceding the terminology Part II (Glossary of Terms), will enable the reader to place in a wider context the various data given in the Handbook, Part III. Those wishing to look up a special term quickly will find it in the Glossary of Terms, with a possible cross reference to the Handbook part, which comprises about 100 key terms of youth work and youth welfare services, listed in alphabetical order and followed in each case by explanations of the respective entry as well as its British equivalent. The Handbook also contains headings taken from other areas, which have been included in order to provide background information. Many years of practical experience made the editing staff of the International Youth Exchange and Visitors' Service of the Federal Republic of Germany (IJAB) realise that some basic information, e.g. on the structural set-up of the State, administration and education system, will facilitate understanding of *Jugendhilfe* and the youth service.

A diagram of the German and English education systems respectively (including Wales), an overview of age limits relevant to youth work, and a list of publications are included as appendices.

The concept of the Glossary was developed by the Language Section of IJAB. The drafts of the texts for the Handbook which were written by IJAB were agreed with the German and British ministries and agencies concerned. The Language Section was also responsible for translating the original texts into English and German respectively and for editing of the Glossary.

A committee of German and British specialists in youth and social work, chaired by the head of the Language Section, drafted part of the explanatory articles (both German and English) and revised the translations.

Members of the committee were Desmond McGlynn, MBE (Chairman, Joint Steering Group, Youth Exchange Centre, London), Christine Jenkins and Tim Gutsell (Youth Exchange Centre), John Prowse (Head of Commonweal Youth and Community Centre, Swindon), Prof. Friedrich W. Seibel (Fachbereich Sozialpädagogik der Fachhochschule des Landes Rheinland-Pfalz, Abt. Koblenz) and Gisela Senssfelder (IJAB).

und Tim Gutsell (Youth Exchange Centre), John Prowse (Head of Commonweal Youth and Community Centre, Swindon), Prof. Friedrich W. Seibel (Fachbereich Sozialpädagogik der Fachhochschule des Landes Rheinland-Pfalz, Abt. Koblenz) und Gisela Senssfelder (IJAB).

Der IJAB weist darauf hin, daß das vorliegende Werk eine Darstellung der Sachverhalte aus deutscher Sicht ist, auf die im Einvernehmen mit den britischen Mitgliedern der Redaktionsgruppe die Entsprechungen im Vereinigten Königreich abgestimmt wurden. Eine vergleichende Untersuchung aus britischer Sicht wäre einer weiteren Veröffentlichung vorbehalten. Durch Einfügen englischer Stichwortverzeichnisse wurde jedoch Sorge dafür getragen, daß das Glossar auch für den englischsprachigen Benutzer die Funktion eines Nachschlagewerkes erfüllt.

Das „Deutsch-englische Glossar der Jugendhilfe" enthält die Summe der Erfahrungen der in den letzten zwanzig Jahren unter der Ägide des „Gemischten Fachausschusses für den deutsch-britischen Jugendaustausch" durchgeführten Fachprogramme. Es wurde aus Mitteln des Bundesjugendplans vom Bundesministerium für Frauen und Jugend gefördert, das den IJAB mit der Erarbeitung beauftragte. Ohne die freundliche Unterstützung zahlreicher britischer Experten und die Übernahme der in Großbritannien entstandenen Kosten durch die britische Seite wäre es sowohl fachlich als auch terminologisch in dieser Form nicht zustande gekommen.

Den nachstehenden britischen und deutschen Ministerien und Einrichtungen sind wir für ihre Mithilfe besonders verpflichtet:
The British Council, London and Cologne
British Embassy, Bonn
Department of Education and Science, London
National Youth Bureau, Leicester
Youth Exchange Centre, London
Gateshead Metropolitan Borough Council, Department of Social Services, Court Office
Bundesministerium für Arbeit und Sozialordnung, Bonn
Bundesministerium für Bildung und Wissenschaft, Bonn
Bundesministerium für Frauen und Jugend, Bonn
Bundesministerium für Raumordnung, Bauwesen und Städtebau, Bonn
Botschaft der Bundesrepublik Deutschland, London
Bundesanstalt für Arbeit, Nürnberg
Deutsch-Französisches Jugendwerk, Bad Honnef

Allen Ministerien, Dienststellen, freien Trägern und Fachkräften in beiden Ländern sei an dieser Stelle für ihren Beitrag zur Erstellung dieses Werkes, insbesondere zur Überprüfung und Aktualisierung der Textentwürfe, aufrichtig gedankt.

Mai 1991
Helga Köhnen
Leiterin des Sprachendienstes des IJAB e.V.

It must be pointed out at this juncture that the publication aims to give a description of the German situation from a German point of view, for which the members of the above committee jointly selected the suitable equivalents in the United Kingdom. A comparative study from the British point of view would be the objective of a later publication. However, care was taken to make the Glossary useful also for the English-speaking reader by inserting English lists of entries in alphabetical order in the appropriate places.

The "German-English Glossary of Youth Services" pools the experience obtained in the special programmes which have been organised in the last two decades under the auspices of the British-German Special Committee on Youth Exchanges. The publication was financed from Federal Youth Plan funds by the Federal Ministry for Women and Youth which commissioned IJAB to produce it. Without the generous assistance provided by various British experts as well as funding made available by the British side for research work and meetings in the United Kingdom, this Glossary and Comparative Handbook would have been linguistically and professionally less authoritative.

The following British and German ministries and bodies provided advice, assistance or research material:
The British Council, London and Cologne
British Embassy, Bonn
Department of Education and Science, London
National Youth Bureau, Leicester
Youth Exchange Centre, London
Gateshead Metropolitan Borough Council, Department of Social Services, Court Office
Bundesministerium für Arbeit und Sozialordnung, Bonn
Bundesministerium für Bildung und Wissenschaft, Bonn
Bundesministerium für Frauen und Jugend, Bonn
Bundesministerium für Raumordnung, Bauwesen und Städtebau, Bonn
Botschaft der Bundesrepublik Deutschland, London
Bundesanstalt für Arbeit, Nürnberg
Deutsch-Französisches Jugendwerk, Bad Honnef

IJAB wishes to pay a special vote of thanks to all ministries, authorities, agencies, voluntary bodies and experts in both countries for their kind contributions to this Glossary and for their generous help in reviewing and updating the texts submitted to them by the Committee.

May 1991
Helga Köhnen
Head of the Language Section of IJAB e.V.

Hinweise für den Benutzer

Das vorliegende Nachschlagewerk ist nach folgenden Gesichtspunkten angeordnet:

1. Der Terminologie-Teil enthält Begriffe, die im Bereich der Jugendhilfe relevant sowie für das Verständnis der Strukturen, Schwerpunkte und Hintergrundinformationen unerläßlich sind. Bedeutungen aus sonstigen Fachgebieten sind nicht berücksichtigt.
2. Im Terminologie-Teil angefügte, kursiv gedruckte Querverweise auf den Handbuch-Teil ermöglichen das Einordnen des jeweiligen Fachterminus in einen weiteren Kontext.
3. Eine alphabetische Auflistung der im Teil III erläuterten britischen Bezeichnungen ohne deutsche Entsprechung enthält das „Englische Register".
4. Begriffe, die wegen der Unterschiedlichkeit der Strukturen in der Bundesrepublik Deutschland und im Vereinigten Königreich nicht übersetzt werden sollten, sind im deutsch-englischen Terminologie-Teil mit dem Symbol ≠ gekennzeichnet (z.B. Fachhochschule, Meisterbrief, Sozialarbeiter/ Sozialpädagoge). Eine kurze Erläuterung folgt in Klammern. In Fällen, in denen der angeführte Begriff mehrere Bedeutungen hat, empfiehlt sich die Lektüre des durch Querverweis zugeordneten Artikels in Teil III. Im englisch-deutschen Terminologie-Teil stehen dann jeweils auch in der englischen Spalte die deutschen Begriffe (Kursiv-Druck).
5. Bei Begriffen und Wendungen, die aus mehr als einem Wort bestehen, ist das Einordnungskriterium der Hauptsinnträger. Enthält ein Terminus mehrere wichtige Sinnträger, wird der Begriff gegebenenfalls an verschiedenen Stellen unter dem jeweiligen Anfangsbuchstaben aufgeführt.
6. In wenigen Ausnahmen, in denen auch die annähernde Übersetzung nicht möglich oder nicht sinnvoll war, wird nur auf Teil III verwiesen (z.B. Garantiefonds, Management Committee, The Duke of Edinburgh's Award Scheme).

Guide for the User

The reference parts of the *Glossary* have been arranged under the following aspects:

1. The terminology part comprises terms which are relevant to youth work and youth welfare services and help the user understand structures, areas of special concern and background information. Meanings belonging to other fields of knowledge are not listed.
2. Cross references printed in italics and added on to entries in the terminology part make it possible to place a given term in a wider context explained under the respective keyword in the Handbook part of the Glossary.
3. An alphabetical list of British terms having no exact German equivalent is included in Part III (English Index).
4. Entries which should not be translated because of the difference in structures in the FRG and the United Kingdom are marked with the symbol ≠ (e.g. Fachhochschule, Meisterbrief, Sozialarbeiter/Sozialpädagoge). Explanations are given in brackets. Where an entry has several meanings, it is advisable to read very carefully the article in Part III to which the term is cross-referenced. In the English-German terminology part, however, the respective German word will appear in the English column as well.
5. Compound entries are listed under the most significant component. Where there are several significant components, the entry will appear under one or the other in the proper alphabetical position.
6. In exceptional cases where an approximate translation was not possible or useful, the respective entry is simply cross-referenced to Part III (e.g. Garantiefonds, Management Committee, The Duke of Edinburgh's Award Scheme).

Teil I
Übersichten

Part I
Overview

Überblick über die Jugendhilfe in der Bundesrepublik Deutschland

Diese Übersicht ist eine Zusammenstellung der für das vorliegende Glossar wichtigen Aspekte der deutschen Jugendhilfe. Sie soll den Zugang zu den Erläuterungen der Fachbegriffe des Teils III erleichtern.

Die Jugendhilfe in der Bundesrepublik Deutschland umfaßt nicht nur die Jugendarbeit oder außerschulische Jugendbildung, die viele Gemeinsamkeiten mit dem britischen *youth service* aufweist, sondern z.B. auch die Kindergartenerziehung, das Pflegekinderwesen und die besonderen Hilfen zur Erziehung, die bei Gefährdungen und Störungen der Entwicklung junger Menschen erforderlich werden. Von zentraler Bedeutung ist in diesem Zusammenhang der Begriff der „Einheit der Jugendhilfe". Diese Einheit der Jugendhilfe stellt eine historisch gewachsene Realität dar, in der die Überzeugung zum Ausdruck kommt, daß jungen Menschen nicht erst bei bereits eingetretenen Beeinträchtigungen und Schädigungen ihrer Entwicklung Hilfe zu leisten ist, sondern daß durch die Bereitstellung geeigneter Erziehungs-, Bildungs- und Betätigungsmöglichkeiten von vornherein das Auftreten solcher Fehlentwicklungen möglichst vermieden werden sollte (Prävention).

Die rechtliche Grundlage stellt das Kinder- und Jugendhilfegesetz (KJHG) vom 26.6.1990 dar. Es löst das Jugendwohlfahrtsgesetz aus dem Jahre 1922 ab. Die Länder passen derzeit ihre Ausführungsgesetze an das neue Bundesgesetz an. Die Jugendhilfe umfaßt in Ergänzung zu Elternhaus und Schule alle gezielten Maßnahmen zur Förderung des Wohles junger Menschen. Sie werden von öffentlichen Trägern und freien Vereinigungen, entsprechend der Struktur der Bundesrepublik Deutschland überwiegend auf Kommunal-, aber auch auf Landes- und Bundesebene in partnerschaftlicher Zusammenarbeit geleistet.

Die Jugendarbeit in den Kreisen und kreisfreien Städten orientiert sich an den örtlichen Gegebenheiten. So schließen sich z.B. die örtlichen Gruppen der Jugendverbände zu Stadt- und Kreisjugendringen zusammen. Auch kommt der kulturellen Jugendarbeit in Freizeit, Geselligkeit und Erholung sowie der sportlichen Jugendarbeit, aber auch der Jugendsozialarbeit, hier eine besondere Bedeutung zu.

Das KJHG verpflichtet alle kreisfreien Städte und Landkreise zur Einrichtung eines Jugendamtes. Es ist unter anderem damit beauftragt, den Bedarf an Jugendarbeit in seinem Einzugsbereich durch Förderung und erforderlichenfalls auch durch eigene Aktivitäten zu decken.

Outline of the Youth Work and Youth Welfare Services in the Federal Republic of Germany

The objective of this outline is to give a survey of the major aspects of the German youth work and youth welfare services (→ *Jugendhilfe*). It should enable the reader to place the comments under each of the specialist terms of *Jugendhilfe* listed in Part III of this Glossary in a wider context.

Jugendhilfe in the Federal Republic of Germany does not only comprise youth work or out-of-school education of the young, which is similar to the British youth service in many respects, but also includes other types of provision such as pre-school education, child fostering and the various forms of specialist socio-educational help which must be made available to young people who are at risk or have to cope with development problems. At this juncture, attention must be drawn to the fact that the basic concept of *Jugendhilfe* is the "unity of youth work and youth welfare services". This concept is rooted in historical development and based on the principle that young people do not only need help when already affected by development problems, but that preventive action is required by placing at their disposal the appropriate socio-educational facilities, educational schemes and activities.

The legal basis of *Jugendhilfe* ist the Child and Youth Services Act, dated 26 June 1990. It replaces the Youth Welfare Act of 1922. The Federal *Länder* are, at present, adapting their implementing statutes to this new Federal Act. Complementing the family and the schools, *Jugendhilfe* comprises all structured provision aiming to promote the welfare of young people. Such provision is made by the public authorities and voluntary organisations who, in keeping with the structure of the Federal Republic of Germany, cooperate on a basis of partnership mainly at the local, but also at *Land* and Federal levels.

Youth work provided by the *Kreise* and *kreisfreie Städte* (→ *Kommunale Selbstverwaltung*) is very much geared to the situation in a given community. For instance, the local groups forming part of a youth organisation come together in standing conferences at the local and above-local level. Emphasis here is also on cultural youth work in leisure time, social gatherings and recreation, on sports as well as socio-educational provision for the young.

The Child and Youth Services Act requires all *kreisfreie Städte* and *Landkreise* to establish a youth work and youth welfare office. Amongst other things, this authority is called upon to supply the necessary youth services within its frame of reference by making available the appropriate funds and, if need be, by creating provision of its own.

Die Ziele der Jugendarbeit als Teil der Jugendhilfe lassen sich wie folgt zusammenfassen: Jugendarbeit stellt die Bedürfnisse und Interessen der jungen Menschen in den Mittelpunkt ihrer vielfältigen Arbeits-, Veranstaltungs- und Organisationsformen. Jugendarbeit hat dabei vorrangig einen Beitrag zur Selbstverwirklichung und zur größeren Freiheit und Gerechtigkeit zu leisten, indem sie den Willen und die Fähigkeit zur verantwortlichen Beteiligung (Partizipation) der jungen Menschen am kulturellen, sozialen und politischen Leben der Gesellschaft entwickelt und stärkt. Sie soll vor allem praktische Erfahrungen im sozialen Engagement vermitteln. Hierzu gehört auch, daß soziale Benachteiligungen und Konflikte aufgegriffen und bearbeitet werden.

In den letzten Jahren galten die Bemühungen der Jugendhilfe vor allem der Bekämpfung der Jugendarbeitslosigkeit, der Integration Behinderter, der Verbesserung der Chancen von Mädchen und jungen Frauen, Programmen zum Abbau der Benachteiligung ausländischer Arbeitnehmer, dem Kampf gegen die Suchtgefahren sowie der Förderung sozialer Randgruppen.

Das Kinder- und Jugendhilfegesetz verpflichtet im übrigen die Jugendämter im Zusammenwirken mit freien Trägern dazu, die Familie zu beraten, zu unterstützen und zu fördern oder sie zu ersetzen, wenn Kinder und Jugendliche keine Eltern mehr haben oder diese sie nicht erziehen können. Dafür steht ein inzwischen weit gefördertes Instrumentarium ambulanter, teil-stationärer und stationärer Erziehungshilfen zur Verfügung. Immer mehr an Bedeutung gewinnt ein bedarfsgerechtes Angebot der Tagesbetreuung für Kinder (z.B. Kindergärten).

Schließlich fördert das Bundesministerium für Frauen und Jugend als oberste Bundesbehörde Aufgaben und Projekte der Jugendhilfe, die für die Entwicklung auf der Ebene des Bundes von Bedeutung sind. Die finanziellen Mittel hierfür sind im Bundesjugendplan enthalten, der zur Unterstützung der Jugendarbeit durch den Bund im Jahre 1950 geschaffen wurde. Er ist seit seiner Verkündung ein Kernstück der Jugendpolitik in der Bundesrepublik Deutschland geworden. Daneben gehört es zu den zentralen Aufgaben des Bundesministeriums, die Gesetzgebung im Bereich Jugend zu initiieren und vorzubereiten. Das KJHG schreibt vor, daß ein Bundesjugendkuratorium die Bundesregierung in grundsätzlichen Fragen der Entwicklung der Jugendhilfe berät. Nach dem gleichen Gesetz ist in jeder Legislaturperiode von einer unabhängigen Expertenkommission ein Jugendbericht zu erarbeiten und mit einer Stellungnahme der Bundesregierung dem Parlament vorzulegen. Das KJHG schreibt weiter vor, daß jeder dritte Bericht einen Überblick über die Gesamtentwicklung der Jugendhilfe zu geben hat. Die beiden anderen Berichte sollen Schwerpunktthemen gewidmet sein. So hat der 1983 vorgelegte Sechste Jugendbericht der Situation der Mädchen in der Jugendhilfe gegolten und eine große Bedeutung erlangt. Der Siebte Jugendbericht hatte das Thema „Familienunterstützende Leistungen der Jugendhilfe". Er stellte eine wichtige Diskussionsgrundlage für die Neuordnung des Jugendhilferechts dar. Der Achte Jugendbericht galt wiederum der Beurteilung der Gesamtsituation der Ju-

The aims and objectives of youth work as an integral part of *Jugendhilfe* may be summarised as follows: Youth work gears its various types of activities, events and organisations to the needs and interests of young people. The weight of effort lies on helping the young to make full use of their abilities and to secure a higher degree of freedom and justice by means of developing and strengthening their desire and capacity for participation in decision-making in the cultural, social and political life of the community. A major priority must be to give young people a chance to gain practical experience in community involvement. This includes the development of the ability to react to and cope with social disadvantages and conflicts.

In recent years, the endeavours undertaken by youth work and youth welfare services were very much aimed at combating youth unemployment, promoting the integration of the disabled, improving opportunities for girls and young women, setting up programmes to counter the discrimination against foreign workers, fighting the risks of drug addiction and assisting marginal groups.

The Child and Youth Services Act requires the youth work and youth welfare office to cooperate with voluntary organisations in their joint task of giving guidance, support and financial assistance to families in need of help. Where children and young people no longer have at least one parent or their parents are not in a position to bring them up, these agencies step in to replace the family. A wide range of largely grant-aided non-residential, partly residential and residential socio-educational provision is available for such purposes. Based on present-day needs, increasing importance is attributed to day care establishments for children (e.g. kindergartens).

School education and youth work are separate fields in Germany. The staff in each are trained in separate establishments with different courses of studies, whilst the need for better cooperation is widely accepted in spite of diverging educational concepts governing each field.

The youth authorities of the *Länder* governments (either the minister of social affairs or the minister of cultural affairs of a given *Land)* make sure that a satisfactory range of youth services is available within their remit. In addition, depending on the size of each Federal *Land,* one or several *Land* youth authorities are responsible for advising, planning and coordinating these services. They also supervise all youth provision (e.g. homes, nursery schools) and administer youth work facilities necessitating the participation of more than one *Land.*

Finally, the Federal Ministry for Women and Youth as the supreme Federal authority assists in tasks and projects in the wider field of *Jugendhilfe* in order to promote youth services at the Federal level. Funds for these purposes are drawn from the Federal Youth Plan, which was created in 1950 as an instrument designed to enable the Federal Government to support youth work. Since its promulgation, the Federal Youth Plan has become a cornerstone of the

gendhilfe. Er hat eine breite Diskussion ausgelöst und vielfältige Umsetzungen seiner Ideen und Vorschläge in der Praxis der Jugendhilfe erfahren.

Zur Vertretung der gemeinsamen Interessen der freien Träger der Jugendhilfe bestehen meist auch Zusammenschlüsse auf Landes- und Bundesebene, von denen als Dachverband der Mehrzahl der deutschen Jugendorganisationen beispielhaft der Deutsche Bundesjugendring genannt sei.

Die internationale Jugendarbeit hatte von Anfang an ihren festen Platz im Bundesjugendplan. Internationale Jugendarbeit trägt durch Begegnung, gemeinsame Aktion, Information und außerschulische Bildung zur Förderung der internationalen Verständigung bei. Hier haben der Deutsche Bundesjugendring und der Ring Politischer Jugend eine wichtige Funktion. Sie bilden das Deutsche Nationalkomitee für internationale Jugendarbeit. An zentraler Stelle der Bemühungen steht die Förderung des europäischen Bewußtseins und der europäischen Zusammenarbeit. Gleichzeitig gewinnt die jugendpolitische Zusammenarbeit mit außereuropäischen Ländern und hier besonders mit den Entwicklungsländern immer größere Bedeutung.

Government's youth policy. The main function of the Federal Ministry is to initiate and prepare legislation in the youth sector. The Child and Youth Services Act stipulates that a Federal Advisory Committee is to advise the Federal Government on principal issues relating to development in the youth field. Under the same Act, a commission of independent experts is required to compile a National Youth Report in every legislative period and to submit it to the German Parliament together with the Government's comments. The Child and Youth Services Act also lays down that every third report must give a survey of the overall depelopment of youth work and youth welfare services. The two other reports should deal with subjects of particular relevance. Thus, the Sixth National Youth Report, which subsequently achieved paramount significance, looked into the situation of girls in the German youth services. The Seventh National Youth Report was entitled "Youth Work and Youth Welfare Provision to Support the Family". It became an important basis for present-day discussions on the revision of existing *Jugendhilfe* legislation. The Eighth National Youth Report made a renewed assessment of the overall situation of youth work and youth welfare services. This report was widely debated and the ideas and suggestions brought forward therein had many repercussions on the day-to-day practice of the different areas of *Jugendhilfe*.

In order to advocate the joint interests of the voluntary organisations concerned with youth work and youth welfare services, various central organisations were formed at *Land* and Federal level. The German Federal Youth Council, which serves as an umbrella for the majority of German youth organisations, may be quoted here as an example.

From the very beginning, international youth work was an integral part of the Federal Youth Plan. Apart from providing contacts with the young of other countries, international youth work contributes to international understanding through joint action, information and out-of-school education. The German Federal Youth Council and the Council of Political Youth Organisations assume an important function in this field. Together they constitute the German National Committee for International Youth Work. One of the central aims of international youth work is to promote the development of a European awareness and to further European cooperation. Increasing importance is equally attributed to cooperation with non-European states, especially with developing countries.

Überblick über den *Youth Service* im Vereinigten Königreich*

Diese Einführung soll einen Überblick über den britischen *youth service* geben und die Ausführungen unter den Stichworten in Teil II des Glossars in einen größeren Zusammenhang stellen.

Der *youth service* ist im allgemeinen Teil des Bildungswesens. Er soll die persönliche Entwicklung und die soziale Erziehung junger Menschen durch ein umfassendes und breit gefächertes Angebot von Freizeitaktivitäten fördern.

Der *Education Act 1944* übertrug den kommunalen Erziehungsbehörden die Aufgabe, Einrichtungen und Angebote des *youth service* in ihrem Verantwortungsbereich sicherzustellen, mit den freien Trägern zusammenzuarbeiten, wo es zweckmäßig erscheint, und für ausreichende Möglichkeiten der sozialen und sportlichen Betätigung Sorge zu tragen.

Die Entwicklungen im *youth service* basieren weitgehend auf den Erkenntnissen des umfangreichen Berichtes *Experience and Participation,* einer 1982 im Auftrag des Ministers für Erziehung und Wissenschaft veröffentlichten Untersuchung und Bestandsaufnahme des *youth service* in England. Der Bericht, nach Alan Thompson, dem Vorsitzenden der für die Erstellung der Studie eingesetzten Arbeitsgruppe, auch als *Thompson Report* bezeichnet, enthielt wichtige Empfehlungen an die Zentralregierung und die Kommunalverwaltungen sowie die freien Träger zur organisatorischen Verbesserung des *youth service* und seiner Anpassung an zeitgemäße Bedürfnisse. Weiterhin wurde die Arbeitsgruppe beauftragt zu prüfen, ob hierzu gesetzliche Maßnahmen erforderlich seien.

Die Regierung übernahm eine Reihe von Empfehlungen des Berichts, sah es jedoch nicht als notwendig an, gesetzliche Maßnahmen zu ergreifen. 1984 wurde eine ähnliche Untersuchung zur Überprüfung der *Youth Provision in Wales* durchgeführt.

Seit einiger Zeit zeigt die Regierung ein verstärktes Interesse an der Jugendarbeit. So fanden auf ministerieller Ebene zwei Konferenzen über die Entwicklung eines Kernstudiums für Fachkräfte der Jugendarbeit statt. Diese Konferenzen bestätigten die pädagogischen Konzepte des *youth service* und umrissen Ziele, Methoden, Zielgruppen und Problemfelder.

Obschon der *Thompson* Bericht über den *youth service* sowie die Reaktion der Regierung sich nur auf England bezogen, lassen sich viele der darin aufgegriffenen Fragen auch auf die Jugendarbeit in anderen Teilen des Vereinigten

---

* „Vereinigtes Königreich von Großbritannien und Nordirland", informell auch als *Britain* bezeichnet. „Großbritannien" umfaßt England, Schottland und Wales.

Outline of the Youth Service in Britain*

The purpose of this introduction is to give a survey of the British youth service and to place the data given under various headings in Part III of the Glossary in a wider context.

The youth service generally forms part of the education system and is concerned with promoting the personal development and social education of young people through a wide and diverse range of leisure-time activities.

The Education Act 1944 placed upon local education authorities the duty to make provision for the youth service in their area, cooperating with voluntary bodies where appropriate and ensuring that facilities for social and physical activities were adequate.

Developments in the youth service have been based to a large extent on the findings of a major review, *Experience and Participation,* published in 1982 on behalf of the Secretary of State for Education and Science, which examined the nature of the youth service in England. The review, also referred to as the *Thompson Report* after the chairman of the review group, Mr. Alan Thompson, made important recommendations on how central und local government and voluntary organisations could ensure that the youth service was better planned and suited to meet present-day requirements. The review group was equally asked to assess the need for legislation.

The Government responded by adopting a number of the Report's recommendations, but did not deem it necessary to take legislative measures. In 1984 a similar review was carried out to look into *Youth Provision in Wales.*

There has since been increasing government interest in youth work with two Ministerial Conferences on a core curriculum for the youth service. These conferences have reaffirmed the Service's educational purposes and clarified objectives, methods, target groups and issues.

While the *Thompson Report* and the Government's response to it related to the youth service in England, many of the issues raised apply also to the service in other parts of Britain. A review on a new youth structure for Northern Ireland was implemented in 1990. In Northern Ireland, the youth service is seen as having a particularly important role since it is in a position to contribute to greater understanding between the two traditions which divide the community there.

Youth services are centrally supported by the education departments in England, Scotland, Wales and Northern Ireland respectively. It must be pointed

---

*   The term *Britain* is used informally to mean the United Kingdom of Great Britain and Northern Ireland; *Great Britain* comprises England, Scotland and Wales.

Königreiches übertragen. Eine Studie über die Jugendarbeit in Nordirland führte dort im Jahre 1990 zur Einführung neuer Strukturen. Der *youth service* in Nordirland hat eine besondere Funktion, da er dazu beitragen kann, die hier bestehende Kluft zwischen zwei gesellschaftlichen Traditionen zu überbrücken.

Die Jugendarbeit wird zentral von den Erziehungsministerien in England, Schottland, Wales bzw. Nordirland gefördert. Dabei ist stets zu berücksichtigen, daß das Ministerium für Erziehung und Wissenschaft auf nationaler Ebene für bestimmte Bereiche, z.B. für die Universitäten und Technischen Hochschulen, zuständig ist, während es auf anderen Gebieten, einschließlich des *youth service,* nur für England verantwortlich ist und hier auf derselben Stufe wie die entsprechenden Ministerien in den übrigen Teilen des Vereinigten Königreiches steht. Dies erklärt auch die Tatsache, daß Strukturen und Terminologie in Schottland und Nordirland abweichen können. Zwischen England und Wales gibt es im Bereich der schulischen Bildung und der Jugend- und Gemeinwesenarbeit kaum Unterschiede.

Die Jugend- und Gemeinwesenarbeit auf der örtlichen Ebene zeigt viele Gemeinsamkeiten mit der → *Jugendarbeit* in der Bundesrepublik Deutschland. Es ist jedoch herauszustellen, daß in Großbritannien die Kommunalbehörden die Hauptlast der Finanzierung der Einrichtungen und Maßnahmen für die Jugend tragen. Dabei ist es ein wichtiges Ziel der Bemühungen, der Jugend Mitwirkungsmöglichkeiten bei der Organisation von Aktivitäten der Jugendclubs und Jugendverbände anzubieten. Erwachsenen Jugendarbeitern soll die Aufgabe zufallen, die von jungen Menschen, besonders von arbeitslosen oder gefährdeten Jugendlichen, häufig benötigte persönliche Hilfestellung und Beratung zu übernehmen. In Jugendzentren, die sich innerhalb oder in der Nähe der Schulen befinden oder die die Schulgebäude mitbenutzen, wird größeres Gewicht auf feste Angebote und weniger Wert auf informelle soziale Aktivitäten gelegt.

Ein weiterer Schwerpunkt ist die politische Bildung oder *active citizenship,* da sie die Entwicklung des Bewußtseins fördert, daß junge Menschen in einer Demokratie die Möglichkeit haben, die Gesellschaft, in der sie leben, zu beeinflussen und ihnen ein Mitspracherecht bei der Ausgestaltung der Demokratie zukommt. Obwohl die Mehrzahl der Jugendlichen die Probleme des Erwachsenwerdens ohne übermäßige Schwierigkeiten meistert und einen breiteren Erfahrungshorizont sowie größere Chancen als jemals zuvor besitzt, gestaltet sich der persönliche Entwicklungsprozeß für eine beträchtliche und voraussichtlich noch wachsende Minderheit alles andere als einfach. Eine Vielzahl von Problemen, einschließlich der Arbeitslosigkeit, der Benachteiligung in Ballungsgebieten, der ländlichen Isolation, der Rassendiskriminierung und Obdachlosigkeit belastet heute das Leben junger Menschen und beeinträchtigt die persönliche Entwicklung entscheidend. Besonders Mädchen und junge Frauen müssen mehr Anreize zur vollen Partizipation erhalten. Dabei geht es besonders um den Abbau sozialer Wertvorstellungen, die die weibliche Jugend daran hindert, ihre Möglichkeiten voll zu nutzen. Ebenso wird

out that the Department of Education and Science (DES) has national responsibilities for some fields, such as universities and polytechnics, but for other
areas, including the youth service, it may only act for England on the same level with the competent ministries in the other parts of Britain. This also ac-
counts for the fact that structures and terminology differ in Scotland and
Northern Ireland. In the field of formal education and youth and community
work, however, the situation is roughly similar in England and Wales.

Youth and community work at the local level has many features in common
with → *Jugendarbeit* in Germany, but attention must be drawn to the fact that in
the UK the local authorities provide the main source of public finance for
youth services. Efforts are made to give young people opportunities for participation in the organisation of activities in youth clubs and youth organisations
and also for adult youth workers to offer the personal counselling and advice
that young people often need, particularly the unemployed or those at risk. In
youth centres, which are located at or near a school or share school premises,
greater emphasis is placed on activities and less on informal social pursuits.

Another priority of youth work is "political education" or "active citizenship",
i.e. the development of an awareness that in a democracy it is possible for
young people to influence the society in which they live and to have a say in
how it is run. It is pointed out that although the majority of young people face
the problems of growing up without undue difficulty, and have wider horizons
and greater opportunities than ever before, for a significant and probably growing minority the process is far from easy. A number of issues impinge upon
the lives of many young people today, including unemployment, urban deprivation, rural isolation, racial discrimination and homelessness, which are serious obstacles to their personal development. The need is recognised for
young women and girls to be given greater encouragement to play a full part
and for efforts to be made to counter those attitudes in society which prevent
them from achieving their full potential. It is also emphasized that measures must be taken to integrate young people with disabilities into youth activities.

In 1989, the Department of Education and Science began a scrutiny of the five
main non-statutory departmental bodies it funds, as it was felt that government support needed to be channelled to achieve higher efficiency. Consequently, a comprehensive National Youth Agency (NYA) was launched in
April 1991 which encompasses the responsibilities of existing bodies such as
the National Youth Bureau, the Council for Education and Training in Youth
and Community Work, the National Council for Voluntary Youth Services
and is to cover the following areas:

– the development of curricular content and methods, especially in advice
  and counselling
– the development, endorsement, accreditation and provision of youth worker training
– the collection, dissemination and publication of information

die Notwendigkeit von Maßnahmen zur Integration junger Behinderter in Aktivitäten der Jugendarbeit unterstrichen.

1989 begann das Ministerium für Erziehung und Wissenschaft mit einer Überprüfung seiner fünf großen Zuwendungsempfänger im Bereich der Jugendarbeit, da Überlegungen angestellt wurden, in verschiedene Richtungen fließende öffentliche Mittel zu bündeln, um sie effektiver einsetzen zu können. Im Zuge dieser Überlegungen wurde im April 1991 eine übergreifende Einrichtung, die *National Youth Agency (NYA),* ins Leben gerufen, auf die die Aufgaben bisheriger Einrichtungen und Träger wie des *National Youth Bureau,* des *Council for Education and Training in Youth and Community Work* und des *National Council for Voluntary Youth Services* nach deren Auflösung übergehen. In der NYA sind folgende Aufgabenbereiche zusammengefaßt:

— die Entwicklung curricularer Inhalte und Methoden, insbesondere im Hinblick auf die Jugendberatung
— die Fortentwicklung, Unterstützung, Anerkennung und Bereitstellung von Ausbildungsangeboten für Mitarbeiter der Jugendarbeit
— das Erheben, Verbreiten und Veröffentlichen von Informationen
— Unterstützung für die Leitung der Organisationen und Maßnahmen der Jugendarbeit, insbesondere der freien Träger, einschließlich einer Ausbildung in Management
— die internationale Jugendarbeit
— die direkte Förderung von Regierungsinitiativen in diesen Bereichen
— die Partizipation Jugendlicher.

Zur Vertretung der Interessen junger Menschen und zur Schaffung einer Diskussionsplattform sowie einer Basis für gemeinsames Vorgehen sind in Großbritannien verschiedene Jugendstrukturen und zentrale Organisationen aufgebaut worden, für die hier der *British Youth Council (BYC)* als wichtigstes Beispiel angeführt sei.

Der *British Youth Council* vertritt als eigenständiger freier Träger die Überzeugungen junger Menschen auf nationaler und internationaler Ebene. Er nimmt aktiv an der Arbeit des Europäischen Jugendrats, des Jugendforums der Europäischen Gemeinschaft und anderer europäischer oder Weltjugendkonferenzen teil. Aber nicht nur der Britische Jugendrat nimmt Aufgaben der internationalen Jugendarbeit wahr. Auch Ministerien, kommunale Behörden und Jugendorganisationen setzen sich gleichermaßen für die internationale Verständigung ein, indem sie alljährlich zahlreiche Jugendkontakte fördern und durchführen.

Abschließend sei darauf hingewiesen, daß schon seit vielen Jahren im Vereinigten Königreich die Notwendigkeit der Schaffung eines umfassenderen *youth service* gesehen wird, der weitgesteckte bildungspolitische Ziele und Hilfen für benachteiligte und sozial unangepaßte Jugendliche miteinander verbindet. Zwar gibt es kein eigenes für Jugendfragen zuständiges Ministerium, doch hat das Ministerium für Erziehung und Wissenschaft die *National Youth Agency* eingerichtet, um den Bedürfnissen der Jugend und der Mitarbeiter der Jugendarbeit gleichermaßen Rechnung zu tragen.

— support for managers of youth service organisations and operations, particularly in the voluntary sector, including management training
— international youth work
— direct support for government initiatives in these areas
— youth participation.

In order to advocate the interests of young people and provide a platform for discussion and joint action, various youth structures and central organisations have been set up in Britain for which the British Youth Council (BYC) may serve as an example as it now plays a major role in the field. BYC functions as an independent voluntary organisation, aiming to represent the views of young people nationally as well as internationally. It takes an active part in the work of the Council of European National Youth Committees, the Youth Forum of the European Community and other European or world youth conferences.

The promotion of international understanding is certainly not limited to the youth work activities of the BYC. Government departments, local authorities and youth organisations alike subscribe to this aim by supporting and organising numerous youth contacts every year.

In conclusion attention should be drawn to the fact that the need for a more comprehensive youth service, combining broad educational aims and those of a service connected with the disadvantaged and alienated has been recognised in the UK for many years. Although there is no single ministry responsible for youth questions, the NYA has been set up by the Department of Education and Science to provide a more effective response to the needs of young people and youth workers alike.

Teil II
Glossar

Part II
Glossary of Terms

Deutsch — englisch
German — English

Abendschule (f)	evening classes, evening institute, evening centre
abweichendes Verhalten (n)	deviant behaviour
Abenteuerspielplatz (m) → *Erlebnispädagogik*	adventure playground
Abitur (n) → *Bildungswesen*	≠ (certificate of qualification for university entrance)
Abrechnung (f) einer Maßnahme (f)	statement of accounts for a programme
Abschlußprüfung (f)	examination at the end of a period of education
Abteilung (f), geschlossene → *Jugendstrafrecht, Maßnahmen des*	secure unit
Abtreibung (f) → *Schwangerschaftsabbruch*	abortion
Adoption (f) → *Adoption*	adoption
Adoptiveltern (pl)	adoptive parents
Adoptionsvermittlung (f) → *Jugendamt*	adoption procedures and implementation
Aktiv-Ferien (pl)	activity and adventure holiday
Alkoholmißbrauch (m) bei Jugendlichen (m/f/pl) → *Alkoholmißbrauch bei Jugendlichen*	alcohol abuse amongst young people
Alkoholiker (m)/Alkoholikerin (f)	alcoholic
Alkoholikerfürsorge (f) → *Drogenmißbrauch*	care for alcoholics
alleinerziehende Eltern (pl)	single-parent family
allgemeinbildende Schule (f)	school providing non-specialist education
Allgemeinbildung (f)	general education
Alternativbewegung (f) → *Alternativbewegung*	alternative life style, alternative movements
Altersgrenze (f) → *Tabelle Altersgrenzen*	age limit

Altersgruppe (f)	age group

ambulant
   ambulante Betreuung (f)
	open, field- . . ., non-residential
	   field support

Amtsvormund (m) → *Vormundschaft*	local authority guardian
Amtsvormundschaft (f) → *Vormundschaft*	guardianship exercised by the local authority
Angestellter (m)/Angestellte (f) → *Bedienstete des Öffentlichen Dienstes*	salaried employee; white collar worker
Angebote (n/pl) Angebote der Jugendarbeit Angebote der Berufsausbildung	provision youth service provision, programmes on offer vocational training activities/ programmes
angelernter Arbeiter (m)/ angelernte Arbeiterin (f)	semi-skilled worker
Anlaufstelle (f)	first contact
Anlernberuf (m)	semi-skilled employment
Anlernling (m)	trainee
anpassungsschwieriges Kind (n)	maladjusted child
Anpassungsschwierigkeit (f)	maladjustment
Ansprechpartner (m)/ Ansprechpartnerin (f)	contact person
Antrag (m)	application
Antragstellung (f)	completion of an application form, submission of an application
Anspruchsberechtigter (m)/ Anspruchsberechtigte (f)	person entitled to receive benefits (services or money)
Anstellungsträger (m)	employing body
Anwesenheitspflicht (f)	compulsory attendance
Arbeiterwohnheim (n)	worker's hostel
Arbeitgeber (m)/Arbeitgeberin (f)	employer
Arbeitnehmer (m)/Arbeitnehmerin (f)	employee, employed person
Arbeitnehmer (m), ausländischer/ Arbeitnehmerin (f), ausländische	foreign worker

Arbeitsamt (n) → *Bundesanstalt für Arbeit*	employment office
Arbeitsbeschaffungsmaßnahme (f) (ABM) → *Jugendarbeitslosigkeit*	Job Creation Scheme
Arbeitserlaubnis (f)	work permit
Arbeitsförderungsgesetz (n) → *Bundesanstalt für Arbeit*	Promotion of Employment Act
Arbeitsgruppe (f)	work group
Arbeitsgemeinschaft (f)	standing conference
Arbeitskreis (m)	working party
Arbeitslosengeld (n) → *Bundesanstalt für Arbeit*	unemployment benefit
Arbeitslosenhilfe (f) → *Bundesanstalt für Arbeit*	reduced unemployment benefit
Arbeitsrecht (n) → *Betriebsrat*	labour law
Arbeitsschutz (m) → *Jugendgesetze*	protection of employment, safety of work regulations
Arbeitsunfall (m)	injury at work
Arbeitsvermittlung (f) → *Bundesanstalt für Arbeit*	job placement, employment service
Arbeitsvermittlungsstelle (f)	jobcentre (UK)
asoziales Verhalten (n)	anti-social behaviour
Asylbewerber (m)/Asylbewerberin (f)	asylum seeker
Asylant (m)/Asylantin (f)	asylant
audio-visuelle Hilfsmittel (n/pl)	audio-visual materials
Aufbaugymnasium (n)	sixth form college
Aufbaulager (n)	work camp
Auferlegung (f) von Pflichten (f/pl) → *Jugendstrafrecht, Maßnahmen des*	community service orders
Auffälligkeit (f)	deviant behaviour
auffällig	behaviourally deviant
Auffangheim (n)	temporary accomodation hostel
Aufklärung (f), sexuelle	sex education, sex instruction

Auflagen (f/pl) → *Jugendstrafrecht, Maßnahmen des*	directions, conditions
Aufnahmeprüfung (f)	entrance examination
Aufsichtspflicht (f) → *Aufsichtspflicht*	supervisory responsibilities
Au-pair-Beschäftigung (f)	au-pair job
Ausbilder (m)/Ausbilderin (f) → *Berufsbildung*	instructor, trainer
Ausbildungsbeihilfe (f)	training grant, education grant
Ausbildungsberuf (m), anerkannter → *Berufsbildung*	recognised training trade
Ausbildungsbetrieb (m) → *Berufsbildung*	recognised training establishment
Ausbildungsförderung (f) → *Ausbildungsförderung*	education grants
Ausbildungslehrgang (m)	training course
Ausbildungsplatz (m)	training vacancy, training position
Ausbildungsvergütung (f)	trainee wage
Ausbildungsverhältnis (n)	training under the conditions of apprenticeship
Ausbildungsvertrag (m)	contract of apprenticeship
Ausländerfeindlichkeit (f)	xenophobia, racism (UK)
ausländischer Arbeitnehmer (m)/ ausländische Arbeitnehmerin (f)	foreign worker, migrant worker
Ausreißer (m)/Ausreißerin (f)	runaway
außerschulische Bildung (f) → *Jugendarbeit*	out-of-school education
Ausschuß (m) für Frauen (f/pl) und Jugend (f) des Deutschen Bundestages (m) → *Ausschuß für Frauen und Jugend des Deutschen Bundestages*	Committee for Women and Youth of the *German Bundestag*
Aussteiger (m)/Aussteigerin (f)	(social) drop out
Austauschprogramm (n)	exchange programme
Auswertungsgespräch (n)	evaluation, appraisal session

Auswertungsseminar (n)	evaluation seminar
Auszubildender (m)/Auszubildende (f) („Azubi") → *Berufsbildung*	apprentice, trainee
Basteln (n)	practical handwork, modelling, amateur constructing
Bastler (m)/Bastlerin (f)	one who enjoys practical handwork
Bediensteter (m)/Bedienstete (f) des öffentlichen Dienstes (m) → *Bedienstete des Öffentlichen Dienstes*	civil service employee
Begegnung (f)	meeting, contact, programme or event with a strong element of mixing and mingling
Begegnungsstätte (f), Begegnungszentrum (n)	conference centre
Begegnungsreise (f)	exchange visit
begleiten	to accompany, to escort, to lead a group
Begleiter (m)/Begleiterin (f)	escort, guide, interpreter-guide, group leader
Begleitung (f)	group leadership
Begleitperson (f)	accompanying staff, accompanying adult
Behinderter (m)/Behinderte (f)	handicapped person, disabled person, person with special needs
geistig Behinderter	mentally handicapped person
Hörbehinderter	person with a hearing impairment
Lernbehinderter	educationally subnormal person, mentally retarded person
Person (f) mit Sinnesschäden (m/pl)	person with impaired vision and/or hearing
seelisch Behinderter	emotionally disturbed person
Sehbehinderter	visually handicapped person
Sprachbehinderter	person with a speech defect

Beihilfe (f)	allowance, grant, subsidy
Behindertenhilfe (f) → *Behindertenhilfe*	services for the handicapped
Beirat (m)	advisory council, advisory board
Bekenntnisschule (f)	denominational school
Benachteiligtenprogramm (n)	programmes for the disadvantaged
Benachteiligung (f), soziale	social disadvantage
Beobachtungsstation (f)	observation unit, observation ward
Beobachtungszentrum (n)	classifying centre, observation and assessment centre
Beratung (f) in Sexual- und Schwangerschaftskonflikten (m/pl) → *Beratungsdienste*	sex and pregnancy counselling
Beratungsdienste (m/pl) → *Beratungsdienste*	advisory services, counselling services
Bereitschaftspflegestelle (f)	short-stay foster family
Beruf (m) a) akademischer Beruf b) Beruf im Sinne von Berufung c) Beruf im Sinne von Gewerbe	occupation a) profession, e.g. lawyer, doctor b) vocation, e.g. priest c) trade, e.g. carpenter, electrician
Berufsakademie (f) → *Sozialarbeiter/Sozialpädagoge*	≠ (polytechnic-type establishment)
Berufsanfänger (m)/Berufsanfängerin (f)	person in the beginning stage of his career
Berufsaufbauschule (f) → *Berufsbildung*	≠ (vocational continuation school)
Berufsausbildungsbeihilfe (f) → *Ausbildungsförderung*	vocational training grant
Berufsberater (m)/Berufsberaterin (f) → *Bundesanstalt für Arbeit*	careers officer
Berufsberatung (f) → *Bundesanstalt für Arbeit*	careers advice, vocational guidance, careers service(s)
Berufsberatungsstelle (f) → *Bundesanstalt für Arbeit*	careers office, careers centre (UK)
Berufsbild (n)	requirements of a trade or profession

berufsbildende Maßnahmen (f/pl) → *Berufsbildung* → *Jugendarbeitslosigkeit, VK*	vocational training schemes, Youth Training
Berufsbildung (f) → *Berufsbildung*	professional training, vocational training
Berufsbildungsgesetz (n) → *Berufsbildung*	Vocational Training Act
Berufsbildungswerk (n)	vocational rehabilitation establishment
Berufseignung (f)	work aptitude
Berufsfachschule (f) → *Berufsbildung*	≠ (full-time vocational school)
Berufsfindung (f) → *Berufsfindung/Berufsvorbereitung*	career choice
Berufsförderung (f)	employment development
berufsfördernde Maßnahmen (f/pl) → *Berufsbildung*	employment promotional schemes, career development
Berufsfortbildung (f)	vocational further education
Berufsfortbildungswerk (n)	college or institute of further education
Berufsgrundbildungsjahr (n) → *Berufsbildung* → *Jugendarbeitslosigkeit*	Basic Vocational Training Year
Berufspraktikum (n) → *Sozialarbeiter/Sozialpädagoge*	full-time work placement, probationary year
Berufspraktikant (m)/ Berufspraktikantin (f)	trainee
berufsqualifizierende Beschäftigungsmaßnahmen (f/pl) → *Bundesanstalt für Arbeit, VK*	Employment Training
berufsqualifizierender Abschluß (m)	vocational qualification
Berufsschule (f)	part-time vocational school
Berufsschulpflicht (f) → *Bildungswesen* → *Berufsbildung*	compulsory part-time vocational education
Berufstätiger (m)/Berufstätige (f)	employed person
Berufsvorbereitung (f) → *Berufsfindung/Berufsvorbereitung*	career preparation

Berufsvorbereitungsjahr (n) → *Jugendarbeitslosigkeit*	vocational training preparatory year
Berufsunterricht (m) → *Berufsfindung/Berufsvorbereitung*	careers education
Berufswahl (f)	choice of a career
Berufswechsel (m)	change of profession or job
Beschäftigungstherapeut (m)/ Beschäftigungstherapeutin (f)	occupational therapist
Betreuer (m)/Betreuerin (f)	accompanying adult, escort, programme organiser
Betreuung (f)	care for / looking after a group or person
Betrieb (m)	shop, factory, firm
betriebliche Ausbildung (f)	in-house training
Betriebsobmann (m) → *Betriebsrat*	shop floor representative
Betriebsjugendvertretung (f) → *Betriebsrat*	youth representation on the works committee
Betriebspraktikum (n)	work experience
Betriebsrat (m) → *Betriebsrat*	work committee
Beschäftigungsprogramm (n)	community project
beschützende Werkstatt (f) (geschützte Werkstatt) → *Behindertenhilfe*	sheltered workshop
Bewährung (f) → *Strafaussetzung zur Bewährung*	probation
Bewährungsaufsicht (f) → *Strafaussetzung zur Bewährung*	probationary supervision
Bewährungsfrist (f) → *Strafaussetzung zur Bewährung*	probation period
Bewährungsheim (n) → *Strafaussetzung zur Bewährung*	hostel for probationers
Bewährungshelfer (m)/Bewährungs- helferin (f) → *Strafaussetzung zur Bewährung*	probation officer

Bewährungshilfe (f) → *Strafaussetzung zur Bewährung*	probation service
bewilligen	to grant, to allocate, to approve
Bewilligung (f)	financial approval, e.g. of a grant
Bewilligungsbescheid (m)	notification of financial approval
Bewilligung (f) eines Zuschusses (m)	approval of grant-aid
Bezirksjugendamt (n) → *Jugendamt*	area youth office
Bezugsperson (f)	≠ (a person to whom one relates specifically)
bilaterales Abkommen (n)	bilateral agreement
bilateraler Jugendaustausch (m)	bilateral youth exchange
Bildung (f)	education
Bildungsauftrag (m)	(the State's) obligation to make educational provision
Bildungschancen (f/pl)	educational opportunities
Bildungsdefizit (n)	educational deficiency, lack of educational opportunities
Bildungsgang (m)	educational path
Bildungsgrad (m)	level of education
Bildungsnotstand (m)	crisis in education
Bildungsplan (m)	governmental proposal to the development of the educational system
Bildungsplanung (f) Bildungspolitik (f) Bildungsreferent (m)/Bildungs-referentin (f)	educational planning educational policy adviser for informal education, training officer
Bildungsreise (f)	educational tour
Bildungsstätte (f)	informal educational establishment
bildungsunfähig	ineducable
Bildungsurlaub (m) → *Weiterbildung*	educational leave
Bildungsweg (m)	educational path

Bildungsweg (m), erster

schooling, formal education, normal progress through the educational system

Bildungsweg (m), zweiter
→ *Weiterbildung*

mature student educational provision

Bildungswesen (n)
→ *Bildungswesen*

education system

Brennpunkt (m), sozialer

socially deprived area

Briefpartner (m)/Briefpartnerin (f)

pen friend

Bürgerinitiative (f)
→ *Bürgerinitiative*

community action group

Bürgerliches Gesetzbuch (n) (BGB)

German Civil Code

Bundesangestelltentarif (m) (BAT)
→ *Bedienstete des Öffentlichen Dienstes*

Federal Employees Salary Scales Agreement

Bundesanstalt (f) für Arbeit (f)
→ *Bundesanstalt für Arbeit*

Federal Institute of Labour

Bundesausbildungsförderungsgesetz (n)
→ *Ausbildungsförderung*

Federal Educational Grants Act

Bundesjugendkuratorium (n)
→ *Bundesjugendkuratorium*

Federal Advisory Committee on Youth Problems

Bundesjugendplan (m)
→ *Bundesjugendplan*

Federal Youth Plan

Bundesjugendspiele (n/pl)
→ *Jugendsport*

Federal Youth Games

Bundesministerium (n) für Frauen (f/pl) und Jugend (f) (BMFJ)
→ *Bundesministerium für Frauen und Jugend*

Federal Ministry for Women and Youth

Bundesprüfstelle (f) für jugendgefährdende Schriften (f/pl)
→ *Jugendschutz*

Federal Board for the Review of Publications Harmful to Young Persons

Bundessozialhilfegesetz (n)
→ *Sozialhilfe*

Federal Social Assistance Act

Chancengleichheit (f)
→ *Chancengleichheit*

equal opportunities

CENYC (Europäischer Jugendrat)　　CENYC (Council of European
→ *Jugendringe*　　　　　　　　　　National Youth Committees)

Dachverband (m)　　　　　　　　　association of voluntary organisa-
→ *Jugendringe*　　　　　　　　　　tions, umbrella organisation

Deutscher Bundesjugendring (m)　　German Federal Youth Council
→ *Jugendringe*

Deutscher Jugendhilfetag (m)　　　National Conference for Child and
→ *Deutscher Jugendhilfetag*　　　 Youth Welfare

Deutsches Jugendherbergswerk (n)　German Youth Hostel Association
→ *Wandern*

Deutsches Jugendinstitut (n)　　　German Youth Institute
→ *Jugendforschung*

Deutsch-Französisches Jugendwerk (n) Franco-German Youth Office
→ *Deutsch-Französisches Jugendwerk*

Deutsches Nationalkomitee (n) (DNK) German National Committee
→ *Jugendringe*

diakonischer Jugendeinsatz (m)　　church voluntary community
→ *Engagement, soziales*　　　　　service

Diplom (n)　　　　　　　　　　　higher education diploma
→ *Bildungswesen*

Diplom-Pädagoge (m)/Diplom-　　≠
Pädagogin (f)　　　　　　　　　　(university-trained youth worker)
→ *Sozialarbeiter/Sozialpädagoge*
→ *Mitarbeiter der Jugendhilfe*

Dorfhelferin (f)　　　　　　　　　rural home help
→ *Mitarbeiter der Jugendhilfe*

Droge (f)　　　　　　　　　　　　drug
→ *Drogenmißbrauch*

Drogenabhängigkeit (f)　　　　　　drug dependency

Drogensüchtiger (m)/Drogensüchtige drug addict
(f)

Drogenbenutzer (m)/Drogenbenut-　drug user
zerin (f), Drogenkonsument (m)/
Drogenkonsumentin (f)

Drogenberatungsstelle (f)　　　　　drug adivsory centre
→ *Beratungsdienste*
→ *Drogenmißbrauch*

Drogenempfänglichkeit (f)	susceptibility to drugs
Drogengefährdeter (m)/Drogenge-fährdete (f)	person at risk from drugs
Drogenmißbrauch (m) → *Drogenmißbrauch*	drug misuse
duales System (n) → *Bildungswesen* → *Berufsbildung*	≠ (day release/sandwich courses)
Duke of Edinburgh's Award Scheme, The → *Duke of Edinburgh' Award Scheme, The*	Duke of Edinburgh's Award Scheme, The
Eheberatung (f) → *Beratungsdienste*	marriage guidance
Eheberatungsstelle (f) → *Beratungsdienste*	marriage guidance centre
Ehemündigkeit (f) → *Tabelle Altersgrenzen*	normal minimum marriage age
ehrenamtlicher Helfer (m)/ehrenamtliche Helferin (f) → *Mitarbeiter der Jugendhilfe*	unpaid full-time or part-time (youth) worker (or helper)
Eigenbeitrag (m)	individual contribution
Eignungsprüfung (f)	aptitude test
Einführungsseminar (n)	briefing seminar
Einführungsvortrag (m)	introductory paper or lecture
Einrichtung (f)	establishment, facility, provision
Einzelfallanalyse (f), Einzelfall-bericht (m)	case work report
Einzelfallhilfe (f)	case work
Einzelwohnen (n), betreutes → *Hilfe zur Erziehung*	living alone with social worker support
elterliche Sorge (f) → *Elterliche Sorge*	parental rights and duties
Elternarbeit (f)	working with parents
Elternbeirat (m)	parents council

Empfängnisverhütung (f)	contraception
Engagement (n), soziales → *Engagement, soziales*	community involvement
Entwicklungshelfer (m)/Entwicklungshelferin (f)	VSO-type of worker (Voluntary Service Overseas worker with a developmental scheme)
Entwicklungshilfe (f)	development aid, Overseas Development
Entziehungsheim (n), Entwöhnungsheim (n)	rehabilitation centre
Entziehungskur (f)	withdrawal therapy
Entzugserscheinungen (f/pl)	withdrawal symptoms
Erholungsheim (n)	convalescent home, rest centre
Erholungsmaßnahme (f)	remedial or recuperative health scheme
Erlaß (m) → *Rechtsinstrumente* ministerieller Erlaß	decree ministerial decree
Erlebnispädagogik (f) → *Erlebnispädagogik*	adventure pursuits, outdoor pursuits
ermäßigter Preis (m), ermäßigter Satz (m)	reduced price, concessionary rate
Erstattung (f)	reimbursement, refund
Erwachsenenbildung (f)	adult education
Erwachsener (m), junger/Erwachsene (f), junge → *Tabelle Altersgrenzen*	≠ (young adult)
Erzieher (m)/Erzieherin (f) → *Erzieher/Erzieherin*	≠ (qualified youth or child care worker)
Erziehung (f) Erziehung durch die Familie Erziehung im Sinne von Bildung	≠ upbringing, child-rearing education
Erziehungsanspruch (m) (des Kindes)	(the child's) right to be brought up and educated
Erziehungsbeistandschaft (f) → *Jugendstrafrecht, Maßnahmen des*	socio-educational provision similar to a supervision order

Erziehungsberatung (f) → *Beratungsdienste* → *Jugendamt*	child guidance
Erziehungsberechtigter (m)/Erziehungsberechtigte (f)	person holding parental authority
Erziehungsheim (n) → *Jugendstrafrecht, Maßnahmen des*	community home (formerly approved school)
Erziehungshilfen (f/pl) → *Hilfe zur Erziehung*	socio-educational provision for children with problems
ambulante Erziehungshilfen	non-residential (out-patient/open) socio-educational provision for children with problems
teilstationäre Erziehungshilfen	partly residential socio-educational provision for children with problems
stationäre Erziehungshilfen	residential socio-educational provision for children with problems
familienunterstützende Erziehungshilfen	socio-educational provision to support the family, supportive provision for the family
familienbegleitende Erziehungshilfen	socio-educational support provided to complement the family
familienergänzende Erziehungshilfen	socio-educational support provided to supplement the family
familienersetzende Erziehungshilfen	socio-educational support provided to replace the family
öffentliche Erziehungshilfen	statutory socio-educational provision for children with problems
Erziehungsjahr (n)	$\neq$ (crediting of periods (a year) devoted to the upbringing of children)
Erziehungsmaßregeln (f/pl) → *Jugendstrafrecht, Maßnahmen des*	socio-educational court orders
Erziehungspflicht (f)	parental educational responsibilities
erziehungsschwieriges Kind (n)	disruptive child
Erziehungsschwierigkeiten (f/pl)	socio-educational difficulties; disruptive behaviour
europäische Jugendstrukturen (f/pl) → *Jugendringe*	European youth structures

Europäischer Jugendrat → *Jugendringe*	Council of European National Youth Committees (CENYC)
Extremistenbeschluß (m)	Decree on Employment of Extremists
Fachausbildung (f) → *Berufsbildung* → *Weiterbildung*	training (for craftsmen in a skilled trade), specialist further training (for a professional), specialist training
Facharbeiterbrief (m)	proficiency certificate for the skilled worker
Fachausschüsse (m/pl), gemischte z.B. Gemischter Fachausschuß für den deutsch-britischen Jugend- austausch → *Fachausschüsse, gemischte*	Special Committees on Youth Exchanges e.g. British-German Special Committee on Youth Exchanges
fachgebundene Hochschulreife (f)	subject-tied university entrance qualification
Fachgymnasium (f) → *Berufsbildung*	≠ (technical grammar school)
Fachhochschule (f) → *Bildungswesen*	≠ (polytechnic-type institution)
Fachhochschulreife (f) → *Bildungswesen*	entrance qualification for a *Fachhochschule*
Fachkräfte (f/pl) der Jugendarbeit (f)	professional youth workers, youth work professionals
Fachoberschule (f) → *Berufsbildung*	≠ (senior technical school)
Fachschule (f) → *Berufsbildung*	≠ (technical school)
Fachtagung (f)	specialist conference
Fachverband (m) der Jugendarbeit (f) (z.B. Musik, Sport)	specialist youth organisation (e.g. music, sport)
Fahrten (f/pl) → *Wandern*	expeditions
Fahrtkosten (pl)	travel expenses

Familienaufenthalt (m)	period spent in staying with a family, home stay
Familienerholungsmaßnahme (f)	family holiday scheme
Familienfürsorge (f) → *Familienfürsorge*	family welfare work
Familienhelfer (m)/Familienhelferin (f)	family aide
Familienplanung (f)	family planning
Familien- und Elternbildung (f) → *Familien- und Elternbildung*	family and parental counselling
Familienverhältnisse (n/pl), gestörte	broken home (s)
Feriendorf (n)	holiday village
Ferienfreizeit (f)	residential event
Ferienheim (n)	holiday home
Ferienkolonie (f), Ferienlager (n)	holiday camp
Ferienmaßnahme (f)	holiday provision, holiday schemes, holiday programmes
Ferienreise (f)	holiday trip
Ferienstätte (f)	holiday centre
Fernunterricht (m)	distance teaching
Föderalismus (m)/Zentralstaatlichkeit (f) → *Föderalismus/Zentralstaatlichkeit*	federalism/unitary government
Förderung (f)	promotion, (financial) support, grant-aid
Förderungsantrag (m)	application for grant-aid
Förderungsbetrag (m)	grant awarded
Förderungsgrundsatz (m), Förderungsprinzip (n)	principle of subsidization
Förderungsmittel (n/pl)	grant-aid available
Förderungsrichtlinien (f/pl)	regulations on grant-aid
Förderungssätze (m/pl)	scales of grant, rates of support
Förderungssumme (f)	sum allocated in grant-aid
Fortbildung (f) → *Weiterbildung*	further education, advanced training
berufsbegleitende Fortbildung	in-service training

Fortbildungskursus (m), Fortbildungslehrgang (m)	further education course
Fortbildungsmaßnahme (f)	further education programme
Frauenbewegung (f) → *Frauenbewegung*	women's movement
Frauenhaus (n) → *Frauenbewegung*	women's refuge
freier Träger (m) → *Träger der Jugendhilfe* die freien Träger	voluntary organisation, voluntary agency the voluntary sector
Freigängerhaus (n)	open prison
Freiheitsstrafe (f)	prison sentence
Freiwilligendienste (m/pl)	voluntary services, volunteering
freiwilliger Arbeitseinsatz (n)	voluntary service in an organised scheme
freiwilliges soziales Jahr (n) → *Freiwilliges Soziales Jahr*	year of voluntary work and community service
Freizeit (f)	a) leisure time b) structured leisure time activity e.g. out-door pursuits, residential event, residential programme
Freizeitangebot (n)	leisure time provision
Freizeitberatung (f) → *Freizeitpädagogik*	leisure counselling
Freizeitbeschäftigung (f), Freizeitbetätigung (f)	leisure time activities, hobbies, pastimes
Freizeitgestaltung (f) → *Freizeitpädagogik*	organisation (or use) of leisure time
Freizeitheim (n)	leisure centre
Freizeitpädagogik (f) → *Freizeitpädagogik*	education for leisure
Freizeitpark (m)	leisure park
Freizeitstätte (f)	leisure centre
Freizeitverhalten (n)	leisure time behaviour
Friedensbewegung (f) → *Friedensbewegung*	peace movement

frühreifes Kind (n)	precocious child
Führungsstile (m/pl)	styles of leadership
→ *Führungsstile*	
autoritärer Führungsstil	directive style of leadership
demokratischer Führungsstil	democratic style of leadership
laissez-faire Führungsstil	non-directive/liberal style of leadership
Fürsorge (f)	welfare work
→ *Fürsorge, öffentliche*	
Fürsorge (f), öffentliche	public welfare
→ *Fürsorge, öffentliche*	
Gammler (m)/Gammlerin (f) (coll.)	drop-out
Ganztagsschule (f)	all-day school
Garantiefonds (m)	≠
→ *Bundesministerium für Frauen und Jugend*	*Garantiefonds*
„Gastarbeiter" (m)/„Gastarbeiterin" (f) (ausländischer Arbeitnehmer (m)/ ausländische Arbeitnehmerin (f)	migrant worker
Gastgeberfamilie (f)	host family
Gefangenenfürsorge (f)	prison welfare and after-care
Gefährdeter (m)/Gefährdete (f)	person at risk
gefährdetes Kind (n)	child at risk
Gemeinde (f)	community
→ *Kommunale Selbstverwaltung*	
Gemeindebehörde (f)	local authority department
Gemeindeverwaltung (f)	local government administration
gemeinnützig	non-profit making
gemeinnützige Arbeit (f)	community service
gemeinnützige Einrichtung (f)	charity
Gemeinschaftsdienst (m)	community service
Gemeinschaftseinrichtung (f)	community centre
Gemeinschaftsleben (n)	community life
Gemeinschaftsschule (f)	non-denominational school

Gemeinwesenarbeit (f) → *Sozialarbeit/Sozialpädagogik*	community organisation, *community work (UK)* community education (Scotland)
Genehmigung (f) von Anträgen (m/pl)	approval of applications
Genossenschaft (f)	cooperative
Gesamthochschule (f)	≠ (combined polytechnic and university)
integrierte Gesamthochschule	integrated polytechnic and university
kooperative Gesamthochschule	cooperative polytechnic and university
Gesamtschule (f) → *Bildungswesen*	comprehensive school
Gesellenbrief (m)	tradesman's certificate
Gesellenprüfung (f) → *Berufsbildung*	trade examination
Gesetz (n) über die Verbreitung (f) jugendgefährdender Schriften (f/pl) → *Jugendgesetze*	Act Concerning the Distribution of Publications Harmful to Young Persons
Gesundheitsamt (n)	local health service department
Gesundheitsbehörde (f)	local health authority
Gesundheitsdienst (m), Gesundheitswesen (n)	health service
Gesundheitserziehung (f)	health education
Gesundheitspflege (f)	health care
Gesundheitsschutz (m)	public health protection
Gleichberechtigung (f)	equality of rights for men and women
Globalförderung (f), Globalmittel (n/pl)	block grant
Graduierung (f) → *Bildungswesen*	graduation from a *Fachhochschule*
Großpflegestelle (f) → *Hilfe zur Erziehung*	large fostering unit
Grundausbildung (f)	basic training
Grundschule (f) → *Bildungswesen*	primary school

Gruppenarbeit (f)	group work
Gruppenbetreuer (m)/Gruppen- betreuerin (f)	group escort, group leader, person looking after a group
Gruppendynamik (f)	group dynamics
Gruppenführer (m)/Gruppenführe- rin (f), Gruppenleiter (m)/Gruppen- leiterin (f)	group leader
Gruppenerziehung (f)	group education, developmental group work
Gruppenpädagogik (f)	group work theory and technique
Gymnasium (n) → *Bildungswesen*	grammar school
Haft (f)	detention, imprisonment
Haftung (f)	liability
hauptamtlicher Mitarbeiter (m)/ hauptamtliche Mitarbeiterin (f) → *Mitarbeiter der Jugendhilfe*	full-time worker
Hauptschule (f)	≠ (secondary school)
Hauptschulabschluß (m) → *Bildungswesen*	*Hauptschule* leaving certificate
Haus (n) der Jugend (f) → *Jugendfreizeitstätten*	youth centre
Haus (n) der offenen Tür (f) (OT) → *Jugendfreizeitstätten*	youth club, open-door youth centre
Haus der teiloffenen Tür (TOT)	youth club, partially open youth centre
Haus der kleinen offenen Tür (KOT)	small door youth centre
Haushaltungsschule (f)	home economics school
Hauspflege (f)	home help
Hauspflegerin (f)	home help
Heilpädagoge (m)/Heilpädagogin (f) → *Mitarbeiter der Jugendhilfe*	remedial teacher
Heilpädagogik (f)	remedial teaching
heilpädagogisch	relating to remedial teaching

Heimaufsicht (f) → *Jugendamt*	supervision of institutions
Heimaufsichtsbehörde (f) → *Jugendamt*	authority responsible for the supervision of institutions
Heimbewohner (m)/Heimbewoh- nerin (f)	hostel resident
Heimerzieher (m)/Heimerzieherin (f) → *Erzieher/Erzieherin*	residential child care worker
Heimerziehung (f)	residential care
Heimkind (n)	child in residential care
Heimleiter (m)/Heimleiterin (f)	warden of a home
Heimunterbringung (f)	residential care
Helfer (m)/Helferin (f)	helper, assistant
Heranwachsender (m)/ Heranwachsende (f) → *Tabelle Altersgrenzen* → *Jugendstrafrecht*	≠ (legal term used for a person of the 18–21 age group)
Hilfe (f) zur Erziehung (f) (H.z.E) → *Hilfe zur Erziehung*	statutory socio-educational provision for children with problems
Hilfe zur Erziehung (Erziehungs- beistandschaft)	socio-educational provision similar to a supervision order
Hilfe zur Erziehung nach § 27 Sozial- gesetzbuch VIII	socio-educational provision under a care order; reception into care
Hilfebedürftiger (m)/ Hilfebedürftige (f)	person in need of help
Hilfsbedürftigkeit (f)	indigence, neediness
Hit-Liste (f)	pop charts
Hochschule (f)	higher education institution
Hochschulreife (f) → *Bildungswesen*	university and technical university entrance qualification
Hort (m) → *Tageseinrichtungen für Kinder*	day care centre
Hortner (m)/Hortnerin (f) → *Erzieher/Erzieherin*	qualified worker in day care centres
Hospitalismus (m)	institutionalization

Hospitation (f)	observation visit
hospitieren	to observe in action, to sit in (on a class)
Informationsaustausch (m)	information sharing, exchange of information
informelle Gruppe (f)	informal group
informelle Gruppenarbeit (f)	informal group work
Inobhutnahme (f) → *Jugendschutz*	provision of shelter and protection
Internat (n)	boarding school
Internationale Jugendarbeit (f) → *Internationale Jugendarbeit*	international youth work
Internationaler Jugendaustausch- und Besucherdienst der Bundesrepublik Deutschland (IJAB) e.V. → *IJAB*	International Youth Exchange and Visitors' Service of the Federal Republic of Germany
Interventionskette (f)	(statutory) process of intervention
Jahrespraktikum (n)	probationary year
jobclub (Beratungsstelle für Arbeitslose) → *Bundesanstalt für Arbeit, VK*	jobclub
Jugendamt (n) → *Jugendamt*	youth welfare and youth service office (youth office)
Jugendarbeit (f) → *Jugendarbeit*	youth work, youth and community work
Jugendarbeit (f), mobile → *Jugendarbeit, mobile*	out-reach youth work, detached youth work
Jugendarbeitslosigkeit (f) → *Jugendarbeitslosigkeit*	youth unemployment
Jugendarbeitsschutz (m) → *Jugendgesetze*	protection of young people at work
Jugendarbeitsschutzgesetz (n) → *Jugendgesetze*	Protection of Young Persons at Work Act

Jugendarrest (m) → *Jugendstrafrecht, Maßnahmen des*	treatment of young offenders at attendance centres
Jugendarrestanstalt (f) → *Jugendstrafrecht, Maßnahmen des*	attendance centre
Jugendaustausch (m)	youth exchange
Jugendbauprogramme (n/pl) → *Bundesministerium für Frauen* *und Jugend*	construction programmes for youth establishments
Jugendbauten (m/pl), Jugend- einrichtungen (f/pl)	youth provision
Jugendbegegnung (f), Jugend- treffen (n)	youth meeting, youth contact
Jugendbehörden (f/pl) → *Jugendbehörden*	youth authorities
Jugendbericht (m) → *Jugendbericht*	National Youth Report
Jugendberufshilfe (f) → *Jugendsozialarbeit*	assistance to young people with a vocational problem
Jugendbewegung (f) → *Jugendkultur*	youth movement
Jugendbildung (f) → *Jugendarbeit*	informal education for young people
Jugendbildungsreferent (m)/ Jugendbildungsreferentin (f)	adviser on informal education for the young
Jugendbildungsgesetz (f)	youth residential training centre
Jugendbuchpreis (m), Deutscher	Award for Children's Books, German
Jugendcafé (n)	drop-in centre
Jugendclub (m)	youth club
Jugendfarm (f)	city farm for young people
Jugendferienwerk (n)	holiday activity schemes
Jugendförderung (f) → *Bundesjugendplan* → *Jugendförderung*	supportive measures for the youth service
Jugendforum (n)	youth forum
Jugendforschung (f) → *Jugendforschung*	youth research

Jugendfreizeitstätten (f/pl)
→ *Jugendfreizeitstätten*

leisure time centres for young people

Jugendfürsorge (f)
→ *Jugendamt*
→ *Jugendfürsorge/Jugendpflege*

welfare work for the young, child care

jugendgefährdend

representing a (moral) risk for the young, harmful to young persons

jugendgefährdende Schriften (f/pl)
→ *Jugendschutz*

publications harmful to young persons

Jugendgemeinschaftsdienste (m/pl)

youth community service

Jugendgericht (n)
→ *Jugendstrafrecht*

juvenile court, young offender's court

Jugendgerichtsgesetz (n)
→ *Jugendstrafrecht*

Juvenile Court Act

Jugendgerichtshelfer (m)
→ *Jugendstrafrecht*

social worker involved in juvenile cases

Jugendgesetze (n/pl)
→ *Jugendgesetze*

laws relating to young people

Jugendgesetzgebung (f)
→ *Jugendgesetze*

youth legislation

Jugendhaus (n)

youth club

Jugendheim (n)

youth club (sometimes with simple overnight facilities)

Jugendhelfer (m)/Jugendhelferin (f)

youth support worker

Jugendherberge (f)

youth hostel

Jugendherbergsausweis (m)

membership card of the Youth Hostel Association

Jugendherbergseltern (pl)

youth hostel wardens

Jugendherbergsleiter (m)/Jugendherbergsleiterin (f)

youth hostel warden

Jugendhilfe (f)
→ *Jugendhilfe*

youth work and youth welfare services,
child and youth services

Jugendhilfeausschuß (m)
→ *Jugendamt*

Youth Services Committee

Jugendhilferecht (n)

child and youth services law

Jugendhilfeträger (m/pl) → *Träger der Jugendhilfe*	bodies responsible for youth work and youth welfare services
Jugendhof (m)	residential youth centre
Jugendinitiativen (f/pl)	youth action
Jugendinformationszentrum (n) → *Beratungsdienste*	information and counselling centre for young people
Jugendkammer (f) → *Jugendstrafrecht*	juvenile court at *Land* level
Jugendkriminalität (f)	juvenile delinquency
Jugendkultur (f) → *Jugendkultur*	youth subculture(s)
Jugendlager (n)	youth camp, residential youth centre
Jugendleiter (m)/Jugendleiterin (f) → *Jugendleiter*	youth leader (voluntary)
Jugendlicher (m)/Jugendliche (f) → *Tabelle Altersgrenzen*	young person
jugendlicher Straffälliger (m)/ jugendliche Straffällige (f)	young offender
Jugendmarke (f) → *Jugendmarke*	Youth Stamp
Jugendmusik (f) → *Jugendarbeit*	young musician's provision
Jugendorganisation (f), Jugendverband (m) → *Jugendverbände*	youth organisation, youth association
Jugendpfarrer (m)/ Jugendseelsorger (m)	youth chaplain
Jugendpflege (f) → *Jugendamt* → *Jugendpflege/Jugendfürsorge*	leisure time provision for the young
Jugendpfleger (m)/Jugendpflegerin (f)	youth officer
Jugendpolitik (f)	youth policy
Jugendpolitiker (m)/ Jugendpolitikerin (f)	policy maker (in the youth field)
Jugendpresse (f)	youth magazines and publications

Jugendprotest (m) → *Jugendprotest*	anti-establishment protest, political protest by the young
Jugendreisedienste (m/pl) → *Jugendreisen*	travel services for young people on a non-profitmaking basis
Jugendreisen (f/pl) → *Jugendreisen*	youth travel, youth tours
Jugendreiseleiter (m)/ Jugendreiseleiterin (f) → *Jugendreisen*	youth courier
Jugendreligionen (f/pl) → *Jugendreligionen*	youth religions
Jugendrichter (m)/Jugendrichterin (f) → *Jugendstrafrecht*	juvenile court magistrate
Jugendring (m) → *Jugendringe*	standing conference of youth organisations
Jugendschöffe (m)/Jugendschöffin (f) → *Jugendstrafrecht*	lay magistrate in a juvenile court
Jugendschutz (m) → *Jugendschutz*	protection of young persons in public
Jugendschutzgesetz (n) → *Jugendgesetze*	Act Concerning the Protection of Young People in Public
Jugendsekten (f/pl) → *Jugendkultur*	youth sects
Jugendsozialarbeit (f) → *Jugendsozialarbeit*	socio-educational provision for young people
Jugendsport (m) → *Jugendsport*	sport for young people
Jugendstaatsanwalt (m)/ Jugendstaatsanwältin (f) → *Jugendstrafrecht*	public prosecutor in juvenile cases
Jugendstrafanstalt (f) → *Jugendstrafrecht, Maßnahmen des*	youth custody centre, youth prison
Jugendstrafe (f) → *Jugendstrafrecht, Maßnahmen des*	committal order, custodial sentence for young people
Jugendstrafrecht (n) → *Jugendstrafrecht*	penal law relating to young offenders
Jugendstrafrecht (n), Maßnahmen (f/pl) des → *Jugendstrafrecht, Maßnahmen des*	measures under penal law relating to young offenders

Jugendstraftat (f) → *Jugendstrafrecht, Maßnahmen des*	juvenile offence
Jugendstrafvollzug (m) → *Jugendstrafrecht, Maßnahmen des*	custodial treatment of young offenders
Jugendtourismus (m) → *Jugendreisen*	tourist services directed at young people
Jugendverbände (m/pl) → *Jugendverbände*	youth organisations
Jugendvertreter (m) → *Betriebsrat*	youth representative of a works committee
Jugendwoche (f)	youth week
Jugendwohnen (n), betreutes → *Hilfe zur Erziehung*	young people living with socio-educational support in the community
Jugendwohnheim (n)	hostel, residential home for young people
Jugendzeitschrift (f)	youth magazine
Jugendzentrum (n) → *Jugendfreizeitstätten*	youth centre
junger Mensch (m) → *Tabelle Altersgrenzen*	≠ (person under 27 years of age)
junger Volljähriger (m)/ junge Volljährige (f) → *Tabelle Altersgrenzen*	young adult
Kind (n) → *Tabelle Altersgrenzen*	child
Kinderarzt (m)/Kinderärztin (f)	pediatrician
Kinderbetreuung (f)	child minding
Kindergarten (m) → *Tageseinrichtungen für Kinder*	kindergarten, nursery school, pre-school play group
Kindergärtnerin (f) → *Erzieher* → *Tageseinrichtungen für Kinder*	nursery (school) teacher, play school leader
Kindergarten-Helfer (m)/ Kindergarten-Helferin (f) → *Tageseinrichtungen für Kinder*	nursery assistant
Kindergeld (n)	family allowance

Kinderheim (n)	children's home
Kinderklinik (f)	pediatric clinic
Kinderkrankenhaus (n)	children's hospital
Kinderkrippe (f) → *Tageseinrichtungen für Kinder*	crêche
Kinderpflegerin (f) → *Tageseinrichtungen für Kinder*	children's nurse
Kinderspielplatz (m)	children's play ground
Kindertagesheim (n) → *Tageseinrichtungen für Kinder*	day care centre for children and young people, day nursery
Kindertagesstätte (f) → *Tageseinrichtungen für Kinder*	day care centre for children and young people
Kinder- und Jugenderholung (f) → *Kinder- und Jugenderholung*	holiday schemes for children and young people
Kinder- und Jugendhilfegesetz (n) (KJHG) → *Jugendgesetze* → *Jugendamt*	Child and Youth Services Act
Kindesmißhandlung (f)	cruelty to children
kirchliche Jugendarbeit (f)	youth work done by the churches
Klassenfahrt (f)	school trip
Kollegschule (f) → *Bildungswesen*	≠ (special educational provision in adult education to reach university entrance qualification)
Kleinheim (n) → *Hilfe zur Erziehung*	small-scale residential provision
Kommune (f) → *Kommunale Selbstverwaltung*	a) local authority b) commune, communal living
kommunale Einrichtungen (f/pl)	services or institutions run by the local authority
kommunale Selbstverwaltung (f) → *Kommunale Selbstverwaltung*	local government (UK), local self-government (FRG)
kommunaler Jugendplan (m) → *Bundesjugendplan*	local authority youth plan
Krabbelstube (f)	toddlers' group

Kreis (m) (Stadtkreis/Landkreis) → *Kommunale Selbstverwaltung*	≠ *Kreis*
Kreisjugendamt (n) → *Jugendamt*	*Kreis* youth office
Kreisjugendring (m) → *Jugendringe*	standing conference of youth organisations at *Kreis* level
Kriegsdienstverweigerer (m) → *Wehrpflicht, allgemeine*	conscientious objector
kulturelle Jugendbildung (f)	youth work in the arts
Kulturhoheit (f) der Länder (n/pl) → *Bildungswesen*	cultural autonomy of the *Länder*
Kurzlehrgang (m)	short course, crash course
Kurzschule (f) → *Erlebnispädagogik*	Outward Bound Trust type establishment
Laienspiel (n)	amateur dramatics
Laienspielgruppe (f)	drama group
Laientheater (n)	amateur theatre
Land (n), Länder (n/pl) → *Föderalismus/Zentralstaatlichkeit*	≠ *Land*, pl. *Länder* (of the FRG)
Landesjugendamt (n) → *Jugendamt* → *Jugendbehörden*	*Land* youth office
Landesjugendplan (m) → *Bundesjugendplan*	*Land* youth plan
Landesjugendring (m) → *Jugendringe*	standing conference of youth organisations at *Land* level
Landesjugendhilfeausschuß (m) → *Jugendamt* → *Jugendbehörden*	Youth Services Committee at *Land* level
Landeskunde (f) (bezogen auf VK)	British studies (UK)
Landjugend (f)	association of rural youth
Lehrstelle (f) → *Berufsbildung*	apprentice training place

Lehrvertrag (m) → *Berufsbildung*	apprenticeship contract
Lehrwerkstätte (f)	training workshop
Leibeserziehung (f)	physical education
Leistung (f)	performance, achievement
Leistungsdruck (m) (im Bildungswesen)	pressure to achieve academically
Leistungsgesellschaft (f)	competitive society, rat race society (coll.)
Lernbeeinträchtiger (m)/ Lernbeeinträchtigte (f), Lernbehinderter (m)/ Lernbehinderte (f)	slow learner
literarischer Jugendschutz (m) → *Jugendschutz*	protection of young people from harmful publications
Mädchenarbeit (f) → *Mädchenarbeit*	work with girls
Management Committee → *Management Committee*	Management Committee
Medienerziehung (f)	education in the use of the media
Medienpädagoge (m)/ Medienpädagogin (f)	media resource officer
Mehrzweckeinrichtung (f)	multi-purpose establishment
Meinungsaustausch (m)	exchange of views, exchange of opinions
Meinungsforschung (f)	opinion research
Meinungsumfrage (f)	opinion poll
Meisterbrief (m) → *Berufsbildung*	≠ (qualified instructor's certificate)
Meisterprüfung (f) → *Berufsbildung*	≠ (examination for qualified instructors in crafts or industry)
milieugeschädigt	socially deprived, underprivileged
Milieuwechsel (m)	change of environment

Mensch (m), junger → *Tabelle Altersgrenzen*	≠ (person under 27 years of age)
Minderjährigkeit (f)	age of minority
Mindestalter (n)	minimum age
Mißhandlung (f)	ill-usage, ill treatment, abuse
mißhandeltes Kind (n)	battered baby, battered child
Mitarbeiter (m)/Mitarbeiterin (f) der Jugendarbeit (f)	youth worker
Mitarbeiter (m/pl)/Mitarbeiterinnen (f/pl) der Jugendhilfe (f) → *Mitarbeiter der Jugendhilfe* (nicht formal qualifizierte) Mitarbeiter der Jugendhilfe	workers in youth and youth welfare services youth work practitioners
Mitbestimmung (f)	co-determination, joint management
Mitbestimmungsrecht (n)	right of co-determination, right to a say in management
Mitglied (n)	member
Mittel (n/pl)	resources, funds
Mitverantwortung (f)	co-responsibility
Mitverwaltung (f)	participation in management
Mitwirkung (f)	participation in decision making
Mitwirkung (f) in der Schule (f) (schulische Mitwirkung) → *Partizipation Jugendlicher*	participation in school government
Mitwirkungsrecht (n)	right to participation in decision making
mobile Jugendarbeit (f) → *Jugendarbeit, mobile*	out-reach youth work, detached youth work
Modellprojekt (n)	pilot project
musische Bildung (f) → *Jugendarbeit*	education in music and the arts
Mütterberatung (f) → *Beratungsdienste*	advice to mothers, instruction of mothers, counselling in child care
Mütterberatungsstelle (f) → *Beratungsdienste*	ante- and post-natal clinic

Nachbarschaftsheim (n)	neighbourhood centre, community centre
Nachbarschaftshilfe (f)	neighbourhood care, community care
Nachbetreuung (f)	after-care
Nachkontakte (m/pl)	follow-up (contact)
National Youth Agency (NYA) → *Überblick über den Youth Service im Vereinigten Königreich (Teil I)*	National Youth Agency (NYA)
nebenamtlicher Mitarbeiter (m)/ nebenamtliche Mitarbeiterin (f)	part-time worker, part-time staff (pl)
Neigungsgruppe (f)	common-interest group
nichteheliches Kind (n)	illegitimate child
numerus clausus (m) → *Bildungswesen*	admission restriction in higher education
Obdachlosenhilfe (f)	help for the homeless
Obdachlosigkeit (f)	homelessness
Oberste Landesjugendbehörde (f)	youth authority of the *Land* government
öffentlicher Träger (m) → *Träger der Jugendhilfe*	statutory authority, statutory agency
offene Einrichtung (f)	establishment without fixed membership
offene Jugendarbeit (f)	activities for young people, mainly in the form of leisure time provision
Pädagoge (m)/Pädagogin (f)	educationist
Pädagogik (f)	educational theory
Partizipation (f) Jugendlicher (m/pl) → *Partizipation Jugendlicher*	participation of young people in decision making
Partnerschaft (f)	partnership, link
Partnerschaftsberatung (f) → *Beratungsdienste*	relationship counselling

Partnerstadt (f)	linked city, twinned city, twinned town
Patenstadt (f)	patron town
Personaljugendvertretung (f) → *Betriebsrat*	youth representatives under the Representation of Staff Act
Personalvertretungsgesetz (n) → *Betriebsrat*	Representation of Staff Act
Personensorge (f) → *Elterliche Sorge*	care and custody of a person
Personensorgeberechtigter (m)/ Personensorgeberechtigte (f) → *Elterliche Sorge*	person who exercises the right of care and custody
Pfadfinder (m)/Pfadfinderin (f)	scout, guide
Pflegebedürftigkeit (f)	(state of being) in need of care
Pflegeeltern (pl), Pflegefamilie (f) → *Pflegekinderbereich/Pflegekinderwesen*	foster parents, foster family
Pflegekind (n) → *Pflegekinderbereich/Pflegekinderwesen*	foster child
Pfleger (m)/Pflegerin (f) → *Pflegschaft*	≠ curator (FRG) custodian (UK)
Pflegestelle (f) → *Pflegekinderbereich/Pflegekinderwesen*	foster home
Pflegschaft (f) → *Pflegschaft*	≠ curatorship (FRG) custodianship (UK)
politische Bildung (f)/ staatsbürgerliche Erziehung (f) → *Jugendarbeit*	political education/education for citizenship (active citizenship)
Pornografie (f)	pornography
Praktikant (m)/Praktikantin (f)	student trainee

Praktikum (n)
  Betriebspraktikum (n)
  Schulpraktikum
	practical placement
	  practical placement
	  work experience

Probandenheim (n)	hostel for ex-prisoners released on probation
Programmfinanzierung (f)	financing of programmes

Programmplanung (f), Programmgestaltung	programme planning
Psychagoge (m)/Psychagogin (f)	≠ (psychiatric child care worker)
Punker (m), Punk (m)	punk
Radikalenerlaß (m)	Decree on Employment of Extremists
Rahmenprogramm (n)	informal element of a programme
Randgruppe (f)	fringe group
Rauschgift (n) → *Drogenmißbrauch*	drugs
Rauschgiftabhängigkeit (f) → *Drogenmißbrauch*	drug dependence
Rauschgifthandel (m)/("dealen") → *Drogenmißbrauch*	trafficking in drugs, drug trafficking
Rauschgiftsucht (f) → *Drogenmißbrauch*	drug addiction
Rauschgiftsüchtiger (m)/ Rauschgiftsüchtige (f) → *Drogenmißbrauch*	drug addict
Rauschmittel (n)	stimulant
Realschule (f) → *Bildungswesen*	≠ (parallels former secondary modern school)
Realschulabschluß (m) → *Bildungswesen*	*Realschule* leaving certificate
Rechtsanspruch (m)	a legal right (to)
Rechtsinstrumente (n/pl) → *Rechtsinstrumente*	legal instruments
Referent (m)/Referentin (f)	a) speaker b) specialist officer
Regelsatz (m), Richtsatz (m) → *Sozialhilfe*	basic benefits
Rehabilitation (f)	rehabilitation

Rehabilitation (f) Behinderter (m/f/pl)
→ *Behindertenhilfe*
→ *Rehabilitation Behinderter*

rehabilitation of the handicapped, integration of disabled persons

Reifezeugnis (n)

≠
(grammar school leaving certificate)

Reisekosten (pl)

travel expenses

Reiseleiter (m)/Reiseleiterin (f)

travel guide, courier

Religionsmündigkeit (f)
→ *Tabelle Altersgrenzen*

age of religious emancipation

Resozialisierung (f)
→ *Jugendstrafrecht*

social rehabilitation, rehabilitation of offenders

Resozialisierungsheim (n)
→ *Rehabilitation Behinderter*

social rehabilitation centre

Richtlinien (f/pl) für den Bundesjugendplan (m)
→ *Bundesjugendplan*

Directives for the Federal Youth Plan

Ring (m) Politischer Jugend (f)
→ *Jugendringe*

Council of Political Youth Organisations

Sachbearbeiter (m)/
Sachbearbeiterin (f)

administrative officer, desk officer

Säuglingsheim (n)
→ *Tageseinrichtungen für Kinder*

home for infants and babies

Säuglingspflege (f)

baby care, infant care

Säuglingsschwester (f)

nursery nurse

Säuglingssterblichkeit (f)

infant mortality

Schlüsselkind (n)

latch-key child

schnüffeln

(glue-)sniffing

Schüffler (m)

sniffer

Schriften (f/pl), jugendgefährdende
→ *Jugendschutz*

publications harmful to young persons

Schüleraustausch (m)

exchange of school children

Schülervertretung (f) (SV)
→ *Partizipation Jugendlicher*

pupil representation, pupils' council

Schulformen (f/pl)	types of schools
Schulkindergarten (m) → *Tageseinrichtungen für Kinder*	school kindergarten, remedial class for slow developers
Schullandheim (n)	country centre, holiday home for pupils
Schullaufbahnberatung (f)	advice on schooling
Schulleiter (m)/Schulleiterin (f)	headmaster, director, principal
Schulleitung (f)	the headmaster of a school and senior staff
Schulpflicht (f) → *Bildungswesen*	compulsory school education
schulpflichtig	having reached statutory school age
schulpsychologischer Dienst (m)	school psychologist
Schulreife (f)	readiness for school
Schulreifetest (m)	school readiness test
Schulschwänzen (n)	truancy
Schulsozialarbeit (f)	school social work, education welfare work
Schulung (f)	schooling, training
Schulungsabend (m)	(staff) training session
Schulungskurs (m)	training course
Schulzeugnis (n)	school report
Schwangerschaftsabbruch (m) → *Schwangerschaftsabbruch*	termination of pregnancy, legal abortion
Schwerbeschädigter (m)/ Schwerbeschädigte (f), Schwerbehinderter (m)/ Schwerbehinderte (f)	severely disabled person, severely handicapped person
schwererziehbares Kind (n)	disruptive child, severely maladjusted child
Schwererziehbarkeit (f)	disruptive behaviour
Sekundarstufenabschluß I (m) → *Bildungswesen*	secondary level stage one leaving certificate
Selbstbestimmung (f)	self-determination
Selbsterfahrungsgruppe (f)	self-awareness group

selbstverwaltet	self-programming
Selbstverwaltung (f)	self-government
Selbstverwaltung (f), kommunale → *Kommunale Selbstverwaltung*	local self-government
Sexualerziehung (f)	sex education
Sonderschule (f) → *Bildungswesen*	special school
Sonderschulunterricht (m)	special education
Sorgeberechtigter (m)/ Sorgeberechtigte (f) → *Elterliche Sorge*	person having custodial rights
Sorgerecht (n) → *Pflegekinderbereich*	right of custody, custodial rights, legal custody (UK)
Sorgerechtsanordnung (f) → *Pflegekinderbereich*	custodianship order (UK)
Sorgerechtsentzug (m) → *Pflegekinderbereich*	withdrawal of (the right of) custody
Sozialabgaben (f/pl)	social insurance contributions, welfare charges, welfare payments
Sozialamt (n)	social services department
Sozialarbeit (f) → *Sozialarbeit/Sozialpädagogik*	≠ (social work, social help)
Sozialarbeiter (m)/Sozialarbeiterin (f) → *Sozialarbeiter/Sozialpädagoge*	≠ (qualified social worker, residential care worker, depending on the respective work situation)
Fachkraft der Sozialen Arbeit/ Sozialarbeiter (D)	professional social worker
Mitarbeiter der Sozialen Arbeit (VK)	social worker
sozial unangepaßt	socially maladjusted, alienated
Soziale Arbeit (f) → *Sozialarbeit/Sozialpädagogik*	social work
soziale Einrichtungen (f/pl)	social service provision, social institutions
soziale Herkunft (f)	social background
soziale Hilfen (f/pl)	social services

soziale Schichtung (f)	social stratification
soziale Sicherung/Sicherheit (f) → *Soziale Sicherung/Sicherheit*	social security
sozialer Dienst (m)	social service provision
sozialer Wandel (m)	social change
sozialer Wohnungsbau (m) → *Sozialer Wohnungsbau*	subsidized housing, council housing
soziales Defizit (n)	social inadequacy
soziales Engagement (n) von Jugendlichen (m/f/pl), freiwilliges → *Engagement, soziales*	youth volunteer action
soziales Jahr (n), freiwilliges → *Freiwilliges Soziales Jahr*	year of voluntary work and community service
soziales Umfeld (n)	social environment
soziales Verhalten (n)	social behaviour
Sozialerziehung (f)	social education
Sozialhilfe (f) → *Soziale Sicherung/Sicherheit* → *Sozialhilfe*	social assistance benefits (FRG), income support (UK)
Sozialhilfeempfänger (m)/ Sozialhilfeempfängerin (f) → *Sozialhilfe*	recipient of social assistance benefits/income support
Sozialhilfeträger (m) → *Soziale Sicherung/Sicherheit* → *Sozialhilfe*	bodies responsible for the discharge of social assistance benefits
Sozialisation (f)	social integration
Sozialkunde (f)	social studies
Sozialleistungen (f/pl)	social security benefits
Sozialpädagoge (m)/ Sozialpädagogin (f) → *Sozialarbeiter/Sozialpädagoge*	≠ (qualified youth worker, child care worker, youth and community worker, depending on the respective work situation)
Sozialpädagogik (f) → *Sozialarbeit/Sozialpädagogik*	≠ (social work, social help)
sozialpädagogische Familienhilfe (f)	socio-educational help for families

Sozialpolitik (f)	social policy and administration
Sozialstation (f)	community care centre
Sozialstruktur (f)	social structure
Sozialversicherung (f) → *Soziale Sicherung/Sicherheit*	social insurance
Sozialversicherungsbeitrag (m) → *Soziale Sicherung/Sicherheit*	social insurance contributions
Sozialversicherungsleistung (f) → *Soziale Sicherung/Sicherheit*	social insurance benefit
Sozialversicherungsträger (m) → *Soziale Sicherung/Sicherheit*	social insurance institution
Sozialwesen (n)	social system
Spielautomat (m)	gaming machine, one-armed bandit
Spielhalle (f)	amusement arcade
Spielplatz (m)	play ground
Spieltherapie (f)	play therapy
Spitzenverbände (m/pl), kommunale → *Kommunale Selbstverwaltung*	≠ (informal (national) associations of local authorities, informal associations of communal units)
Sportabzeichen (n) → *Jugendsport*	sports proficiency badge
Sportjugend (f), Deutsche → *Jugendsport*	German Sport Youth
Sportjugendleiter (m)/ Sportjugendleiterin (f) → *Jugendarbeit*	(voluntary) youth worker in the sport sector
Sportlehrer (m)/Sportlehrerin (f)	sports teacher, physical education teacher
sportliche Jugendbildung (f) → *Jugendarbeit*	education of the young through sports
Sportmannschaft (f)	sports team
Sportplatz (m)	sports field, playing field
Sportschau (f)	TV/radio sports programmes
Sprachheilkunde (f)	speech therapy

Sprachhelfer (m)/Sprachhelferin (f)	helper with interpreting
Städtepartnerschaft (f)	city link, town twinning arrangement, linked local authorities, city partnership, civic links
Städtetag (m), Deutscher → *Kommunale Selbstverwaltung*	Association of German Cities and Towns
Stadtjugendamt (n) → *Jugendamt*	municipal youth office
Stadtjugendring (m) → *Jugendringe*	local standing conference of voluntary youth organisations
Stadtranderholung (f)	suburban holiday play schemes
Stadtstreicher (m)/Stadtstreicherin (f), Penner (coll.)	vagrant, single homeless
stadtteilbezogene Jugendarbeit (f)	neighbourhood-orientated youth work
Stadtverwaltung (f)	local government administration in a town
Stipendium (n)	scholarship, fellowship, bursary
Strafaussetzung (f) zur Bewährung (f) → *Strafaussetzung zur Bewährung*	sentence suspended whilst on probation
Straferlaß (m) → *Jugendstrafrecht* → *Strafaussetzung zur Bewährung*	remission of sentence
Straffälliger (m), jugendlicher/ Straffällige (f), jugendliche	young offender
Straffälligenhilfe (f)	welfare and after-care for offenders
strafmündig → *Jugendstrafrecht*	having reached the age of criminal responsibility
Strafmündigkeit (f) → *Jugendstrafrecht*	criminal responsibility
Straftäter (m), jugendlicher/ Straftäterin (f), jugendliche	juvenile delinquent
Straßensozialarbeit (f)	street work
Straßensozialarbeiter (m)/ Straßensozialarbeiterin (f), Streetworker (m)	street worker, detached worker

Streuner, jugendliche (m/pl)	homeless young people
Studentenverband (m)	student organisation
Studentenvertretung (f)	student council, student representation
Studentenwerk (n)	student union
Studienabschluß (m)	degree/diploma
Studienreise (f)	study tour, study visit
Subkultur (f)	subculture
Subsidiaritätsprinzip (n) → *Subsidiaritätsprinzip*	≠ (a principle which establishes the priority rights and responsibilities of individuals, voluntary bodies and the State)
Suchtstoffe (m/pl)	narcotics
Supervision (f) → *Sozialarbeit/Sozialpädagogik*	tutorial supervision
Tageseinrichtungen (f/pl) für Kinder (n/pl) → *Tageseinrichtungen für Kinder*	day care establishments for children and young people
Tagesmutter (f) → *Pflegekinderbereich*	child minder
Tagespflege (f) → *Pflegekinderbereich*	child minding
Tagung (f)	conference, meeting
Tagungsstätte (f)	conference centre
Teamer (m) → *Jugendleiter*	youth leader in youth tourism/ outdoor pursuits
Teestube (f)	drop-in centre
Teilnahmebescheinigung (f)	certificate of attendance
Träger (m)	a body/organisation/agency responsible for a sector of work, provider
Ausbildungsträger freier Träger öffentlicher Träger die freien und öffentlichen Träger	provider of training voluntary organisation statutory body the statutory and voluntary sectors

Träger der öffentlichen Jugendhilfe	bodies responsible for the statutory youth services, bodies responsible for youth work and youth welfare services
Träger (m/pl) der Jugendhilfe (f) → *Träger der Jugendhilfe*	bodies responsible for youth work and youth welfare services
trägerübergreifend	jointly organised
trampen	to go hitch-hiking
Trimmpfad (m)	fitness trail

überbetriebliche Ausbildung (f)	inter-firm training
überbetriebliche Ausbildungsstätte (f)	inter-firm training centre
überörtlich	above local (FRG), local (UK)
Umschulung (f)	vocational retraining, occupational rehabilitation
Umweltbedingungen (f/pl)	environmental conditions
Umwelteinfluß (m)	influence of the environment
Umweltschutz (m) → *Umweltschutz*	protection of the environment, environmental and nature conservation
unangepaßt	alienated
unerziehbar	uneducable, unsuitable for education at school
uniformierte Jugendgruppen (f/pl) → *Jugendverbände (UK)*	uniformed youth
Unterhaltspflicht (f)	responsibility for maintenance of dependents
Unterhaltszahlung (f)	maintenance payment
Unterkunft (f)	accommodation, shelter
Untersuchungshaft (f)	remand in custody pending further enquiries
Untersuchungsrichter (m)/ Untersuchungsrichterin (f)	investigating magistrate
unvollständige Familie (f)	incomplete family

Veranstaltung (f)	event, function
kulturelle Veranstaltung	cultural event
Verband (m)	association (organisational form)
→ *Verband*	
→ *Jugendverbände*	
verbandsgebunden	being member of a (youth) organisation
nicht verbandsgebundene Jugendliche (pl)	unattached young people, young people outside of youth organisations
nicht organisierte Jugendliche (pl)	young people not being members of youth clubs or organisations
Verbandsjugend (f)	organised youth
Verein (m)	association (legal form), club, society
→ *Verein*	
eingetragener Verein	registered association
Verfügung (f)	order
→ *Rechtsinstrumente*	
gerichtliche Verfügung	court order, order of the court
Verführung (f) von Minderjährigen (m/f/pl)	sexual interference with a minor
Vergewaltigung (f)	rape
Verhalten (n)	behaviour
Verhaltensstörung (f)	behaviour(al) disorder, behavioural disturbance
verhaltensgestörtes Kind (n)	child showing disturbed behaviour
Vernachlässigung (f)	neglect
vernachlässigtes Kind (n)	neglected child
Verordnung (f)	statutory order
→ *Rechtsinstrumente*	
Vertrauensmann (m)	shop steward
→ *Betriebsrat*	
verwahrlost	destitute
Verwahrlosung (f)	state of destitution
Verwarnung (f)	caution
→ *Jugendstrafrecht, Maßnahmen des*	
Verwendungsnachweis (m)	statement of expenditure

Volksbildungswerk (n)	adult education body
Volkshochschule (f) → *Weiterbildung*	adult education centre
Volljährigkeit (f) → *Tabelle Altersgrenzen*	age of majority
Vollzug (m) der Jugendstrafe (f) → *Jugendstrafrecht, Maßnahmen des*	custodial treatment of young offenders
Vorbereitungsseminar (n)	briefing seminar
Vorbereitungstreffen (n)	briefing meeting
Vorbeugungsmaßnahme (f)	preventive measure
Vormund (m) → *Vormundschaft*	guardian
Vormundschaft (f) → *Vormundschaft*	guardianship
Vormundschaftsgericht (n) → *Vormundschaft*	guardianship court
Vormundschaftsrichter (m) → *Vormundschaft*	magistrate in a guardianship court
Vorschule (f)	pre-school education establishment
Vorschulerziehung (f) → *Tageseinrichtungen für Kinder*	pre-school education
Vorsitzende (f)	chairwoman, chair person
Vorsitzender (m)	chairman, chair person
Vorstand (m) → *Verband* → *Verein*	executive committee
Vorstrafe (f)	previous conviction
wählbar	eligible for election
wahlberechtigt	entitled to vote, enfranchised
Wahlrecht (n) → *Tabelle Altersgrenzen*	right to vote, enfranchisement
wandern → *Wandern*	to go hiking, to go on a walking tour
Wanderung (f) → *Wandern*	hike, walking tour

Wehrdienst (m)
→ *Wehrpflicht, allgemeine*

military service

Wehrdienstverweigerer (m)
→ *Wehrpflicht, allgemeine*

conscientious objector

Wehrdienstverweigerung (f)
→ *Wehrpflicht, allgemeine*

conscientious objection

Wehrpflicht (f), allgemeine
→ *Wehrpflicht, allgemeine*

liability for military service

Wehrpflichtiger (m)
→ *Wehrpflicht, allgemeine*

person liable to serve in the armed forces, person liable for military service

Weisungen (f/pl)
→ *Jugendstrafrecht, Maßnahmen des*

directions by a judge or magistrate

Weiterbildung (f)
→ *Weiterbildung*

further education

weiterführende Schulen (f/pl)
→ *Bildungswesen*

secondary education establishments

Werkarbeit (f), Werken (n)

craft(s), handiwork

Werklehrer (m)/Werklehrerin (f)

craft teacher

Werkstatt (f)

workshop

Werktätiger (m), junger/
Werktätige (f), junge

young worker

Werkunterricht (m)

craft classes

Wiedereingliederung (f)
→ *Rehabilitation Behinderter*

reintegration, rehabilitation

Wohlfahrtspflege (f), freie
→ *Sozialhilfe*
→ *Wohlfahrtsverbände, freie*

voluntary welfare work

Wohlfahrtsverbände (m/pl)
→ *Wohlfahrtsverbände, freie*

welfare organisations

Wohngemeinschaft (f)
  betreute Jugendwohngemeinschaft (f)

communal living
  communal living (of young people) with social worker support

Wohnheim (n)

residential home, residential centre, hostel

Wohnungsbaugesellschaft (f)
→ *Sozialer Wohnungsbau*

housing association

wohnungslose alleinstehende Jugendliche (m/f/pl)	homeless young people
zelten	to go camping
Zeltlager (n)	tented camp
Zentralstelle (f)	central agency
Zentralverband (m)	central organisation
Zivildienst (m), ziviler Ersatzdienst (m) → *Wehrpflicht, allgemeine*	compulsory non-military national service
Zivildienstleistender (m) (ZDL) → *Wehrpflicht, allgemeine*	person on compulsory non-military national service
Zivildienstpflichtiger (m) → *Wehrpflicht, allgemeine*	person subject to compulsory non-military national service
Zuchtmittel (n/pl) → *Jugendstrafrecht, Maßnahmen des*	correctional treatment
Zusatzausbildung (f) → *Weiterbildung*	additional training
Zuschuß (m), Zuwendung (f)	subsidy, grant
Zuwendungsempfänger (m)	recipient of a grant
zwischenstaatlich	intergovernmental

Englisch — deutsch
English — German

Abitur (certificate of qualification for university entrance)	Abitur (n) → *Bildungswesen*
abortion	Abtreibung (f)
abortion, legal	Schwangerschaftsabbruch (m) → *Schwangerschaftsabbruch*
above local (FRG)	überörtlich
abuse	Mißhandlung (f)
accommodation, shelter	Unterkunft (f)
accompany, to	begleiten
accompanying adult	Betreuer (m)/Betreuerin (f), Begleitperson (f)
accompanying staff	Begleitperson (f)
achieve academically, pressure to	Leistungsdruck (m) (im Bildungswesen)
achievement	Leistung (f)
active citizenship	politische Bildung (f) → *Jugendarbeit*
activities for young people, mainly in the form of leisure time provision	offene Jugendarbeit (f) → *Jugendarbeit*
activity and adventure holiday	Aktiv-Ferien (pl)
administrative officer	Sachbearbeiter (m)/ Sachbearbeiterin (f)
admission restriction in higher education	numerus clausus (m) → *Bildungswesen*
adoption	Adoption (f) → *Adoption*
adoption procedures and implementation	Adoptionsvermittlung (f)
adoptive parents	Adoptiveltern (pl)
adult education	Erwachsenenbildung (f)
adult education body	Volksbildungswerk (n)
adult education centre	Volkshochschule (f) → *Weiterbildung*
advanced training	Fortbildung (f)

adventure playground	Abenteuerspielplatz (m)
adventure pursuits	Erlebnispädagogik (f) → *Erlebnispädagogik*
advice to mothers	Mütterberatung (f)
advice on schooling	Schullaufbahnberatung (f)
adviser on informal education	Bildungsreferent (m)/ Bildungsreferentin (f)
adviser on informal education for the young	Jugendbildungsreferent (m)/ Jugendbildungsreferentin (f)
advisory board, advisory council	Beirat (m)
advisory services	Beratungsdienste (m/pl) → *Beratungsdienste*
after-care	Nachbetreuung (f)
age group	Altersgruppe (f)
age limit	Altersgrenze (f) → *Tabelle Altersgrenzen*
age of criminal responsibility, having reached the	strafmündig → *Jugendstrafrecht*
agency responsible for a sector of work	Träger (m)
agreement, bilateral	bilaterales Abkommen (n)
alcohol abuse amongst young people	Alkoholmißbrauch (m) bei Jugendlichen (m/f/pl) → *Alkoholmißbrauch bei Jugendlichen*
alcoholic	Alkoholiker (m)/Alkoholikerin (f)
alcoholics, care for	Alkoholikerfürsorge (f)
alienated	sozial unangepaßt
all-day school	Ganztagsschule (f)
allocate, to	bewilligen
alternative life style, alternative movements	Alternativbewegung (f)
amateur constructing	Basteln (n)
amateur dramatics	Laienspiel (n)

amateur theatre	Laientheater (n)
amusement arcade	Spielhalle (f)
ante- and post-natal clinic	Mütterberatungsstelle (f)
anti-social behaviour	asoziales Verhalten (n)
application	Antrag (m)
application form, completion of an	Antragstellung (f)
application, submission of an	Antragstellung (f)
appraisal session	Auswertungsgespräch (n)
apprentice/trainee	Auszubildender (m)/ Auszubildende (f) („Azubi") → *Berufsbildung*
apprenticeship contract, contract of apprenticeship	Lehrvertrag (m), Ausbildungsvertrag (m)
apprentice training place	Lehrstelle (f)
approval of applications	Genehmigung (f) von Anträgen (m/pl)
approval of grant-aid	Bewilligung (f) eines Zuschusses (m)
approve, to	bewilligen
aptitude test	Eignungsprüfung (f)
area youth office	Bezirksjugendamt (n) → *Jugendamt* → *Jugendbehörden*
assistant	Helfer (m)/Helferin (f)
association (legal form)	Verein (m) → *Verein*
association (organisational form)	Verband (m) → *Verband* → *Jugendverbände*
Association of German Cities and Towns	Deutscher Städtetag (m)
association of voluntary organisations	Dachverband (m)
association, registered	eingetragener Verein (m) → *Verein*
asylant	Asylant (m)/Asylantin (f)

asylum seeker	Asylbewerber (m)/ Asylbewerberin (f)
attendance centre	Jugendarrestanstalt (f) → *Jugendstrafrecht, Maßnahmen des*
attendance centres, treatment of young offenders at	Jugendarrest (m)
audio-visual materials	audio-visuelle Hilfsmittel (n/pl)
au-pair job	Au-pair-Beschäftigung (f)
Award for Children's Books, German	Deutscher Jugendbuchpreis (m)

baby care	Säuglingspflege (f)
basic benefits	Regelsatz (m), Richtsatz (m)
basic training	Grundausbildung (f) → *Berufsbildung*
Basic Vocational Training Year	Berufsgrundbildungsjahr (n) → *Berufsbildung* → *Jugendarbeitslosigkeit*
battered baby, battered child	mißhandeltes Kind (n)
behaviour	Verhalten (n)
behaviour(al) disorder, behavioural disturbance	Verhaltensstörung (f)
behaviour, deviant	abweichendes Verhalten (n)
behaviour, disruptive	Erziehungsschwierigkeit (f), Schwererziehbarkeit (f)
benefits, basic	Regelsatz (m), Richtsatz (m)
Berufsfachschule (full-time vocational school)	Berufsfachschule (f) → *Berufsbildung*
Berufsakademie (polytechnic-type establishment)	Berufsakademie (f) → *Sozialarbeiter/Sozialpädagoge*
Berufsaufbauschule (vocational continuation school)	Berufsaufbauschule (f) → *Berufsbildung*
Bezugsperson (a person to whom one relates specifically)	Bezugsperson (f)
bilateral agreement	bilaterales Abkommen (n)

bilateral youth exchange	bilateraler Jugendaustausch (m)
block grant	Globalförderung (f), Globalmittel (n/pl)
boarding school	Internat (n)
bodies responsible for youth work and youth welfare services	Träger (m/pl) der Jugendhilfe (f) → *Träger der Jugendhilfe*
briefing meeting	Vorbereitungstreffen (n)
briefing seminar	Einführungsseminar (n), Vorbereitungsseminar (n)
British studies (UK)	Landeskunde (f) (bezogen auf VK)
broken home(s)	gestörte Familienverhältnisse (n/pl)
bursary	Stipendium (n)
camping, to go	zelten
care and custody of a person	Personensorge (f)
care and custody, person who exercises the right of	Personensorgeberechtigter (m)/ Personensorgeberechtigte (f)
career choice	Berufsfindung (f)
career development	berufsfördernde Maßnahmen (f/pl) → *Berufsbildung*
career preparation	Berufsvorbereitung (f)
careers education	Berufsunterricht (m)
careers advice	Berufsberatung (f) → *Bundesanstalt für Arbeit*
careers office	Berufsberatungsstelle (f)
careers officer	Berufsberater (m)/ Berufsberaterin (f)
careers service	Berufsberatung (f)
care for a group or person	Betreuung (f)
care order	Sorgerechtsanordnung (f) → *Pflegekinderbereich* → *Elterliche Sorge*
case work	Einzelfallhilfe (f)

case work report	Einzelfallanalyse (f), Einzelfallbericht (m)
caution	Verwarnung (f) → *Jugendstrafrecht, Maßnahmen des*
central agency	Zentralstelle (f)
central organisation	Zentralverband (m)
CENYC (Council of European National Youth Committees)	Europäischer Jugendrat (CENYC) → *Jugendringe*
certificate of attendance	Teilnahmebescheinigung (f)
chairman, chair person	Vorsitzender (m)
chairwoman, chair person	Vorsitzende (f)
change of profession or job	Berufswechsel (m)
change of environment	Milieuwechsel (m)
charity	gemeinnützige Einrichtung (f)
child	Kind (n) → *Tabelle Altersgrenzen*
Child and Youth Services Act	Kinder- und Jugendhilfegesetz (n) (KJHG) → *Jugendgesetze*
child and youth services law	Jugendhilferecht (n)
child at risk	gefährdetes Kind (n)
child care	Jugendfürsorge (f) → *Jugendamt* → *Jugendfürsorge/Jugendpflege*
child care worker	Erzieher (m)/Erzieherin (f) → *Erzieher/Erzieherin*
child fostering	Pflegekinderbereich (m), Pflegekinderwesen (n) → *Pflegekinderbereich/ Pflegekinderwesen*
child guidance	Erziehungsberatung (f) → *Beratungsdienste* → *Jugendamt*
child minder	Tagesmutter (f)
child minding	Kinderbetreuung (f), Tagespflege (f)

child raising allowance	Erziehungsgeld (n)
child raising leave	Erziehungsurlaub (m)
children's home	Kinderheim (n)
children's hospital	Kinderkrankenhaus (n)
children's nurse	Kinderpflegerin (f) → *Tageseinrichtungen für Kinder*
children's playground	Kinderspielplatz (m)
child showing disturbed behaviour	verhaltensgestörtes Kind (n)
choice of a career	Berufswahl (f)
church voluntary community service	diakonischer Jugendeinsatz (m) → *Engagement, soziales*
city farm for young people	Jugendfarm (f)
city link, city partnership, civic links	Städtepartnerschaft (f)
civil service employee	Bediensteter (m)/ Bedienstete (f) des öffentlichen Dienstes (m) → *Bedienstete des öffentlichen* *Dienstes*
classifying centre	Beobachtungszentrum (n)
co-determination	Mitbestimmung (f)
college or institute of further education	Berufsfortbildungswerk (n)
Committee for Women and Youth of the *German Bundestag*	Ausschuß (m) für Frauen (f/pl) und Jugend (f) des Deutschen Bundestages (m) → *Ausschuß für Frauen und Jugend* *des Deutschen Bundestages*
committal order	Jugendstrafe (f) → *Jugendstrafrecht, Maßnahmen des*
common interest group	Neigungsgruppe (f)
communal living	Wohngemeinschaft (f)
communal living (of young people) with social worker support	betreute Jugendwohngemeinschaft (f)
commune, communal living	Kommune (f)
community	Gemeinde (f) → *Kommunale Selbstverwaltung*

community action group	Bürgerinitiative (f) → *Bürgerinitiative*
community care	Nachbarschaftshilfe (f)
community care centre	Sozialstation (f)
community centre	Gemeinschaftseinrichtung (f), Nachbarschaftsheim (n)
community education (Scotland)	Gemeinwesenarbeit (f) → *Jugendarbeit, VK* → *Sozialarbeit, VK*
community home	Erziehungsheim (n)
community involvement	soziales Engagement (n) → *Engagement, soziales*
community life	Gemeinschaftsleben (n)
community organisation	Gemeinwesenarbeit (f) → *Jugendarbeit, VK*
community project	Beschäftigungsprogramm (n)
community service	Gemeinschaftsdienst (m)
community service order	Auferlegung (f) von Pflichten (f/pl) → *Jugendstrafrecht, Maßnahmen des*
community work	Gemeinwesenarbeit (f)
competitive society	Leistungsgesellschaft (f)
compulsory attendance	Anwesenheitspflicht (f)
compulsory non-military national service	Zivildienst (m), ziviler Ersatzdienst (m) → *Wehrpflicht, allgemeine*
compulsory non-military national service, person on	Zivildienstleistender (m) (ZDL)
compulsory non-military national service, person subject to	Zivildienstpflichtiger (m)
compulsory part-time vocational education	Berufsschulpflicht (f) → *Berufsbildung*
compulsory school education	Schulpflicht (f) → *Bildungswesen*
comprehensive school	Gesamtschule (f) → *Bildungswesen*

concessionary rate	ermäßigter Preis (m), ermäßigter Satz (m)
conditions	Auflagen (f/pl)
conference	Tagung (f)
conference centre	Tagungsstätte (f); internationale Jugendarbeit auch: Begegnungsstätte (f), Begegnungszentrum (n)
conscientious objector	Kriegsdienstverweigerer (m), Wehrdienstverweigerer (m) → *Wehrpflicht, allgemeine*
conscientious objection	Wehrdienstverweigerung (f)
consciousness raising	Bewußtseinsbildung (f)
construction programmes for youth establishments	Jugendbauprogramme (n/pl) → *Bundesministerium für Frauen und Jugend*
contact	Begegnung (f)
contact person	Ansprechpartner (m)/ Ansprechpartnerin (f)
contraception	Empfängnisverhütung (f)
convalescent home	Erholungsheim (n)
cooperative	Genossenschaft (f)
cooperative polytechnic and university	kooperative Gesamthochschule (f) → *Bildungswesen*
co-responsibility	Mitverantwortung (f)
correctional treatment	Zuchtmittel (n/pl) → *Jugendstrafrecht, Maßnahmen des*
council housing	sozialer Wohnungsbau (m) → *sozialer Wohnungsbau*
Council of Political Youth Organisations	Ring (m) Politischer Jugend (f) → *Jugendringe*
counselling in child care	Mütterberatung (f)
counselling services	Beratungsdienste (m/pl) → *Beratungsdienste*
country centre	Schullandheim (n)
courier	Reiseleiter (m)/Reiseleiterin (f)

court order	gerichtliche Verfügung (f)
craft classes	Werkunterricht (m)
craft(s)	Werkarbeit (f), Werken (n)
craft teacher	Werklehrer (m)/Werklehrerin (f)
crash course	Kurzlehrgang (m)
crêche	Kinderkrippe (f) → *Tageseinrichtungen für Kinder*
crediting of periods (a year) devoted to the upbringing of children	Erziehungsjahr (n)
criminal responsibility	Strafmündigkeit (f) → *Tabelle Altersgrenzen*
crisis in education	Bildungsnotstand (m)
cruelty to children	Kindesmißhandlung (f)
cultural autonomy of the *Länder*	Kulturhoheit (f) der Länder (n/pl)
cultural event	kulturelle Veranstaltung (f)
curator	Pfleger (m)/Pflegerin (f)
curatorship	Pflegschaft (f) → *Pflegschaft*
custodial rights	Sorgerecht (n) → *Pflegekinderbereich/ Pflegekinderwesen*
custodial rights, person having	Sorgeberechtigter (m)/ Sorgeberechtigte (f) → *elterliche Sorge*
custodial sentence for young people	Jugendstrafe (f) → *Jugendstrafrecht, Maßnahmen des*
custodial treatment of young offenders	Jugendstrafvollzug (m), Vollzug (m) der Jugendstrafe (f)
custodian	Pfleger (m)/Pflegerin (f)
custodianship	Pflegschaft (f) → *Pflegschaft*
custodianship order	Sorgerechtsanordnung → *Pflegekinderbereich/ Pflegekinderwesen*
custody, right of	Sorgerecht (n) → *Elterliche Sorge*

custody, withdrawal of (the right of)	Sorgerechtsentzug (m) → *Pflegekinderbereich/* *Pflegekinderwesen*
day care centre	Hort (m) → *Tageseinrichtungen für Kinder*
day care centre for children and young people	Kindertagesheim (n)
day care establishments for children and young people	Tageseinrichtungen (f/pl) für Kinder (n/pl) → *Tageseinrichtungen für Kinder*
decision making, right to participation in	Mitwirkungsrecht (n)
decree	Erlaß (m) → *Rechtsinstrumente*
Decree of Employment of Extremists	Extremistenbeschluß (m), Radikalenerlaß (m)
degree/diploma	Studienabschluß (m)
denominational school	Bekenntnisschule (f)
desk officer	Sachbearbeiter (m)/ Sachbearbeiterin (f)
destitute	verwahrlost
destitution, state of	Verwahrlosung (f)
detached youth work	mobile Jugendarbeit (f) → *Jugendarbeit, mobile*
detention	Haft (f)
development aid	Entwicklungshilfe (f)
development of the educational system, governmental proposal to the	Bildungsplan (m)
deviant behaviour	Auffälligkeit (f)
Diplom-Pädagoge (university-trained youth worker)	Diplom-Pädagoge (m)/ Diplom-Pädagogin (f) → *Sozialarbeiter/Sozialpädagoge*
directions	Auflagen (f/pl) → *Jugendstrafrecht, Maßnahmen des*
directions by a judge or magistrate	Weisungen (f/pl)

Directives for the Federal Youth Plan	Richtlinien (f/pl) für den Bundesjugendplan (m) → *Bundesjugendplan*
director (of a school)	Schulleiter (m)/Schulleiterin (f)
disabled person	Behinderter (m)/Behinderte (f) → *Behindertenhilfe*
disabled persons, integration of	Rehabilitation (f) Behinderter (pl) → *Rehabilitation Behinderter*
disadvantaged, programmes for the	Benachteiligtenprogramm (n)
disruptive behaviour	Schwererziehbarkeit (f)
disruptive child	schwererziehbares Kind (n), erziehungsschwieriges Kind (n)
distance teaching	Fernunterricht (m)
disturbed behaviour, child showing	verhaltensgestörtes Kind (n)
drama group	Laienspielgruppe (f)
drop-in centre	Jugendcafé (n), Teestube (f)
drop out	Gammler (m)/Gammlerin (f) (coll)
drop out, social	Aussteiger (m)/Aussteigerin (f)
drug	Droge (f) → *Drogenmißbrauch*
drug addict	Drogensüchtiger (m)/ Drogensüchtige (f), Rauschgift- süchtiger (m)/Rauschgiftsüchtige (f)
drug addiction	Rauschgiftsucht (f)
drug advisory centre	Drogenberatungsstelle (f)
drug dependence	Rauschgiftabhängigkeit (f)
drug dependency	Drogenabhängigkeit (f)
drug misuse	Drogenmißbrauch (m) → *Drogenmißbrauch*
drugs	Rauschgift (n)
drugs, addicted to	rauschgiftsüchtig
drugs, person at risk from	Drogengefährdeter (m)/ Drogengefährdete (f)
drugs, susceptibility to	Drogenempfänglichkeit (f)

drug trafficking	Rauschgifthandel (m), („dealen", coll.)
drug user	Drogenbenutzer (m)/Drogenbenutzerin (f), Drogenkonsument (m)/Drogenkonsumentin (f)
„dual system" (day release/sandwich courses)	duales System (n) → *Berufsbildung*
Duke of Edinburgh's Award Scheme, The	*The Duke of Edinburgh's Award Scheme* → *Duke of Edinburgh's Award Scheme, The*
education	Bildung (f), Erziehung (f)
educational deficiency	Bildungsdefizit (n)
educational establishment, informal	Bildungsstätte (f)
educational leave	Bildungsurlaub (m)
educationally subnormal person	Lernbehinderter (m)
educational opportunities	Bildungschancen (f/pl)
educational path	Bildungsgang (m), Bildungsweg (m)
educational planning	Bildungsplanung (f)
educational policy	Bildungspolitik (f)
educational provision similar to a supervision order	Erziehungsbeistandschaft (f)
educational provision under a care order	Fürsorgeerziehung (f)
educational system, normal progress through the	erster Bildungsweg (m) → *Bildungswesen*
educational theory	Pädagogik (f)
educational tour	Bildungsreise (f)
education, crisis in	Bildungsnotstand (m)
education for citizenship	politische Bildung (f) → *Jugendarbeit*
education for leisure	Freizeitpädagogik (f)
education, formal	erster Bildungsweg (m)

education grant	Ausbildungsbeihilfe (f) → *Ausbildungsförderung*
education in the use of the media	Medienerziehung (f)
education in music and the arts	musische Bildung (f) → *Jugendarbeit*
educationist	Pädagoge (m)/Pädagogin (f)
education, level of	Bildungsgrad (m)
education of the young through sports	sportliche Jugendbildung (f) → *Jugendarbeit*
education system	Bildungswesen (n)
education welfare work	Schulsozialarbeit (f)
eligible for election	wählbar
emotionally disturbed person	seelisch Behinderter (m)
employed person	Arbeitnehmer (m)/Arbeitnehmerin (f), Berufstätiger (m)/Berufstätige (f)
employee	Arbeitnehmer (m)/ Arbeitnehmerin (f)
employer	Arbeitgeber (m)/Arbeitgeberin (f)
employing body	Anstellungsträger (m)
employment development	Berufsförderung (f)
employment office	Arbeitsamt (n) → *Bundesanstalt für Arbeit*
employment promotional schemes	berufsfördernde Maßnahmen (f/pl)
employment, protection of	Arbeitsschutz (m)
employment service	Arbeitsvermittlung (f) → *Bundesanstalt für Arbeit, VK*
Employment Training	berufsqualifizierende Beschäftigungsmaßnahmen (f/pl) → *Bundesanstalt für Arbeit, VK*
enfranchised	wahlberechtigt
enfranchisement	Wahlrecht (n)
entitled to vote	wahlberechtigt
entrance qualification for a *Fachhochschule*	Fachhochschulreife (f) → *Bildungswesen*

entrance examination	Aufnahmeprüfung (f)
environmental and nature conservation	Umweltschutz (m) → *Umweltschutz*
environmental conditions	Umweltbedingungen (f/pl)
environment, influence of the	Umwelteinfluß (m)
environment, protection of the	Umweltschutz (m) → *Umweltschutz*
equality of rights for men and women	Gleichberechtigung (f)
equal opportunities	Chancengleichheit (f) → *Chancengleichheit*
Erzieher/Erzieherin (qualified youth or child care worker)	Erzieher (m)/Erzieherin (f) → *Erzieher/Erzieherin*
escort	Begleiter (m)/Begleiterin (f), Betreuer (m)/Betreuerin (f)
escort, to	begleiten
establishment	Einrichtung (f)
establishment without fixed membership	offene Einrichtung (f)
European youth structures	europäische Jugendstrukturen (f/pl)
evaluation	Auswertungsgespräch (n)
evaluation seminar	Auswertungsseminar (n)
evening centre, evening classes, evening institute	Abendschule (f) → *Bildungswesen*
examination at the end of a period of education	Abschlußprüfung (f)
exchange of opinions, exchange of views	Meinungsaustausch (m)
exchange of school children	Schüleraustausch (m)
exchange programme	Austauschprogramm (n)
exchange visit	Begegnungsreise (f), Austausch (m)
executive committee	Vorstand (m)
expeditions	Fahrten (f/pl) → *Wandern*

Fachgymnasium (technical grammar school)	Fachgymnasium (n) → *Bildungswesen*
Fachhochschule (polytechnic-type institution)	Fachhochschule (n) → *Bildungswesen*
Fachoberschule (senior technical school)	Fachoberschule (f) → *Bildungswesen*
Fachschule (technical school)	Fachschule (f) → *Bildungswesen*
facility	Einrichtung (f)
factory/firm/shop	Betrieb (m)
family aide	Familienhelfer (m)/ Familienhelferin (f)
family allowance	Kindergeld (n)
family and parental counselling	Familien- und Elternbildung (n) → *Familien- und Elternbildung*
family holiday scheme	Familienerholungsmaßnahme (f)
family planning	Familienplanung (f)
family welfare work	Familienfürsorge (f)
Federal Advisory Committee on Youth Problems	Bundesjugendkuratorium (n) → *Bundesjugendkuratorium*
Federal Educational Grants Act	Bundesausbildungsförderungs- gesetz (n) → *Jugendgesetze*
Federal Employees Agreed Salary Scales	Bundesangestelltentarif (m) (BAT) → *Bedienstete des Öffentlichen Dienstes*
Federal Institute of Labour	Bundesanstalt (f) für Arbeit (f) → *Bundesanstalt für Arbeit*
federalism/unitary government	Föderalismus (m)/ Zentralstaatlichkeit (f) → *Föderalismus/Zentralstaatlichkeit*
Federal Ministry for Women and Youth	Bundesministerium (n) für Frauen (f/pl) und Jugend (f) (BMFJ) → *Bundesministerium für Frauen und Jugend*
Federal Social Assistance Act	Bundessozialhilfegesetz (n) → *Sozialhilfe*

Federal Board for the Review of Publications Harmful to Young Persons	Bundesprüfstelle (f) für jugendgefährdende Schriften (f/pl)
Federal Youth Games	Bundesjugendspiele (n/pl) → *Jugendsport*
Federal Youth Plan	Bundesjugendplan (m) → *Bundesjugendplan*
fellowship	Stipendium (n)
field support	ambulante Betreuung (f)
financial approval, eg of a grant	Bewilligung (f)
financial approval, notification of	Bewilligungsbescheid (m)
financing of programmes	Programmfinanzierung (f)
firm/factory/shop	Betrieb (m)
first contact	Anlaufstelle (f)
fitness trail	Trimmpfad (m)
follow-up (contact)	Nachkontakte (m/pl)
foreign worker	ausländischer Arbeitnehmer (m)/ ausländische Arbeitnehmerin (f)
formal education	erster Bildungsweg (m) → *Bildungswesen*
foster child	Pflegekind (n) → *Pflegekinderbereich/* *Pflegekinderwesen*
foster family	Pflegeeltern (pl), Pflegefamilie (f)
foster home	Pflegestelle (f)
fostering, child	Pflegekinderbereich (m), Pflegekinderwesen (n) → *Pflegekinderbereich/* *Pflegekinderwesen*
fostering unit, large	Großpflegestelle (f) → *Hilfe zur Erziehung*
foster parents	Pflegeeltern (pl)
Franco-German Youth Office	Deutsch-Französisches Jugendwerk (n) → *Deutsch-Französisches Jugendwerk*
fringe group	Randgruppe (f)

full-time worker	hauptamtlicher Mitarbeiter (m)/ hauptamtliche Mitarbeiterin (f)
funds	Mittel (n/pl)
further education	Fortbildung (f), Weiterbildung (f) → *Weiterbildung*
further education course	Fortbildungskursus (m), Fortbildungslehrgang (m)
further education programme	Fortbildungsmaßnahme (f)
gaming machine	Spielautomat (m)
Garantiefonds	Garantiefonds (m) → *Bundesministerium für Frauen und Jugend*
general education	Allgemeinbildung (f)
German Civil Code	Bürgerliches Gesetzbuch (n) (BGB)
German Federal Youth Council	Deutscher Bundesjugendring (m) → *Jugendverbände*
German National Committee	Deutsches Nationalkomitee (n) (DNK) → *Jugendverbände*
German Sport Youth	Deutsche Sportjugend (f) → *Jugendsport*
German Youth Hostel Association	Deutsches Jugendherbergswerk (n) → *Wandern*
German Youth Institute	Deutsches Jugendinstitut (n) → *Jugendforschung*
Gesamthochschule (combined polytechnic and university)	Gesamthochschule (f) → *Bildungswesen*
gluesniffing	schnüffeln
graduation from a *Fachhochschule*	Graduierung (f) → *Bildungswesen*
grammar school	Gymnasium (n)
grant	Zuschuß (m), Zuwendung (f), Beihilfe (f)
grant-aid	Förderung (f)
grant-aid, application for	Förderungsantrag (f)

grant-aid, approval of	Bewilligung eines Zuschusses (m)
grant-aid available	Förderungsmittel (n/pl)
grant-aid, regulations on	Förderungsrichtlinien (f/pl)
grant-aid, sum allocated in	Förderungssumme (f)
grant awarded	Förderungsbetrag (m)
grant, education	Ausbildungsbeihilfe (f) → *Ausbildungsförderung*
grant, recipient of a	Zuwendungsempfänger (m)
grant, scales of	Förderungssätze (m/pl)
grants, education	Ausbildungsförderung (f) → *Ausbildungsförderung*
grant, to	bewilligen
grant, training	Ausbildungsbeihilfe (f) → *Ausbildungsförderung*
group dynamics	Gruppendynamik (f)
group education	Gruppenerziehung (f)
group escort	Gruppenbetreuer (m)/ Gruppenbetreuerin (f)
group leader	Begleiter (m)/Begleiterin (f), Gruppenbetreuer (m)/Gruppen- betreuerin (f), Gruppenführer (m)/ Gruppenführerin (f), Gruppenleiter (m)/Gruppenleiterin (f)
group leadership	Begleitung (f)
group, person looking after a	Gruppenbetreuer (m), Gruppen- betreuerin (f)
group work	Gruppenarbeit (f)
group work, developmental	Gruppenerziehung (f)
group work theory and technique	Gruppenpädagogik (f)
guardian	Vormund (m) → *Vormundschaft*
guardian, local authority	Amtsvormund (m) → *Vormundschaft*
guardianship	Vormundschaft (f) → *Vormundschaft*

guardianship court	Vormundschaftsgericht (n)
guardianship exercised by the local authority	Amtsvormundschaft (f)
guidance, child	Erziehungsberatung (f) → *Beratungsdienste*
guide	Begleiter (m)/Begleiterin (f)
Guide	Pfadfinderin (f) → *Jugendverbände*

handicapped person	Behinderter (m)/Behinderte (f)
handicapped, services for the	Behindertenhilfe (f) → *Behindertenhilfe*
handiwork	Werkarbeit (f), Werken (n)
Hauptschule (secondary school)	Hauptschule (f) → *Bildungswesen*
Hauptschule leaving certificate	Hauptschulabschluß (m)
headmaster	Schulleiter (m)/Schulleiterin (f)
headmaster of a school and senior staff	Schulleitung (f)
health authority, local	Gesundheitsbehörde (f)
health care	Gesundheitspflege (f)
health education	Gesundheitserziehung (f)
health service	Gesundheitsdienst (m), Gesundheitswesen (n)
health service department, local	Gesundheitsamt (n)
hearing impairment, person with a	Hörbehinderter (m)/Hörbehinderte (f)
helper	Helfer (m)/Helferin (f)
help for the homeless	Obdachlosenhilfe (f)
help, person in need of	Hilfebedürftiger (m)/Hilfebedürftige (f)
Heranwachsender (legal term used for a person of the 18–21 age group)	Heranwachsender (m)/Heranwachsende (f) → *Jugendstrafrecht*

higher education, admission restriction in	numerus clausus (m) → *Bildungswesen*
higher education diploma	Diplom (n)
higher education institution	Hochschule (f)
hike	Wanderung (f)
hiking, to go	wandern → *Wandern*
hitch-hiking, to go	trampen
hobbies	Freizeitbeschäftigung (f), Freizeitbetätigung (f)
holiday activity schemes	Jugendferienwerk (n)
holiday camp	Ferienkolonie (f), Ferienlager (n)
holiday centre	Ferienstätte (f)
holiday home	Ferienheim (n)
holiday programmes, holiday provision, holiday scheme	Ferienmaßnahme (f)
holiday schemes for children and young people	Kinder- und Jugenderholung (f) → *Kinder- und Jugenderholung*
holiday trip	Ferienreise (f)
holiday village	Feriendorf (n)
home for infants and babies	Säuglingsheim (n)
home economics school	Haushaltungsschule (f)
home help	Hauspflege (f), Hauspflegerin (f)
homelessness	Obdachlosigkeit (f)
homeless young people	jugendliche Streuner (m/pl), wohnungslose alleinstehende Jugendliche (pl)
home stay, period spent in staying with a family	Familienaufenthalt (m)
hostel	Wohnheim (n), Jugendwohnheim (n)
hostel for ex-prisoners released on probation	Probandenheim (n) → *Jugendstrafrecht*
hostel resident	Heimbewohner (m)/ Heimbewohnerin (f)

host family	Gastgeberfamilie (f)
housing association	Wohnungsbaugesellschaft (f) → *Sozialer Wohnungsbau*
illegitimate child	nichteheliches Kind (n)
ill-usage, ill treatment	Mißhandlung (f)
impaired vision and/or hearing, person with	Person (f) mit Sinnesschäden (m/pl)
imprisonment	Haft (f) → *Jugendstrafrecht, Maßnahmen des*
income support (UK)	Sozialhilfe (f) → *Sozialhilfe*
incomplete family	unvollständige Familie (f)
indigence	Hilfsbedürftigkeit (f)
individual contribution	Eigenbeitrag (m)
ineducable	bildungsunfähig, unerziehbar
infant care	Säuglingspflege (f)
infant mortality	Säuglingssterblichkeit (f)
infants and babies, home for	Säuglingsheim (n)
informal education for the young, adviser on	Jugendbildungsreferent (m)/ Jugendbildungsreferentin (f)
informal education for young people	Jugendbildung (f)
informal educational establishment	Bildungsstätte (f)
informal element of a programme	Rahmenprogramm (f)
informal group	informelle Gruppe (f)
informal group work	informelle Gruppenarbeit (f)
information sharing	Informationsaustausch (m)
in-house training	betriebliche Ausbildung (f)
injury at work	Arbeitsunfall (m)
in-service training	berufsbegleitende Fortbildung (f) → *Weiterbildung*
institutionalization	Hospitalismus (m)

instruction of mothers	Mütterberatung (f)
instructor	Ausbilder (m)/Ausbilderin (f)
integrated polytechnic and university	integrierte Gesamthochschule (f) → *Berufsbildung*
integration of disabled persons	Rehabilitation (f) Behinderter (pl) → *Rehabilitation Behinderter*
inter-firm training	überbetriebliche Ausbildung (f) → *Berufsbildung*
inter-firm training centre	überbetriebliche Ausbildungsstätte (f)
intergovernmental	zwischenstaatlich
international youth work	internationale Jugendarbeit (f) → *Internationale Jugendarbeit*
International Youth Exchange and Visitors' Service of the Federal Republic of Germany	Internationaler Jugendaustausch- und Besucherdienst der Bundesrepublik Deutschland (IJAB) e.V. → *Internationaler Jugendaustausch- und Besucherdienst der Bundesrepublik Deutschland (IJAB) e.V.*
interpreter-guide	Begleiter (m)/Begleiterin (f)
interpreting, helper with	Sprachhelfer (m)/Sprachhelferin (f)
intervention, (statutory) process of	Interventionskette (f)
introductory paper or lecture	Einführungsvortrag (m)
investigating magistrate	Untersuchungsrichter (m)/ Untersuchungsrichterin (f)
jobcentre (UK)	Arbeitsvermittlungsstelle (f) → *Bundesanstalt für Arbeit, VK*
jobclub (UK)	*jobclub* (Beratungsstelle für Arbeitslose)
Job Creation Scheme	Arbeitsbeschaffungsmaßnahme (f) (ABM) → *Jugendarbeitslosigkeit*
job placement	Arbeitsvermittlung (f) → *Bundesanstalt für Arbeit*
joint management	Mitbestimmung (f) → *Partizipation Jugendlicher*

jointly organised	trägerübergreifend
juvenile cases, public prosecutor in	Jugendstaatsanwalt (m)/ Jugendstaatsanwältin (f)
juvenile cases, social enquiry in	Jugendgerichtshilfe (f) → *Jugendstrafrecht*
juvenile cases, social worker involved in	Jugendgerichtshelfer (m)
juvenile court	Jugendgericht (n)
Juvenile Court Act	Jugendgerichtsgesetz (n)
juvenile court at *Land* level	Jugendkammer (f)
juvenile court magistrate	Jugendrichter (m)/ Jugendrichterin (f)
juvenile delinquency	Jugendkriminalität (f)
juvenile delinquent	jugendlicher Straftäter (m)/ jugendliche Straftäterin (f)
juvenile offence	Jugendstraftat (f) → *Jugendstrafrecht, Maßnahmen des*
kindergarten	Kindergarten (m)
Kollegschule (special educational provision in adult education to reach university entrance qualification)	Kollegschule (f) → *Bildungswesen*
Kommunale Spitzenverbände (informal (national) associations of local authorities, informal associations of communal units)	Kommunale Spitzenverbände (m/pl) → *Kommunale Selbstverwaltung*
Kreis	Kreis (m) (Stadtkreis/Landkreis) → *Kommunale Selbstverwaltung*
Kreis youth welfare and youth service office	Kreisjugendamt (n)
labour law	Arbeitsrecht (n)
Land, pl. *Länder* (of the FRG)	Land (n), Länder (n/pl) → *Föderalismus/Zentralstaatlichkeit*
Land youth office	Landesjugendamt (n) → *Jugendbehörden*

Land youth plan	Landesjugendplan (m) → *Bundesjugendplan*
latch-key child	Schlüsselkind (n)
law relating to young people	Jugendgesetze (n/pl) → *Jugendgesetze*
lay magistrate in a juvenile court	Jugendschöffe (m)/ Jugendschöffin (f) → *Jugendstrafrecht*
lead a group, to	begleiten
leadership, democratic style of	demokratischer Führungsstil (m)
leadership, directive style of	autoritärer Führungsstil (m)
leadership, group	Begleitung (f)
leadership, non-directive/liberal style of	laissez-faire Führungsstil (m)
leadership, styles of	Führungsstile (m/pl) → *Führungsstile*
legal abortion	Schwangerschaftsabbruch (m) → *Schwangerschaftsabbruch*
legal custody (UK)	Sorgerecht (n)
legal instruments	Rechtsinstrumente (n/pl) → *Rechtsinstrumente*
legal right (to)	Rechtsanspruch (m)
legislation, youth	Jugendgesetzgebung (f) → *Jugendgesetze*
leisure centre	Freizeitheim (n), Freizeitstätte (f) → *Jugendfreizeitstätten*
leisure counselling	Freizeitberatung (f)
leisure park	Freizeitpark (m)
leisure time	Freizeit (f)
leisure time activities	Freizeitbeschäftigung (f), Freizeitbetätigung (f)
leisure time behaviour	Freizeitverhalten (n)
leisure time centres for young people	Jugendfreizeitstätten (f/pl) → *Jugendfreizeitstätten*

leisure time, organisation (or use) of	Freizeitgestaltung (f)
leisure time provision	Freizeitangebot (n)
leisure time provision for the young	Jugendpflege (f) → *Jugendfürsorge/Jugendpflege*
level of education	Bildungsgrad (m)
liability	Haftung (f)
liability for military service	allgemeine Wehrpflicht (f) → *Wehrpflicht, allgemeine*
liable for military service, person	Wehrpflichtiger (m)
link	Partnerschaft (f)
linked city	Partnerstadt (f)
linked local authorities	Städtepartnerschaft (f)
living alone with social worker support	betreutes Einzelwohnen (n) → *Hilfe zur Erziehung*
local authority	Kommune (f) → *Kommunale Selbstverwaltung*
local authority department	Gemeindebehörde (f)
local authority guardian	Amtsvormund (m) → *Vormundschaft*
local authority, guardianship exercised by the	Amtsvormundschaft (f) → *Vormundschaft*
local authority, services or institutions run by the	kommunale Einrichtungen (f/pl)
local authority youth plan	kommunaler Jugendplan (m) → *Bundesjugendplan*
local government (UK)	Kommunale Selbstverwaltung (f) → *Kommunale Selbstverwaltung*
local government administration	Gemeindeverwaltung (f)
local government administration in a town	Stadtverwaltung (f)
local health authority	Gesundheitsbehörde (f)
local health service department	Gesundheitsamt (n)
local standing conference of voluntary youth organisations	Stadtjugendring (m)

magazines and publications, youth	Jugendpresse (f)
magazine, youth	Jugendzeitschrift (f)
magistrate in a guardianship court	Vormundschaftsrichter (m) → *Vormundschaft*
maintenance of dependents, responsibility for	Unterhaltspflicht (f)
maintenance payment	Unterhaltszahlung (f)
majority, age of	Volljährigkeit (f)
maladjusted child	anpassungsschwieriges Kind (n)
maladjustment	Anpassungsschwierigkeit (f)
Management Committee (UK)	*Management Committee* → *Management Committee*
management, joint	Mitbestimmung (f) → *Partizipation Jugendlicher*
management, participation in	Mitverwaltung (f)
management, right to a say in	Mitbestimmungsrecht (n)
marriage age, normal minimum	Ehemündigkeit (f) → *Tabelle Altersgrenzen*
marriage guidance	Eheberatung (f) → *Beratungsdienste*
marriage guidance centre	Eheberatungsstelle (f)
mature student educational provision	zweiter Bildungsweg (m) → *Bildungswesen*
media resource officer	Medienpädagoge (m)/ Medienpädagogin (f)
meeting	Begegnung (f), Tagung (f)
Meisterbrief (qualified instructor's certificate)	Meisterbrief (m) → *Berufsbildung*
Meisterprüfung (examination for qualified instructors in crafts or industry)	Meisterprüfung (f) → *Berufsbildung*
member	Mitglied (m)
mentally handicapped person	geistig Behinderter
mentally retarded person	Lernbehinderter

migrant worker	ausländischer Arbeitnehmer (m)/ ausländische Arbeitnehmerin (f), „Gastarbeiter" (m)/„Gastarbeiterin" (f)
military service	Wehrdienst (m) → *Wehrpflicht, allgemeine*
military service, liability for	allgemeine Wehrpflicht (f)
military service, person liable for	Wehrpflichtiger (m)
minimum age	Mindestalter (n)
ministerial decree	ministerieller Erlaß (m) → *Rechtsinstrumente*
minor	Minderjähriger (m) → *Tabelle Altersgrenzen*
minority, age of	Minderjährigkeit (f)
modelling	Basteln (n)
mothers, advice to	Mütterberatung (f)
mothers, instruction of	Mütterberatung (f)
multi-purpose establishment	Mehrzweckeinrichtung (f)
municipal youth office	Stadtjugendamt (n) → *Jugendamt*
music and the arts, education in	musische Bildung (f) → *Jugendarbeit*
narcotics	Suchtstoffe (m/pl) → *Drogenmißbrauch*
National Conference for Child and Youth Welfare	Deutscher Jugendhilfetag (m) → *Deutscher Jugendhilfetag*
national service, compulsory non military	Zivildienst (m), ziviler Ersatzdienst (m) → *Wehrpflicht, allgemeine*
national service, person on compulsory non-military	Zivildienstleistender (m) (ZDL)
national service, person subject to compulsory non-military	Zivildienstpflichtiger (m)
National Youth Report	Jugendbericht (m) → *Jugendbericht*
neediness	Hilfsbedürftigkeit (f)
need of care, (state of being) in	Pflegebedürftigkeit (f)

neglect	Vernachlässigung (f)
neglected child	vernachlässigtes Kind (n)
neighbourhood care	Nachbarschaftshilfe (f)
neighbourhood centre	Nachbarschaftsheim (n)
neighbourhood-orientated youth work	stadtteilbezogene Jugendarbeit (f)
non-denominational school	Gemeinschaftsschule (f)
non-profit making	gemeinnützig
non-specialist education, school providing	allgemeinbildende Schule (f)
nursery assistant	Kindergarten-Helfer (m)/ Kindergarten-Helferin (f) → *Tageseinrichtungen für Kinder*
nursery nurse	Säuglingsschwester (f)
nursery school	Kindergarten (m) → *Tageseinrichtungen für Kinder*
nursery(school)teacher	Kindergärtnerin (f) → *Erzieher, VK*
obligation to make educational provision, (the State's)	Bildungsauftrag (m)
observation and assessment centre	Beobachtungszentrum (n)
observation unit, observation ward	Beobachtungsstation (f)
observation visit	Hospitation (f)
observe in action, to	hospitieren
occupation a) profession, eg lawyer, doctor b) vocation, eg priest c) trade, eg carpenter, electrician	Beruf (m) akademischer Beruf Beruf im Sinne von Berufung Beruf im Sinne von Gewerbe
occupational therapist	Beschäftigungstherapeut (m)/ Beschäftigungstherapeutin (f)
one-armed bandit	Spielautomat (m)
open-door youth centre	Haus (n) der offenen Tür (f) (OT) → *Jugendfreizeiteinrichtungen*
open prison	Freigängerhaus (n)

opinion poll	Meinungsumfrage (f)
opinion research	Meinungsforschung (f)
order of the court	gerichtliche Verfügung (f)
organised youth	Verbandsjugend (f)
outdoor pursuits	Erlebnispädagogik (f) → *Erlebnispädagogik*
outdoor pursuits, youth leader in	Teamer (m)
out-reach youth work	mobile Jugendarbeit (f) → *Jugendarbeit, mobile*
Overseas Development	Entwicklungshilfe (f)
parental authority, person holding	Erziehungsberechtigter (m)/ Erziehungsberechtigte (f)
parental educational responsibilities	Erziehungspflicht (f)
parental rights and duties	elterliche Sorge (f) → *Elterliche Sorge*
parents council	Elternbeirat (m)
parents, working with	Elternarbeit (f)
participation in decision making	Mitwirkung (f) → *Partizipation Jugendlicher*
participation in management	Mitverwaltung (f)
participation in school government	Mitwirkung (f) in der Schule (f) (schulische Mitwirkung)
participation of young people in decision making	Partizipation (f) Jugendlicher (pl) → *Partizipation Jugendlicher*
partnership	Partnerschaft (f)
part-time vocational school	Berufsschule (f) → *Bildungswesen* → *Berufsbildung*
part-time worker, part-time staff	nebenamtlicher Mitarbeiter (m)/ nebenamtliche Mitarbeiterin (f)
pastimes	Freizeitbeschäftigung (f), Freizeitbetätigung (f)
patron town	Patenstadt (f)

peace movement	Friedensbewegung (f) → *Friedensbewegung*
pediatric clinic	Kinderklinik (f)
pediatrician	Kinderarzt (m)/Kinderärztin (f)
penal law relating to young offenders	Jugendstrafrecht (n) → *Jugendstrafrecht*
pen friend	Briefpartner (m)/ Briefpartnerin (f)
performance	Leistung (f)
person at risk	Gefährdeter (m)/Gefährdete (f)
person entitled to receive benefits (services or money)	Anspruchsberechtigter (m)/ Anspruchsberechtigte (f)
person in need of help	Hilfebedürftiger (m)/ Hilfebedürftige (f)
person in the beginning stage of his career	Berufsanfänger (m)/ Berufsanfängerin (f)
person to whom one relates specifically	Bezugsperson (f)
person with a hearing impairment	Hörbehinderter (m)
person who exercises the right of care and custody	Personensorgeberechtigter (m)/ Personensorgeberechtigte (f) → *Elterliche Sorge*
person with a speech defect	Sprachbehinderter (m)
person with impaired vision and/or hearing	Person (f) mit Sinnesschäden (m/pl)
person with special needs	Behinderter (m)/Behinderte (f)
physical education	Leibeserziehung (f)
physical education teacher	Sportlehrer (m)/Sportlehrerin (f)
pilot project	Modellprojekt (n)
playground	Spielplatz (m)
playing field	Sportplatz (m)
play school leader	Kindergärtnerin (f) → *Erzieher, VK*
play therapy	Spieltherapie (f)

political education, education for citizenship	politische Bildung (f), staatsbürgerliche Erziehung (f) → *Jugendarbeit*
political protest by the young	Jugendprotest (m) → *Jugendprotest*
polytechnic and university, co-operative	kooperative Gesamthochschule (f) → *Bildungswesen*
polytechnic and university, integrated	integrierte Gesamthochschule (f)
pop charts	Hit-Liste (f)
pornography	Pornografie (f)
post-natal clinic, ante- and	Mütterberatungsstelle (f) → *Beratungsdienste*
practical handwork	Basteln (n)
practical handwork, one who enjoys	Bastler (m)/Bastlerin (f)
practical placement	Praktikum (n), Betriebspraktikum (n)
precocious child	frühreifes Kind (n)
pregnancy, termination of	Schwangerschaftsabbruch (m) → *Schwangerschaftsabbruch*
pre-school class	Vorklasse (f), Vorschulklasse (f)
pre-school education	Vorschulerziehung (f) → *Tageseinrichtungen für Kinder*
pre-school education establishment	Vorschule (f)
pre-school play group	Kindergarten (m)
pressure to achieve academically	Leistungsdruck (m) (im Bildungswesen)
preventive measure	Vorbeugungsmaßnahme (f)
primary school	Grundschule (f)
principal (of a school)	Schulleiter (m)/Schulleiterin (f)
prison sentence	Freiheitsstrafe (f) → *Jugendstrafrecht, Maßnahmen des*
prison welfare and after-care	Gefangenenfürsorge (f)
probation	Bewährung (f) → *Strafaussetzung zur Bewährung*

probationary supervision	Bewährungsaufsicht (f)
probationary year	Jahrespraktikum (n), Berufs-praktikum (n) von einem Jahr (n)
probationers, hostel for	Bewährungsheim (n) → *Strafaussetzung zur Bewährung*
probation officer	Bewährungshelfer (m)/ Bewährungshelferin (f)
probation period	Bewährungsfrist (f)
probation service	Bewährungshilfe (f)
problem children, statutory educational provision for	öffentliche Erziehungshilfen (f/pl) → *Erziehungshilfen, öffentliche*
professional training	Berufsausbildung (f)
professional youth workers	Fachkräfte (f/pl) der Jugendarbeit (f)
programme or event with a strong element of mixing and mingling	Begegnung (f)
programme organiser	Betreuer (m)/Betreuerin (f)
programme planning	Programmplanung (f), Programmgestaltung (f)
programmes for the disadvantaged	Benachteiligtenprogramm (n)
programmes on offer	Angebote (n/pl) der Jugendarbeit (f)
promotion	Förderung (f)
Promotion of Employment Act	Arbeitsförderungsgesetz (n) → *Bundesanstalt für Arbeit*
protection of employment	Arbeitsschutz (m)
protection of the environment	Umweltschutz (m) → *Umweltschutz*
protection of young people at work	Jugendarbeitsschutz (m) → *Jugendgesetze*
protection of young people from harmful publications	literarischer Jugendschutz (m) → *Jugendschutz*
protection of young persons in public	Jugendschutz (m) → *Jugendschutz*

Protection of Young People in Public, Act Concerning the	Jugendschutzgesetz (n) → *Jugendschutz* → *Jugendgesetze*
Protection of Young Persons at Work Act	Jugendarbeitsschutzgesetz (n) → *Jugendgesetze*
protest, anti-establishment	Jugendprotest (m) → *Jugendprotest*
provision	Angebote (n/pl), Einrichtung (f)
provision, youth service	Angebote der Jugendarbeit
Psychagoge (psychiatric child care worker)	Psychagoge (m)/Psychagogin (f)
publications harmful to young persons	jugendgefährdende Schriften (f/pl) → *Jugendschutz*
Publications Harmful to Young Persons, Act Concerning the Distribution of	Gesetz (n) über die Verbreitung (f) jugendgefährdender Schriften (f/pl) → *Jugendschutz*
public health protection	Gesundheitsschutz (m)
public prosecutor in juvenile cases	Jugendstaatsanwalt (m)/ Jugendstaatsanwältin (f) → *Jugendstrafrecht*
public welfare	öffentliche Fürsorge (f) → *Fürsorge, öffentliche*
punk	Punker (m), Punk (m)
pupil representation, pupils' council	Schülervertretung (f) (SV)
qualification, vocational	berufsqualifizierender Abschluß (m)
qualified worker in day care centres	Hortner (m)/Hortnerin (f) → *Tageseinrichtungen für Kinder*
racism (UK)/xenophobia	Ausländerfeindlichkeit (f)
rape	Vergewaltigung (f)
rates of support	Förderungssätze (m/pl)
rat race society (coll)	Leistungsgesellschaft (f)
readiness for school	Schulreife (f)

Realschule (parallels former secondary modern school)	Realschule (f) → *Bildungswesen*
Realschule leaving certificate	Realschulabschluß (m)
recipient of a grant	Zuwendungsempfänger (m)
recipient of social assistance benefits	Sozialhilfeempfänger (m)/ Sozialhilfeempfängerin (f) → *Sozialhilfe*
recognised training establishment	Ausbildungsbetrieb (m) → *Berufsbildung*
recognised training trade	anerkannter Ausbildungsberuf (m)
reduced unemployment benefit	Arbeitslosenhilfe (f) → *Bundesanstalt für Arbeit*
reduced price	ermäßigter Preis (m), ermäßigter Satz (m)
refund	Erstattung (f)
registered association	eingetragener Verein (m) → *Verein*
regulations on grant-aid	Förderungsrichtlinien (f/pl)
rehabilitation	Rehabilitation (f)
rehabilitation centre	Rehabilitationszentrum (n), Entziehungsheim (n), Entwöhnungsheim (n)
rehabilitation of offenders	Resozialisierung (f)
rehabilitation of the handicapped	Rehabilitation (f) Behinderter (pl) → *Rehabilitation Behinderter*
Reifezeugnis (grammar school leaving certificate)	Reifezeugnis (n) → *Bildungswesen*
reimbursement	Erstattung (f)
reintegration, rehabilitation	Wiedereingliederung (f)
relationship counselling	Partnerschaftsberatung (f) → *Beratungsdienste*
remand in custody pending further enquiries	Untersuchungshaft (f)
remedial or recuperative health scheme	Erholungsmaßnahme (f)

remedial teacher	Heilpädagoge (m)/Heilpädagogin (f) → *Mitarbeiter der Jugendhilfe*
remedial teaching	Heilpädagogik (f)
remedial teaching, relating to	heilpädagogisch
remission of sentence	Straferlaß (m) → *Jugendstrafrecht* → *Strafaussetzung zur Bewährung*
Representation of Staff Act	Personalvertretungsgesetz (n) → *Bedienstete des öffentlichen Dienstes*
representing a (moral) risk for the young	jugendgefährdend
requirements of a trade or profession	Berufsbild (n)
residential care	Heimerziehung (f), Heimunterbringung (f)
residential care, child in	Heimkind (n)
residential centre	Wohnheim (n)
residential child care worker	Heimerzieher (m)/ Heimerzieherin (f) → *Erzieher*
residential event	Freizeit (f)
residential home	Wohnheim (n)
residential home for young people	Jugendwohnheim (n)
residential provision, small-scale	Kleinheim (n) → *Hilfe zur Erziehung*
residential youth centre	Jugendhof (m)
resources	Mittel (n/pl)
responsibility for maintenance of dependents	Unterhaltspflicht (f)
right of co-determination	Mitbestimmungsrecht (n)
right of custody	Sorgerecht (n) → *Elterliche Sorge*
right to a say in management	Mitbestimmungsrecht (n)
right to be brought up and educated, (the child's)	Erziehungsanspruch (m) (des Kindes)

right to participation in decision making	Mitwirkungsrecht (n)
risk, person at	Gefährdeter (m)/Gefährdete (f)
runaway	Ausreißer (m)/Ausreißerin (f)
rural home help	Dorfhelferin (f)
rural youth, association of	Landjugend (f)
safety of work regulations	Arbeitsschutz (m)
salaried employee	Angestellter (m)/Angestellte (f) → *Bedienstete des Öffentlichen Dienstes*
scholarship	Stipendium (n)
schooling	(Schul-)ausbildung (f), Schulung (f), erster Bildungsweg (m)
schooling, advice on	Schullaufbahnberatung (f)
school kindergarten	Schulkindergarten (m) → *Tageseinrichtungen für Kinder*
school psychologist	Schulpsychologe (m)/ Schulpsychologin (f); schulpsychologischer Dienst (m)
school readiness test	Schulreifetest (m)
school report	Schulzeugnis (n)
school social work	Schulsozialarbeit (f)
school trip	Klassenfahrt (f)
Scout	Pfadfinder (m)
secondary education establishment	weiterführende Schule (f)
secondary level stage one leaving certificate	Sekundarstufenabschluß I (m) → *Bildungswesen*
secure unit	geschlossene Abteilung (f)
self-awareness group	Selbsterfahrungsgruppe (f)
self-determination	Selbstbestimmung (f)
self-government	Selbstverwaltung (f)
self-government, local	Kommunale Selbstverwaltung (f) → *Kommunale Selbstverwaltung*

self-programming	selbstverwaltet
semi-skilled employment	Anlernberuf (m)
semi-skilled worker	angelernter Arbeiter (m)/ angelernte Arbeiterin (f)
sentence suspended whilst on probation	Strafaussetzung zur Bewährung (f)
services for the handicapped	Behindertenhilfe (f) → *Behindertenhilfe*
severely disabled person, severely handicapped person	Schwerbeschädigter (m)/ Schwerbeschädigte (f), Schwerbehinderter (m)/ Schwerbehinderte (f)
sex and pregnancy counselling	Beratung (f) in Sexual- und Schwangerschaftskonflikten (m/pl) → *Beratungsdienste*
sex education	Sexualerziehung (f)
sex education, sex instruction	sexuelle Aufklärung (f)
shelter/accomodation	Unterkunft (f)
shelter and protection, provision of	Inobhutnahme (f) → *Jugendschutz*
sheltered workshop	beschützende Werkstatt (f) (geschützte Werkstatt) → *Behindertenhilfe*
shop/factory/firm	Betrieb (m)
shop floor representative	Betriebsobmann (m) → *Betriebsrat*
shop steward	Vertrauensmann (m) → *Betriebsrat, VK*
short course	Kurzlehrgang (m)
short-stay foster family	Bereitschaftspflegestelle (f)
single homeless	Stadtstreicher (m)/ Stadtstreicherin (f), Penner (coll)
single-parent family	alleinerziehende Eltern (pl)
sit in (on a class), to	hospitieren
sixth form college	Aufbaugymnasium (n)

slow learner	Lernbehinderter (m)/ Lernbehinderte (f), Lernbeeinträchtigter (m)/Lernbeeinträchtigte (f)
sniffer	Schnüffler (m)
sniffing (glue-)	schnüffeln
Social Assistance Act, Federal	Bundessozialhilfegesetz
social assistance benefits, bodies responsible for the discharge of	Sozialhilfeträger (m/pl) → *Sozialhilfe*
social assistance benefits (FRG)	Sozialhilfe (f) → *Sozialhilfe*
social assistance benefits, recipient of	Sozialhilfeempfänger (m) Sozialhilfeempfängerin (f) → *Sozialhilfe*
social background	soziale Herkunft (f)
social behaviour	soziales Verhalten (n)
social change	sozialer Wandel (m)
social disadvantage	soziale Benachteiligung (f)
social education	Sozialerziehung (f)
social enquiry in juvenile cases	Jugendgerichtshilfe (f) → *Jugendstrafrecht*
social environment	soziales Umfeld (n)
social inadequacy	soziales Defizit (n)
social institutions	soziale Einrichtungen (f/pl)
social insurance	Sozialversicherung (f) → *Soziale Sicherung*
social insurance benefit	Sozialversicherungsleistung (f)
social insurance contributions	Sozialversicherungsbeitrag (m), Sozialabgaben (f/pl)
social insurance institution	Sozialversicherungsträger (m)
social integration	Sozialisation (f)
socially deprived	milieugeschädigt
socially deprived area	sozialer Brennpunkt (m)
socially maladjusted	sozial unangepaßt

social policy and administration	Sozialpolitik (f)
social rehabilitation	Resozialisierung (f)
social rehabilitation centre	Resozialisierungsheim (n)
social security	soziale Sicherung/Sicherheit (f) → *Soziale Sicherung*
social security benefits	Sozialleistungen (f/pl)
social service provision	sozialer Dienst (m), soziale Einrichtungen (f/pl)
social services	soziale Hilfen (f/pl)
social services department	Sozialamt (n)
social stratification	soziale Schichtung (f)
social structure	Sozialstruktur (f)
social studies	Sozialkunde (f)
social system	Sozialwesen (f)
social work, social help	Soziale Arbeit (f) → *Sozialarbeit/Sozialpädagogik*
social worker	≠ (Mitarbeiter der Sozialen Arbeit (VK)) → *Sozialarbeiter/Sozialpädagoge*
professional social worker	Fachkraft der Sozialen Arbeit
social worker involved in juvenile cases	Jugendgerichtshelfer (m) → *Jugendstrafrecht*
society	Verein (m) → *Verein,* VK
socio-educational court orders	Erziehungsmaßregeln (f/pl) → *Jugendstrafrecht, Maßnahmen des*
socio-educational provision for children with problems	Hilfe (f) zur Erziehung (f) → *Hilfe zur Erziehung*
socio-educational provision similar to a supervision order	Hilfe zur Erziehung (Erziehungsbeistandschaft)
socio-educational provision under a care order, reception into care	Hilfe zur Erziehung nach § 27 Sozialgesetzbuch VIII
non-residential (out-patient/open) socio-educational provision for children with problems	ambulante Erziehungshilfen

partly-residential socio-educational provision for children with problems	teilstationäre Erziehungshilfen
residential socio-educational provision for children with problems	stationäre Erziehungshilfen
socio-educational provision for young people	Jugendsozialarbeit (f) → *Jugendsozialarbeit*
speaker	Referent (m)/Referentin (f)
Special Committees on Youth Exchanges, eg British-German Special Committee on Youth Exchanges	Gemischte Fachausschüsse (m/pl), z.B. Gemischter Fachausschuß für den deutsch-britischen Jugendaustausch → *Fachausschüsse, gemischte*
special education	Sonderschulunterricht (m)
specialist conference	Fachtagung (f)
specialist further training (for a professional)	Fachausbildung (f)
specialist training	Fachausbildung (f)
special school	Sonderschule (f)
speech defect, person with a	Sprachbehinderter (m)
speech therapy	Sprachheilkunde (f)
sport for young people	Jugendsport (m)
sports field	Sportplatz (m)
sports proficiency badge	Sportabzeichen (n)
sports programmes, TV/radio	Sportschau (f)
sports teacher	Sportlehrer (m)/Sportlehrerin (f)
sports team	Sportmannschaft (f)
standing conference	Arbeitsgemeinschaft (f)
standing conference of voluntary youth organisations, local	Stadtjugendring (m)
standing conference of youth organisations	Jugendring (m) → *Jugendringe*
standing conference of youth organisations at *Kreis* level	Kreisjugendring (m)
standing conference of youth organisations at *Land* level	Landesjugendring (m)

statement of accounts for a programme	Abrechnung (f) einer Maßnahme (f)
statement of expenditure	Verwendungsnachweis (m)
statutory authority, statutory agency	öffentlicher Träger (m)
statutory educational provision for problem children	öffentliche Erziehungshilfen (f/pl) → *Erziehungshilfen, öffentliche*
statutory order → *Rechtsinstrumente*	Verordnung (f)
statutory school age, having reached	schulpflichtig
statutory socio-educational provision for children with problems	Hilfe (f) zur Erziehung (f) → *Hilfe zur Erziehung*
stimulant	Rauschmittel (n)
street work	Straßensozialarbeit (f)
street worker	Straßensozialarbeiter (m)/ Straßensozialarbeiterin (f), Streetworker (m)
structured leisure time acitivity e.g. out-door pursuits, residential event, residential programme	Freizeit (f)
student council, student representation	Studentenvertretung (f)
student organisation	Studentenverband (m)
student trainee	Praktikant (m)/Praktikantin (f)
student union	Studentenwerk (n)
study tour, study visit	Studienreise (f)
subculture	Subkultur (f)
subject-tied university entrance qualification	fachgebundene Hochschulreife (f) → *Bildungswesen*
submission of an application	Antragstellung (f)
Subsidiaritätsprinzip (a principle which establishes the priority rights and responsibilities of individuals, voluntary bodies and the State)	Subsidiaritätsprinzip (n) → *Subsidiaritätsprinzip*
subsidization, principle of	Förderungsgrundsatz (m), Förderungsprinzip (n)

subsidized housing	sozialer Wohnungsbau (m) → *sozialer Wohnungsbau*
subsidy	Zuschuß (m), Zuwendung (f), Beihilfe (f)
suburban holiday play schemes	Stadtranderholung (f)
supervision of institutions	Heimaufsicht (f)
supervision of institutions, authority responsible for the	Heimaufsichtsbehörde (f) → *Jugendamt*
supervisory responsibilities	Aufsichtspflicht (f) → *Aufsichtspflicht*
support, financial	Förderung (f)
supportive measures for the youth service	Jugendförderung (f) → *Jugendförderung*
temporary accommodation hostel	Auffangheim (n)
tented camp	Zeltlager (n)
termination of pregnancy	Schwangerschaftsabbruch (m)
toddlers' group	Krabbelstube (f)
tourist services directed at young people	Jugendtourismus (m) → *Jugendreisen*
town twinning arrangement	Städtepartnerschaft (f)
trade examination	Gesellenprüfung (f) → *Berufsbildung*
tradesman's certificate	Gesellenbrief (m) → *Berufsbildung*
trafficking in drugs	Rauschgifthandel (m) → *Drogenmißbrauch*
trainee	Auszubildender (m) ohne Lehr- vertrag (m) (VK), Anlernling (m), → *Berufsbildung*
trainee wage	Ausbildungsvergütung (f) → *Berufsbildung*
trainer	Ausbilder (m)/Ausbilderin (f) → *Berufsbildung*
training, additional	Zusatzausbildung (f)

training course	Ausbildungslehrgang (m), Schulungskurs (m)
training establishment, recognised	Ausbildungsbetrieb (m)
training (for craftsmen in a skilled trade)	Fachausbildung (f)
training grant	Ausbildungsbeihilfe (f)
training position	Ausbildungsplatz (m)
training session	Schulungsabend (m)
training trade, recognised	anerkannter Ausbildungsberuf (m) → *Berufsbildung*
training under the conditions of apprenticeship	Ausbildungsverhältnis (n) → *Berufsbildung*
training vacancy	Ausbildungsplatz (m)
training workshop	Lehrwerkstätte (f)
travel expenses	Fahrtkosten (pl), Reisekosten (pl)
travel guide	Reiseleiter (m)/Reiseleiterin (f)
travel services for young people on a non-profit making basis	Jugendreisedienste (m/pl) → *Jugendreisen*
treatment of young offenders at attendance centres	Jugendarrest (m) → *Jugendstafrecht, Maßnahmen des*
truancy	Schulschwänzen (n)
tutorial supervision	Supervision (f)
TV/radio sports programmes	Sportschau (f)
twinned city, twinned town	Städtepartnerschaft (f)
types of schools	Schulformen (f/pl) → *Bildungswesen*
umbrella organisation	Dachverband (m)
underprivileged	milieugeschädigt
unemployment benefit	Arbeitslosengeld (n) → *Bundesanstalt für Arbeit*
unemployment benefit, reduced	Arbeitslosenhilfe (f) → *Bundesanstalt für Arbeit*

uniformed youth	uniformierte Jugendgruppen (f/pl) → *Jugendverbände, VK*
university and technical university entrance qualification	Hochschulreife (f) → *Bildungswesen*
university entrance qualification, subject-tied	fachgebundene Hochschulreife (f)
unsuitable for education at school	unerziehbar
upbringing	Erziehung (f) (durch die Familie)
vagrant	Stadtstreicher (m)/ Stadtstreicherin (f), Penner (coll.)
visually handicapped person	Sehbehinderter
vocational education, compulsory part-time	Berufsschulpflicht (f) → *Bildungswesen* → *Berufsbildung*
vocational further education	Berufsfortbildung (f)
vocational guidance	Berufsberatung (f) → *Bundesanstalt für Arbeit*
vocational qualification	berufsqualifizierender Abschluß (m)
vocational rehabilitation establishment	Berufsbildungswerk (n) → *Rehabilitation Behinderter*
vocational training	Berufsbildung (f) → *Berufsbildung*
Vocational Training Act	Berufsbildungsgesetz (n) → *Berufsbildung*
vocational training activities/ programmes	Angebote (n/pl) der Berufsausbildung (f)
vocational training grant	Berufsausbildungsbeihilfe (f) → *Ausbildungsförderung*
vocational training preparatory year	Berufsvorbereitungsjahr (n)
vocational training schemes	berufsbildende Maßnahmen (f/pl) → *Berufsbildung*
vocational training year, basic	Berufsgrundbildungsjahr (n)
vocational retraining	Umschulung (f)
voluntary agency, voluntary organisation	freier Träger (m)

voluntary work and community service, year of	freiwilliges soziales Jahr → *Freiwilliges Soziales Jahr*
voluntary sector, the	die freien Träger
voluntary service in an organised scheme	freiwilliger Arbeitseinsatz (m)
voluntary welfare work	freie Wohlfahrtspflege (f)
voluntary youth worker in the sport sector	Sportjugendleiter (m)/ Sportjugendleiterin (f)
volunteering	Freiwilligendienste (m/pl)
VSO-type of worker (Voluntary Services Overseas), worker with a development scheme	Entwicklungshelfer (m)/ Entwicklungshelferin (f)
walking tour	Wanderung (f) → *Wandern*
walking tour, to go on a	wandern
warden of a home	Heimleiter (m)/Heimleiterin (f)
welfare and after-care for offenders	Straffälligenhilfe (f)
welfare charges	Sozialabgaben (f/pl)
welfare organisations	Wohlfahrtsverbände (m/pl) → *Wohlfahrtsverbände*
welfare payments	Sozialabgaben (f/pl)
welfare, public	öffentliche Fürsorge (f) → *Fürsorge, öffentliche*
welfare work	Fürsorge (f)
welfare work for the young	Jugendfürsorge (f) → *Jugendfürsorge/Jugendpflege*
welfare work, voluntary	freie Wohlfahrtspflege (f)
white collar worker	Angestellter (m)/Angestellte (f) → *Bedienstete des Öffentlichen Dienstes*
withdrawal of (the right of) custody	Sorgerechtsentzug (m) → *Pflegekinderbereich/Pflegekinderwesen*
withdrawal symptoms	Entzugserscheinungen (f/pl)
withdrawal therapy	Entziehungskur (f)

women's movement	Frauenbewegung (f) → *Frauenbewegung*
women's refuge	Frauenhaus (n)
work aptitude	Berufseignung (f)
work camp	Aufbaulager (n)
work experience	Betriebspraktikum (n), Schulpraktikum (n)
work group	Arbeitsgruppe (f)
work, injury at	Arbeitsunfall (m)
work permit	Arbeitserlaubnis (f)
work placement	Berufspraktikum (n) → *Bildungswesen*
work with girls	Mädchenarbeit (f) → *Mädchenarbeit*
worker's hostel	Arbeiterwohnheim (n)
workers in youth and youth welfare services	Mitarbeiter (m/pl)/Mitarbeiterinnen (f/pl) der Jugendhilfe (f) → *Mitarbeiter/Mitarbeiterinnen der Jugendhilfe*
working party	Arbeitskreis (m)
working with parents	Elternarbeit (f)
works committee	Betriebsrat (m) → *Betriebsrat*
works committee, youth representation on the	Betriebsjugendvertretung (f) → *Betriebsrat*
workshop	Werkstatt (f)
xenophobia/racism (UK)	Ausländerfeindlichkeit (f)
young adult	junger Volljähriger (m)/ junge Volljährige (f) → *Tabelle Altersgrenzen*
young musician's provision	Jugendmusik (f)
young offender	jugendlicher Straffälliger (m)/ jugendliche Straffällige (f) → *Jugendstrafrecht*

young offenders, custodial treatment of	Vollzug (m) der Jugendstrafe (f)
young offenders' court	Jugendgericht (n)
young offenders, measures under penal law relating to	Jugendstrafrecht (n), Maßnahmen (f/pl) des → *Jugendstrafrecht, Maßnahmen des*
young offenders, penal law relating to	Jugendstrafrecht (n) → *Jugendstrafrecht*
young people at work, protection of	Jugendarbeitsschutz (m) → *Jugendgesetze*
young people, informal education of	Jugendbildung (f)
young people, information and counselling centre for	Jugendinformationszentrum (n) → *Beratungsdienste*
young people, laws relating to	Jugendgesetze (n/pl) → *Jugendgesetze*
young people living with socio-educational support in the community	betreutes Jugendwohnen (n) → *Hilfe zur Erziehung*
young people outside youth organisations	nicht organisierte Jugendliche (pl)
young people, publications morally dangerous to	jugendgefährdende Schriften (f/pl) → *Jugendschutz*
young people, residential home for	Jugendwohnheim (n)
young people, tourist services directed at	Jugendtourismus (m) → *Jugendreisen*
young people, unattached	nicht verbandsgebundene Jugendliche (pl)
young people with a vocational problem, assistance to	Jugendberufshilfe (f) → *Jugendsozialarbeit*
young person	Jugendlicher (m)/Jugendliche (f)
young persons, harmful to	jugendgefährdend → *Jugendschutz*
young worker	junger Werktätiger (m)/ junge Werktätige (f)
youth action	Jugendinitiativen (f/pl)
youth and child welfare	Jugendwohlfahrt (f) → *Jugendwohlfahrt*

youth and community worker	Jugend- und Gemeinwesen-arbeiter (m) → *Sozialarbeiter/Sozialpädagoge, VK*
youth and youth welfare services, workers in	Mitarbeiter (m/pl)/Mitarbeiterinnen (f/pl) der Jugendhilfe (f) → *Mitarbeiter/Mitarbeiterinnen der Jugendhilfe*
youth association	Jugendorganisation (f), Jugendverband (m) → *Jugendverbände*
youth authorities	Jugendbehörden (f/pl) → *Jugendbehörden*
youth authority of the *Land* government	Oberste Landesjugendbehörde (f)
youth camp	Jugendlager (n)
youth centre	Haus der Jugend (n), Jugendzentrum (n) → *Jugendfreizeitstätten*
youth centre, open-door	Haus (n) der offenen Tür (f) (OT) → *Jugendfreizeitstätten*
youth centre, residential	Jugendhof (m), Jugendlager (n)
youth centre, small door	Haus (n) der kleinen offenen Tür (f) (KOT) → *Jugendfreizeitstätten*
youth chaplain	Jugendpfarrer (m), Jugendseelsorger (m)
youth club	Haus (n) der offenen Tür (f) (OT), Jugendclub (m), Jugendhaus (n) → *Jugendfreizeitstätten*
youth club, partially open youth centre	Haus (n) der teiloffenen Tür (f) (TOT) → *Jugendfreizeitstätten*
youth club (sometimes with simple overnight facilities)	Jugendheim (n)
youth community service	Jugendgemeinschaftsdienste (m/pl)
youth courier	Jugendreiseleiter (m)/ Jugendreiseleiterin (f) → *Jugendreisen*
youth custody centre, youth prison	Jugendstrafanstalt (f) → *Jugendstrafrecht, Maßnahmen des*

youth establishments, construction programmes for	Jugendbauprogramme (n/pl)
youth exchange	Jugendaustausch (m)
youth exchange, bilateral	bilateraler Jugendaustausch (m)
Youth Exchanges, Special Committees on	Gemischte Fachausschüsse (m/pl) → *Fachausschüsse, gemischte*
youth forum	Jugendforum (n)
youth hostel	Jugendherberge (f) → *Wandern*
Youth Hostel Association, membership card of the	Jugendherbergsausweis (m)
youth hostel warden	Jugendherbergsleiter (m)/ Jugendherbergsleiterin (f)
youth hostel wardens	Jugendherbergseltern (pl)
youth leader (voluntary)	Jugendleiter (m)/Jugendleiterin (f) → *Jugendleiter*
youth leader in outdoor pursuits	Teamer (m)
youth legislation	Jugendgesetzgebung (f)
youth magazine	Jugendzeitschrift (f)
youth magazines and publications	Jugendpresse (f)
youth meeting, youth contact	Jugendbegegnung (f), Jugendtreffen (n)
youth movement	Jugendbewegung (f)
youth office, area	Bezirksjugendamt (n) → *Jugendamt*
youth officer	Jugendpfleger (m)/Jugendpflegerin (f) → *Jugendamt*
youth organisation	Jugendorganisation (f), Jugendverband (m) → *Jugendverbände*
youth organisation, being member of a	verbandsgebunden
youth organisation, specialist (eg music, sport)	Fachverband (m) der Jugendarbeit (f) (z.B. Musik, Sport)
youth organisations	Jugendverbände (m/pl) → *Jugendverbände*

youth organisations at *Land* level, standing conference of	Landesjugendring (m) → *Jugendringe*
youth plan, local authority	Kommunaler Jugendplan (m) → *Bundesjugendplan*
youth policy	Jugendpolitik (f)
youth provision	Jugendbauten (m/pl), Jugendeinrichtungen (f/pl)
youth religions	Jugendreligionen (f/pl) → *Jugendreligionen*
youth representation on the works committee	Betriebsjugendvertretung (f) → *Bedienstete des Öffentlichen Dienstes*
youth representative of a works committee	Jugendvertreter (m) → *Bedienstete des Öffentlichen Dienstes*
youth representatives under the Representation of Staff Act	Personaljugendvertretung (f)
youth research	Jugendforschung (f) → *Jugendforschung*
youth residential training centre	Jugendbildungsstätte (f)
youth sects	Jugendsekten (f/pl) → *Jugendreligionen*
youth service provision	Angebote (n/pl) der Jugendarbeit (f) → *Jugendamt*
Youth Services Committee	Jugendhilfeausschuß (m)
Youth Stamp	Jugendmarke (f) → *Jugendmarke*
youth subculture(s)	Jugendkultur (f)
youth support worker	Jugendhelfer (m)/ Jugendhelferin (f)
youth tours, youth travel	Jugendreisen (f/pl) → *Jugendreisen*
Youth Training	berufsbildende Maßnahmen (f/pl) für Jugendliche (pl) → *Jugendarbeitslosigkeit, VK*
youth volunteer action	freiwilliges soziales Engagement (n) von Jugendlichen (pl) → *Engagement, soziales*

youth week	Jugendwoche (f)
youth welfare and youth service office (youth office)	Jugendamt (n(n)) → *Jugendamt*
Youth Services Committee at *Land* level	Landesjugendhilfeausschluß (m)
youth work	Jugendarbeit (f) → *Jugendarbeit*
youth work and youth welfare services, child and youth services	Jugendhilfe (f) → *Jugendhilfe*
youth work and youth welfare services, bodies responsible for	Jugendhilfeträger (m/pl) → *Träger der Jugendhilfe*
youth work, detached	mobile Jugendarbeit (f) → *Jugendarbeit, mobile*
youth work done by the churches	kirchliche Jugendarbeit (f)
youth work in the arts	kulturelle Jugendbildung (f) → *Jugendarbeit*
youth work, out-reach	mobile Jugendarbeit (f) → *Jugendarbeit, mobile*
youth work practitioners	(nicht formal qualifizierte) Mitarbeiter der Jugendhilfe → *Mitarbeiter/Mitarbeiterinnen der Jugendhilfe*
youth worker	Mitarbeiter (m)/Mitarbeiterin (f) der Jugendarbeit (f)
youth worker, qualified	Sozialpädagoge (m)/ Sozialpädagogin (f) → *Sozialarbeiter/Sozialpädagoge*
youth worker in the sport sector, voluntary	Sportjugendleiter (m)/ Sportjugendleiterin (f) → *Jugendarbeit*
youth worker (or helper), unpaid full-time or part-time	ehrenamtlicher Helfer (m)/ehren- amtliche Helferin (f) → *Mitarbeiter/Mitarbeiterinnen der Jugendhilfe*
youth work professionals	Fachkräfte (f/pl) der Jugendarbeit (f)
youth unemployment	Jugendarbeitslosigkeit (f) → *Jugendarbeitslosigkeit*

Teil III
Handbuch

Part III
Handbook

Fachbegriffe der deutschen Jugendhilfe mit Erläuterungen und britische Entsprechungen

Adoption (f)

D

Bei der Adoption eines Kindes durch ein verheiratetes Paar nehmen in der Regel beide Ehegatten das Kind an. Ausnahmsweise können auch Ledige adoptieren, vor allem Vater und Mutter eines nichtehelichen Kindes.

Zumindest einer der Annehmenden muß 25, der andere kann 21 Jahre alt sein. Ein nichteheliches oder ein Stiefkind kann man mit 21 Jahren annehmen.

Bei einem ehelichen Kind ist die Zustimmung der Eltern und des Kindes selbst erforderlich, wenn es über 14 Jahre alt ist. Bei einem nichtehelichen Kind bedarf es der Zustimmung der Mutter, nicht aber der des Vaters. Die Adoption des Kindes durch Dritte ist jedoch nicht auszusprechen, wenn der Vater die Ehelicherklärung oder die Annahme seines nichtehelichen Kindes beantragt hat. Über diese Rechte muß das Jugendamt den Vater beraten. Die Zustimmung zur Adoption kann erst erteilt werden, wenn das Kind acht Wochen alt ist.

Der Annahme wird ein Pflegeverhältnis (→ *Pflegschaft)* vorgeschaltet. Mit der Einwilligung eines Elternteils in die Annahme ruht grundsätzlich die → *elterliche Sorge* dieses Elternteils.

Zuständig für den Ausspruch der Adoption ist das Vormundschaftsgericht, das in erster Linie das Wohl des Kindes zu berücksichtigen hat.

Durch staatlichen Akt erhält das adoptierte Kind die Stellung und den Namen eines ehelichen Kindes und wird mit der Familie des Annehmenden verwandt. Die Adoption begründet ein Ehehindernis. Das Verwandtschaftsverhältnis mit der Ursprungsfamilie erlischt.

Die Adoption von Minderjährigen darf nur von Fachkräften der Adoptionsvermittlungsstellen der → *Jugendämter* und Landesjugendämter sowie einiger anerkannter freier Träger vermittelt werden (→ *Träger der Jugendhilfe).*

VK

Nach geltendem Recht können nicht verehelichte Personen unter 18 Jahren durch Gerichtsbeschluß adoptiert werden. Ein Adoptionsbeschluß bewirkt die Übertragung der elterlichen Sorge auf die Annehmenden. Dem adoptierten Kind wird dadurch insbesondere die Unehelichkeit erspart. Durch den Adoptionsbeschluß erlischt das Verwandtschaftsverhältnis zwischen dem adoptier-

Specialist Terms of the German Youth Services with Explanations and British Equivalents

Adoption

G

A child is normally adopted by both marital partners. Exceptionally, it is also possible for unmarried persons to adopt, in particular for the father and mother of an illegitimate child.

At least one of the adopting parties must be 25, the other 21 years of age; an illegitimate child or a stepchild may be adopted at 21.

It is necessary to obtain the consent of a legitimate child's parents and that of the child himself if he/she is over 14. In case of an illegitimate child the mother must agree. The father's consent, however, is not required. But if the father of an illegitimate child has applied for a declaration of legitimacy or for an adoption order, the child may not be adopted by a third person. The youth office must advise the father on his rights. Agreement to an adoption is only valid if given at least eight weeks after the child's birth.

Prior to adoption, a curatorship (→ *Pflegschaft*) is established. When a parent has consented to an adoption, his or her parental rights are suspended as a matter of principle (→ *Elterliche Sorge*).

Adoption lies within the competence of the guardianship court, which endeavours to resolve the matter in the best interests of the child.

By a formal legal act the adopted child obtains the status and name of a child born in wedlock and is henceforth next of kin to the adopting party. This kinship constitutes an impediment to marriage within the adopting family. Kinship with the familiy of origin ceases.

Adoption services in respect of minors may only be provided by the specialists of those sections of the youth offices (→ *Jugendamt*), the *Land* youth offices and some recognised voluntary organisations which are responsible for adoption procedures and implementation (→ *Träger der Jugendhilfe*).

UK

In accordance with the applicable legislation, any child under the age of 18 who has not been married may be adopted pursuant to an order of the court. An adoption order has the effect of vesting parental rights and duties in the adopters. An adopted child is specifically prevented from being illegitimate. An adoption order does not sever the links between an adopted child and his former

ten Kind und seinen natürlichen Eltern nicht. Auch die den Inzest betreffenden gesetzlichen Bestimmungen werden nicht außer Kraft gesetzt.

Ein Adoptionsbeschluß kann auf Antrag eines verheirateten Paares, bei dem beide Ehegatten mindestens 21 Jahre alt sind, erfolgen. Er ist auch möglich auf Antrag von unverheirateten oder ständig getrennt lebenden Paaren von 21 Jahren und darüber.

Die Zustimmung der Mutter ist erforderlich, wenn das Kind zur Adoption freigegeben werden soll. Auch Mütter unter 16 Jahren besitzen auf ihr Kind die Rechte einer Volljährigen. Die Einwilligung der Mutter ist unwirksam, wenn sie vor Ablauf von sechs Wochen nach der Geburt des Kindes erteilt wird. Die Zustimmung des Vaters eines unehelichen Kindes ist nicht erforderlich. Er kann jedoch während der Zeit, in der über die Frage der Adoption entschieden wird, das Sorgerecht für das Kind beantragen.

Wenn eine Entscheidung über die Adoption eines Kindes getroffen wird, muß das Gericht vor allem die Schutzwürdigkeit des Kindes bedenken und sein Wohl in den Jahren der Kindheit fördern.

Jede Kommune ist verpflichtet, in ihrem Zuständigkeitsbereich einen Adoptionsdienst zu schaffen, der die Interessen der bereits adoptierten oder der zur Adoption freigegebenen Kinder sowie der Eltern wahrt. Die Behörden müssen entweder unmittelbar oder durch einen anerkannten freien Träger der Adoptionsvermittlung entsprechende Strukturen schaffen und z.B. für Möglichkeiten der Unterbringung und Verpflegung, der Prüfung der Eignung der Kinder und der Adoptionswilligen sowie der Beratung von Personen sorgen, bei denen die Kindesannahme mit Schwierigkeiten verbunden ist. Eine kommunale Behörde oder ein anerkannter freier Träger, die die Aufgaben der Adoptionsvermittlung übernehmen, wird als *adoption agency* (Adoptionsvermittlungsstelle) bezeichnet.

Alkoholmißbrauch (m) bei Jugendlichen (m/f/pl)

D

Der regelmäßige Alkoholkonsum junger Menschen zwischen 12 und 24 Jahren ist seit Anfang der 80er Jahre deutlich zurückgegangen; die Abnahme zeigt sich bei beiden Geschlechtern. Dem Rückgang des Trinkens von Alkoholika entspricht eine Zunahme der alkoholfreien Getränke: bei Mineralwasser z.B. von 32% auf 50%.

Allerdings findet dieser positive Trend keinen Niederschlag bei dem kleinen Kreis der jungen Leute, die Alkoholmißbrauch betreiben und als alkoholgefährdet einzustufen sind. Diese Problemgruppe junger Menschen ist im genannten Zeitraum ungefähr gleich groß geblieben. Dazu gehören rund 4% der 12- bis 14jährigen, wobei der Anteil der Jungen größer ist als der der Mädchen.

Der Staat versucht, durch die im Gesetz zum Schutze der Jugend in der Öffentlichkeit *(→ Jugendgesetze)* festgelegten Altersgrenzen für den Verkauf und

parents for the purposes of kindred and affinity or for the purposes of the law of incest.

An adoption order may be made upon application by a married couple where each has attained the age of 21. An order may also be made on the application of one person aged 21 or over where the person is not married or is permanently separated.

The mother's agreement is required if the child is to be placed for adoption. Even if she is under 16 years she has full adult rights concerning the child. Agreement by the mother is ineffective if given less than six weeks after the child's birth. The consent of the father of an illegitimate child is not required, although the father may apply for custody of the child at the time that the question of adoption is decided.

In reaching any decision relating to the adoption of a child, a court must give priority to the need of safeguard and promote the welfare of the child throughout his childhood.

Every local authority has a duty to establish in its area an adoption service to meet the needs of children who have been or may be adopted and the needs of parents and prospective parents. The local authority must provide, either directly or through an approved adoption society, facilities such as temporary board and lodging, arrangements for assessing children and prospective adopters and counselling for persons with problems relating to adoption. A local authority or approved adoption society carrying out these functions is known as an adoption agency.

Alcohol Abuse Amongst Young People

G

The percentage of 12–24 year-olds who drink alcohol regularly has gone down significantly since the beginning of the 80s. This downward trend may be observed with both sexes. The decline in the consumption of alcoholic beverages is set off by an increase in the use of non-alcoholic beverages: the consumption of mineral water, e.g., rose from 32% to 50%.

This positive trend, however, has not affected the small group of young people who abuse alcohol and must be considered as being at risk. During the same period there has been practically no change in the size of the problem group which comprises 4% of the 12 – 14 year-olds. The proportion of boys is higher than that of girls in this age bracket.

The State has attempted to protect young people from the harmful effects of alcohol by laying down age limits for the sale and serving of alcoholic beverages, as

Ausschank von alkoholischen Getränken zumindest junge Menschen vor den schädlichen Einflüssen des Alkohols zu schützen. Dieses Gesetz allein kann aber den Alkoholmißbrauch nicht eindämmen. Ihm kann langfristig nur entgegengewirkt werden, wenn die Prävention intensiver betrieben wird. Dazu gehört ein verantwortungsbewußterer Umgang der Bezugspersonen des Kindes oder Jugendlichen mit dem Alkohol, die Einschränkung der Werbung für alkoholische Getränke, eine bessere Aufklärung der Jugend über die Gefahren des Alkoholmißbrauchs und ihre Erziehung zum kritischen Umgang mit der Droge Alkohol.

Die freien und öffentlichen Träger der Gesundheitsfürsorge bemühen sich vor allem um die Förderung der Prävention. So stellen z.B. das Bundesministerium für Frauen und Jugend, die Deutsche Hauptstelle gegen die Suchtgefahren, die Bundeszentrale für gesundheitliche Aufklärung und die Aktion Jugendschutz Informationsmaterial zur Verfügung. Von Zeit zu Zeit finden Schulungskurse für Multiplikatoren und Informationsveranstaltungen in Schulen und Jugendeinrichtungen statt.

Für Eltern, bei deren Kindern Alkoholprobleme auftreten, bestehen Beratungsstellen. Die entsprechend qualifizierten Mitarbeiter bemühen sich, in Ergänzung zu einer ggfs. erforderlichen ärztlichen Betreuung bei der Lösung der persönlichen Konflikte behilflich zu sein.

VK

Im Vereinigten Königreich sind Herstellung, Verkauf, Erwerb und Vertrieb von alkoholischen Getränken strengen gesetzlichen Bestimmungen unterworfen. Nach dem *Children and Young Persons Act* von 1933 ist die Verabreichung von Alkohol an Kinder unter fünf Jahren eine strafbare Handlung. Kinder unter 14 Jahren haben keinen Zutritt zu Orten, an denen Alkohol verkauft und konsumiert wird. Ab 16 Jahren ist der Genuß von Bier und Apfelwein (in Schottland auch Wein) gestattet, jedoch nur als Getränk zu einer Mahlzeit, die nicht im Schankbereich serviert wird. Erst ab 18 Jahren ist es jungen Menschen gesetzlich erlaubt, Alkohol zu kaufen (→ *Jugendgesetze).*

Trotz dieser gesetzlichen Regelung kann davon ausgegangen werden, daß 60% der 13–17jährigen in einem *pub* oder in Gaststätten mit Schankkonzession über die Straße alkoholische Getränke käuflich erworben haben. In der Altersgruppe der 13–16jährigen trinken ein Drittel der Kinder mindestens einmal pro Woche, jedoch meist zu Hause und im allgemeinen in kleinen Mengen.

Entsprechende Träger des *youth service,* die mit Gruppen- und Einzelbetreuung arbeiten, bieten Unterstützung, Beratung, Sozialerziehung und Freizeitprogramme an. Sie sind in der Lage, über die Gefahren des Alkoholmißbrauchs grundsätzlich zu informieren. Landesweite Träger wie das *National Youth Bureau,* die *National Association of Youth Clubs* und die *National Association of Young People's Counselling and Advisory Services* stellen den Mitarbeitern zeitgemäßes Informationsmaterial, Veröffentlichungen sowie Anregun-

embodied in the Act concerning the Protection of Young People in Public (→ *Jugendgesetze*). However, this Act alone cannot control the abuse of alcohol. A long-term effect may only be achieved if prevention is taken more seriously. This also means that the persons to whom children and young people relate must be more responsible in their own use of alcohol. Advertisements for alcoholic beverages need to be controlled and young people better informed of the risks involved in alcohol abuse and be brought up to use the drug alcohol with great caution.

Statutory and voluntary organisations responsible for health care are making real efforts to promote preventive measures. Thus, for example, the Federal Ministry for Women and Youth, the German Central Office for the Prevention of Addiction, the Federal Association for Information on Health, and the Federal Association for the Protection of Young People provide information on the dangers of drug abuse. Periodically, schools and youth establishments organise courses for opinion leaders and provide information programmes.

Parents whose children have problems with alcohol may consult the drug advisory centres. Their staff, who are trained in this field, try to assist the parents in obtaining medical care and help in solving the personal conflicts involved.

UK

In the UK the manufacture, sale, purchase and distribution of alcoholic beverages are controlled by strict regulations. It is an offence under the Children and Young Persons Act 1933 to give alcohol to a child under five. No child under 14 is allowed to enter a place where alcohol is bought and consumed. 16-year-olds are allowed to have a beer or cider (in Scotland also wine), but only to drink with a meal not served in a bar. Only at the age of 18 can a young person legally purchase alcohol (→ *Jugendgesetze, UK*)

Despite these laws, around 60% of children aged between 13 and 17 are likely to have bought alcohol in a pub or off-licence. In the 13–16 years age range, about a third of children drink at least once a week, but mostly in the home and generally small amounts.

Youth service agencies working with groups and individuals offer support, counselling, social education and recreational programmes. They are in a position to provide basic information about the danger of alcohol misuse. National organisations like the National Youth Bureau, the National Association of Youth Clubs and the National Association of Young People's Counselling and Advisory Services are able to provide workers with up-to-date information, publications and descriptions of current examples of work with young people at risk. Social education programmes with a health education component play an important role, both in schools and in the youth service.

gen mit aktuellen Beispielen für die Arbeit mit gefährdeten Jugendlichen zur Verfügung. Die Sozialerziehung einschließlich der Gesundheitserziehung spielt sowohl in der Schule als auch in der Jugendarbeit eine wichtige Rolle.

Alternativbewegung (f)

D

Die Alternativbewegung ist eine weitgehend unorganisierte, nicht institutionalisierte Bewegung. Das Spektrum der Alternativbewegung reicht von Hausbesetzern über Anhänger der Friedens- und Ökologiebewegung bis hin zu Atomkraftgegnern. Die Anhänger der Alternativbewegung lassen sich weder einer politischen Partei, noch einer einheitlichen Altersgruppe zuordnen. Überrepräsentiert sind jedoch Wähler der Partei „Die Grünen" und Jugendliche/junge Erwachsene bis ca. 30 Jahre. Obwohl ein Teil der Alternativbewegung mit einer apathisch-provokanten „No-future-Attitüde" auftritt, ist sie mehrheitlich einem konstruktiven zukunftsorientierten Anspruch verpflichtet. Ausdruck findet dies in der Entwicklung und Praktizierung alternativer Wert- und Symbolsysteme (z.B. → *Jugendreligionen*), die im Widerspruch zu den Werten der industriell-kapitalistischen Gesellschaft stehen und in der Gegenüberstellung ihre politische Dimension entfalten.

Im Zusammenhang mit der wachsenden (Jugend-)Arbeitslosigkeit und finanziellen Kürzungen im sozialen Bereich ist es in den letzten Jahren zu verstärkten Gründungen von Selbsthilfeprojekten/Alternativprojekten mit Modellcharakter gekommen. Diese werden zum Teil durch öffentliche Mittel gefördert, zum Teil aber auch mit erheblichem finanziellen Risiko von den Beteiligten selbst getragen (z.B. Tee-, Ökoladen, Fahrradwerkstatt, Jugend-, Frauencafé, Freizeit-Bildungsheime).

VK

Im VK gibt es ähnliche Erscheinungen.

Aufsichtspflicht (f)

D

Die Aufsichtspflicht ist die Verpflichtung von Personen, denen Minderjährige oder Behinderte anvertraut sind, darüber zu wachen, daß der betreute Personenkreis keinen Schaden nimmt oder andere Personen zu Schaden kommen.

Die Aufsichtspflicht ergibt sich aus dem Gesetz oder sonstigen rechtlichen oder vertraglichen Bestimmungen. Sie gilt für Eltern, Lehrer, Jugendarbeiter, etc. Welche Vorsichtsmaßnahmen zu erfüllen sind, um bei einem Unfall dem Vorwurf der Fahrlässigkeit (zivil- und strafrechtliche Konsequenzen) zu entgehen, hängt von den Umständen des Einzelfalles ab. Bei der Beurteilung ei-

Alternative Movement

G

The alternative movement generally lacks a firm organisational or institutional structure. Its wide spectrum comprises squatters, followers of the peace movement and ecologists as well as those who campaign against atomic energy. The followers of the alternative movement may belong neither to a given political party nor a homogeneous group. The majority are those who vote for the ecology party, "The Greens", and are mainly young people/young adults up to 30 years of age. Even though some of them profess an apathetic or provocative "no-future attitude", most of the alternatives have a constructive concept orientated towards the future. The aim to develop and practise alternative values and symbols (see e.g. → *Jugendreligionen*), which are inconsistent with the values embraced by the industrial-capitalist society. Their political dimension develops by contrasting these conflicting values.

Because of growing youth unemployment and financial cut-backs in the social field, an increasing number of self-help/alternative pilot projects have been founded in recent years. Some of these are grant-aided from public funds, others are self-supporting and involve a considerable element of financial risk (examples: tea or organic food shops, bicycle workshops, youth cafés, womens' cafés, homes providing educational leisure time activities).

UK

The situation is reflected in the UK.

Supervisory Responsibilities

G

Adults supervising minors or the handicapped are obliged to make sure that the group entrusted to their care will come to no harm nor cause damage to others.

Supervisory responsibilities are laid down by law or other legal or contractual provision. Parents, teachers, youth workers etc. are obliged to fulfill their supervisory responsibilities. The particular circumstances determine the precautions needed to be taken in order to avoid responsibility for negligence in the case of an accident consequent under civil and penal law. On the hearing of a case the educational function i.e. the aim of teaching those being supervised to

nes Falles wird die pädagogische Aufgabe berücksichtigt, die darin besteht, die Betreuten zu selbständigem Handeln zu erziehen. Der Betreuer muß aber auch das Alter der Betreuten, die Gruppensituation und örtliche und räumliche Gegebenheiten in Betracht ziehen. Wichtig ist außerdem, daß auf gefährliche Situationen vorbereitet wird (Warnungen, Übungen, bei Kindern und Jugendlichen auch Unterrichtung der Eltern über mögliche Gefahren).

Die Aufsichtspflicht bedeutet nicht unbedingt Anwesenheitspflicht. Es wird aber verlangt, daß der Aufsichtspflichtige den Überblick über das Geschehen behält, um gegebenenfalls schnell eingreifen zu können. Er muß auf einen Unfall vorbereitet sein und die gesetzlichen Schutzbestimmungen beachten.

VK

Im Vereinigten Königreich gibt es keine gesonderten Bestimmungen über die Beaufsichtigung von Kindern. Nach der Rechtsprechung *(case law)* sind jedoch Personen, denen Kinder anvertraut sind, verpflichtet, für das Wohl der Beaufsichtigten angemessen Sorge zu tragen. Sie können für Fahrlässigkeit zur Verantwortung gezogen werden, wenn sie die Aufsichtspflicht nicht erfüllen. Was im Einzelfall als angemessene Sorge anzusehen ist, hängt von den gegebenen Umständen ab (z.B. Alter und Zahl der Kinder, Art der Aktivität, usw.).

Die Eltern können Personen, die ihre Kinder in Obhut nehmen, das Recht übertragen, Einfluß auf deren Verhalten zu nehmen und angemessene disziplinarische Maßnahmen zu ergreifen.

Ausbildungsförderung (f)

D

In der Bundesrepublik Deutschland besteht ein umfassendes System der finanziellen Förderung zur Sicherung der Existenz von Jugendlichen und Erwachsenen für die Dauer ihrer Aus- und Weiterbildung. Da der Besuch von öffentlichen Schulen und Hochschulen in der Regel kostenlos ist, soll die Ausbildungsförderung vorrangig den Lebensunterhalt sowie Sachkosten abdekken. Die schulische Ausbildung wird nach dem Bundesausbildungsförderungsgesetz (BAFÖG, letzte Änderung 1990), die berufliche und betriebliche nach dem Arbeitsförderungsgesetz (AFG) geregelt. Neben diesen Bundesgesetzen gibt es zusätzliche Unterstützungsmöglichkeiten auf Länderebene.

Die Förderung nach BAFÖG setzt voraus, daß die Auszubildenden oder ihre Unterhaltsverpflichteten nicht über die erforderlichen Eigenmittel verfügen. Schüler haben Anspruch auf einen (nicht zurückzahlbaren) Zuschuß, wenn sie Ausbildungsstätten des zweiten Bildungsweges oder Fach- und Berufsfachschulklassen, die zu einem berufsqualifizierenden Abschluß führen, besuchen oder die Schule der gymnasialen Oberstufe in unzumutbarer Entfernung vom Wohnsitz der Eltern liegt. Studenten erhalten Ausbildungsförderung je zur Hälfte als Zuschuß bzw. als zinsloses Darlehen, das fünf Jahre nach

use their own initiative is a prime consideration. The supervisor, however, must always take into account the age of his charges, the group situation as well as the actual place and environmental factors. It is equally important to give thorough briefing to those under supervision to cope with potentially dangerous situations and to similarly brief the parents.

Supervisors are required to be constantly aware of the situation and prepared for immediate intervention if necessary, but their physical presence at all times ist not essential. They must take measures to prevent accidents and always observe legal provision of health and safety acts.

UK
There ist no separate set of rules in the United Kingdom concerning the supervision of children, but according to case law persons in charge of children are under a duty to take proper care of them and may be liable for negligence if they fail to do so. What constitutes proper care must depend upon the circumstances of the case (e.g. age and number of children, nature of the activity being undertaken, etc.).

Parents may delegate to persons taking charge of their children the right to control their conduct and to exercise reasonable discipline.

Education Grants

G
In the Federal Republic of Germany there is a comprehensive system of financial assistance designed to safeguard the livelihood of young people and adult persons while attending courses of vocational training or further education. As attendance at state schools and universities is normally free of charge, education grants are given to cover the cost of living as well as study materials. Regulations concerning school education are embodied in the Federal Educational Grants Act ("BAFÖG", as amended in 1990). Vocational training under the dual system (→ Berufsbildung) is regulated by the Promotion of Employment Act. In addition to these Federal laws there are other schemes providing education grants at *Land* level.

BAFÖG education grants are only available on condition that the student or those responsible for his maintenance do not have the necessary means. School pupils are entitled to an outright grant when attending training establishments for mature students, courses provided by technical schools or full-time vocational schools leading to a vocational qualification. Education grants are equally available to those attending the upper stage of a grammar school which is at a distance from their parents' home where ist would be unreasona-

Ende der Förderungshöchstdauer in Monatsraten von mindestens DM 200,– zurückgezahlt werden muß. Hochschulabsolventen mit besonders guten Leistungen wird ein Schuldenerlaß eingeräumt.

Für die betriebliche und überbetriebliche Ausbildung in anerkannten Ausbildungsberufen oder die Teilnahme an berufsvorbereitenden Maßnahmen kann die Bundesanstalt für Arbeit auf Antrag Berufsausbildungsbeihilfe nach dem AFG gewähren. Bei der Festsetzung der Beihilfe werden in der Regel Eigenmittel ebenfalls angerechnet. Behinderte haben Anspruch auf zusätzliche Leistungen aufgrund von Sonderregelungen. Auch die berufliche Fortbildung und Umschulung wird nach AFG gefördert. Darüber hinaus können nach dem AFG ausländische Auszubildende und Lernbeeinträchtigte oder sozial benachteiligte deutsche Auszubildende Zuschüsse zur Berufsausbildung erhalten. Bestimmte Personengruppen können auch finanzielle Hilfen aufgrund anderer Gesetze wie das Bundessozialhilfegesetz, das Häftlingshilfegesetz, das Soldatenversorgungsgesetz u.a. erhalten.

VK

Im Vereinigten Königreich sind die kommunalen Erziehungsbehörden nach den *Education (Mandatory Awards) Regulations* gesetzlich verpflichtet, Ausbildungsförderung zu gewähren. Dabei werden die Begriffe *grant* und *award* oft austauschbar verwandt. Die Förderungsbestimmungen unterscheiden jedoch zwischen *award,* wobei sowohl die Ausbildungsgebühren als auch der Lebensunterhalt berücksichtigt werden, und *grant,* wodurch nur Mittel zur Deckung des Lebensunterhaltes bereitgestellt werden.

Alle Studenten, die vornehmlich mit dem Ziel, den ersten akademischen Grad zu erwerben, entsprechende Einrichtungen besuchen und die Förderungsvoraussetzungen erfüllen, erhalten die gesetzliche Ausbildungsförderung.

Der Anspruch auf Ausbildungsförderung setzt voraus, daß der Antragsteller seinen Wohnsitz im Vereinigten Königreich hat und den Nachweis erbringt, daß er nicht über ausreichende Eigenmittel verfügt. Gegegebenenfalls haben der/die Studierende und seine/ihre Eltern einen Teil der Kosten zu übernehmen. Die gesetzliche Ausbildungsförderung wird für einen ganzen Ausbildungsgang ungeachtet seiner Dauer und nicht für eine bestimmte Anzahl von Jahren gewährt.

Die Kommunalverwaltungen stellen auch nach eigenem Ermessen Förderungsmittel zur Verfügung, die gegebenenfalls nach einem Ausleseverfahren und auf der Grundlage eigener Richtlinien vergeben werden.

Zahlreiche gewerbliche Organisationen sowie einige Ministerien haben Ausbildungsförderungsprogramme für Studenten, die in der Regel die Teilnahme

ble for them to be required to commute. Students in higher education receive a grant, 50% of which is given as an interest-free loan. This has to be paid back in monthly instalments (of at least 200,– DM) starting five years after completion of the maximum applicable period for a particular education grant. University graduates who do exceptionally well in their final exams are allowed a remission of part of their debt.

Persons in in-firm vocational training for recognised training trades, attending an inter-firm vocational training establishment, or taking part in vocational training preparatory schemes may apply to the Federal Institute of Labour for a vocational training grant under the Promotion of Employment Act. The amount of the grant is determined after a means test. Additional benefits are available to the handicapped on the basis of special regulations. The Promotion of Employment Act also provides for grant-aid to those following programmes of further education and retraining. Equally, under this Act, foreign trainees and slow learners or socially disadvantaged German apprentices may be granted a subsidy for vocational training. Certain groups of persons can also obtain financial aid under other laws, such as the Social Services Act, the Detained Persons Assistance Act, and the Care of Soldiers Act.

UK

In the UK, the local education authorities (LEAs) are required by law to pay grants under the Education (Mandatory Awards) Regulations. The words "grant" and "award" are often used interchangeably, but the regulations make a distinction between the award, which comprises both a fee and a maintenance element, and the grant, which represents only the maintenance element.

All students who are attending advanced, i.e. primarily first-degree courses, and who satisfy the qualifying conditions receive a mandatory grant.

Eligibility depends on residence in the UK and a means test. Depending on the respective financial situation, the student or his/her parents may have to contribute. A mandatory grant is given for a course, of any length, not for a particular number of years.

Discretionary grants which are sometimes competitive are also available, but each local authority decides its own policy on these.

Many industrial organisations, and some government departments, have schemes, which are usually competitive, for assisting students. There are also educational trust funds and charities which give grants for specific purposes.

Postgraduate studies, non-degree courses, courses of adult education and non-advanced further education do not qualify under the above regulations. There is no general statutory grant entitlement for non-advanced vocational training as in the FRG.

an einem Ausleseverfahren erfordern. Außerdem bestehen Studienstiftungen und gemeinnützige Einrichtungen, die Förderungsmittel für bestimmte Zwecke vergeben.

Für die Fortsetzung des Studiums nach Erwerb des ersten akademischen Grades sowie die Teilnahme an nicht-akademischen Ausbildungsprogrammen, an Kursen der Erwachsenenbildung und nicht-akademischen Fortbildungsmaßnahmen können nach den oben genannten Förderungsbestimmungen keine finanziellen Hilfen bereitgestellt werden. Es besteht kein allgemeiner gesetzlicher Anspruch auf Ausbildungsförderung für die berufliche Bildung wie in der Bundesrepublik Deutschland.

Ausschuß (m) für Frauen (f/pl) und Jugend (f) des Deutschen Bundestages (m)

D

Der Deutsche Bundestag hat einen ständigen Ausschuß für Frauen und Jugend eingesetzt. Dieser Ausschuß berät — federführend oder mitberatend — alle Vorlagen und Gesetzentwürfe, die sich auf Frauen- und Jugendfragen beziehen. Seine Entscheidungen legt der Ausschuß in Form von Beschlußempfehlungen und Berichten dem Plenum des Deutschen Bundestages vor. Der Ausschuß für Frauen und Jugend entspricht als Fachausschuß des Deutschen Bundestages der Aufgabenstellung des → *Bundesministeriums für Frauen und Jugend.*

VK

Es gibt keine Entsprechung im VK.

Bedienstete (m/f/pl) des öffentlichen Dienstes (m)

D

Als öffentliche Bedienstete gelten die in einem besonderen Dienst- und Treueverhältnis stehenden Beschäftigten bei Bund, Ländern, Gemeinden sowie öffentlich-rechtlichen Körperschaften, Anstalten und Stiftungen. Unterschieden wird zwischen Beamten, Angestellten des öffentlichen Dienstes und Arbeitern (Lohnempfängern). Beamte werden berufen für hoheitliche Aufgaben zur Sicherung des Staates und des öffentlichen Lebens; sie sind nicht Arbeitnehmer, sondern Funktionsträger ohne Streikrecht, und beziehen dafür eine monatliche Besoldung. Dem steht eine Fürsorgepflicht des Dienstherrn gegenüber.

Angestellte nehmen aufgrund eines Dienstvertrages öffentlich-rechtliche Aufgaben wahr, soweit diese nicht nach den genanten Grundsätzen Beamten übertragen werden müssen; sie erhalten für diese Dienstleistung eine monatliche Vergütung nach dem Bundesangestelltentarif BAT (zeitlich befristetes

Committee for Women and Youth of the *German Bundestag*

G

The *German Bundestag* (the elected parliamentary respresentation of the Federal Republic of Germany) has set up a standing Committee for Women and Youth. This committee acts in an advisory or executive capacity in all matters dealing with motions and bills relating to women's and youth issues, and submits its recommendations and reports to the Full Assembly of the *Bundestag*. As a specialist body the Committee for Women and Youth is the parliamentary counterpart to the Federal Ministry for Women and Youth *(→ Bundesministerium für Frauen und Jugend)*.

UK

There is no UK equivalent.

Civil Service Employees

G

Those working in the Civil Service for statutory bodies under public law at Federal, *Land* and local authority level, institutions and foundations are bound by a particular relationship of service and loyalty. A distinction is made between civil servants, Civil Service salaried employees and workers (wage earners). Civil servants are appointed to carry out specific governmental tasks designated to ensure the proper functioning of the State and society for which they are remunerated on a monthly basis. They are not considered as employees but as office holders, and are debarred from the right to strike. The employer, for his part, has certain legal responsibilities to provide for the welfare of his staff and to set up personnel schemes.

Civil Service salaried employees work on the basis of a contract of employment. They fulfil public responsibilities in as much as these do not devolve on the civil servants. Under the Federal Employees Salary Scales *(Bundes-*

Abkommen über Vergütungsgruppen, Arbeitszeit, Urlaub etc. zwischen Bund und den Tarifpartnern des öffentlichen Dienstes). Lohnempfänger werden aufgrund eines Arbeitsvertrages für manuelle Dienstleistungen beschäftigt; sie erhalten einen nach Arbeitsstunden berechneten Lohn.

Die Mitarbeiter der Jugendhilfe sind entweder Bedienstete von Kommunalbehörden oder Angestellte bei freien Trägern.

VK

Civil servants sind Diener der Krone. Von ihnen wird ein besonderes Dienst- und Treueverhältnis zur jeweiligen Regierung erwartet, ungeachtet deren politischer Zusammensetzung.

Auf der obersten Ebene des Staatsdienstes in Großbritannien besteht eine offene und vereinheitlichte Struktur, die die überwiegende Mehrzahl der Stellen umfaßt und alle Aufgabengebiete einbezieht.

Auf den anderen Ebenen sind die nicht manuell tätigen Bediensteten (Arbeiter werden meist in den Dienstleistungsbetrieben der Regierung beschäftigt) in 12 Kategorien und nach Beschäftigungsgruppen unterteilt, die maßgeblich sind für Einstellungsbedingungen, Gehaltseinstufung usw.

Den Staatsbediensteten wird nahegelegt, der Gewerkschaft der Gruppe beizutreten, der sie angehören. Die Bedingungen des Dienstverhältnisses und der Bezahlung werden zwischen leitenden Beamten und Vertretern der Gewerkschaften ausgehandelt (→ *Betriebsrat,* VK).

Civil servants genießen nicht die besonderen Rechte und den Status des Beamten in der Bundesrepublik Deutschland. Ihr Recht zu streiken ist nicht generell eingeschränkt (obwohl Streiks im öffentlichen Dienst selten sind); auch haben sie keinen besonderen gesetzlichen Kündigungsschutz, der über die Bestimmungen hinausgeht, die allgemein für Arbeitnehmer gelten.

In Großbritannien sind *civil servants* nur die Bediensteten der Zentralregierung. Die Beschäftigten *(employees)*[1] der Kommunalbehörden (*counties, cities, districts,* → *Kommunale Selbstverwaltung,* VK) werden nicht als *civil servants,* sondern als *local government officers* bezeichnet. Die Mehrzahl der hauptamtlichen Mitarbeiter des *youth service* der Kommunalbehörden haben diesen Status.

---

1) Der Begriff des *employee* geht weiter als der deutsche Begriff des Angestellten. Er umfaßt auch Arbeiter eines Betriebes.

angestelltentarif — BAT) Agreement (concluded for limited periods on salary scales, working hours, holiday entitlement, etc., between the Federation and the negotiating parties on the employees' side) they draw a monthly salary. Wage earners are employed for manual services under a contract of work. They receive wages which are calculated on the basis of the number of hours worked.

Youth workers are either local authority employees or employees of a voluntary organisation.

UK

Civil servants are servants of the Crown. They are expected to serve the Government of the day, regardless of its political composition.

At the top of the Home Civil Service there is an open and unified structure which, with very few exceptions, covers all posts whatever the nature of their duties.

At other levels the structure of the non-industrial Civil Service (manual workers are mainly employed in government industrial establishments) is based on a system of 12 categories and occupational groups which are the basic groupings of staff for the purposes of recruitment, pay, etc.

Civil servants are encouraged to join the trade union which represents the grade to which they belong. Conditions of service of staff and pay are discussed between senior officials and representatives of the unions (→ *Betriebsrat,* UK).

Civil servants in Britain do not have the special rights and status accorded to *Beamte* in the Federal Republic of Germany. There is no general restriction on their right to strike (although strikes in the Civil Service are rare); and they have no special legal protection against dismissal beyond that in force for employees in general.

In Britain the term "civil servant" applies only to employees of central government. Employees of local authorities (counties, cities, districts etc., → *Kommunale Selbstverwaltung,* UK) are recruited directly by the individual local authorities and are called local government officers rather than civil servants. Most full-time employees of the youth service are local government officers.

Behindertenhilfe (f)

D

Der Begriff der Behinderung umfaßt Körper- und Sinnesschäden sowie geistige und seelische Beeinträchtigungen. Hilfen für Behinderte sind in einer Vielzahl von Gesetzen normiert. Sie umfassen neben Maßnahmen der Früherkennung, Frühförderung und Frühbehandlung für Säuglinge und Kleinkinder die medizinische Rehabilitation von Kindern, Jugendlichen und Erwachsenen, Bildungsmaßnahmen, berufliche Rehabilitation, besondere Beschäftigungsmöglichkeiten für behinderte Menschen und Maßnahmen zur Eingliederung Behinderter in die Gesellschaft.

Behinderte Kinder werden überwiegend in Sonderkindergärten und -schulen unterrichtet. Darüber hinaus gibt es Bestrebungen und Modelle, behinderte Kinder, vor allem in der Vorschulerziehung, in Regeleinrichtungen des → *Bildungswesens* zu integrieren.

Jugendliche erhalten eine ihrer Behinderung angemessene Berufsberatung und Berufsausbildung. Für Personen mit einer im Erwachsenenalter erworbenen Behinderung gibt es Maßnahmen der Umschulung und → *Rehabilitation.* Verantwortlich für diese Maßnahmen und Leistungen sind je nach Zuständigkeit die Krankenversicherung, die Rentenversicherung, die Unfallversicherung, die Versorgungsämter und Fürsorgestellen, die → *Bundesanstalt für Arbeit,* die → *Sozialhilfe* und die → *Jugendhilfe.*

Vorrangig sind die Bemühungen darauf gerichtet, behinderten Menschen den Zugang zum allgemeinen Arbeitsmarkt zu öffnen. Wo dies nicht möglich ist, steht die Eingliederung in Werkstätten für Behinderte offen. Dennoch sind behinderte Menschen wesentlich mehr als andere von Arbeitslosigkeit betroffen.

Um soziale Kontakte zu erhalten und zu erweitern, haben Freizeit und Urlaub für behinderte Mitbürger ein besonderes Gewicht. Auf kommunaler Ebene bestehen Selbsthilfeeinrichtungen für Behinderte und Nichtbehinderte (Teestuben, Freundschaftskreise der Behinderten und Nichtbehinderten etc.).

Durch den Bau von behindertengerechten Einrichtungen wie Familienferienstätten, Jugendherbergen etc. und das Angebot vom Bundesministerium für Frauen und Jugend geförderter Broschüren („Familienferien", „Ferienführer") wird behinderten Menschen das Reisen erleichtert. Die Behindertenverbände bieten individuelle Urlaubsberatung an. Die Bestrebungen gehen heute dahin, Behinderten die Teilnahme an Ferienangeboten für alle zu ermöglichen.

Nationale und internationale Behindertenorganisationen (z.B. *Mobility International)* sowie die Jugendverbände fördern Gruppen- und Begegnungsreisen von Behinderten mit Hilfe von öffentlichen Mitteln. Dem ebenfalls staatlich geförderten Behindertensport als wirkungsvolle Lebenshilfe kommt eine besondere Bedeutung zu.

Services for the Handicapped
G

The term disablement covers the permanent impairment of physical, sensory (irreversible hearing, visual and speech problems) or mental retardation as well as emotional disturbances. Services for and assistance to the handicapped are embodied in numerous legal instruments. In addition to measures aiming at the early detection, prevention and treatment of a disablement with infants and small children, such legal provision comprises the medical rehabilitation of children, young people and adults, educational programmes, vocational rehabilitation, special employment for disabled men and women, and their social integration.

Handicapped children are mainly taught in special kindergartens and special schools. Attempts are being made and pilot projects set up aiming to integrate disabled children into the regular education system, especially in the field of pre-school education *(→ Bildungswesen).*

Young people receive vocational guidance and training suited to their handicap. Persons disabled as adults may take part in retraining and rehabilitation programmes *(→ Rehabilitation).* Depending on the respective competence, such programmes and benefits are provided by health insurance funds, retirement pension schemes, accident insurance schemes, war victims' pensions authorities, social welfare offices, the Federal Institute of Labour *(→ Bundesanstalt für Arbeit),* and social assistance *(→ Sozialhilfe).*

Particular efforts are made to open the general labour market to disabled men and women. Where this is impossible, the alternative is sheltered employment. However, disabled persons are more frequently affected by unemployment than others.

In order to maintain and increase social contact, leisure time and holidays have a special importance for handicapped men and women. At local level there are self-help establishments for the disabled (tea rooms, friendship circles for the disabled and the able-bodied, etc.).

Mobility is made easier for the handicapped by the provision of establishments adapted to their needs such as family holiday centres, youth hostels and the like, and the publication of brochures ("Family Holidays", "Holiday Guide") grant-aided by the Federal Ministry for Women and Youth. Organisations for the disabled provide individual counselling on suitable holidays. Every effort is now being made so that disabled persons may take ordinary holidays.

National and international organisations for the handicapped (e.g. Mobility International) and youth organisations promote group travel and inter-group contacts for the disabled with the help of public funds. The significance of participation in sport by the handicapped is widely recognized and receives support from public funds.

Ziel aller Maßnahmen muß die berufliche und soziale Integration der behinderten Mitbürger sein. Trotz aller Bemühungen – auch von Seiten der Bundesregierung – ist die allgemeine gesellschaftliche Eingliederung durch Sozialleistungen allein nicht zu erreichen. Vielmehr muß jeder einzelne dazu beitragen, die Gemeinsamkeit von behinderten und nichtbehinderten Menschen zu verwirklichen.

VK

Im Vereinigten Königreich umfaßt der Begriff der Behinderung dieselben Beeinträchtigungen oder Mehrfachbehinderungen wie in der Bundesrepublik Deutschland. Die Hilfen für Behinderte und die Ziele der → *Rehabilitation* sind fast identisch.

Behinderte werden entweder in Sonderschulen oder in Sonderschulzentren unterrichtet. In jüngster Zeit gehen jedoch die politischen Bestrebungen dahin, Einheiten oder Klassen für Behinderte in den Regelschulen zu schaffen. Das Vereinigte Königreich befindet sich in einer Phase der Neuorientierung vom Sonderschulunterricht zum integrierten Unterricht. Vorerst bleiben die Sonderschulen jedoch weiter bestehen.

Junge Behinderte erhalten eine Berufsberatung und eine Ausbildung, die auf die jeweilige Behinderung abgestimmt ist. Für Personen mit einer im Erwachsenenalter erworbenen Behinderung gibt es Maßnahmen der Umschulung und Rehabilitation.

Je nach Zuständigkeit werden solche Programme angeboten und finanziert von der *Training Agency,* den regionalen Gesundheitsbehörden oder den kommunalen Sozialämtern.

Finanzielle Unterstützung bietet das System der sozialen Sicherung, z.B. das staatliche Altersruhegeld, die Hilfen für Behinderte, die Mobilitätshilfen, usw. Die kommunalen Erziehungsbehörden führen im Rahmen des Bildungswesens allgemeinbildende und berufsbildende Maßnahmen durch. Im Einzelfall bestehen auch Ansprüche aus einer privaten Rentenversicherung, Unfallversicherung oder der Kriegsopferversorgung.

Behinderte finden Arbeitsplätze auf dem allgemeinen Arbeitsmarkt oder in beschützenden Werkstätten (Programme auf nationaler und örtlicher Ebene). Weitere Maßnahmen sind die Schaffung von Kooperativen sowie der Einsatz von *disablement resettlement officers,* die versuchen, die Arbeitgeber zur Einstellung von Behinderten zu veranlassen, indem sie ihnen besondere Zuschüsse für die bauliche Anpassung sowie für technische Hilfsmittel anbieten, die Behinderten die Aufnahme einer Erwerbstätigkeit ermöglichen.

Zur Förderung von Sozialkontakten stellen die Kommunalbehörden Einrichtungen für die Tagesbetreuung, Förderungsmittel für die Teilnahme an Urlaubsangeboten, Unterstützung für die behindertengerechte Ausstattung von Wohnungen sowie Informationsdienste bereit. Die freien Träger sind eine wichtige Säule der Behindertenhilfe. Sie unterhalten Schulen und Heime,

All endeavours undertaken must aim at the vocational and social integration of disabled fellow citizens. In spite of all efforts made also by the Federal Government — general social integration cannot be achieved by social benefits alone. Society as a whole needs to recognise the necessity for integration of the disabled into its midst.

UK

In the United Kingdom, the term disablement covers the same handicaps or combination of impairments (multiple handicap) as in the Federal Republic of Germany. Services for the disabled and aims of → *Rehabilitation* are almost identical.

Handicapped children are taught either in special schools or centres but current policy aims to provide an integrated education through the provision of special units or classes in ordinary schools. The United Kingdom is passing through a period of change from special schooling to integrated schooling. However, special schools will continue to exist in the immediate future.

Young people are given vocational guidance and training suited to their handicap. Persons who become disabled as adults may take part in retraining and rehabilitation programmes.

Depending on the respective competence, such programmes may be offered and financed by the Training Agency, the regional health authorities or social services departments of local authorities.

Benefits are paid through the Social Security System including State retirement pensions, disability allowances, mobility allowances, etc. Local education authorities may offer courses for training and education through the education system. Some people may also receive pensions or benefits through private retirement pensions, accident insurance or war pensions.

Employment opportunities include those available through the open labour market or sheltered workshops (national and local schemes). Other possibilities include the establishment of co-operative schemes and official support is given by the disablement resettlement officers who try to encourage employers to accept disabled persons by offering grants for the adaptation of premises and any special equipment which may help a person to work.

In order to encourage social contact local authorities provide day care, grants for holidays, assistance with home adaptions and general information services. The voluntary organisations form an important source of help and may provide schools, homes, holidays, car purchase schemes plus a wide range of general and specific services. To encourage integration in leisure activities youth clubs exist in many areas such as PHAB, Gateway Clubs and Breakthrough for the Deaf. Such organisations as the Holiday Care Centre, Mobility International, Day Care Centres provide opportunities for travel, exchange and holidays. The general trend is to persuade holiday companies to accept disabled people

schaffen Ferienprogramme und geben Hilfestellung für den Kauf eines Autos. Die unterschiedlichsten allgemeinen und spezifischen Dienste werden von den freien Trägern erbracht. Zur Förderung der Integration im Freizeitbereich bestehen vielerorts Jugendclubs wie PHAB *(Physically Handicapped and Able-Bodied), Gateway Clubs* and *Breakthrough for the Deaf.* Organisationen wie das *Holiday Care Centre, Mobility International, Day Care Centres* verfügen über Reise-, Austausch- und Ferienangebote. Die Bestrebungen gehen heute dahin, kommerzielle Reiseveranstalter zu veranlassen, Behinderte in ihr Urlaubsangebot einzubeziehen. In ähnlicher Weise sind Fluggesellschaften, Hotels und sonstige kommerzielle Träger im Tourismussektor dabei, ihre Dienstleistungen für behinderte Kunden zu erweitern.

Im Vereinigten Königreich sind hinsichtlich der Integration der Behinderten bereits beträchtliche Erfolge erzielt worden. Dennoch bleibt viel zu tun, bis behinderte Menschen ein erfülltes Leben in der Gemeinschaft führen können.

Beratungsdienste (m/pl)

D

Das Gesamtfeld der Beratung läßt sich in folgende Teilbereiche aufteilen: Erziehungsberatung, Berufsberatung, Bildungsberatung und Freizeitberatung. Innerhalb der einzelnen Teilbereiche sind verschiedene Stufen der Beratung festzustellen: Ressourcenberatung, Lebensstilberatung, therapeutische Beratung. Diese Aufzählung zeigt, daß die therapeutische Beratung nur einen Sonderfall im Gesamtbereich darstellt. Die Ausbreitung des Beratungswesens in vielen Lebensbereichen ist nicht zufällig. Sie ist eine Antwort auf gesellschaftliche Wandlungsprozesse.

Beratung wird in der Bundesrepublik im wesentlichen von freien Trägern (→ *Wohlfahrtsverbände)* sowie von Kreisen und Gemeinden (→ *Kommunale Selbstverwaltung)* angeboten. → *Sozialarbeiter/-pädagogen,* Psychologen, Ärzte und Geistliche haben sich in den Beratungsstellen die Aufgabe gestellt, in allgemeinen Lebensfragen und in besonderen Lebenssituationen Gespräch und Hilfe anzubieten. Beratungsdienste umfassen z.B. die psycho-soziale Beratung, Partnerschafts-, Ehe-, Familien- und Lebensberatung, Familienplanungsberatung, Schwangerschafts- und Konfliktberatung, Sexualberatung, Freizeitberatung (→ *Freizeitpädagogik)* sowie die Beratung in Trennungs- und Scheidungssituationen.

Im Bereich der Jugendberatung ist zuerst auf die in einigen deutschen Städten bestehenden Jugendinformationszentren zu verweisen. Sie dienen generell als Anlaufstelle für Ratsuchende. In vielen Fällen können die Mitarbeiter dieser Zentren selbst die gewünschte Auskunft geben. Andernfalls vermitteln sie an geeignete Fachstellen.

Wichtig für junge Menschen ist die Schullaufbahn- und Berufsberatung, die sie normalerweise beim Schulpsychologischen Dienst oder bei den Arbeits-

on their regular holidays. Likewise airlines, hotels and others involved in the tourist industry are developing their services for disabled clients.

In the United Kingdom great strides have been made for the integration of disabled persons. However, much still needs to be done to provide a full and integrated life to disabled persons.

Counselling Services

G

The field of counselling may be subdivided into the following areas: child guidance, careers advice, educational counselling and recreational counselling. Within these areas different levels of counselling may be distinguished: resource counselling, lifestyle advice and therapeutic counselling. Thus it can be seen that therapeutic counselling is only one aspect of the overall field. The increase of counselling services is not accidental. It is a response to processes of social change.

In the Federal Republic, counselling is mainly provided by voluntary bodies (→ *Wohlfahrtsverbände*), by the *Kreise* and by local authorities (→ *Kommunale Selbstverwaltung*). Professional youth and social workers, child care officers (→ *Sozialarbeiter/Sozialpädagoge*), psychologists, and clergymen working in advice centres offer verbal counselling and assistance in general problems and in specific situations. Counselling services comprise, among others, psycho-social advice, marriage guidance, relationship, family and personal counselling, family planning advice, pregnancy, sexual and recreational counselling (→ *Freizeitpädagogik*) as well as advice in cases of separation and divorce.

Counselling services for young people may take the form of youth information centres which are to be found in some German towns. They generally provide a first contact for those seeking advice. In many cases, the staff of the centres can provide the information required. When this is not the case, they must refer their clients to the appropriate specialist agencies.

Advice on schooling and careers guidance which young people usually obtain from the school psychologists or the jobcentres are of particular importance. There is an increasing demand for the services provided by voluntary bodies

ämtern erhalten. Zunehmend gefragt sind hier die Angebote der freien Träger oder Selbsthilfe-Einrichtungen für jene Gruppen, die den Gang zu „Ämtern" scheuen. Außerdem bestehen Einrichtungen der Drogenberatung und der Beratung bei → *Alkoholmißbrauch*. Eltern, die in der Familie mit Erziehungsproblemen zu kämpfen haben, können sich an Erziehungsberatungsstellen wenden, die in den Verantwortungsbereich der → *Jugendämter* fallen.

VK

Seit mehr als zwanzig Jahren gehören Informations- und Beratungsdienste für Jugendliche zu den wichtigsten Angeboten des *youth service* in Großbritannien. Von den Fachkräften der Jugendarbeit wird erwartet, daß sie im Rahmen ihrer Tätigkeit in Clubs und Jugendzentren über Fragen der Berufstätigkeit, des Familienlebens und der Sexualität informieren und beraten. In den letzten fünfzehn Jahren sind viele neue Zentren wie *Open-Door* und *Contact* entstanden, die im persönlichen Gespräch, über das Telefon oder durch Briefe ihre Hilfe anbieten. *Drop-in*-Beratungszentren richten sich besonders an arbeitslose Jugendliche. Die Berater aller dieser Zentren überweisen die Ratsuchenden erforderlichenfalls an Fachstellen wie Arbeitsämter, Berufsberatung, Schwangerschaftsberatung, Wohnungsvermittlungsbüros oder die Drogenberatung.

In Schottland, wo der Einstieg in die Jugendberatung viel später als in England erfolgte, entstand der *Youth Enquiry Service*. YES ist ein Netz der Jugendinformation, das als Beitrag zur persönlichen, sozialen und beruflichen Entwicklung junger Menschen die kostenlose Bereitstellung von Auskünften, Hilfen und Anregungen fördert. Auf der örtlichen Ebene wurden in ganz Schottland in zahlreichen Jugendclubs, Jugendcafés, Kirchen und Zentren der Gemeinwesenarbeit YES-Stellen eingerichtet.

Nordirland orientierte sich bei der Schaffung eines eigenen Förderungsprogramms für Jugendinformation unter der Bezeichnung YIPLINKS an den in Schottland und auf dem europäischen Kontinent gesammelten Erfahrungen. Gegenwärtig wird eine Datenbank errichtet. Ein EDV-System soll die Entwicklung eines flächendeckenden Netzes von Jugendinformationsstellen fördern.

Für die Gesamtheit der Maßnahmen zur Fortentwicklung der Jugendinformation und -beratung ist die *National Youth Agency (NYA)* verantwortlich. Zu ihren Aufgaben gehört auch die Durchführung eines Pilotprojektes mit der Intention, an gezielt ausgewählten Standorten sogenannte Informations-Shops von hoher fachlicher Leistungsfähigkeit einzurichten (→ *Überblick über den Youth Service im Vereinigten Königreich*).

and organisations from those groups afraid of contacting the authorities. In addition, there are establishments which give advice on drug problems (→ *Drogenmißbrauch*) and alcohol abuse (→ *Alkoholmißbrauch*). Parents experiencing difficulties with their children may consult the child guidance clinics, which come within the remit of the youth office (→ *Jugendamt*).

UK

For more than twenty years, the provision of information, advice and counselling services for young people has been one of the major offerings of the youth service in Britain. Professional youth workers find themselves called upon to provide information and advice on such matters as jobs, family life and sex as an integral part of their work in clubs and centres. Over the past fifteen years many new centres such as "Open Door" or "Contact" have come into existence to provide youth counselling on a personal basis or by phone or letter. "Drop-in" advice centres cater especially for the young unemployed. The advice given at all these centres may involve contacting such specialist centres as the jobcentre, careers advisory service, pregnancy advisory services, housing agencies or agencies concerned with drug misuse.

Scotland, which came much later than England to the youth counselling field, developed the *Youth Enquiry Service*. YES is a youth information network which promotes free information, support and ideas of young people as a contribution to their personal, social and vocational development. Local YES points were set up in a variety of youth clubs, cafés, church halls and community centres throughout Scotland.

Northern Ireland has drawn on the Scottish and other European experience to develop its own Youth Information Development Programme called YIPLINKS. A resource bank is being established and a computerised system will encourage the development of a network of youth information points throughout Northern Ireland.

The National Youth Agency (NYA) has overall responsibility for the development of information, advice and counselling services for young people, including a pilot project to establish high-quality information shops in selected areas (→ *Outline of the Youth Service in Britain*).

Berufsbildung (f)

D

Unter Berufsbildung versteht man die berufliche Ausbildung an Einrichtungen außerhalb der Hochschulen (→ *Bildungswesen*). Nach Erwerb des Abschlußzeugnisses in einer der Schulen der Sekundarstufe I/II kann der Jugendliche seine Berufsausbildung beginnen. Der Regelfall ist der Abschluß eines Ausbildungsvertrages (auch: Lehrvertrag) mit einem anerkannten Ausbildungsbetrieb. Im Rahmen der zwei bis dreieinhalb Jahre umfassenden praktischen Ausbildung am Arbeitsplatz wird der Auszubildende (früher: Lehrling) von seinem Ausbilder (früher: Lehrherr) bis zum Erreichen des festgelegten Ausbildungszieles geschult. Parallel zur praxisorientierten Ausbildung läuft die theoretische Unterweisung in der Berufsschule an einem oder zwei Tagen wöchentlich oder in zusammenhängenden Teilabschnitten (Blockunterricht). Eine Berufsausbildungspflicht besteht nicht; die Berufsschule ist jedoch auch von denen zu besuchen (meist bis zum 18. Lebensjahr), die in keinem Ausbildungsverhältnis stehen (Berufsschulpflicht). Diese Kombination von Theorie und Praxis nennt man das duale System.

Die Rechte und Pflichten der an der Ausbildung Beteiligten regelt das Berufsbildungsgesetz (letzte Fassung 23.12.1981). Es enthält Vorschriften über die Festlegung des Ausbildungsvertrages sowie über Maßnahmen der Fortbildung und Umschulung. In der Bundesrepublik gibt es etwa 380 anerkannte Ausbildungsberufe.

Verschiedene öffentliche und freie Träger bieten den Jugendlichen, die nach Beendigung der Schulpflicht keinen Ausbildungsplatz finden, berufsfördernde, -orientierende und -bildende Maßnahmen an, die ihnen den Einstieg in eine geeignete Berufsausbildung erleichtern sollen.

Die berufliche Ausbildung wird durch eine Abschlußprüfung beendet, die im Bereich des Handwerks vor der Handwerkskammer, der Industrie und des Handels vor der Industrie- und Handelskammer, im Bereich der Landwirtschaft, des öffentlichen Dienstes, der freien Berufe, der Hauswirtschaft und der Seeschiffahrt vor einem entsprechenden Gremium abgelegt wird. Die fachliche Qualifizierung geschieht durch den Erwerb des Gesellen-, Gehilfen- oder Facharbeiterbriefes, der die Voraussetzung für eine entsprechende tarifliche Bezahlung ist. Der Meistertitel (Industrie- oder Handwerksmeister) kann erst nach mehrjähriger beruflicher Praxis, dem Besuch der Meisterschule und dem Ablegen der Meisterprüfung vor der Handwerkskammer erworben werden.

Neben der Ausbildung im dualen System gibt es auch die Möglichkeit des Besuchs von Theorie und Praxis verbindenden Vollzeitschulen.

Das Berufsgrundbildungsjahr bietet eine allgemeine sowie fachtheoretische und -praktische Orientierung in einem bestimmten Berufsfeld und soll den Zugang zu mehreren Ausbildungsberufen eröffnen. Die ein bis drei Jahre umfassende Berufsfachschule führt zur Fachschulreife. Fachschulen vermitteln

Vocational Training

G

Vocational training is provided by educational establishments other than universities (→ *Bildungswesen*). After obtaining his/her leaving certificate of secondary education, level I/II, a young person may commence vocational training. As a rule, a contract of apprenticeship is entered into with a recognised training establishment. The training period may last from two to three and a half years. The apprentice is taught on the job by his instructor until he attains the appropriate trade qualification. Parallel to this practical work experience the apprentice attends day release classes once or twice a week for theoretical studies or sometimes for a longer spell (block release). Vocational training is not compulsory, but even those who do not have a contract of apprenticeship must attend the part-time vocational school (compulsory part-time vocational education mostly up to 18 years). This combination of theory and practice is called the "dual system".

The rights and obligations of those in vocational training are laid down in the Vocational Training Act (last amended 23 December 1981). It regulates contracts of apprenticeship and further education and retraining. In the Federal Republic there are about 380 recognised training trades.

Various statutory and voluntary bodies provide employment promotional, orientation and vocational training schemes for those young people unable to find a training vacancy after completion of compulsory education. These schemes help them to get started on a suitable career.

Vocational training ends with a final examination. This is taken before a board of representatives of the Chamber of Crafts, the Chamber of Industry and Commerce, or other boards of examiners for a given field such as Chamber of Agriculture, Civil Service, the liberal professions, domestic science, and ocean shipping. Proof of vocational qualification is shown by the tradesman's certificate, the proficiency certificate for the assistent worker or the skilled worker, on the basis of which the wage scales are established. The title of "master" (qualified instructor in industry or crafts) may only be awarded after several years' vocational experience, the attendance of the "master" school and the passing of the master's examination before the Chamber of Trade.

Besides training under the dual system there is the alternative of attending full-time schools combining theory and practice.

The Basic Vocational Training Year provides a general as well as job-specific theoretical and practical orientation in a given field. It is intended to provide access to several training trades. Successful completion of study at a full-time vocational school (1–3 years) gives access to the technical schools. The latter award the advanced qualifications of master and technician normally after three years of study.

Educational provision for mature students corresponding to that of the full-time vocational school is made by the vocational continuation school (→ *Bil-*

ihren Absolventen in der Regel nach zwei Jahren gehobene Berufsabschlüsse wie die des Meisters oder Technikers.

Die der Berufsfachschule entsprechende Einrichtung des Zweiten Bildungsweges (→ *Bildungswesen)* ist die Berufsaufbauschule, die ebenfalls die Fachschulreife verleiht.

Auszubildende im Besitz eines Realschulabschlusses oder der Fachschulreife können die Fachoberschule besuchen (auch das in einigen Ländern bestehende Fachgymnasium), um dort die Fachhochschulreife zu erwerben. Die Fachoberschule umfaßt zwei Jahre und ist auf die Anforderungen der Fachhochschule abgestimmt (Fachhochschulreife).

VK

Nach Erwerb des Bildungsabschlusses an einer allgemeinbildenden Schule können Jugendliche einen Ausbildungsvertrag (Lehrvertrag) mit einem geeigneten Betrieb abschließen. Der Auszubildende (Lehrling) erhält die Gewähr, in dem Betrieb über eine gewisse Zeit fachlich ausgebildet zu werden. Die Ausbildung (Lehre) führt zu einer allgemein anerkannten Qualifikation und in vielen Fällen schließlich zu einer Anstellung in dem betreffenden Betrieb.

Wie in Deutschland gibt es einen theoretischen Teil der Ausbildung, der an einer Fortbildungseinrichtung einmal wöchentlich oder im Blockunterricht von etwa sechs bis acht Wochen pro Jahr absolviert wird. Jugendliche mit einem im 18. Lebensjahr erworbenen höheren Bildungsabschluß (→ *Bildungswesen)* genießen in den Betrieben eine Ausbildung als *graduate apprentice.* Diese Auszubildenden verbringen das erste Ausbildungsjahr in ihrem Betrieb, um dort Erfahrungen zu sammeln, und besuchen anschließend drei Jahre lang eine Universität oder ein *polytechnic* bis zum Erwerb eines akademischen Grades. In den Semesterferien arbeiten sie gewöhnlich in dem Betrieb, der sie fördert.

Da die Zahl der Lehrstellen zurückgeht, weil Betriebe, die diese Ausbildung finanzieren müssen, zunehmend mit wirtschaftlichen Schwierigkeiten zu kämpfen haben, gibt es jetzt immer mehr *trainees,* deren Ausbildung nach einem ähnlichen Muster verläuft. Diese Auszubildenden besitzen jedoch keinen Lehrvertrag und erhalten auch keine Zusicherung einer späteren Anstellung.

Die Berufsausbildung endet mit der Qualifikation des *skilled worker* (Facharbeiter) oder *journeyman* (Geselle). Dieser kann dann je nach Fähigkeiten und Erfahrung eine Tätigkeit als Facharbeiter oder Handwerker ausüben. Im VK gibt es keinen Meisterbrief für den Industrie- und Handwerksmeister wie in der Bundesrepublik Deutschland. Ausbilden darf jeder, der dazu die tatsächliche Fähigkeit besitzt.

Berufsbildende Maßnahmen für arbeitslose und benachteiligte Jugendliche sind unter → *Jugendarbeitslosigkeit, VK* aufgeführt.

dungswesen), which also provides the entrance qualification for technical schools.

Apprentices possessing a General Certificate of Secondary Education or the entrance qualification for technical schools may attend the senior technical school (as well as the technical grammar school which exists in some of the *Länder*) in order to obtain the entrance qualification for the *Fachhochschule* which is similar to a polytechnic. The senior technical school provides a two-year course and is geared to the needs of the *Fachhochschule*.

UK

After completing formal education a young person may follow an apprentice-ship on a contract basis with a suitable factory or firm. The apprentice is guaranteed a period of skilled training by the firm, leading to a nationally recognised qualification and, in many cases, a job in the firm at the end.

Also, as in Germany, there is theoretical training, either day release or block release of generally six to eight weeks each year, provided by a college of fur-ther education. Well qualified young people leaving school at 18 (→ *Bildungs-wesen)* are trained as graduate apprentices by a firm. Such apprentices will spend the first year with the firm gaining experience, and then three years at a university or polytechnic to obtain a degree. Normally vacations are spent working for the sponsoring firm.

As the number of apprenticeships decreases because of economic difficulties encountered by firms having to finance this training, there are now more and more trainees, whose training follows a similar pattern. However, trainees do not have a training contract nor do they have the guarantee of future employ-ment.

As a rule, at the end of vocational training the qualification of skilled worker or journeyman may be obtained. According to their ability and experience, per-sons so qualified may then become tradesmen. In the UK there is no qualified instructors' certificate for industry or crafts as in the FRG. Everyone who has the factual ability may provide training.

For vocational training schemes directed at unemployed or disadvantaged young people see → *Jugendarbeitslosigkeit, UK.*

Berufsfindung (f)/Berufsvorbereitung (f)

D

Die Angebote der Berufsvorbereitung sollen Jugendlichen bei der Berufsfindung helfen. Zu diesem Zweck werden in enger Zusammenarbeit mit der Berufsberatung der Arbeitsämter (→ *Bundesanstalt für Arbeit)* in den Schulen Gespräche, Berufserkundungen, Betriebsbesichtigungen, Betriebspraktika usw. veranstaltet, oder es wird Berufsunterricht erteilt. Das Berufsgrundbildungsjahr nach Abschluß der allgemeinbildenden Schulen (→ *Berufsbildung)* ist ebenfalls zu den Angeboten der Berufsvorbereitung zu zählen. Dazu gehören auch Förderlehrgänge mit sozialpädagogischem Charakter für noch nicht berufsreife Jugendliche. Die letztgenannten Formen der Berufsvorbereitung dienen häufig denjenigen, die nach Verlassen der allgemeinbildenden Schule kein Ausbildungsverhältnis eingehen können.

Im Rahmen der → *Rehabilitation Behinderter* bezeichnet Berufsfindung eine gesetzlich verankerte Maßnahme, in der durch medizinische und psychologische Untersuchung sowie durch eine berufspraktische Erkundung ein für Behinderte geeigneter Beruf ermittelt wird.

VK

Die Beratung bei der Berufswahl ist neben den freien Trägern fast ausschließlich Aufgabe der Berufsberatung (→ *Bundesanstalt für Arbeit,* VK) der kommunalen Erziehungsbehörden (engl. Abk.: LEA's).

Die Berufsberater der kommunalen Berufsberatungsstellen arbeiten mit den Beratungslehrern in den Schulen eng zusammen. Schülern ab Vollendung des 13. Lebensjahres stehen sie auch selbst für in der Schule (ggfs. mit den Eltern) durchgeführte Beratungsgespräche zur Verfügung. Obwohl die Berufsberatung nicht unmittelbar organisatorisch beteiligt ist, berät sie die Schulen bei der Durchführung von Betriebspraktika. Diese können sich über zwei vollzeitlich in einem Betrieb verbrachte Wochen oder einen halben Tag pro Woche über ein ganzes *term*[1] erstrecken.

Die meisten Berufsberatungsstellen betreuen Personen jeder Altersstufe, auch wenn ihre gesetzliche Aufgabe hauptsächlich darin besteht, Jugendlichen im allgemeinen Bildungswesen (mit Ausnahme der Universitäten) bei der Berufsfindung beizustehen und Schulabgängern zu einem Arbeitsplatz zu verhelfen.

Betriebsrat (m)

D

Das Betriebsverfassungsgesetz von 1972 sieht vor, daß in Betrieben mit mindestens fünf ständig wahlberechtigten Arbeitnehmern alle drei Jahre ein Be-

---

1) Das Schuljahr ist in drei *terms* aufgeteilt.

Career Choice/Career Preparation

G

These vocational training preparatory schemes aim to help young people to choose a suitable career. To this end interviews, vocational orientation sessions, factory visits, practical placements etc. or career education classes are organised by the schools in close cooperation with careers officers (→ *Bundesanstalt für Arbeit)*. The Basic Vocational Training Year (following the completion of formal education → *Berufsbildung)* also forms part of such provision. For those unable to find a training position on leaving formal education and those seen as not yet ready to enter employment, development courses of a marked socio-educational content are provided.

A handicapped individual has legal entitlement to medical and psychological tests as well as a practical work period to enable him to make a proper choice of a career (→ *Rehabilitation Behinderter)*.

UK

Advice on the choice of a career, apart from private organisations, is almost totally the remit of the careers services (→ *Bundesanstalt für Arbeit, UK)* of the local education authorities (LEA's).

Careers officers from the LEA's Careers Centres maintain close contact with the careers teachers in the schools and are themselves available for consultation in the schools with pupils (and parents) from the end of a pupil's thirteenth year of age. Although not directly involved in its organisation the Service also advises schools on work experience for pupils; this can be in the form of two weeks full time on the job experience or a half day a week for a whole term.

Most careers services will see people of any age although the statutory requirement is to provide guidance for people in the education system (except universities) and an employment service for people leaving it.

Works Committee

G

The Works Constitution Act of 1972 stipulates that in all establishments or companies employing at least five persons who are entitled to vote, a shop floor representative may be elected every three years. Establishments or companies employing over 20 staff members may elect a works committee. This does not

triebsobmann, ab 21 Mitarbeiter ein Betriebsrat gewählt werden kann. Rechtlich ist er kein gewerkschaftliches Gremium. Dies schließt jedoch nicht aus, daß auch Gewerkschaftsvertreter in den Betriebsrat gewählt werden können.

Nach dem Betriebsverfassungsgesetz hat der Betriebsrat bestimmte Mitwirkungsrechte, z.B. bei Einstellungen und Entlassungen sowie Mitbestimmungsrechte bei sozialen Angelegenheiten. In Betrieben mit mindestens fünf Arbeitnehmern, die das 18. Lebensjahr noch nicht vollendet haben, werden Jugendvertretungen gewählt. Wahlberechtigt und wählbar sind die jugendlichen Mitarbeiter ab 14 Jahren.

Entsprechende Bestimmungen gelten für den öffentlichen Dienst und sind geregelt in den Personalvertretungsgesetzen des Bundes und der Länder.

VK

In der britischen Industrie gibt es kein dem Betriebsverfassungsgesetz entsprechendes Rechtsinstrument.

Es bestehen natürlich Gesetze, die die Beschäftigten am Arbeitsplatz schützen (z.B. der *Industrial Relations Act,* der *Safety at Work Act,* der *Race Relations Act*), doch sind diese integraler Bestandteil des gesamten Rechtssystems. Die Interessen der Beschäftigten am Arbeitsplatz werden von der jeweiligen Gewerkschaft oder einer ähnlichen Organisation vertreten. Jugendlichen wird nahegelegt, einer Gewerkschaft beizutreten. Gewerkschaften haben jedoch keine spezielle Jugendvertretung.

Kein Arbeitnehmer ist verpflichtet, Mitglied einer Gewerkschaft zu werden. Die Bezeichnung für die Gewerkschaftsvertreter in den Betriebsabteilungen ist *shop steward* (Vertrauensmann). Die weiblichen oder männlichen Inhaber dieses Amtes werden in der Regel alle zwei Jahre von den Gewerkschaftsmitgliedern der Betriebsabteilungen gewählt. Der *shop steward* hat ähnliche Aufgaben wie der Betriebsrat, jedoch nur zur Vertretung der Interessen der Gewerkschaftsmitglieder.

In größeren Firmen wählen die *shop stewards* Führungskräfte aus ihren Reihen, die sog. *convenors,* die bei Verhandlungen mit der Betriebsleitung im Auftrag und im Interesse ihrer Wähler agieren. Die Gewerkschaftsvertreter sind zuständig für bestimmte Fragen wie Arbeitslohn, soziale Angelegenheiten, Arbeitsbedingungen, Sicherheit, Dauer der Arbeitswoche, Entlassungen, Versetzungen, usw. Einige dieser Angelegenheiten, z.B. Arbeitslohn, Urlaub, Dauer der Arbeitswoche, unterliegen übergeordneten Abkommen, die zwischen Vertretern der nationalen Zusammenschlüsse der Gewerkschaften (vergleichbar dem DGB) und der Arbeitgeber (vergleichbar mit den Arbeitgeberverbänden in der Bundesrepublik Deutschland) ausgehandelt werden.

Im britischen *Civil Service (→ Bedienstete des öffentlichen Dienstes)* gibt es verschiedene Gewerkschaften sowie Berufsverbände für die Bediensteten. Als zwei der größten wären in diesem Zusammenhang die *National Union of Civil and Public Servants* und die *Civil and Public Servants Association* zu nennen.

exclude, however, that trade union representatives may be elected as members. Legally, it is not a trade union body.

Under the Works Constitution Act, the works committee enjoys certain rights of participation, e.g. when staff is hired or dismissed. It also has the right of co-determination in social matters. In establishments or companies with at least five young people (form 14 to 17 years) the young workers are entitled to vote for youth representatives and are themselves eligible for election.

Similar conditions apply for the Civil Service as specified in the Staff Representation Acts at Federal and *Land* level.

UK

There is no legal instrument in British Industry which corresponds to the *Betriebsverfassungsgesetz*.

There are, of course, laws which protect workers in their work places (e.g. the Industrial Relations Act, the Health and Safety at Work Act, the Race Relations Act), but these are an integral part of the overall legal system. The interests of the workers in the work place are represented by the appropriate trade union or similar organisation. Young people are encouraged to join trade unions but they have no special youth representation.

No worker is compelled to join a trade union. The union representative in each section of a firm is the shop steward and he or she is normally elected by the union members of the section every two years. The shop steward has similar functions to the *Betriebsrat* but only on behalf of union members.

In a firm of reasonable size, the shop stewards will elect senior representatives from their number who will act on their behalf and under their instruction in negotiations with senior management. These are called convenors. The union representatives are responsible for aspects of pay, welfare, conditions of work, safety, the length of the working week, dismissals, transferrals, etc. Some of these aspects, e.g. pay, holidays, length of working week, are pursued under national agreements between national union representatives (comparable to the DGB) and national employers' representatives (comparable to the *Arbeitgeberverbände*).

The British Civil Service (→ *Bedienstete des öffentlichen Dienstes*) has several staff unions and staff associations. Two of the largest are the National Union of Civil and Public Servants and the Civil and Public Servants Association.

Bildungswesen (n)

D

(s. auch Anhang, → *Bildungswesen,* Schema)

Aufgrund der föderativen Staatsstruktur der Bundesrepublik Deutschland sind die Zuständigkeiten im Bereich des Bildungswesens zwischen Bund und Ländern aufgeteilt. Weite Teile des Bildungswesens, wie z.B. die allgemeinbildenden und berufsbildenden Schulen, unterstehen der Zuständigkeit der Länder.

Gesetzgebungskompetenzen des Bundes im Bildungswesen bestehen im wesentlichen auf folgenden Gebieten: außerschulische Berufsbildung, Förderung der wissenschaftlichen Forschung, Ausbildungsförderung, Rahmenplanung und -gesetzgebung im Hochschulbereich, auswärtige Kulturpolitik, überregionale Bildungsplanung (in Zusammenarbeit mit den Ländern).

Die Schulpflicht beginnt mit dem sechsten Lebensjahr. Zur Grundstufe (Primarstufe) gehören die vier Jahrgangsstufen umfassende Grundschule oder entsprechende Jahrgänge der Sonderschule *(→ Behindertenhilfe).*

Sonderschulen gibt es für Kinder mit körperlichen und geistigen Behinderungen sowie schweren Lernstörungen. Sie umfassen in einer Einrichtung eine Grund- und Hauptschule.

Mittel- und Oberstufe des Schulwesens werden als Sekundarbereich bezeichnet. Die Mittelstufe (Sekundarstufe I) kann an den Schularten Hauptschule, Realschule und Gymnasium besucht werden. In einigen Bundesländern (u.a. in Niedersachsen) bestehen für die 5. und 6. Klasse schulartübergreifende Orientierungsstufen, die den Übergang von der Grund- in die Sekundarstufe erleichtern sollen, damit die Schüler bei der Wahl der ihren Fähigkeiten angemessenen Schulart genügend vorbereitet sind. Werden Hauptschule, Realschule und Gymnasium zu einer Schule zusammengefaßt, spricht man von integrierter Gesamtschule.

Die Vollzeitschulpflicht ist in den Bundesländern unterschiedlich geregelt; sie dauert in Berlin, Bremen und Nordrhein-Westfalen zehn Jahre, in den übrigen Ländern neun Jahre. In Hessen besteht die Besonderheit einer auf zehn Jahre verlängerten Vollzeitschulpflicht für die Jugendlichen, die nach Beendigung der neunten Klasse weder eine weiterführende Schule besuchen noch ein Ausbildungsverhältnis eingehen. Die Hauptschule dauert bis zur 9., in den genannten Ländern bis zur 10. Jahrgangsstufe. Die Realschule ist bis zur 10. Jahrgangsstufe angelegt, das Gymnasium bis zur 13.

Den Erwerb des Abschlußzeugnisses dieser drei Schulformen nennt man Hauptschul-, Realschulabschluß (oder Fachoberschulreife) bzw. Abitur (Reifezeugnis). Diese Abschlüsse ermöglichen den Besuch von Bildungseinrichtungen der nächsthöheren Stufe. Bis zum Abschluß der Sekundarstufe I liegt das Hauptgewicht auf der Vermittlung einer Allgemeinbildung. Die Schulfor-

Education System

G

(cf. Appendix, → *Bildungswesen,* FRG)

In accordance with the structure of the Federal Republic of Germany responsibilities for the education system are divided between the Federation and the *Länder.* Broad sectors of the education system, e.g. the establishments of formal education and the vocational schools, fall within the terms of reference of the *Länder.*

The Federation has legislative competence for the education system mainly in the following areas: out-of-school vocational training, promotion of scientific research, over-all planning and legislation for higher education, foreign cultural policy, and for educational planning (in cooperation with the *Länder*).

Compulsory education begins at six years of age. The basic primary level covers the primary school for four years, or the corresponding years of the special school *(→ Behindertenhilfe).*

Special schools are provided for children with severe physical and mental handicaps as well as serious learning difficulties. Special schools have a basic level and a secondary level in one establishment.

The middle and upper stages of the school system are referred to as secondary level. Secondary level stage I is provided by the school types of *Hauptschule* (basic secondary school), *Realschule* (former secondary modern school) and *Gymnasium* (grammar school). In some of the Federal Länder (in particular in Lower Saxony) there are orientation stages in years five and six for all school types whose aim is to facilitate transition from the primary to the secondary level and to enable pupils to choose a type of school that is best suited to their abilities. Where *Hauptschule, Realschule* and *Gymnasium* are combined, the establishment is called an integrated comprehensive school.

The duration of compulsory education varies from *Land* to *Land.* In Berlin, Bremen and North Rhine-Westphalia it is ten years, in the remaining *Länder* nine years. In Hesse compulsory education is extended to ten years for those who, having completed the ninth year, neither move on to a continuation school nor begin an apprenticeship. The *Hauptschule* goes up to the 9th year except for the *Länder* just named. The *Realschule* also goes up to the 10th year, the *Gymnasium* to the 13th year.

On successful completion of their secondary education pupils receive either the *Hauptschule,* the *Realschule* or *Gymnasium* leaving certificate *(Abitur/Reifezeugnis).* These certificates qualify for admission to educational establishments at the next higher level.

Until the end of secondary level stage I emphasis is on providing an all-round education. The school forms of the secondary level stage II, with the exception

men der Sekundarstufe II dienen vornehmlich, mit Ausnahme des Gymnasiums, der beruflichen Aus- und Fortbildung (→ *Berufsbildung*).

Die Oberstufe des Gymnasiums umfaßt die Klassen 11 bis 13 und ist als Kurssystem organisiert. Der Klassenverband ist aufgelöst; die Schüler wählen gemäß ihren Neigungen Leistungs- und Grundkurse. Dabei müssen der sprachliche wie der naturwissenschaftliche Bereich angemessen berücksichtigt werden. Die gymnasiale Oberstufe dient als Propädeutikum für das Hochschulstudium. Mit dem Gymnasialabschluß, dem Abitur (Reifezeugnis), wird die allgemeine Hochschulreife erworben. In einigen Ländern kann an Wirtschaftsgymnasien, Fachoberschulen oder ähnlichen Einrichtungen eine fachgebundene Hochschulreife, bzw. Fachhochschulreife erworben werden.

Als zweiten Bildungsweg bezeichnet man den Besuch von Einrichtungen, an denen Schul- und Bildungsabschlüsse nachgeholt werden können. Dies ist in Direkt- und/oder Fernunterricht möglich. Direktunterricht geben tagsüber oder abends z.B. die Abendrealschulen, Berufsaufbauschulen, Abendgymnasien sowie Kollegs zur Erlangung der Hochschulreife. Fernlehrinstitute sind meist in privater Hand. Dort ist eine externe Abschlußprüfung vor einer staatlichen Kommission abzulegen.

Der Hochschulbereich (Tertiärer Bereich) umfaßt Universitäten, Technische Hochschulen, Pädagogische Hochschulen, Kunst- und Musikhochschulen und Fachhochschulen, außerdem einige Gesamthochschulen, in denen die Aufgaben der verschiedenen Hochschularten verbunden sind.

Für eine Reihe von Studiengängen bestehen örtliche oder bundesweite Zulassungsbeschränkungen (numerus clausus). In diesen Fällen ist die Zulassung aufgrund des Hochschulrahmengesetzes (HRG) von den Ländern im Zusammenwirken mit den Hochschulen geregelt.

Die Hochschulen sind mit wenigen Ausnahmen staatliche Einrichtungen der Länder. Sie haben das Recht der Selbstverwaltung, für die das Prinzip der funktionsgerechten (abgestuften) Mitwirkung aller Mitglieder (Professoren, wissenschaftliche und nicht-wissenschaftliche Mitarbeiter, Studenten) gilt.

Aufgaben der Universitäten sind Forschung, Lehre und Heranbildung des wissenschaftlichen Nachwuchses in allen wissenschaftlichen Fachrichtungen. Der Nachweis eines erfolgreichen Studiums wird entweder mit einer Staatsprüfung (Staatsexamen) oder einer Hochschulprüfung (Diplom- oder Magisterprüfung) erbracht. Staatsprüfungen werden von staatlichen Prüfungskommissionen, denen auch Hochschullehrer angehören, abgenommen. Die Universitäten und die Gesamthochschulen können Doktorgrade verleihen (Promotionsrecht).

Fachhochschulen haben die Aufgabe, eine stärker anwendungsbezogene Ausbildung zu vermitteln, vor allem in den Bereichen Ingenieurwesen, Wirtschaft, Sozialwesen. Das Studium ist kürzer als an Universitäten (in der Regel drei Studienjahre; bis zu vier Jahren einschließlich des Praxissemesters). Nach

of the grammar school, are devoted to vocational and further education (→ *Berufsbildung*).

The upper stage of the grammar school covers years 11–13. It is organised on a course basis and the former close class teaching ceases. Pupils may select from a core of academic courses and have a choice of complementary studies. Within this choice, a proper balance of languages and natural sciences must exist. The upper stage of the grammar school is intended as a preparation for university studies. Successful completion of the *Reifeprüfung/Abitur* provides a general entrance qualification for university. In some of the *Länder, Wirtschaftsgymnasien* (economics grammar school), *Fachoberschulen* (senior technical schools), and similar establishments may award a university entrance qualification for relevant university studies.

Mature students may obtain appropriate certificates at adult education establishments offering full-time day courses and/or courses at evening institutes *(Abendschulen, Abendgymnasien), Berufsaufbauschulen* (vocational continuation schools), and colleges providing the university entrance qualifications. Distance teaching, concluding with a final State examination, offers another possibility. For the most part distance teaching establishments are privately owned.

Institutions of higher education (the tertiary level) include universities, technical universities, teacher training colleges, art and music academies, *Fachhochschulen* (similar to a polytechnic), and some *Gesamthochschulen* which embrace some or all of the above-mentioned higher education institutions.

Access to most degree courses in the higher education institutions is limited by either local or Federal regulations *(numerus clausus)*. Admission to available places is governed by regulations of the respective *Länder* and establishments in accordance with the *Hochschulrahmengesetz* (Framework Act for Higher Education).

With few exceptions, the higher education establishments are statutory institutions of the *Länder*. They are self-governing bodies which are regulated by the principle of graduated participation by all members (i.e. professors, academic and non-academic staff, students).

The universities are responsible for research, teaching and the education of the younger generation of academics in all fields. Completion of studies is marked by the passing of a State examination *(Staatsexamen)* or an examination *(Diplom/Magister)* set by the higher education establishments themselves. State examinations are taken before a State examination board which includes representatives of the teaching staff of the respective higher education institution. Universities as well as combined polytechnics and universities have the right of conferment of doctorates.

The *Fachhochschulen* provide degree courses much more related to practice especially in the fields of engineering, economics, and social studies. The *Fach-*

Bestehen der Abschlußprüfung wird ein Diplomgrad mit dem Zusatz (FH) verliehen. Voraussetzung ist die Fachhochschulreife (Fachabitur an Fachoberschulen) oder eine allgemeine Hochschulreife in Verbindung mit einem Berufspraktikum.

VK

(s. auch Anhang → *Bildungswesen,* VK)

Die Zuständigkeit des Ministers für Erziehung und Wissenschaft umfaßt das gesamte Bildungswesen in England, die Beziehungen der Zentralregierung zu den Universitäten in ganz Großbritannien sowie ihre finanzielle Unterstützung. Die Minister für Wales, Schottland und Nordirland besitzen in ihrem jeweiligen Land die volle Zuständigkeit für den Bildungssektor mit Ausnahme der Universitäten.

Die Verwaltung der öffentlichen Schulen und der Weiterbildung ist dezentralisiert. Es besteht eine Aufteilung der Zuständigkeiten auf die Ministerien der Zentralregierung, die kommunalen Erziehungsbehörden und verschiedene freie Träger.

Die Eltern sind gesetzlich verpflichtet, dafür zu sorgen, daß ihre Kinder entweder im Schulwesen oder in sonstiger Form vom 5. bis zum 16. Lebensjahr eine ordnungsgemäße Allgemeinbildung erhalten.

Mit fünf Jahren kommen die Kinder in England und Wales in *infant schools* oder *infant departments,* von denen viele Schüler mit 7 Jahren in die *junior schools* oder *junior departments* überwechseln. Im allgemeinen ist das Übergangsalter von der Grundschule zur Sekundarstufe in England, Wales und Nordirland bei 11 Jahren; einige Kommunen in England haben jedoch sogenannte „Erstschulen" für Kinder von 5 bis 8, 9 oder 10 Jahren eingerichtet sowie „Mittelschulen" für unterschiedliche Altersgruppen zwischen 8 und 14 Jahren. In Schottland werden die Kinder mit fünf Jahren eingeschult und besuchen die *primary school* bis zum 12. Lebensjahr.

Etwa 90% der Schülerpopulation der öffentlichen Schulen in England und Wales besuchen *comprehensive schools* (Gesamtschulen), die alle Schüler ohne Ansehen ihrer besonderen Befähigung oder Eignung aufnehmen und ein breites Unterrichtsangebot der Sekundarstufe für alle oder die meisten Kinder eines *district* (→ *Kommunale Selbstverwaltung,* VK) bereitstellen. Die übrigen Kinder besuchen meist die *grammar school* (Gymnasium) oder die *secondary modern school* (Realschule), in die sie nach einem Auswahlverfahren im Alter von 11 Jahren aufgenommen werden.

Die *independent schools* (unabhängigen Schulen) für Schüler jeden Alters sind nicht Teil des öffentlichen Schulwesens, unterliegen jedoch der Schulaufsicht und benötigen die Eintragung beim zuständigen Bildungsministerium auf Re-

hochschule course which normally extends over three years and, if one includes the mandatory practical placement work of one semester, may come up to four years, is shorter than a university course. Those having passed the final examination are awarded a *Diplom* to which the letters FH are added in brackets. Successful completion of a senior technical school or the general university entrance qualification plus a full-time work placement serves as entrance qualification to a *Fachhochschule*.

UK
(cf. Appendices → *Bildungswesen,* UK)

The Secretary for Education and Science is responsible for all aspects of education in England, and for the Government's relations with and support for universities throughout Great Britain. The Secretaries of State for Wales, Scotland and Northern Ireland have full responsibility in their respective countries for non-university education.

Administration of publicly provided schools and further education is decentralised. Responsibilities are divided between the central government departments, local education authorities and various voluntary organisations.

Parents are required by law to see that their children receive efficient full-time education, at school or elsewhere, between the ages of 5 and 16.

At five children in England and Wales go to infant schools or departments; many go on to junior schools or departments at seven years. The usual age of transfer from primary to secondary school is 11 in England, Wales and Northern Ireland, but a number of local authorities in England have established "first" schools for pupils aged 5 to 8, 9 or 10 and "middle" schools covering various age ranges between 8 and 14. In Scotland the primary schools take children from 5 to 12.

Some 90% of the maintained secondary school population in England and Wales attend comprehensive schools, which take pupils without reference to ability or aptitude and provide a wide range of secondary education for all or most of the children of a district (→ *Kommunale Selbstverwaltung,* UK). Most other children receive secondary education in grammar and secondary modern schools to which they are allocated after selection procedures at the age of 11.

Independent schools catering for pupils of all ages are outside the publicly supported sector, but are open to inspection and must register with the appropriate government education department. Among these are about 550 "public schools", most of which have boarding pupils between the ages of 11 and 19, and are single sex. Almost all independent schools charge fees at or near the cost of provision. In individual cases local education authorities may assist with the payment of fees.

Special schools for the handicapped exist as separate establishments. Current policy aims to provide integrated education for them (→ *Behindertenhilfe*).

gierungsebene. Darunter befinden sich ungefähr 550 *public schools,* die meist ein Internat besitzen und nur Kinder eines Geschlechts von etwa 11 – 19 Jahren erziehen. In fast allen unabhängigen Schulen ist zur ungefähren Deckung der Unkosten der jeweiligen Einrichtung Schulgeld zu zahlen. In Einzelfällen stellen die kommunalen Erziehungsbehörden Zuwendungen für den Besuch einer Privatschule bereit.

Für behinderte Kinder bestehen eigene Sonderschulen. Gegenwärtig gehen die politischen Bestrebungen dahin, sie in die Regelschulen zu integrieren *(→ Behindertenhilfe).*

In England, Wales und Nordirland können die Schüler nach erfolgreicher Beendigung ihrer Schulbildung folgende Abschlußzeugnisse erwerben:

– Das *General Certificate of Secondary Education / G.C.S.E.* (früher *C.S.E.* und *G.C.E. O-level),* in der Regel mit 16 Jahren. Es ist die Zugangsvoraussetzung für Einrichtungen der Weiterbildung und der Berufsbildung;

– nach Beendigung von zwei weiteren Jahren der Sekundarstufe und in der Regel mit 18 Jahren kann das *General Certificate of Education (G.C.E.) Advanced (A) level* erworben werden.

– Ein neuer Schulabschluß mit der Bezeichnung *Advanced Supplementary (AS) levels* wurde neben dem *G.C.E. A level* 1987 in England und Wales und 1989 in Nordirland eingeführt. *A level* oder eine Mischung von *A* und *AS levels* sind die Mindestanforderungen für die Zulassung zur Universität und anderen Hochschulen sowie viele Formen der beruflichen Bildung.

– Das *Certificate of Pre-Vocational Education* bietet denjenigen, die mit 16 noch ein weiteres Jahr die Schule besuchen möchten, die Möglichkeit, sich auf einen Beruf, eine Berufsausbildung oder sonstige Ausbildungsangebote vorzubereiten. Es kann auch als Überbrückung für den Besuch einer Hochschule genutzt werden.

Schottische Schüler erwerben das *Scottish Certificate of Education (S.C.E.) at Ordinary grade* am Ende des vierten Jahres der Sekundarstufe. Im fünften und sechsten Jahr legen die Schüler die Prüfungen des *S.C.E. Higher grade* ab. Dieser Schulabschluß wird als Zugangsvoraussetzung für die Universität sowie andere Formen des Hochschulstudiums und der qualifizierten Fachausbildung anerkannt. Manche Schüler besuchen die Schule noch ein weiteres Jahr, um das *Certificate of Sixth Year Studies* zu erwerben.

Der Begriff *further education (→ Weiterbildung)* bezeichnet im allgemeinen jede Form organisierten Lernens nach Abschluß der Schule mit Ausnahme des Universitätsstudiums, bezieht sich jedoch oft auf berufsspezifische Ausbildungsangebote für 16–19jährige, die die Schule verlassen haben. Der Hochschulbereich (*post-graduate, first-degree* und sonstige Studiengänge für Teilnehmer im Besitz der Hochschulreife) umfaßt die Universitäten, *polytechnics* und sonstige *colleges.*

Es gibt 47 Universitäten in Großbritannien einschließlich der *Open University* (Fernuniverstität). Jede Universität besitzt eine Charta, die bis zur Mitte des 19. Jahrhunderts religiösen Ursprungs war, heute hingegen durch königlichen

In England, Wales and Northern Ireland, pupils having successfully completed their formal education may obtain the following certificates:

- The General Certificate of Secondary Education / G.C.S.E. (previously C.S.E. and G.C.E. O level), normally taken at 16 years of age, which is the entrance qualification for establishments of further education and vocational training.
- Upon completion of two further years of secondary education and normally at the age of 18, pupils take the General Certificate of Education (G.C.E.) Advanced (A) level.
- New examinations, Advanced Supplementary (AS) levels, were introduced alongside the G.C.E. A level in 1987 (England and Wales) and in 1989 (Northern Ireland). A or a mixture of A and AS levels are the standard for entrance to university and other higher education and to many forms of professional training.
- The Certificate of Pre-Vocational Education is intended for those who wish to continue for a year after the age of 16 to prepare either for work or for vocational or other courses. It can serve as a stepping stone for higher education.

Scottish pupils take the Scottish Certificate of Education (S.C.E.) at Ordinary grade at the end of their fourth year of secondary education. Pupils in the fifth and sixth year sit the S.C.E. Higher grade. Passes at this grade are the basis for entry to university and other forms of higher education and professional training. Some continue for a further year to take the Certificate of Sixth Year Studies.

The term further education (→ Weiterbildung) is usually used to define all post-school education outside the universities, but often refers specifically to non-advanced vocational courses for 16 to 19-year-olds who have left school. Higher education (post-graduate, first degree and other courses of post A-level standard) is provided at universities, polytechnics and other colleges.

There are 47 universities in Britain, including the Open University. Each one has a charter which prior to the mid-19th century was religious in origin but now is granted either by Royal Decree or Act of Parliament (→ Rechtsinstrumente, UK). Funded at least in part by the Department of Education and Science (increasing links with industry are also a major source of finance), within the terms of their charters they are completely autonomous. Although degree titles vary accordingly, first degrees are usually titled Bachelor of Arts (BA) or Bachelor of Science (BSc), second degrees Master of Arts (MA), Master of Science (MSc), and Doctor of Philosophy (PhD). In Scotland Master is used for a first degree in arts subjects.

The practice of employing external examiners (whose appointment is at the discretion of the universities) for all university examinations maintains a uniformity of standard of degrees between the universities. Research, which many staff combine with their teaching duties (as in the Federal Republic) is an important feature of university work.

Erlaß oder Parlamentsgesetz (→ *Rechtsinstrumente,* VK) verliehen wird. Die Universitäten werden zumindest teilweise vom Ministerium für Erziehung und Wissenschaft finanziert (wobei immer zahlreicher werdende Verbindungen mit der Industrie eine ebenfalls sehr wichtige Finanzierungsquelle darstellen), sind jedoch im Rahmen der Bedingungen der Charta völlig autonom. Obwohl aus diesem Grund bei den akademischen Titeln eine gewisse Uneinheitlichkeit herrscht, sind folgende Bezeichnungen als allgemein üblich anzusehen: *Bachelor of Arts* (BA) oder *Bachelor of Science* (BSc) für den ersten akademischen Grad. *Master of Arts* (MA), *Master of Science* (MSc) und *Doctor of Philosphy* (PhD) für den zweiten. In Schottland wird der *Master* für einen ersten akadamischen Grad in den geisteswissenschaftlichen Fächern verliehen.

Die Praxis, externe Prüfer (über deren Benennung die Universitäten nach eigenem Ermessen entscheiden) für alle Universitätsprüfungen zu berufen, sichert ein einheitliches Niveau der akademischen Grade. Die Forschung, die viele Mitarbeiter der Universitäten mit ihren Lehraufgaben verbinden, ist (wie auch in der Bundesrepublik Deutschland) ein entscheidendes Merkmal der wissenschaftlichen Arbeit.

Jede Universität besitzt ein *governing body* (Selbstverwaltungsgremium), das je nach den Bestimmungen der Charta unterschiedlich zusammengesetzt ist und meist aus Vertretern der wissenschaftlichen Arbeit, der Verwaltung sowie der Studentenschaft besteht.

Die Zulassung zur Universität ist an ein Auswahlverfahren oder eine Prüfung gebunden. Bis zum ersten akademischen Grad ist in der Regel ein drei- bis vierjähriges Vollzeitstudium zu absolvieren.

Die *Open University* ist eine Einrichung, die nicht die persönliche Anwesenheit erfordert und Teilzeit-Kurse für den Erwerb des ersten akademischen Grades und anderer Qualifikationen anbietet. Sie arbeitet mit einer Kombination von Funk- und Fernsehprogrammen, brieflichem Fernunterricht und Sommerkursen. Die Teilnahme an diesen Kursen setzt zwar keine akademische Qualifikation voraus, aber der Standard der verliehenen Grade ist derselbe wie an anderen Universitäten.

Eine wichtige Funktion im Bereich der Fortbildung erfüllen in England und Wales die 30 *polytechnics,* die seit 1967 geschaffen wurden. Sie haben ein breit gefächertes Angebot an Ausbildungsgängen in vielen Fächern und auf allen Ebenen, obschon in jüngster Zeit ein Übergewicht bei den wissenschaftlichen Studiengängen zu verzeichnen ist. Diese können zum ersten und zweiten akademischen Grad führen, zu bestimmten Qualifikationen, die ihnen entsprechen, zu den Abschlußprüfungen der wichtigsten Berufsverbände und sonstigen Qualifikationen. Die *polytechnics* unterhalten enge Beziehungen zu Handel und Industrie. Viele Studenten gehen einer Erwerbstätigkeit nach und besuchen Kurse auf Teilzeit-Basis. Vergleichbare Einrichtungen sind die 15 schottischen *central institutions* und eine gewisse Anzahl von Fortbildungs-Colleges. In Nordirland bietet die Universität von Ulster Fortbildungsprogramme an.

Each university has a governing body which, according to its charter, is composed variously of academic staff, administrative staff, and student representatives.

Admission to university is by selection or by examination. First degree courses are mainly full-time and usually last three to four years.

The Open University is a non-residential university which provides part-time degree and other courses, using a combination of television and radio broadcasts, correspondence texts and summer schools. No formal academic qualifications are required to register for these courses, but the standard of its degrees are the same as those of other universities.

A major contribution to post-school education in England and Wales is made by the 30 polytechnics which have been established since 1967. They provide courses in a wide range of subjects at all levels, though the trend is towards a concentration on advanced work. Courses may lead to first and higher degrees, certain graduate-equivalent qualifications, the examinations of the main professional bodies and to other qualifications. Polytechnics have close links with commerce and industry, and many polytechnic students have jobs and attend on a part-time basis. Similar provision is made in Scotland in the 15 central institutions and a number of further education colleges, and in Northern Ireland by the University of Ulster.

Bürgerinitiative (f)

D

Zusammenschluß (mit unterschiedlicher Rechtsform) von Bürgern zur Abänderung eines sie gemeinsam betreffenden Zustandes oder zur Durchsetzung eines gemeinsamen Zieles. Die Bestrebungen richten sich zum Beispiel auf die Erhaltung alter Bausubstanz, den Umweltschutz oder die Vertretung der Interessen benachteiligter Gruppen. Bürgerinitiativen sind nur in Ausnahmefällen parteipolitisch gebunden. In der Mehrzahl der Fälle lösen sie sich nach Erreichung des Zieles wieder auf.

VK

Gilt grundsätzlich für beide Länder.

Bundesanstalt (f) für Arbeit (f)

D

In der Bundesrepublik Deutschland sind nach dem Arbeitsförderungsgesetz die Aufgaben der öffentlichen Arbeitsvermittlung, der Berufsberatung und Vermittlung beruflicher Ausbildungsstellen, der Förderung der beruflichen Bildung sowie der Arbeitslosenversicherung der Bundesanstalt für Arbeit mit Sitz in Nürnberg gesetzlich übertragen. Als Körperschaft des öffentlichen Rechts unterliegt sie der Rechtsaufsicht des Bundesministers für Arbeit und Sozialordnung.

Die Bundesanstalt für Arbeit gliedert sich in die Hauptstelle mit ihrem Institut für Arbeitsmarkt- und Berufsförderung, neun Landesarbeitsämter und 146 Arbeitsämter. Die Hauptstelle in Nürnberg organisiert, plant und überwacht die Durchführung der fachlichen Aufgaben im gesamten Bundesgebiet. Den Landesarbeitsämtern untersteht jeweils eine Zahl von Arbeitsämtern, deren Aufgaben auf kommunaler Ebene sie koordinieren. Diese Aufgaben umfassen die Berufsberatung und Arbeitsvermittlung, die Förderung der beruflichen Aus- und Fortbildung, die Gewährung von berufsfördernden Leistungen zur Rehabilitation, zur Erhaltung und Schaffung von Arbeitsplätzen, die Gewährung von Arbeitslosengeld und – im Auftrag und auf Kosten des Bundes – die Gewährung von Arbeitslosenhilfe sowie die Gewährung von Konkursausfallgeld. Darüber hinaus betreibt die Bundesanstalt für Arbeit Arbeitsmarkt- und Berufsforschung.

Das Arbeitsförderungsgesetz bietet eine Vielzahl von Förderungsmöglichkeiten, deren Ziel es ist, dem einzelnen – entsprechend seiner Eignung und Neigung – zu einer Anpassung an geänderte berufliche Voraussetzungen, einem Aufstieg im Beruf oder zu einer beruflichen Neuorientierung zu verhelfen, um damit seine Chancen auf dem Arbeitsmarkt zu verbessern und ihn vor Arbeitslosigkeit zu schützen.

Die Berufsberatung der Arbeitsämter erteilt Jugendlichen und Erwachsenen Auskunft und individuellen Rat in Fragen der Berufswahl. Die Berufsberater

Community Action Group

G

Groupings of citizens aiming to change a situation which represents a general grievance or to attain a common objective. These groupings may take a varying legal form. Their aims may be to preserve old buildings, protect the environment or to support the interests of disadvantaged groups. Community action groups are linked only in exceptional cases to a political party. For the most part, they dissolve after having achieved their objective.

UK

This principle applies to both countries.

Federal Institute of Labour

G

Under the Employment Promotion Act in the Federal Republic of Germany the responsibility for placement of workers, vocational guidance, the provision of places for vocational training, the promotion of vocational training and the administration of unemployment insurance is legally vested in the Federal Institute of Labour, the seat of which is in Nuremberg. It is a statutory body under the legal supervision of the Federal Ministry of Labour and Social Affairs.

The Federal Institute of Labour is subdivided into a head office to which the Institute for the Promotion of the Labour Market and Career Development is attached, nine *Land* employment agencies and 146 employment offices. The head office in Nuremberg organises, plans, and supervises the implementation of the regulations governing the above responsibilities throughout the Federal Republic. The *Land* employment agencies coordinate the work of a number of employment offices at the local level. The latters' tasks include vocational guidance and job placement, the promotion of vocational training and further education, the granting of benefits for the purposes of vocational rehabilitation, the creation and conservation of jobs, as well as the payment of unemployment benefits. Acting as an agent of the Federation and drawing on Federal funds, they are also responsible for the payment of reduced unemployment benefit (see below) and a special form of compensation in case of bankruptcy.

The Promotion of Employment Act provides for a large number of promotional programmes whose main objective is to help individuals – according to their interests and abilities – to adapt to changing conditions in their vocation or profession, to advance in their career or to find an opportunity for vocational reorientation in order to improve their chances on the labour market and to protect them from unemployment.

The employment offices have a vocational guidance section providing vocational orientation and individual counselling to young persons as well as adults.

sind ausgebildete Fachkräfte der Berufs- und Betriebskunde, Psychologie und Pädagogik. Für die Vermittlung in Ausbildungsstellen sind Ausbildungsvermittler tätig, die speziell für diese Aufgabe ausgebildet wurden.

Die Arbeitsvermittlung in den Arbeitsämtern steht allen Arbeitnehmern und Arbeitgebern zur freiwilligen Benutzung kostenlos offen. Sie bringt Arbeitssuchende mit Arbeitgebern zur Begründung von Arbeitsverhältnissen zusammen. Dabei werden die besonderen Verhältnisse der Betriebe und der zu besetzenden Arbeitsplätze ebenso beachtet wie die Eignung der Bewerber, z.B. ihre schulische und berufliche Aus- und Fortbildung. Bestimmte, vor allem schutzbedürftige Personengruppen wie Schwerbehinderte, werden dabei besonders berücksichtigt. Die Arbeitsvermittlung von Jugendlichen bis zum Alter von 20 Jahren, die nicht für eine Berufsausbildung in Betracht kommen, bzw. eine solche nicht anstreben, wird von Arbeitsvermittlern wahrgenommen, die neben ihrer fachlichen Qualifikation in aller Regel auch über jugendpflegerische Erfahrung verfügen.

Eine weitere Leistung nach dem Arbeitsförderungsgesetz ist die Zahlung von Arbeitslosengeld bzw. Arbeitslosenhilfe an Arbeitslose, denen nicht sofort zumutbare Arbeit vermittelt werden kann. Arbeitslosengeld erhalten Personen, die beitragspflichtig beschäftigt waren. Die Dauer des Anspruchs auf Arbeitslosengeld hängt von den Beschäftigungszeiten ab. Nach Ablauf des Anspruchs wird unter bestimmten Voraussetzungen Arbeitslosenhilfe gezahlt.

VK

Gruppe Arbeitsministerium

Die Umsetzung der Beschäftigungspolitik der Regierung ist Aufgabe des Arbeitsministeriums und dreier Behörden, des *Adivsory, Conciliation and Arbitration Service* (Schlichtungsstelle für Arbeitsstreitigkeiten), der *Health and Safety Commission* (Kommission für Arbeitsschutz) sowie des *Employment Service* (Arbeitsvermittlung), die die Gruppe Arbeitsministerium bilden. Die umfassende Zielsetzung der Gruppe ist es, durch die Schaffung eines wettbewerbsfähigen, effizienten und flexiblen Arbeitsmarktes das Wirtschaftswachstum zu unterstützen.

Neben der Beschäftigungsförderung und der verstärkten Qualifizierung der Ausbildung hat das Arbeitsministerium die Aufgabe, Anreize für unternehmerische Initiativen und die Schaffung von Arbeitsplätzen zu geben sowie gleiche Beschäftigungschancen für Arbeitnehmer ungeachtet ihrer Rasse, Hautfarbe, Herkunft und ihres Geschlechts sicherzustellen. Das Ministerium ist weiterhin verantwortlich für die zentrale Aufsichtsführung über die Berufsberatung, die junge Menschen vor oder nach dem Verlassen der Schule oder des College bei den kommunalen Erziehungsbehörden erhalten.

Die Hauptstelle des Arbeitsministeriums hat sechs „Direktorate" (Abteilungen) mit weitreichenden Aufgaben, zu denen auch die öffentliche Arbeitsver-

The careers officers are fully qualified in career and business theory, psychology and pedagogics. The provision of training places is administered by training officers who are specially schooled for this purpose.

Job placement is available to all persons seeking employment and to all employers. Calling on these services is voluntary and free of charge. Contact is arranged between job seekers and employers with a view to concluding a contract of employment. When vacancies are to be filled, the details of a given firm and the respective job are considered, as is the aptitude of the applicant for the job, e.g. his formal education and vocational training. Special provision is made for certain groups of persons in need of protection, such as the severely handicapped. Job placement for young people up to the age of 20 who do not qualify for vocational training or do not intend to train, is in the hands of placement officers who, in addition to their special qualifications, as a rule have some experience in youth work.

A further provision made under the Promotion of Employment Act is the payment of unemployment benefit (of which there are two forms, *Arbeitslosengeld* and *Arbeitslosenhilfe*) to unemployed persons for whom a suitable job cannot be found immediately. Eligible for *Arbeitslosengeld* are all persons who have been employed and liable to pay contributions. The period during which unemployment benefit may be claimed depends on the duration of previous gainful employment. When this period has expired, a reduced unemployment benefit *(Arbeitslosenhilfe)* may be drawn under certain conditions.

UK

Employment Department Group (EDG)
The Government's policy on employment is implemented by the Employment Department (ED) and three statutory agencies, the Advisory, Conciliation and Arbitration Service, the Health and Safety Commission and the Employment Service. Together the four bodies form the Employment Department Group (EDG). The general objective of the EDG is to support economic growth by promoting a competitive, efficient and flexible labour market.

In addition to its wider concerns of furthering employment and qualified training, the Employment Department aims to promote enterprise and job creation and safeguard equal employment opportunities for workers regardless of race, colour, origin or sex. It is responsible for the central supervision of the careers advice and guidance given by the local education authorities to young people attending or leaving schools and colleges (careers service).

The six directorates of the ED Headquarters perform a wide range of functions, amongst which the Employment Service Agency and the Training, Education and Enterprise Directorate provide the services that would mirror those of the *Bundesanstalt für Arbeit* to the extent in which comparison is possible in view of the structural differences existing between the German and the British system.

mittlung sowie die Ausbildung, Bildung und Unternehmensförderung gehören. Deren Aufgabenstellung entspricht der der Bundesanstalt für Arbeit, soweit angesichts der zwischen Deutschland und Großbritannien bestehenden strukturellen Unterschiede ein Vergleich möglich ist.

1. Employment Service

Der *Employment Service* verfügt über ein Netz von 1.800 örtlichen Arbeitsämtern, 59 überörtlichen Ämtern sowie neun regionalen Dienststellen. In 1.032 *jobcentres* (Arbeitsvermittlungsstellen) wird Arbeitssuchenden Hilfe zuteil, entweder unmittelbar durch Vermittlung in freie Stellen oder durch Unterstützung im Rahmen anderer Initiativen der Regierung.

Die Arbeitsvermittlung führt jetzt umfassende Programme durch, um eine fundierte Eignungsprüfung der Bewerber sowie eine sorgfältige Beratung der Arbeitslosen auf der Suche nach Wegen zu einem neuen Arbeitsplatz sicherzustellen. Berater für bestimmte Personenkreise wie Arbeitslose, die einen neuen Anlauf nehmen wollen, Empfänger von Arbeitslosenunterstützung und neu auf den Arbeitsmarkt gekommene Arbeitslose übernehmen eine wichtige Funktion in diesem Prozeß. Ihre Tätigkeit wird unterstützt von den *jobclubs,* die langfristig Arbeitslose und Benachteiligte beraten, um sie in die Lage zu versetzen, bestehende Angebote zu nutzen (→ *Jugendarbeitslosigkeit,* VK).

2. Arbeitslosenunterstützung

Die Auszahlung der Arbeitslosenunterstützung erfolgt durch örtliche Dienststellen des *Employment Service,* die im Auftrag des Ministeriums für Soziale Sicherheit tätig sind.

Im britischen System der sozialen Sicherung bestehen zwei Kategorien der finanziellen Unterstützung für Arbeitslose: einerseits die Leistungen des Nationalen Versicherungsfonds, der aus Beiträgen der Beschäftigten und ihrer Arbeitgeber sowie der Selbständigen und der Regierung gespeist wird, und andererseits die Leistungen aus dem allgemeinen Steueraufkommen. Anspruchsberechtigte der ersten Kategorie erhalten aus dem Versicherungsfonds Arbeitslosenunterstützung für einen Zeitraum von bis zu einem Jahr. Leistungen der zweiten Kategorie, deren Auszahlung durch örtliche Dienststellen des Ministeriums für Soziale Sicherheit erfolgt, können von allen nicht vollzeitbeschäftigten Personen ab 16 Jahren im Rahmen der Sozialhilfe und der Kinderzulage für einkommensschwache Arbeitnehmer in Anspruch genommen werden.

Der *Employment Service* ist zunehmend bestrebt, die Arbeitsvermittlungsstellen und die Dienststellen für die Auszahlung der Arbeitslosenunterstützung in einer Einrichtung zusammenzufassen, damit Arbeitssuchende nur mit einer Stelle zu tun haben.

3. Training and Enterprise Councils (TECs)

Unter der allgemeinen Aufsichtsführung der Abteilung für Ausbildung, Bildung und Unternehmensförderung werden die Aufgaben, die bislang in England und Wales auf örtlicher Ebene der *Training Agency* übertragen waren,

1. The Employment Service (ES)

The Employment Service has a network of 1,800 local offices, 59 area offices and nine regional offices. Its 1,032 jobcentres provide help for people seeking a job, either directly via employers' vacancies or by assistance available through other government initiatives.

The Employment Service now delivers major programmes of in-depth interviewing and counselling designed to assist unemployed people find routes back into work. Restart, claimant advisers and new client advisers are vital elements in this process, together with jobclubs which provide guidance to long-term unemployed and disadvantaged people on how to apply for the oppurtunities available to them (→ *Jugendarbeitslosigkeit*, UK).

2. Benefits

Local offices of the Employment Service are responsible for the payment of unemployment benefits to those entitled to them, acting as an agent for the Department of Social Security.

Financial benefits for the unemployed under the UK social security system fall into two categories: those paid from the National Insurance Fund which consists of contributions from employed people and their employers, self-employed people and the Government, and those financed from general taxation revenue. Under the former a previous contributor may claim unemployment benefit for up to one year. Benefits under the latter (paid by local offices of the Department of Social Security) can be claimed by any person of the age 16 and over who is not in full-time employment under such headings as income support and family credit.

The Employment Service is working progressively to bring jobcentres and unemployment benefit offices together under one roof to provide a one-stop employment service to help people back to work.

3. Training and Enterprise Councils (TECs)

Under the general supervision of the Training, Education and Enterprise Directorate the functions previously performed by the Training Agency at local level in England and Wales are now carried out by Training and Enterprise Councils at local level, and at regional and national level by the Employment Department itself. In Scotland, the functions of the Training Agency were transferred to the Scottish Enterprise or the Highlands and Islands Enterprise Board.

A national network of approximately 100 TECs and LECs (Scotland) is being established. TECs cover an average working population of 250,000.

Every TEC is an independent legal entity. They operate under a performance contract with the Employment Department to manage the delivery of training activities and help for small businesses in their locality. Their main tasks are:

jetzt von den *Training and Enterprise Councils* wahrgenommen. Auf regionaler und nationaler Ebene übernimmt sie das Arbeitsministerium selbst. In Schottland gingen die Verantwortlichkeiten der *Training Agency* auf das *Scottish Enterprise* oder das *Highlands and Islands Enterprise Board* über.

Gegenwärtig wird ein Netz von etwa 100 TECs und LECs (Schottland) eingerichtet. Die TECs betreuen durchschnittlich 250.000 Erwerbstätige.

Jeder TEC ist eine rechtlich unabhängige Einheit. Die TECs arbeiten mit dem Arbeitsministerium auf der Basis eines Leistungsvertrages zusammen, im Rahmen dessen sie auf örtlicher Ebene Ausbildungs- und Hilfsangebote für kleine Firmen bereitstellen. Ihr Aufgabenbereich umfaßt:

— die Förderung einer effektiveren Ausbildung durch Arbeitgeber und Einzelpersonen in ihrem Bereich unter Einbeziehung öffentlicher Programme und privater Mittel;
— die Durchführung und Fortentwicklung der berufsbildenden Maßnahmen des *Youth Training* (→ *Jugendarbeitslosigkeit,* VK);
— die Durchführung und Fortentwicklung von berufsqualifizierenden Beschäftigungsmaßnahmen für Arbeitslose *(Employment Training);*
— die Bereitstellung von praktischen Hilfen und Anschubförderung für Arbeitgeber, insbesondere für kleine Betriebe, über andere Programme, z.B. das *Enterprise Allowance Scheme.*

Bundesjugendkuratorium (n)

D
Gemäß Art. 1 § 83 Abs. 2 des Kinder- und Jugendhilfegesetzes wurde zur Beratung der Bundesregierung in grundsätzlichen Fragen der Jugendhilfe das Bundesjugendkuratorium gebildet. Dem Kuratorium gehören 20 Vertreter der wesentlichen Bereiche der Jugendhilfe an, die vom Bundesminister für Frauen und Jugend jeweils auf drei Jahre berufen werden. Das Ministerium trägt die Kosten des Bundesjugendkuratoriums und erledigt die laufenden Geschäfte.

VK
Hierzu gibt es im Vereinigten Königreich keine Entsprechung. Einen Hinweis verdient jedoch die *Parliamentary Youth Affairs Lobby,* die 1977 ins Leben gerufen wurde. Sie ist eine Partnerschaft zwischen Parlamentsabgeordneten, *Peers* (die dem Hochadel angehörenden Mitglieder des Oberhauses) und Jugendverbänden. Die Lobby will jungen Menschen helfen, die Jugend betreffende Fragen aufzugreifen, und ist bemüht, ihnen ein besseres Verständnis des parlamentarischen Systems zu vermitteln.

— to promote more effective training by employers and individuals in their area, using public programmes and private funds;
— to deliver and develop Youth Training (→ *Jugendarbeitslosigkeit, UK);*
— to deliver and develop programmes to train unemployed people for jobs (Employment Training);
— to provide practical help and give incentives to employers and, in particular, to small firms through various other programmes, e.g. the Enterprise Allowance Scheme.

Federal Advisory Committee on Youth Problems

G

The Federal Advisory Committee on Youth Problems was formed to advise the Federal Government on principal issues relating to the youth work and youth welfare services in accordance with art 1, section 83, subs. 2 of the Child and Youth Services Act. It consists of 20 representatives of the important fields of youth work and youth welfare services, who are appointed by the Federal Minister for Women and Youth, each for a period of three years. The Ministry is responsible for the running costs and the expenses of the Federal Advisory Committee on Youth Problems.

UK

There is no equivalent in the UK. Reference should be made, however, to the Parliamentary Youth Affairs Lobby which started in 1977. It is a partnership between MPs, Peers and youth organisations. The Lobby aims to help young people raise issues which concern them in Parliament and understand how the system works.

Bundesjugendplan (BJP) (m)

D

Für die Förderung der Jugendarbeit durch den Bund wurde 1950 der Bundesjugendplan geschaffen. Er ist als gesetzesfreie Fondsverwaltung das Hauptinstrument der Jugendförderung durch den Bund und ist seit seiner Verkündung ein Kernstück der Jugendpolitik in der Bundesrepublik Deutschland geworden.

Durch den Bundesjugendplan werden Bestrebungen der Jugendhilfe, vor allem aber der Jugendarbeit, angeregt und gefördert, soweit sie über die Verpflichtungen der Länder und Gremien hinausgehen.

Der Bundesjugendplan wird vom Gesetzgeber mit einem jährlichen Finanzvolumen ausgestattet (1990: 125,2 Mio. DM) und vom → *Bundesministerium für Frauen und Jugend* nach dem Subsidiaritäts- und Pluralitätsprinzip *(→ Subsidiaritätsprinzip)* auf der Grundlage der Richtlinien zum Bundesjugendplan vom 6. November 1985 verwaltet.

Die Vielfalt der Aktivitäten, die aus Mitteln des Bundesjugendplans gefördert werden, gibt ein lebendiges Bild von den Bedürfnissen und Notwendigkeiten der freien und öffentlichen Jugendhilfe, die im außerschulischen Bereich einen breiten Erziehungs- und Bildungsauftrag zu erfüllen hat. Ergänzt wird dieses Programm durch Landesjugendpläne und kommunale Jugendpläne.

VK

Es gibt zwar keine Entsprechung zum Bundesjugendplan im Vereinigten Königreich, aber die nationalen freien Träger der Jugendarbeit erhalten Zuwendungen von den zentralen Erziehungsministerien für die Unterhaltung ihrer Geschäftsstelle, für Innovationen, Modellprojekte und nationale Bauprojekte. Weiterhin fließen ihnen von anderen Ministerien Mittel für spezifische Belange der Jugendarbeit zu. So stellen z.B. das Innenministerium, das Schottische Innen- und Gesundheitsministerium, und das *North Ireland Office* Zuschüsse für die Arbeit mit jungen Straffälligen und die Freiwilligen-Aktion zur Verfügung. Das Arbeitsministerium fördert Maßnahmen für junge Arbeitslose über die *Training Agency*. Die *Cadet Forces* (Heer, Marine und Luftwaffe) erhalten Zuwendungen vom Verteidigungsministerium, und das Außenministerium bezuschußt den internationalen Jugendaustausch über das → *Youth Exchange Centre (→ Internationaler Jugendaustausch- und Besucherdienst der Bundesrepublik Deutschland (IJAB) e.V.; VK Youth Exchange Centre)*.

Weitere Förderungsmittel vergeben der *Sports Council* und der *Royal Jubilee Trust* für die freiwilligen sozialen Dienste Jugendlicher bis zum Alter von 25 Jahren. Hinzu tritt der *Prince's Trust,* der zur Unterstützung benachteiligter Jugendlicher von 14–25 Jahren eingerichtet wurde und finanzielle Hilfen für einzelne oder kleine ad hoc gebildete Gruppen bereitstellt.

Einige Kommunalbehörden stellen Mittel für Städtepartnerschaften zur Verfügung, wozu allerdings keinerlei Verpflichtung besteht.

Federal Youth Plan

G

In 1950, the Federal Youth Plan was instituted by the Federation in order to help promote youth work. It is not an Act, but a fund administered at Federal Ministry level. This fund is the central instrument for the promotion of youth by the Federation. Since its promulgation it has become the mainstay of youth policy in the Federal Republic of Germany.

Through the Federal Youth Plan incentives to develop youth work and youth welfare services are encouraged and financially supported in as much as they exceed the responsibilities of the *Länder* and local authorities.

Parliament votes a yearly budget (1990: 125.2 mill. DM) for the Federal Youth Plan, which is then administered by the Federal Ministry for Women and Youth on the basis of the principle of subsidiarity (→ *Subsidiaritätsprinzip*) and plurality according to the Directives concerning the Federal Youth Plan dated 6 November 1985.

The wide spectrum of activities grant-aided from Federal Youth Plan funds presents a vivid picture of the needs of voluntary and statutory youth work and youth welfare services, which have a comprehensive educational mission in out-of-school provision for the young. This programme is supplemented by youth plans devised by the *Länder* and local authorities.

UK

There is no parallel to the *Bundesjugendplan* in the UK, but the national voluntary youth organisations receive grants from the central education departments for headquarters expenses, for innovatory developments and experimental projects, and for national building projects. They are also assisted by other government departments for specific aspects of youth work. For example, the Home Office, the Scottish Home and Health Department and the Northern Ireland Office make funds available for work connected with young offenders and voluntary action, and the Department of Employment, through the Training Agency, for projects involving unemployed young people. Support is given to the Cadet Forces (army, navy and air force) by the Ministry of Defence, and the Foreign and Commonwealth Office, through the Youth Exchange Centre, provides grants for international youth exchange (→ *Internationaler Jugendaustausch- und Besucherdienst der Bundesrepublik Deutschland (IJAB) e.V.; UK Youth Exchange Centre*).

Other sources of financial aid include the Sports Council and the Royal Jubilee Trust, which help fund voluntary community service work by young people up to the age of 25. In addition the Prince's Trust, which was set up to help disadvantaged young people aged 14 to 25, makes grants to individuals or small ad hoc groups.

Some local authorities make funds available for twinning links, but they are under no obligation to do so.

Bundesministerium (n) für Frauen (f/pl) und Jugend (f)

D

Das Bundesministerium für Frauen und Jugend (BMFJ) hat wichtige Bereiche der Gesellschafts- und Jugendpolitik abzudecken. Innerhalb der Abteilung Kinder und Jugend, Zivildienst (→ *Wehrpflicht*) befassen sich zwei Unterabteilungen speziell mit der Kinder- und Jugendpolitik sowie der → *Jugendarbeit*. Sie sind in folgende Arbeitsbereiche aufgeteilt:

- Allgemeine Fragen der Jugendpolitik, Jugendforschung (→ *Jugendforschung*)
- Kinder- und Jugendhilferecht, Erziehungshilfen
- Jugend und Arbeit, Jugendsozialrecht, (→ *Jugendsozialarbeit*), Mädchen in der Jugendhilfe
- Kinder und Jugend im Recht, Jugendschutz (→ *Jugendschutz*)
- Allgemeine Fragen der Jugendarbeit, Bundesjugendplan (→ *Bundesjugendplan*)
- Jugendarbeit in den neuen Bundesländern
- Eingliederungsprogramme (Garantiefonds), Jugendbauprogramme, vor allem in den neuen Bundesländern
- Internationale Jugendpolitik und Jugendarbeit (→ *Internationale Jugendarbeit*)
- Allgemeine Fragen der Kindheit, Tageseinrichtungen (→ *Tageseinrichtungen für Kinder*).

Näheres über die mit Pfeil gekennzeichneten Bereiche findet sich unter den jeweiligen Stichworten.

Eingliederungsmaßnahmen sind Hilfen zur schulischen, beruflichen und gesellschaftlichen Integration junger Menschen aus den Aussiedlungsgebieten sowie anerkannter ausländischer Flüchtlinge. Hierfür besteht ein besonderer Förderungsfonds (sog. Garantiefonds).

Jugendbauprogramme des → *Bundesjugendplans* fördern die Errichtung und Einrichtung von zentralen Jugendbildungs- und Begegnungsstätten und Jugendherbergen.

VK

Die Situation im Vereinigten Königreich ist unter → *Jugendbehörden* beschrieben.

Chancengleichheit (f)

D

Chancengleichheit ist seit den 60er Jahren ein zentraler Begriff in der deutschen Bildungspolitik. Er beinhaltet die gesellschafts- und bildungspolitische Forderung, allen Kindern und Jugendlichen unabhängig von ihrer sozialen

Federal Ministry for Women and Youth

G

The Federal Ministry for Women and Youth deals with vital policies in respect of social and youth matters. Within its department of Children and Young People, Compulsory Non-military National Service (→ *Wehrpflicht)* two subdivisions are responsible for child and youth policy and youth work (→ *Jugendarbeit).* Their tasks include:

- general problems of youth policy and responsibility for youth research (→ *Jugendforschung)*
- child and youth services law, socio-educational provision for children with problems
- youth and vocational problems, socio-educational provision for young people (→ *Jugendsozialarbeit),* girls in the youth services
- legal provisions for children and young people, protection of young persons in public (→ *Jugendschutz)*
- general problems of youth work, Federal Youth Plan (→ *Bundesjugendplan)*
- youth work in the new Federal *Länder*
- integration programmes (*Garantiefonds,* see below), construction programmes for youth establishments, particularly in the new *Länder*
- international youth policy and youth work (→ *Internationale Jugendarbeit)*
- general problems of childhood, day care establishments (→ *Tageseinrichtungen für Kinder).*

Details about the areas marked with an arrow may be found under the respective headings.

Integration programmes cover educational, vocational and social schemes helping young resettlers from East European countries as well as recognised foreign refugees to get settled in the Federal Republic. This is supported from a special fund called *Garantiefonds.*

Construction programmes for youth establishments are projects which are financed from Federal Youth Plan funds (→ *Bundesjugendplan)* to build and equip central and international youth residential centres, conference centres and youth hostels.

UK

For UK situation see → *Jugendbehörden.*

Equal Opportunities

G

The provision of equal opportunities has been an essential part of German educational policy. The aim is to provide for all children and young people the same educational opportunities irrespective of social and/or ethnic back-

und/oder ethnischen Herkunft, ihres Geschlechtes oder ihrem Wohnort gleiche Bildungschancen zu gewähren. Dahinter stand die Einsicht, daß das rigide dreigliedrige Schulsystem dazu nicht in der Lage war, da es schichtspezifisch konzipiert ist und schichtspezifisch Bildung vermittelt.

Die Forderung nach Chancengleichheit ist im Zusammenhang mit anderen Einrichtungen in Gesellschaft und Wissenschaft zu betrachten. Sie geht einher mit der Forderung nach Demokratisierung und Reformierung des Bildungssystems und korrespondiert mit den Theorien, die den Umweltfaktoren größeren Einfluß auf die Entwicklungsmöglichkeiten des Menschen zusprechen als Vererbungsfaktoren.

Der ausschlaggebende Faktor für die persönliche und berufliche Entwicklung sollte also bei der individuellen Leistungsfähigkeit des einzelnen liegen.

Da bestimmte Bevölkerungsgruppen aufgrund ihres gesellschaftlichen Status und der fehlenden finanziellen Möglichkeiten nicht in der Lage sind, die Voraussetzungen für eine adäquate Ausschöpfung der Bildungsreserven zu schaffen, wurden kompensatorische Bildungsprogramme entwickelt, die diese Mißstände ausgleichen sollen. Der ihrem Bevölkerungsanteil entsprechende Prozentsatz von Arbeiterkindern, die Abitur machen und studieren, gilt als Indikator für die Einlösung der Forderung nach Chancengleichheit.

VK
In Großbritannien ist der Grundsatz der Chancengleichheit in der Jugendarbeit und in der Schule von großer Bedeutung. Nach dem Thompson-Bericht (1982) sollen Mädchen und Jungen völlig gleich behandelt werden (→ *Mädchenarbeit*). Außerdem wird in der Jugendarbeit kein Unterschied zwischen schwarzen und weißen Jugendlichen gemacht. Die Integration von Weißen und jungen Mitgliedern ethnischer Minderheiten ist einer der Schwerpunkte. Weiterhin bemüht man sich zunehmend, Behinderte und Nicht-Behinderte zu integrieren. Angesichts der besonderen Situation in Nordirland hat es sich der *youth service* dort zur Aufgabe gemacht, katholische und protestantische Jugendliche zusammenzuführen.

Deutscher Jugendhilfetag (m)

D
Alle vier Jahre veranstaltet die Arbeitsgemeinschaft für Jugendhilfe, ein bundeszentraler Zusammenschluß öffentlicher und freier Träger der Jugendhilfe, zur Förderung des fachlichen Gesprächs und der Fortbildung den Deutschen Jugendhilfetag (DJHT). Diese Veranstaltung richtet sich sowohl an die Vertreter der Träger der Jugendhilfe als auch an Öffentlichkeit und Politik. Unter einem zentralen Thema werden aktuelle Fragen und Probleme der jungen Generation sowie der Jugendhilfe diskutiert und Lösungsansätze für vorhandene Probleme entwickelt. In der Regel werden die Jugendhilfetage durch eine Publikation dokumentiert.

ground, sex or place of residence. This concept is based on the discovery that the rigid tripartite system of education is not in a position to secure equal opportunities as it is founded within social stratification.

The demand for equal opportunities must be seen in relation to other scientific and social institutions. It goes hand in hand with the demand to democratize and reform the educational system, and reflects the theory that environmental factors have a stronger influence on human development than heredity.

Thus, the decisive factor for personal and vocational or professional development should be the individual's own potential.

As certain groups of the population, because of their lack of social status and financial means, are unable to make maximum use of educational opportunities, supplementary educational programmes have been set up to compensate for this unsatisfactory state of affairs. The percentage of working-class children obtaining a university entrance qualification and receiving a university level education is considered to be an indicator of the extent to which the demand for equal opportunities is met.

UK

The principle of equal opportunities is very important in youth work and schools in Britain. Following the Thompson Report (1982) boys and girls are to be given completely equal treatment (→ *Mädchenarbeit*). Similarly, in the youth service there is no discrimination between black and white youths. The emphasis is on integrating white and ethnic young people. Likewise, efforts are increasingly being made to integrate the handicapped and able-bodied. In Northern Ireland there is a special situation and the youth service aims to involve both Catholic and Protestant young people jointly.

National Conference for Child and Youth Welfare

G

Every four years the Standing Conference of Youth Work and Youth Welfare Services, a federation of national central voluntary and statutory bodies concerned with youth work and youth welfare services, organises a national conference for child and youth welfare matters the aim of which is to provide a platform for an exchange of opinions among specialists and to promote further training. The Conference is aimed at representatives of the bodies concerned with youth work and youth welfare services, the general public and politicians. Each event is placed under a central subject in connection with which present-day questions and problems relating to the younger generation as well as youth

VK

Keine Entsprechung im VK

Deutsch-Französisches Jugendwerk (DFJW) (n)

D

Zwischenstaatliche, autonome Organisation mit eigener Rechtspersönlichkeit, gegründet 1963 durch die Regierungen der Bundesrepublik Deutschland und Frankreichs, um die Begegnung und die Zusammenarbeit von Jugendlichen und Verantwortlichen der Jugendarbeit beider Länder im Rahmen der beruflichen, schulischen und außerschulischen Bildung anzuregen und zu fördern.

Jährlich unterstützt das DFJW ca. 5000 Programme mit über 140.000 Teilnehmern. Bestimmte Programme können für Jugendliche aus anderen Ländern geöffnet werden. Sitz des Generalsekretariats ist Bad Honnef; ein Büro befindet sich in Paris.

VK

Keine Entsprechung im VK

Drogenmißbrauch (m)

D

Als Droge werden alle Stoffe bezeichnet, die auf das zentrale Nervensystem des Menschen einwirken. Dabei handelt es sich zum Teil um legale Drogen wie Alkohol und Nikotin. Alkohol ist in der Bundesrepublik Deutschland das am weitesten verbreitete Rauschmittel, auch unter Jugendlichen, und dasjenige, das die meisten Probleme verursacht. Der Genuß und Erwerb von Alkohol und Tabak wird für Jugendliche teilweise durch das Gesetz eingeschränkt (→ *Jugendgesetze).*

Legal ist auch der Erwerb chemischer Lösungsmittel, nur das Schnüffeln dieser Mittel stellt einen Mißbrauch dar. Schnüffler findet man hauptsächlich in der Altersgruppe der 12- bis 15jährigen; die empirischen Daten sind allerdings lückenhaft.

Nach einem leichten Rückgang zu Beginn der 80er Jahre ist der Konsum illegaler Drogen in der Bundesrepublik Deutschland seit 1982 wieder angestiegen, gerade auch unter Jugendlichen. Außergewöhnlich stark zugenommen hat der Konsum synthetischer Rauschgifte wie Amphetamine.

Nach den Strafbestimmungen des Betäubungsmittelgesetzes (BtMG) vom 1.1.1982 müssen Personen, die Betäubungsmittel wie Haschisch, Marihuana,

work and youth welfare services are discussed. Its aim is to provide solutions for current problems. Conference reports are compiled and published.

UK
No UK equivalent

Franco-German Youth Office (OFAJ)

G

This is an intergovernmental independent organisation with a special legal status, founded in 1963 by the Governments of the Federal Republic of Germany and France to stimulate and promote the contact and cooperation of young people and those responsible for youth work in the two countries within the framework of both formal and out-of-school education, and vocational training.

Every year the Franco-German Youth Office subsidizes approximately 5,000 programmes with over 140,000 participants. Certain programmes may be available to young people from other countries. The head office is in Bad Honnef with a sub-office in Paris.

UK
No UK equivalent

Drug Misuse

G

Drugs are substances which influence the central nervous system of a person. Some drugs like alcohol and tobacco are legal drugs. In the Federal Republic of Germany, alcohol is the most common stimulant, also amongst young people, and the one that causes the most problems. The consumption and purchase of alcohol and tobacco by young people is partly restricted by law (→ *Jugendgesetze).*

The purchase of chemical solvents is legal, but sniffing of such solvents is considered to be a misuse. Sniffing is mainly common in the 12—15 age range, but factual data is scarce.

Following a slight decrease in the early 80s the consumption of illegal drugs has again been growing since 1983, especially among young people. The increase in the misuse of synthetic drugs such as amphetamines is marked.

By the Narcotic Drugs Act dated 1 January 1982 persons who, without authorization, possess, cultivate, manufacture, traffic, import, export, give away or otherwise put into circulation, purchase or otherwise obtain narcotic drugs such as hashish, marihuana, LSD, heroin, cocaine or others, may be fined or

LSD, Heroin, Kokain, usw. ohne Erlaubnis besitzen, anbauen, herstellen, mit
ihnen Handel treiben, sie einführen, ausführen, abgeben oder in den Verkehr
bringen, erwerben oder sich in sonstiger Weise verschaffen, mit einer Geldstrafe oder einer Freiheitsstrafe bis zu vier Jahren, in besonders schwerwiegenden Fällen bis zu 15 Jahren rechnen.

Zur Bekämpfung des Alkohol- und Drogenmißbrauchs hat die Bundesregierung besondere Aktionsprogramme verabschiedet. Hier wird der gesundheitlichen Aufklärung und der vorbeugenden Drogenerziehung besonderer Wert
zugemessen. Verantwortlich für die Drogenprävention sollten sich alle füh-
len, die beruflich oder ehrenamtlich in der Jugendarbeit und der Familienbildung tätig sind. Drogenprävention sollte als Bestandteil der gesamten Erziehung aufgefaßt werden.

Ein wichtige Neuerung im BtMG sind die Bestimmungen für drogenabhängige Straftäter. Sie eröffnen die Möglichkeit einer Zurückstellung der Strafvoll-
streckung, bzw. einer Einstellung eines Ermittlungs- oder Strafverfahrens,
wenn sich der Angeklagte bereits in Therapie befindet oder eine Therapie aufnehmen möchte.

VK

Im VK wächst der Drogenmißbrauch. Immer mehr Jugendliche nehmen Drogen, besonders Heroin.

Es ist ein großes soziales Anliegen, dem Drogenmißbrauch unter Jugendlichen vorzubeugen. Die Träger der Jugendhilfe können hier grundlegende Informationen über die Gefahren des Drogenmißbrauchs sowie Stellen, die Hilfe anbieten, vermitteln.

Das Gesetz gegen den Drogenmißbrauch von 1971 enthält Bestimmungen
über die Herstellung und Verteilung legaler Drogen für den medizinischen
Gebrauch sowie über Straftaten im Hinblick auf die illegale Herstellung, Verteilung und den Besitz von Drogen.

Die Höchststrafen sind hart. Ersttäter, die des Besitzes einer auch noch so kleinen Menge von Drogen überführt werden, kommen oft mit einer Geldstrafe
davon, die allerdings ins Strafregister eingetragen wird. Regeltäter müssen mit
Freiheitsstrafen rechnen. Für Rauschgifthändler und -schmuggler werden fast
ausschließlich Freiheitsstrafen verhängt, wobei die Höchststrafe für Drogen-
handel lebenslänglicher Freiheitsentzug sowie Beschlagnahme und Einzug
von Vermögenswerten ist *(Drug Trafficking Offences Act, 1987)*.

In England und Wales werden strafbare Handlungen Jugendlicher zwischen
10 und 16 Jahren vor den Jugendgerichten verhandelt, die die Eltern zu einer
Geldstrafe verurteilen oder den Jugendlichen in ein Erziehungsheim einwei-
sen können.

Das Gesetz gegen den Drogenmißbrauch enthält außerdem Bestimmungen
über strafbare Handlungen von Personen, die für eine Schule oder ein Ju-

sentenced to imprisonment for up to four years or in more serious cases up to 15 years.

In order to combat the abuse of alcohol and drugs, the Federal Government has initiated special programmes in which the emphasis is on health and preventive drug education. Professionals and volunteers working with young people and their families should realise their responsibility for preventing drug misuse and should consider drug education an integral part of education.

An important amendment to the Narcotic Drugs Act allows for a sentence to be suspended or even the case to be dismissed where an offender is currently undergoing treatment or is shown to intend to do so.

UK

Drug misuse in the UK is growing. More and more young people are using drugs, particularly heroin.

Preventing drug misuse by the young is of broad social concern. The youth service agencies are in a position to provide basic information about the dangers of drug misuse and where to go for help.

The Misuse of Drugs Act 1971 governs the manufacture and supply of controlled drugs for legitimate medical use. It also defines offences in respect of the unlawful manufacture, supply and possession of drugs.

Maximum sentences are severe. First offenders, convicted of the possession of a small quantity of drugs may only be fined, but they would still have a criminal record. Regular offenders might well be imprisoned. Those selling drugs and drug smugglers are almost without exception given sentences of imprisonment – the maximum penalty for trafficking offences being a life sentence and forfeiture of property (Drug Trafficking Offences Act 1987).

In England and Wales 10 to 16 year-olds are usually dealt with by a Juvenile Court which has power to fine parents or to make the offender attend an institution designed to keep young people »in detention« but out of prison.

The Misuse of Drugs Act also defines offences which can be committed by those responsible for schools and youth clubs. Knowingly permitting the smoking of cannabis or opium on the premises for which one is responsible is also an offence.

gendzentrum verantwortlich sind. Wer wissentlich das Rauchen von Cannabis oder Opium in seinem Zuständigkeitsbereich zuläßt, macht sich strafbar.

Duke of Edinburgh's Award Scheme, The

VK

Ursprünglich vom Herzog von Edinburgh im Jahre 1956 mit der Absicht gegründet, die offenbar wenig zielgerichteten Energien junger Männer aller sozialer Schichten auf sinnvolle Tätigkeiten zu lenken, ist der *Award* kein Club oder Verband, sondern ein Programm freiwilliger Freizeitaktivitäten, dessen Anforderungen auf die Leistungsfähigkeit des einzelnen Teilnehmers abgestimmt sind. Es dauerte nicht lange, bis auch auf die spezifischen Interessen und Fähigkeiten von Mädchen zugeschnittene Aktivitäten entwickelt wurden. Mit der Zeit jedoch und im Zuge des Wandels sozialer Wertvorstellungen wurde das Programm vereinheitlicht, so daß heute die gleichen Bedingungen für junge Menschen beiderlei Geschlechts zwischen 14 und 25 Jahren gelten.

Der *Award* basiert auf den pädagogischen Grundsätzen Kurt Hahns, der im Jahre 1938 Deutschland verließ und in Schottland die *Gordonstoun School* gründete. Jeder Jugendliche, der am Programm des *Award* teilnimmt, um eine bronzene, silberne oder goldene Auszeichnung zu erwerben, muß eine Aufgabe in den vier Bereichen *Service* (Dienste für die Gemeinschaft), *Expedition* (Expeditionen nach den Grundsätzen der → *Erlebnispädagogik), Skills* (Entwicklung persönlicher Fähigkeiten) und *Physical Recreation* (Sport) erfüllen. Neben der Abstimmung der Projekte auf die Leistungsfähigkeit des einzelnen ist der Zeitraum, der für jede einzelne Aufgabe zur Verfügung steht, je nach Anforderungsstufe sorgfältig festgelegt. Bewerber um die goldene Auszeichnung müssen sich bei einem fünftägigen Projekt bewähren, das auch Gemeinschaftsunterbringung mit den ihnen unbekannten Mitbewerbern vorsieht. Prinz Phillip konzipierte das Programm ursprünglich für fünf Jahre. Heute geht der *Award* in sein fünftes Jahrzehnt.

Keine deutsche Entsprechung

Elterliche Sorge (f)

D

Ehe und Familie, insbesondere das Elternrecht, stehen unter dem besonderen Schutz des Staates (Art. 6 GG).

Gesetzgebung und Rechtsanwendung müssen dem entsprechen. Dem Elternrecht ist als einzigem Grundrecht eine Verpflichtung beigegeben. Der Staat hat in diesem Bereich nur ein „Wächteramt", das in das Grundrecht nur eingreifen darf, wenn Kinder zu verwahrlosen drohen.

The Duke of Edinburgh's Award Scheme

UK

Founded in 1956 by the Duke of Edinburgh originally as a channel for the seemingly aimless energies of adolescent and young adult males of all social levels, the Award is not a club or association but a voluntary programme of activities whose standards are set to match the level of achievement of the individual participant. It was not long before specifically female activities were developed and the Award was opened to young women. In time, however, and with changing social values, the differences were removed and now one set of conditions applies equally to both male and female participants aged between 14 and 25.

Based on the educational principles of Kurt Hahn who moved from Germany to Scotland in 1938 and there founded Gordonstoun School, every young person participating in the Award, whether at Bronze, Silver or Gold level, has to complete an activity in each of the four sections Service, Expedition, Skill and Physical Recreation. Standards are set to match the ability of the participants, but the duration for which each activity has to be followed is carefully specified according to the level of participation. At Gold level the participant also has to complete a five day residential period with unfamiliar companions. Originally conceived by Prince Phillip as serving a useful purpose for about five years, the Award is now in its fourth decade.

No German equivalent

Parental Rights and Duties

G

Marriage and the family, in particular parental rights, are placed under the special protection of the State (Section 6, Basic Law).

Legislation and its implementation must make allowance for this. Parental rights are the only constitutional rights which also carry a legal responsibility. The State's function here is merely that of a "watchdog" and it may only interfere when children are at risk of destitution.

Die elterliche Sorge für einen Minderjährigen (→ *Tabelle Altersgrenzen*) umfaßt die Personensorge und die Vermögenssorge sowie das Recht zur Vertretung.

Sie steht Vater und Mutter gemeinsam zu. Bei Nichteinigung weist das Vormundschaftsgericht auf Antrag einem der beiden die Entscheidungsbefugnis zu.

Zur Personensorge gehören die Sorge für das leibliche Wohl (Unterbringung, Verpflegung, Bekleidung, Gesundheit), die Erziehung, die Aufsicht, das Aufenthaltsbestimmungsrecht und die Regelung des Umgangs. − Die Vermögenssorge umfaßt die (mündelsichere) Vermögensverwaltung und nur noch in sehr beschränktem Umfang ein Nutzungsrecht.

Bei Ehescheidung bestimmt das Familiengericht, welchem Elternteil die elterliche Sorge zusteht; nur ausnahmsweise sollen Personen- und Vermögenssorge geteilt werden. Nach einer Entscheidung des Bundesverfassungsgerichtes kann die elterliche Sorge auch beiden Eltern belassen werden.

Die elterliche Sorge über ein nichteheliches Kind hat die Mutter; das Jugendamt ist Pfleger (→ *Pflegschaft*), insbesondere für die Regelung des Verhältnisses zum Vater. Ist die Mutter minderjährig, so hat sie nur die Personensorge. Auf Antrag der volljährigen Mutter kann auch die Pflegschaft aufgehoben werden.

Einige wenige Rechtsakte können auch die Inhaber der elterlichen Sorge nur mit Genehmigung des Vormundschaftsgerichts vornehmen. Dieses schreitet u.a. ein, wenn das Wohl des Kindes gefährdet ist (→ *Jugendhilfe*).

VK

Der Begriff „elterliche Sorge" wird im *Children Act 1975* als die Rechte und Pflichten definiert, die die Mutter und der Vater nach dem Gesetz in bezug auf ein eheliches Kind und sein Vermögen besitzen. Der Umfang der elterlichen Sorge wird jedoch zum größten Teil durch *common law* (→ *Rechtsinstrumente*, VK) und nicht durch Gesetz bestimmt. Die Eltern sind gesetzlich verpflichtet, im Rahmen ihrer Möglichkeiten für das leibliche Wohl (Ernährung, Kleidung, usw.) ihrer Kinder angemessen zu sorgen.

Mutter und Vater eines ehelichen Kindes stehen die gleichen Rechte und Pflichten zu, und jeder kann diese Rechte ohne den anderen ausüben, es sei denn, es wurde gerichtlich anläßlich der Eheschließung der Eltern anders verfügt. In diesem Fall überträgt der Richter in der Regel *custody* (das Sorgerecht) sowie *care and control* (Recht auf Betreuung und Aufsicht) für die Kinder einem Elternteil. *Custody* umfaßt das Recht, langfristig wirksame Entschei-

Parental rights and duties towards a minor (→ *Tabelle Altersgrenzen)*, comprise the care and custody of a child, the statutory duty to care for the minor's property, and the right to act in lieu of the child.

Parental rights and duties are equally vested in the father and the mother. In cases of disagreement, the guardianship court, upon submission of an apllication, assigns the authority to make decisions for and on behalf of the child to one of them.

The care and custody of a child encompass the care for the child's physical well-being, which includes the duty to house, feed, clothe the child and provide for his/her health, raising and educating the child, supervising him/her, and the right to decide where the child is to live and with whom he/she may associate. The statutory duty to care for a minor's property means that a child's possessions must be safely administered and the right of usufruct is strictly limited.

Following a divorce the family court decides which parent has custodial rights. Only in exceptional cases may care and custody and the statutory duty to care for the child's property be divided. According to a ruling of the Federal Constitutional Court it is also possible to leave parental rights and duties vested in both parents.

Parental rights and duties towards an illegitimate child are normally attributed to the mother. The youth office acts as "curator" (→ *Pflegschaft)*, particularly where the relationship with the father is concerned. If the mother is a minor, she will only be given the right of care and custody. On application, the youth office's curatorship may be annulled.

There is a small number of legal transactions in which those exercising parental rights and duties may engage only upon authorization by the guardianship court. Amongst other things, the latter takes action when the child is at risk (→ *Jugendhilfe)*.

UK

The term "parental rights and duties" is defined in the Children Act 1975 as all the rights and duties which by law the mother and father have in relation to a legitimate child and his property, but the scope of parental rights and duties is determined for the most part by the common law and not by statute. Parents have a legal obligation to feed, clothe, and provide properly for their children according to their means.

The mother and father of a legitimate child have equal rights and duties with respect to the child and either parent can exercise the rights without the other, unless a different arrangement is made by the court, for example on the parents' divorce. In this case, the judge normally grants custody and "care and control" of the children to one parent. "Custody" means the right to take long-term decisions affecting their lives (such as the manner and style of their children's lives, including upbringing, education, residence, dress, religion and all

dungen für das Leben der Kinder zu treffen (Lebenszuschnitt und Lebensstil einschließlich Erziehung und Bildung, Aufenthaltsbestimmung, Kleidung, Religion und Verhalten). *Care and control* bedeutet die tägliche Verantwortung für ihre Betreuung. Der Richter kann beiden Eltern das Sorgerecht gemeinsam zusprechen und *care and control* nur einem Elternteil.

Eltern haben kein Recht auf das Einkommen aus dem Grundbesitz eines Kindes. Es steht ihnen auch nicht zu, das persönliche Vermögen des Kindes für eigene Zwecke zu verwenden. Sie können jedoch als sein Vormund oder Bevollmächtigter auftreten. Solange Minderjährige bei ihren Eltern leben und von ihnen unterhalten werden, haben die Eltern Anspruch auf das Arbeitseinkommen ihrer Kinder.

Zur Behandlung der elterlichen Sorge im Strafrecht → *Jugendstrafrecht, Maßnahmen des,* VK.

Engagement (n), soziales

D

Das soziale Engagement auf örtlicher, nationaler und internationaler Ebene entwickelt und stärkt das demokratische Verantwortungsbewußtsein junger Menschen.

Soziales Engagement ist eine praktische Form sozialen Lebens. Die breite Skala der Möglichkeiten des sozialen Engagements umfaßt u.a. die freiwilligen sozialen Dienste, den diakonischen Jugendeinsatz, Maßnahmen der Jugendarbeit in Entwicklungsländern und die Mitgliedschaft in Jugendverbänden, deren konkrete Aufgabe der Dienst an der Gemeinschaft ist (z.B. Jugendfeuerwehr, Samariterjugend, Jugendrotkreuz, Jugendabteilungen von Lebensrettungsgesellschaften und Deutscher Entwicklungsdienst/DED).

VK

Gilt grundsätzlich für beide Länder

Erlebnispädagogik (f)

D

Erziehungskonzept, das auf Kurt Hahn zurückgeht. Neben der Erfahrung mit hohen körperlichen, geistigen und persönlichen Anforderungen will es auch sittliche Normen wie Selbstdisziplin, Eigeninitiative und Sorgfalt vermitteln.

Die Erlebnispädagogik will ein Gegengewicht gegen einseitige kognitive Lernprozesse in Schule und Beruf bilden. Sie benutzt Formen der Selbstorganisation, der Mitgestaltung und Mitverantwortung sowie bewußt herbeigeführte Situationen, in denen junge Menschen Wissen und Entscheidungen in Handeln umsetzen und authentische Erfahrungen sammeln können.

kinds of behaviour). "Care and control" means the day-to-day responsibility of looking after them. The judge may grant joint custody to both parents and care and control to one.

A parent has no right to the income from a child's real estate or to deal with the child's personal property for his own ends but can act as the guardian or agent of the child. While infant children live with their parents and are maintained by them the parents are entitled to the earnings of their children's labour.

For the treatment of parental rights under penal law → *Jugendstrafrecht, Maß-nahmen des,* UK.

Community Involvement

G

Involvement in the community at local, national, and international levels develops and strengthens young persons' sense of democratic responsibility.

It is a practical form of social learning which includes such things as voluntary social service, church voluntary community service, work in the developing countries, and membership of youth organisations directly involved in service to the community (e.g. Community Service Volunteers, Royal Life Saving Society, Voluntary Service Overseas).

UK

Principle applies to both countries

Adventure/Outdoor Pursuits

G

Erlebnispädagogik (adventure/outdoor pursuits) comprises an educational concept which goes back to Kurt Hahn. Its objective is to unite physical, intellectual and personal challenges with ethical norms such as self-discipline, personal initiative and thoroughness.

Erlebnispädagogik is intended to counterbalance one-sided cognitive learning processes at school and at work. It uses the techniques of self-organisation, participation and joint responsibility combined with planned situations in which young people may translate their knowledge and decisions into action and gain authentic experience.

Aus der Erlebnispädagogik abgeleitete Arbeitsformen liegen den Einrichtungen bestimmter Träger wie Kurzschulen (entsprechen etwa dem *Outward Bound Trust)*, den Jugendherbergen und Sportorganisationen zugrunde. Zahlreiche Aktivitäten der außerschulischen → *Jugendarbeit* (Wanderfahrten, Lager, Kanusport, Kletter- und Orientierungstouren, Wanderungen, Abenteuerfahrten, Stadtrallyes, Überlebenstraining) basieren ebenfalls auf diesem Konzept.

VK
Die im Vereinigten Königreich bestehenden *outdoor pursuits centres* arbeiten mit einer vergleichbaren Zielsetzung. Sie dienen der Erweiterung des Horizontes und bieten in Verbindung mit Übernachtungskapazitäten jungen Menschen eine Möglichkeit, ihre persönlichen und sozialen Fähigkeiten zu erforschen. Die Teilnahme an Sportarten wie Kanufahrten, Segeln, Abseilen, Skilaufen, Klettern, Zelten, Bergwandern als eigene Aktivität oder in Form von Expeditionen in Verbindung mit der Benutzung von Wanderkarten und dem Zubereiten der eigenen Mahlzeiten stellt vielfältige Anforderungen an Selbstvertrauen, Selbstdisziplin und Eigeninitiative.

Das *outdoor pursuits centre* vereinigt diese Elemente unter einem Dach. Die Einrichtungen werden von zahlreichen kommunalen Erziehungsbehörden oder freien Trägern wie der *Youth Hostel Association,* dem *Outward Bound Trust,* dem *Ocean Youth Club,* der *Sail Training Association* sowie den Jugendverbänden unterhalten. Sie stehen Schulen, Jugendclubs, freien Trägern, der Industrie und ganz allgemein jeder Organisation offen, die bestrebt ist, die Lebensqualität junger Menschen zu verbessern.

Erzieher (m)/Erzieherin (f)

D
Im weitesten Sinne sind Erzieher alle an der Erziehung junger Menschen beteiligten Personen wie Eltern, Lehrer, Mitarbeiter der Jugendarbeit, usw.

In der Bundesrepublik Deutschland gibt es einen eigenen Ausbildungslehrgang für den staatlich anerkannten Erzieher. Die Ausbildung an der Fachschule für Sozialpädagogik *(→ Berufsbildung; → Sozialarbeit/Sozialpädagogik)* dauert drei Jahre, in die eine einjährige, überwiegend fachpraktische Ausbildung (Berufspraktikum) einbezogen ist. Zugangsvoraussetzungen für die Ausbildung sind ein mittlerer Bildungsabschluß und eine abgeschlossene Berufsausbildung von mindestens zweijähriger Dauer, bzw. eine mindestens einjährige einschlägige praktische Tätigkeit. Tätigkeitsfelder sind u.a. Gruppenerziehung in Kinderheimen und Anleitung von Jugendlichen in Häusern der offenen Tür (Jugendarbeiter), Freizeiterziehung in Heimen aller Art, Kindertagesstätten (Kindergärtner/-in, Hortner/-in), Betreuung von erziehungsschwierigen Kindern (Heimerzieher).

Approaches derived from *Erlebnispädagogik* are used at the establishments run by certain organisations such as the *Kurzschulen* (similar to the Outward Bound Trust), the German Youth Hostel Association and sports organisations. A wide range of activities provided in out-of-school youth work (→ *Jugendarbeit)* such as hiking tours, camps, canoeing, rock climbing and orienteering, walks, adventure trips, city rallyes and survival training are also based on this concept.

UK
The outdoor pursuits centres existing in the UK have a comparable objective. As well as being a means of broadening horizons and providing opportunities for adventure outdoor pursuits, when combined with a residential element they provide the possibility for young people to extend and explore their own personal and social skills. Participation in such activities as canoeing, sailing, abseiling, ski-ing, rock climbing, camping, mountain walking in their own right or combined with mapreading and cookery in the form of expeditions provides a variety of challenges to self-reliance, self-discipline and initiative.

These elements, brought together under one roof in the form of the outdoor pursuits centre, are run by many local education authorities as well as such organisations as the Youth Hostel Association, the Outward Bound Trust, the Ocean Youth Club, the Sail Training Association and the voluntary youth organisations. The centres are used by schools, youth clubs, voluntary organisations, industry and, in fact, by any organisation that seeks to improve the quality of the lives of young people.

≠
(qualified youth or child care worker)
G
In the widest sense of the term, *Erzieher* are all those involved in bringing up and educating young people, e.g. parents, teachers, youth workers, etc.

In the Federal Republic of Germany, there is a separate training course for the *Erzieher,* with state recognition. This three-year training course, provided by the technical school for *Sozialpädagogik (→ Berufsbildung; → Sozialarbeit/ Sozialpädagogik),* includes a one-year full-time work placement. The entrance qualification for this type of training is a medium-level certificate of secondary education and the completion of a vocational training course of at least two years duration or an appropriate practical occupation of at least one year. *Erzieher* may work in the following areas of activity: group education in children's homes, leadership of young people in open-door youth centres (youth workers), education for leisure in all kinds of homes, day care centres for children (nursery school teacher/qualified child care worker in day centres), and care of maladjusted children (residential child care worker).

VK

Im Vereinigten Königreich bezeichnet der Begriff *youth educator* im weitesten Sinne eine Person, deren Aufgabe die Erziehung von Kindern und Jugendlichen ist. Eine anerkannte Entsprechung zum Berufsbild des deutschen „Erziehers" gibt es nicht. In England wird eine vergleichbare Tätigkeit zum Beispiel von Lehrern, Fachkräften der Jugendarbeit, der britischen Ausprägung des Sozialarbeiters, Kindergärtnerinnen und Leiter(n)/-innen von Spielgruppen ausgeübt. Die Ausbildungsgänge für diese Berufe werden in den Erklärungen der britischen Entsprechungen zum → *Sozialarbeiter/Sozialpädagogen* sowie unter → *Mitarbeiter/-innen der Jugendhilfe* dargestellt.

Lehrer sind in Grundschulen und weiterführenden Schulen, Sonderschulen für geistig und körperlich Behinderte sowie Heimen für schwererziehbare Kinder tätig.

Social worker sind überwiegend in den Sozialämtern der Kommunalbehörden, in der Bewährungshilfe, im Schulsozialdienst oder bei freien Trägern beschäftigt.

Kindergärtnerinnen und Leiter/-innen von Spielgruppen arbeiten hauptsächlich bei privaten Trägern, bei deren Vorschulangeboten für Drei- und Vierjährige die Mitwirkung der Eltern stark ausgeprägt ist.

Anstellungsträger der Fachkräfte der Jugendarbeit sind die Kommunalbehörden. Ihr Wirkungsfeld sind Jugendclubs oder die mobile Jugendarbeit. Die Kommunalbehörden legen meist als Richtlinien für die Mitarbeiter die allgemeinen Erziehungsziele der Jugendarbeit fest. In der Praxis der Jugendclubs wenden die Jugendarbeiter je nach Fachausbildung jedoch ihre eigenen sozialpädagogischen Methoden an.

Fachausschüsse (m/pl), gemischte

D

Regierungsabsprachen über den Jugendaustausch bestehen zur Zeit mit Ägypten, Belgien, Finnland, Griechenland, Großbritannien, Israel, Italien, Japan, Marokko, den Niederlanden, Polen, Portugal, der Sowjetunion, Spanien, der Tschechoslowakei, Tunesien, Ungarn und den Vereinigten Staaten von Amerika. Mit der Mehrzahl dieser Staaten sind gemischte Fachausschüsse bzw. Fachgespräche für den Jugendaustausch eingerichtet worden, um den bilateralen Jugendaustausch durch gezielte Programme zu qualifizieren, neue Impulse zu geben und Schwerpunkte zu setzen. Von deutscher Seite nehmen an den Fachausschußsitzungen, die in Abständen von einem bis zwei Jahren stattfinden, Vertreter des Bundesministeriums für Frauen und Jugend, der obersten Landesjugendbehörden, der Jugendverbände und des → *IJAB* teil.

VK

Auch das Vereinigte Königreich hat Regierungsabsprachen über den Jugendaustausch getroffen. Es bestehen jedoch nur drei gemische Fachausschüsse

UK

In the UK, a "youth educator" in the widest sense of the term is a person responsible for bringing up and educating children and young people. No one recognised profession parallels the German *Erzieher*. In England, for example,
equivalent work is done by teachers, youth workers, social workers, nursery
teachers and play-school leaders. Training programmes for these professions
are explained in the UK parts of the German headings → *Sozialarbeiter/Sozial-
pädagoge* and → *Mitarbeiter/-innen der Jugendhilfe*.

Teachers work in primary and secondary schools, special schools for the mentally and physically handicapped, and residential schools for the severely mal-
adjusted.

Social workers are mainly employed by local authorities' social services departments. Others work in the probation service, the education welfare service or
in voluntary organisations.

Nursery teachers and play-school leaders work chiefly in the non-statutory sector with high parent involvement in providing pre-school activities for children
who are three and four years old.

Youth workers are employed by local authorities as club-based or outreach
workers. The local authority will have a youth work curriculum as guidelines
for its employees, but youth workers will structure their approach to the social
education of their club members through their own specialisms.

Special Committees on Youth Exchanges

G

At present, there are agreements at government level on youth exchanges with
Belgium, Czechoslovakia, Egypt, Finland, Greece, Hungary, Israel, Italy, Japan, Morocco, the Netherlands, Poland, Portugal, the Soviet Union, Spain,
Tunisia, the United Kingdom and the USA. With the majority of these countries, joint special committees on youth exchanges have been appointed or
expert meetings are held in order to improve bilateral youth exchanges by
providing appropriate programmes, offering new incentives and establishing
priorities. The special committees meet at regular intervals of one to two years.
The German delegation attending these meetings consists of representatives
of the Federal Ministry for Women and Youth, the youth authorities of the
Land governments, the youth organisations and → *IJAB*.

UK

The UK has also concluded youth exchange agreements at government
level. However, there are only three Special Committees (Federal Republic of

(Bundesrepublik Deutschland, Frankreich, Italien), deren wichtigster der deutsche ist.

An den Fachausschußsitzungen, die ein- bis zweimal jährlich stattfinden, nehmen britischerseits Vertreter des *Youth Exchange Centre* sowie Beobachter des *British Council* und des britischen Außenministeriums teil.

Familienfürsorge (f)

D

Familienfürsorge ist ein heute noch in der Jugend- und Familienhilfe verwendeter Begriff, der aber zunehmend durch die Bezeichnung „Allgemeiner Sozialdienst (ASD)" in den Behörden oder „Sozialer Dienst" bei den → *freien Wohlfahrtsverbänden* für alle personenbezogenen Dienste, die als Organisationseinheit angesehen werden, abgelöst wird.

Die Aufgaben der Sozialen Dienste umfassen die personale, soziale und wirtschaftliche Beratung sowie die Betreuung von Familien in Notlagen, in denen oft mehrere Problembereiche gleichzeitig auftreten. Durch Hilfe zur Selbsthilfe, Informationen über Hilfsangebote sowie Unterstützung bei der Bewältigung von Konflikten soll zur Vorbeugung oder Beseitigung der Probleme beigetragen werden. Diese Tätigkeit wird von → *Sozialarbeitern* oder → *Sozialpädagogen* ausgeübt.

Falls erforderlich, ersetzt der Sozialdienst auch die Familie, wenn Kinder und Jugendliche keine Eltern mehr haben oder die Familie sie nicht erziehen kann.

VK

Keine genaue britische Entsprechung

Familien- und Elternbildung (f)

D

Nach dem Kinder- und Jugendhilfegesetz *(→ Jugendgesetze)* ist die Elternbildung Aufgabe der Jugendhilfe. Elternbildung ist andererseits nicht auf die Jugendhilfe beschränkt, sondern gehört auch zur Erwachsenenbildung. Über die Ziele dieser Bildungsarbeit bestehen unterschiedliche Vorstellungen, die von der Entwicklung und Förderung der Sozialisation der Familie im Hinblick auf das Kind bis zur Beratung und Unterstützung *aller* Familienmitglieder gehen. Die Spannung spiegelt sich in der begrifflichen Vielfalt, die Arbeitsansätze wie Mütterschulung, Elternschulung, Familienerziehung, Elternarbeit und anderes einschließen. Für die Elternbildung wurden zum Teil eigene Einrichtungen geschaffen (Familienbildungsstätten, Eltern-, Mütterschulen). Zum Teil wird die Elternbildung funktional gesehen, wobei die Eltern z.B. in die

of Germany, France, Italy), of which the German one is the most important.

The committees meet at regular intervals of one or two years with representatives on the British side from the Youth Exchange Centre and observers from
the British Council and the Foreign and Commonwealth Office.

Family Welfare Work

G

This expression is still in use in youth and family welfare services. However,
the public authorities are more and more replacing it by the term "General Social Service", and the voluntary welfare organisations (→ *Wohlfahrtsverbände)*
by "Social Service". If refers to the personal social services which are seen as an
organisational unit.

The responsibilities of these services comprise personal, social as well as economic counselling and guidance for families in difficult circumstances whereby
the staff are frequently confronted with several types of problems at the same
time. Moreover, the Social Service gives incentives for self-help, provides information on available support, and aims to assist its clients in coping with conflicts. This work, for which the Social Service employs → *Sozialarbeiter* and →
Sozialpädagogen, is both preventive and remedial.

If necessary, the Social Service may also substitute the family in cases where
children and young people no longer have at least one parent or the family is
not in a position to bring them up.

UK
No exact UK equivalent

Family and Parental Counselling

G

Under the Child and Youth Services Act (→ *Jugendgesetze)* family and parental
counselling is a responisbility of the youth work and youth welfare services.
However, it is not exclusively covered by these services but also provided by
adult education establishments. There are different views on the aims of such
counselling, which range from the encouragement of the family's development as it affects the child to the counselling and support of the whole family.
This is reflected in the diversity of existing provision such as classes for mothers, classes for parents, family education, work with parents etc. In some cases,
separate establishments have been set up for parental counselling (family
counselling centres, schools for parents, schools for mothers). In other cases, a
functional approach is taken to parental counselling whereby parents are asked

Kindergartenarbeit oder Freizeitaktivitäten einbezogen werden. Dieser Arbeitsansatz ist der → *Sozialarbeit* strukturell verwandt und führt zum Konzept der Familienarbeit oder Familienbildung. Durch verstärkten Einsatz von pädagogisch geschulten Fachkräften geht die Tendenz vom schulisch orientierten Kurssystem zu zeitgemäßeren Methoden wie Gruppenarbeit, Elternbriefen und gruppentherapeutischen Elterngesprächen.

VK
Wo Angebote der Familien- und Elternbildung bestehen, sind sie bei den Sozialen Diensten des Ministeriums für Gesundheit und Soziale Sicherheit angesiedelt. Die Sozialbehörden leisten durch ihre Mitarbeiter für Soziale Arbeit praktische Hilfe und beraten Familien in besonderen Lebenslagen. So stehen bei gesundheitlicher Gefährdung oder drohender Vernachlässigung von Kindern, die außerhalb der Familie untergebracht werden müssen, oder aber für Betreuer von älteren oder sonstigen Familienmitgliedern, die eine Erholungspause benötigen, Hilfen zur Verfügung. Auch alleinerziehende Elternteile können Beratung und Unterstützung durch die Mitarbeiter der Sozialen Dienste in Anspruch nehmen. Viele Behörden leisten einen Beitrag zu den Kosten der von freien Trägern übernommenen sozialen Arbeit mit Familien (z.B. für Eheberatung).

Föderalismus (m)/Zentralstaatlichkeit (f)

D
Aufgrund des seit 1949 die Funktion einer Verfassung erfüllenden Grundgesetzes ist die Bundesrepublik Deutschland nach dem föderativen Staatsprinzip aufgebaut. Sie besteht aus den Ländern Baden-Württemberg, Bayern, Bremen, Hamburg, Hessen, Niedersachsen, Nordrhein-Westfalen, Rheinland-Pfalz, Saarland und Schleswig-Holstein sowie dem Land Berlin. Durch den Beitritt der Deutschen Demokratischen Republik wurde nach einer über 40jährigen Teilung am 3. Oktober 1990 die Einheit Deutschlands vollzogen. Mit dem Beitritt wurden die wiedererrichteten Länder Brandenburg, Mecklenburg-Vorpommern, Sachsen, Sachsen-Anhalt und Thüringen Länder der Bundesrepublik Deutschland und übernahmen, von wenigen Teilbereichen abgesehen, deren Rechtsordnung.

Die Bundesländer besitzen eine eigene Staatlichkeit und haben nicht den Charakter von Provinzen eines Einheitsstaates. Sie sind als Gliedstaaten in dem Gesamtstaat (Bund) in der Weise zusammengeschlossen, daß sowohl der Gesamtstaat als auch die Gliedstaaten Staatscharakter haben.

Die gewählte Volksvertretung des Gesamtstaates Bundesrepublik Deutschland ist der Bundestag. Der Bundestag besteht aus 662 Abgeordneten, die an Aufträge und Weisungen nicht gebunden sind. Der Bundestag ist Gesetzgebungsorgan; er beschließt die Bundesgesetze, soweit das Grundgesetz dem Bund die Kompetenz zur Gesetzgebung zuweist.

to take part in nursery schools or leisure time activities. This approach is more akin to social work (→ *Sozialarbeit*) and leads on to the concept of work with families or family counselling. As more and more trained specialists are employed for this kind of work, it tends to move away from the school-system approach towards more up-to-date methods such as group work, letters to parents, and group therapy discussions with parents.

UK

Where it exists, this provision is made by the Social Services, Department of Health and Social Security (DHSS). Social services authorities, through their own social workers, give practical help and advice to families facing special problems. This help includes services for children at risk of injury or neglect who require accommodation, and support for family carers who look after elderly and other family members in order to give them a respite. They also help and counsel single parent families. Many authorities contribute to the cost of social work with families (such as marriage guidance) carried out by voluntary organisations.

Federalism/Unitary Government

G

The Federal Republic of Germany is based on the principle of the federal state. Its constitution is the *Grundgesetz* (Basic Law), which was enacted in 1949. The Federal Republic of Germany is composed of the *Länder* Baden-Wuerttemberg, Bavaria, Bremen, Hamburg, Hesse, Lower Saxony, North Rhine-Westphalia, Rhineland-Palatinate, Saarland, Schleswig-Holstein, and the *Land* Berlin. Through the accession of the German Democratic Republic, Germany's unification was achieved on 3 October 1990 following a separation of over 40 years. As a consequence, the reestablished *Länder* of Brandenburg, Mecklenburg-Western Pommerania, Saxony, Saxony-Anhalt and Thuringia became *Länder* of the Federal Republic of Germany and, except in a very limited number of aspects, took over its legal system.

The Federal *Länder* are states in their own right, unlike the provinces of a unitary state. At the same time, they are integrated in the overall state *(Bund)* in a manner which gives state character to the overall state as well as its component parts *(Gliedstaaten)*.

The elected parliament of the Federal Republic of Germany is the *Bundestag*. It has 662 members who are free to vote as they wish. The *Bundestag* is the legislative body; it enacts the Federal laws within the frame of reference in which the Basic Law entitles the national government to make laws.

Die Bundesregierung besteht aus dem Bundeskanzler, der die Richtlinien der Politik bestimmt, sowie den Bundesministern, die innerhalb dieser Richtlinien ihre Geschäftsbereiche selbständig und unter eigener Verantwortung leiten.

Die Bundesländer haben neben dem Bund ein eigenes Recht zur Gesetzgebung. Sie wirken durch ihre Vertreter im Bundesrat entscheidend bei der Gesetzgebung und Verwaltung des Bundes mit. Die Länder haben das Recht zur Gesetzgebung insbesondere im Bereich der Erziehung und des Schulwesens, der Bildung und Wissenschaft sowie in kulturellen Angelegenheiten (sog. Kulturhoheit der Länder). Materien von Bedeutung sind für die Landesgesetzgebung ferner noch das Kommunal- und Polizeirecht sowie Teilbereiche des Umweltschutz- und Medienrechts. Für Aufgaben der Länder im Bereich der Jugendhilfe und sozialer Angelegenheiten sind in den einzelnen Bundesländern zumeist verschiedene Landesministerien ressortmäßig zuständig.

Der Bundesrat besteht aus 68 instruierten Vertretern der Landesregierungen, die die Politik der Bundesländer zum Tragen bringen. Jedes Land entsendet je nach Größe drei bis sechs Abgeordnete, die die Stimmen ihres Landes nur einheitlich abgeben können.

Die vom Bundestag beschlossenen Gesetze kommen in der Regel zustande, wenn ihnen auch der Bundesrat zugestimmt hat, wenn dieser gegen sie keinen Einspruch erhebt oder wenn er nach Einspruch vom Bundestag überstimmt wird.

Jedes Bundesland hat eine eigene Landesverfassung. Die Legislative ist der Landtag, die Exekutive die Landesregierung (Staatsregierung in Bayern).

In den Stadtstaaten traten an die Stelle des Landtages die Bürgerschaft (Bremen und Hamburg) oder das Abgeordnetenhaus (Berlin), an die Stelle der Landesregierung der Senat.

Die Bundesländer führen nicht nur ihre eigenen Gesetze, sondern auch Bundesgesetze als landeseigene Angelegenheiten aus, soweit das Grundgesetz nichts anderes bestimmt oder zuläßt.

VK

Die Verfassung des Vereinigten Königreichs (England, Wales, Schottland, Nordirland) ist nicht in einem einzigen Dokument niedergelegt. Sie ist teils in den Parlamentsgesetzen, teils im *Common Law (→ Rechtsinstrumente, VK)* sowie in Überlieferung und Brauchtum verankert.

Das Parlament ist die oberste Legislative. Seine drei Organe, d.h. die Königin, das Oberhaus und das gewählte Unterhaus, sind äußerlich getrennt und nach unterschiedlichen Grundsätzen konstituiert. Sie kommen nur bei Anlässen symbolischer Bedeutung zusammen.

The Federal Government consists of the Federal Chancellor who decides policy guidelines, and the Federal ministers who run their departments independently and on their own responsibility within these guidelines.

The Federal *Länder* are entitled to legislate in their own right side by side with the national government. Through their respective representatives in the *Bundesrat* they participate in decisions on the legislation and administration of the *Bund*. In particular, the *Länder* may legislate in the field of school and general education, science, and cultural affairs (so-called cultural autonomy of the *Länder*). *Länder* acts may also be concerned with the local authorities and the police as well as some areas of environmental protection and the rights of the media. *Länder* responsibilities for youth work and youth welfare services as well as social affairs are vested in different ministries from one *Land* to the next.

The *Bundesrat* is composed of 68 representatives of the *Länder* governments. Through it, the *Länder* have a voice in national affairs. Depending on its size, each *Land* sends three to six representatives who may only vote together as a delegation and in accordance with the instructions of their *Land* government.

The laws enacted by the *Bundestag* will, as a rule, be adopted if the *Bundesrat* also agrees with them, does not object to them or if its objections are overruled by the *Bundestag*.

Every *Land* has a separate constitution. Legislative power is vested in the *Landtag* or *Land* parliament, executive power in the *Land* government ("state government" in Bavaria).

In the city states the *Bürgerschaft* (Bremen and Hamburg) or the *Abgeordnetenhaus* (Berlin) take the place of the *Landtag,* the Senate replaces the *Land* government.

The Federal *Länder* implement not only their own acts but also Federal laws as affairs of their own wherever the Basic Law does not provide or allow for a different course of action.

UK

The constitution of the United Kingdom (England, Wales, Scotland, Northern Ireland) is not contained in any single document. It is formed partly by statute, partly by Common Law and partly by convention *(→ Rechtsinstrumente,* UK).

Parliament is the supreme legislative authority. Its three elements, the Queen, the House of Lords and the elected House of Common, are outwardly separate and constituted on different principles, and meet together only on occasions of symbolic significance.

Das Unterhaus hat 650 Abgeordnete. Von den 650 Sitzen entfallen 523 auf England, 38 auf Wales, 72 auf Schottland und 17 auf Nordirland.

Das Oberhaus besteht aus den *Lords Spiritual* (Vertreter der Geistlichkeit) und den *Lords Temporal* (weltliche Mitglieder, d.h. Vertreter des hohen Adels). 1989 hatte es einschließlich der Erzbischöfe von York und Canterbury sowie der 24 Bischöfe insgesamt 1184 Mitglieder.

Gesetzesvorlagen müssen grundsätzlich von beiden Häusern verabschiedet werden. In der Regel durchlaufen politisch kontroverse Gesetzesvorlagen der Regierung zuerst das Unterhaus, bevor sie dem Oberhaus zugeleitet werden, während komplizierte, aber nicht kontroverse Gesetzesvorlagen zuerst vor dem Oberhaus verhandelt werden. Gesetze, die Steuern oder nationale Ausgaben betreffen, passieren das Oberhaus gewöhnlich ohne Änderungsvorschläge.

Die Einschränkung der Vollmachten des Oberhauses durch die Parlamentsgesetze von 1911 und 1949 beruht auf der Auffassung, daß die wichtigste legislative Aufgabe des nicht gewählten Hauses heute darin besteht, als Revisionsinstanz zu fungieren. Es wird als Ergänzung zur gewählten Volksvertretung und nicht als ihre Konkurrenz angesehen.

Wenn eine Gesetzesvorlage alle parlamentarischen Stadien durchlaufen hat, wird sie der Königin mit der Bitte um die königliche Zustimmung zugeleitet. Mit Erteilung dieser Zustimmung, die seit 1707 nicht verweigert worden ist, erhält die Vorlage Gesetzeskraft und wird ein förmliches Parlamentsgesetz.

Im Gegensatz zu Wales, Schottland und Nordirland besitzt England keinen eigenen Minister, bzw. kein Ministerium für die zentrale Verwaltung oder die inneren Angelegenheiten. Statt dessen sind die Verantwortlichkeiten für diese Belange auf verschiedene Ministerien der Zentralregierung verteilt.

Das Vereinigte Königreich wird im allgemeinen in dem Sinne zentralstaatlich verwaltet, daß es keine mittlere Regierungsebene gibt, die den deutschen Ländern und Länderparlamenten vergleichbar wäre. Träger der Kommunalverwaltung ist ein in zwei Ebenen untergliedertes System von 45 *counties,* die in *districts* eingeteilt sind. Die kommunale Selbstverwaltung gründet sich auf besondere Vollmachten, die das Parlament und die vom Parlament erlassenen Gesetze den Kommunalbehörden übertragen haben (→ *Kommunale Selbstverwaltung,* VK).

Die englischen *regions* (South East, East, East Anglia, South West, West Midlands, East Midlands, Yorkshire, Humberside, North West and North) entsprechen den administrativen Zuständigkeitsbereichen der *Regional Advisory Councils for Further Education* (Fortbildungsbeiräte). Dieses sind von den Kommunen finanzierte Gremien, die die Bediensteten der Kommunalverwaltungen zusammenführen, um ihnen die Koordinierung bestimmter Bereiche wie Curriculum-Entwicklung oder berufliche Fortbildung der Arbeitnehmer zu ermöglichen.

The House of Commons consists of 650 Members of Parliament (MPs). Of the 650 seats, 523 are for England, 38 for Wales, 72 for Scotland, and 17 for Northern Ireland.

The House of Lords consists of the Lords Spiritual and the Lords Temporal. In 1989, there were 1,184 members of the House of Lords, including the Archbishops of York and Canterbury and 24 bishops.

Bills must, in principle, be passed by each House. As a rule, government bills likely to raise political controversy go through the Commons before the Lords, while those of an intricate but uncontroversial nature often pass through the Lords first. Normally the Lords pass without amendments bills authorizing taxation or national expenditure.

The limitation on the power of the Lords, contained in the Parliament Acts 1911 und 1949, are based on the belief that the principal legislative function of the non-elected House nowadays is to act as a chamber of revision, complementing, not rivalling, the elected House.

When a bill has passed through all its parliamentary stages it is sent to the Queen for royal assent, after which it becomes an Act of Parliament. The royal assent has not been refused since 1707.

England has no government minister or department exclusively responsible for its central administration or domestic affairs, in contrast to Wales, Scotland and Northern Ireland. Instead responsibility is shared among a number of government departments.

The United Kingdom is in general administered centrally in the sense that there is no intermediate government level comparable to the German *Länder* and *Länder* parliaments. Administrative responsibilities are vested in the two-tier system of 45 counties subdivided into districts. Local government administration is based on specific powers which Parliament and the laws enacted by Parliament have conferred upon the local authorities.

The English regions (South East, East, East Anglia, South West, West Midlands, East Midlands, Yorkshire, Humberside, North West and North) are based on the administrative areas of the Regional Advisory Council for Further Education which are bodies, funded by local government, that bring together local government officials to enable them to co-ordinate their work in specific fields like curriculum development or in-service training for further education.

It is important to recognise that these regions do not have separate political identities in the way that German *Länder* do. Indeed, local authorities do not have to participate in their work whilst, in a few instances, counties belong to two regions.

(For Regional Committes for Youth Exchanges cf. → *Internationaler Jugend-austausch- und Besucherdienst der Bundesrepublik Deutschland (IJAB) e.V.; UK Youth Exchange Centre)*

Wichtig ist zudem der Hinweis, daß die *regions* keine eigene politische Identität besitzen, wie es bei den Ländern der Bundesrepublik Deutschland der Fall ist. Die Kommunalbehörden sind nicht verpflichtet, bei der Arbeit der *regions* mitzuwirken. Es gibt auch Fälle, in denen eine *county* zwei *regions* angehört.

(Zu den Regionalausschüssen für den Jugendaustausch → *Internationaler Jugendaustausch- und Besucherdienst der Bundesrepublik Deutschland (IJAB) e.V.;* *VK Youth Exchange Centre*)

Frauenbewegung (f)

D

Im Unterschied zu ihrer historischen Vorläuferin ist die heutige Frauenbewegung weniger eine Frauenrechts- als eine Befreiungsbewegung. Trotz formalrechtlicher Gleichberechtigung dauert die soziale und familiäre Unterordnung und Fremdbestimmung von Frauen an. Die Frauenbewegung kämpft vor allem um die weibliche Mitwirkung in allen gesellschaftlichen Bereichen und gegen Rollenklischees von Frau und Mann.

Insbesondere setzen sich Frauen für die Gleichberechtigung am Arbeitsplatz ein (Frauenförderung, Quotenregelung etc.). Als Teil der → *Alternativbewegung* engagieren sie sich in der Ökologie-und Friedensbewegung. Frauen fordern einen gleichberechtigten Anteil an Arbeitsplätzen trotz steigender Arbeitslosigkeit und eine prozentual angemessene Zahl von Frauen in politischen Vertretungsgremien sowie in Leistungsfunktionen in Wirtschaft und Verwaltung.

In den 70er Jahren entwickelte sich eine Art feministische Gegenkultur mit zahlreichen anfangs isolierten, dann aber weithin aufgegriffenen Initiativen. Dazu gehören insbesondere die Frauenzentren, die Selbsterfahrungsgruppen, in denen Frauen versuchen, ihre Probleme gemeinsam zu lösen und sich von ihrer Rollenfixierung zu befreien, die Frauenhäuser zur Aufnahme von physisch oder psychisch mißhandelten Frauen mit ihren Kindern und Notrufinitiativen für vergewaltigte Frauen und Mädchen.

Der Einstellungswandel in der Gesellschaft zur Rolle der Frau vollzieht sich nur langsam, führt aber doch allmählich zu einigen positiven Ergebnissen. So nimmt z.B. die Zahl der Politikerinnen nicht nur insgesamt, sondern auch in Führungspositionen zu. Fast alle Parteien haben entsprechende Zielvorgaben oder Quoten beschlossen. Viele Berufe, die bislang dem männlichen Geschlecht vorbehalten waren, stehen heute auch den Mädchen und Frauen offen. In anderen Bereichen jedoch hält die Benachteiligung der Frau weiter an.

VK

Die Situation im Vereinigten Königreich ist sehr ähnlich.

Women's Movement

G

In contrast with earlier days, today's women's movement is geared not so much to fighting for women's rights as to striving for women's liberation. Although legally women today have equal rights, their inferior position in society and within the family persists. Meanwhile, the conditioning of women to accept a secondary rôle continues. The movement now primarily seeks to achieve full participation by women in all social fields and to eliminate the traditional rôles attributed to men and women.

Women are most insistent on the demand for equal opportunities at work. As part of the alternative movement (→ *Alternativbewegung*), they are committed to the aims of the environmental protection and peace. Women demand an equal proportion of jobs in spite of rising unemployment figures. They want to see an appropriate number of women as political representatives as well as in leading positions in industry and administration.

In the 70s a feminist anti-culture developed generating numerous initiatives which were isolated at the beginning but later widely adopted. Amongst these there were the women's centres and the self-awareness groups, where women attempt to solve their problems jointly and cast off their conditioning. Other initiatives included the establishment of refuge houses for battered and emotionally maltreated women and their children, and the emergency rape helplines.

Society's attitude to women and their rôles is slow to change. But some positive developments can be seen. Thus, for example, not only is the actual number of female politicians increasing but also the number in senior positions. Most political parties accept the aim of adequate representation by women and have set appropriate quotas for this for themselves. Many trades and professions which were a male preserve are today also open to girls and women. However, equal opportunities for women have not yet been achieved.

UK

In the UK the situation is very much as that in Germany.

Freiwilliges Soziales Jahr (n)

D

Jungen Menschen, die sich noch nicht sicher sind, welchen Weg sie nach der Schulzeit einschlagen möchten, die einen Dienst am Nächsten leisten und damit vielleicht auch etwas über sich selbst erfahren wollen, bietet sich die Möglichkeit des Freiwilligen Sozialen Jahres (FSJ), einer Einrichtung, die 1965 entstanden ist. Mehr als 6.000 Helfer und Helferinnen beginnen jedes Jahr mit einer Tätigkeit vor allem in der Altenhilfe, in Kinderheimen und Tagesstätten, in Krankenhäusern und Einrichtungen für Behinderte.

Diese Tätigkeit vermittelt soziale Erfahrung, stärkt das Verantwortungsbewußtsein und fördert die Weiterentwicklung der Persönlichkeit. Zugleich bietet sie eine Orientierung in den sozialen und pflegerischen Berufen. Jugendliche können in der täglichen Praxis prüfen, ob sie sich für einen solchen Beruf eignen.

Das FSJ wird für die Zulassung zum Studium ebenso begünstigend anerkannt wie der Wehr- oder Zivildienst. In den sozialen Berufen wird es im allgemeinen als Praktikum angerechnet.

Das FSJ wird aus dem Bundesjugendplan des Bundesministeriums für Frauen und Jugend gefördert. Die Träger des FSJ zahlen kein Entgelt, wohl aber ein monatliches Taschengeld – im Durchschnitt um DM 200,–, manche auch ein kleines Urlaubs- oder Weihnachtsgeld. Unterkunft und Verpflegung sind frei. In der gesetzlichen Sozialversicherung und Urlaubsregelung (mindestens 26 Werktage) sind die Helfer den Jugendlichen in der Berufsausbildung gleichgestellt. Sie sind also kranken-, unfall-, renten- und arbeitslosenversichert. Es gelten ferner die Bestimmungen des Jugendarbeitsschutzgesetzes. Voraussetzung sind ein Alter von 17 bis 25 Jahren und soziales Engagement.

VK

Keine Entsprechung in Großbritannien

Freizeitpädagogik (f)

D

„Freizeit umfaßt die individuell frei disponible Zeit, die nach Erledigung aller sozialer und individueller Verpflichtungen dem Einzelnen täglich verbleibt" (Opaschowski).

Die zunehmende Freizeit führt zur Entwicklung neuer Güter und Dienstleistungen, für deren Produktion sonst kein Anlaß bestanden hätte. Der „Freizeitwert" einer Kommune kann zu einem wesentlichen Qualitätsmerkmal einer Stadt werden. Dabei besteht jedoch die Gefahr, Freizeit und Konsum-

Year of Voluntary Work and Community Service

G

Young people who do not quite know what they want to do after leaving school, who wish to serve their fellow man and, by doing so, hope to learn more about themselves, may sign up for the *Freiwilliges Soziales Jahr (FSJ)*. This scheme, the Year of Voluntary Work and Community Service, was set up in 1965. Every year, more than 6,000 helpers commit themselves to a year's voluntary work for the elderly or service in children's homes, day care centres, hospitals and establishments for the handicapped.

The participants largely benefit in terms of social experience, a growing sense of responsibility and personality development. They also obtain first-hand information about the professions engaged in social work and nursing care. Day-to-day practical experience will enable them to find out whether they are suited for such a profession.

Just like the completion of military service or non-military national service, a year's work under the FSJ is taken into account when young people apply for admission to a study course. It is generally recognised as a practical placement for all types of social work training.

The FSJ is financed from the Federal Youth Plan funds administered by the Federal Ministry for Women and Youth. Participants do not receive payment from the organisers of the FSJ but pocket money averaging DM 200,— per month. Some bodies also provide leave pay and a Christmas bonus. Room and board are free. For the purposes of statutory social security and holiday entitlement (a minimum of 26 workdays) FSJ helpers are in the same category as young people undergoing vocational training. They are also covered by a sickness, accident and unemployment insurance as well as the provisions of the Protection of Young Persons at Work Act. Participants must be between 17 and 25 years of age. Another prerequisite is social commitment.

UK

No UK equivalent

Education for Leisure

G

"Leisure is the time which every day is at the individual's free disposal after having fulfilled all his social and personal commitments" (Opaschowski).

As leisure time has increased, new goods and services have been developed for which there was no previous demand. The quality of leisure provision in a town can become a major attraction. However, there is always the risk that leisure and consumer opportunities are not differentiated. Seeing leisure time in terms of consumption is criticized by those who believe in the idea of self-determining education for leisure. The tendency to overburden extra-curricular

möglichkeiten gleichzusetzen. Gerade die konsumorientierte Freizeitgestaltung wird im Rahmen einer emanzipatorischen Freizeitpädagogik kritisiert. Aber auch die Überfrachtung des außerschulischen Freizeitbereiches mit sozialen Lernzielen und Kompensationsfunktionen ist ein Kritikpunkt. Demgegenüber soll Freizeitpädagogik ein Gegengewicht zu kognitiven Lerninhalten und Streßsituationen schaffen und Freiräume für angst- und zwangfreies Lernen sichern sowie vorhandene Nischen für Selbstbestimmung und Eigeninitiative ausweiten. Um dies umzusetzen, bedarf es einer „animativen Didaktik" – einer Alternative zur Zwangsbelehrung (Opaschowski).

Gerade in diesem Bereich haben die → *Träger der Jugendhilfe* durch geeignete Angebote und Beratung *(→ Beratungsdienste)* eine wichtige Aufgabe zu übernehmen.

Schließlich muß noch hinzugefügt werden, daß die anhaltende Arbeitslosigkeit vielen Menschen unfreiwillig freie Zeit beschert. Das macht deutlich, daß Freizeit kein Wert an sich ist, sondern gesellschaftlich und individuell gestaltet werden kann und muß.

VK

Die Entwicklungstendenzen in der Freizeitpädagogik sind im Vereinigten Königreich ähnlich wie in der Bundesrepublik Deutschland. Es ist jedoch die Aufgabe der Schulen, des *youth service* und der freien Träger, den Erfordernissen der Freizeitpädagogik Rechnung zu tragen. Das Fach „Freizeit-Management" wird jetzt an Universitäten angeboten.

Friedensbewegung (f)

D

In verschiedene ideologische Richtungen einteilbare und weitgehend auch von Jugendlichen getragene Protestbewegungen gegen den Rüstungswettlauf.

Die Friedensbewegung hat sich hauptsächlich in Friedensappellen sowie in vielfältigen öffentlichen Aktionen in Form von Demonstrationen und Menschenketten artikuliert. Sie hat dazu beigetragen, den Informationsstand der Bevölkerung in Rüstungsfragen zu verbessern, und deutlich gemacht, daß in einem demokratischen Staat außerparlamentarische Volksbewegungen Einfluß auf die Politik nehmen können. Die Friedensbewegung wird als ein wichtiger Bestandteil der Friedenssicherung betrachtet.

VK

Abgesehen von der Kampagne für die Nukleare Abrüstung wird eine erkennbare Friedensbewegung im Vereinigten Königreich nur von kleinen Gruppen vertreten. Ihr Ziel ist, die Öffentlichkeit auf das Problem des Wettrüstens, insbesondere im Bereich der atomaren Rüstung, aufmerksam zu machen. Die Kampagne für Nukleare Abrüstung tritt vor allem für die nukleare Abrüstung

leisure time with the objective of social learning and compensatory activities is equally subject to criticism. Education for leisure should balance out cognitive learning processes, relieve stress and open up opportunities for stress-free learning, extending existing possibilities for self-determination and personal initiative. To achieve this, we need "animative didactics" (Opaschowski) rather than compulsory instruction.

It is precisely to this task that bodies responsible for youth work and youth welfare services (→ Träger der Jugendhilfe) must respond by providing suitable programmes and counselling services (→ Beratungsdienste).

Moreover, it must be pointed out that many people are faced with a lot of undesired free time as unemployment continues. This demonstrates that leisure time is not an asset in itself but can and must be structured socially and individually.

UK

The trends in education for leisure in the UK are similar to those in Germany. However, it is the task of schools, the youth service and the voluntary sector to respond to the demands for leisure education. Education for leisure management is now studied in universities.

Peace Movement

G

Protest movement against the arms race which may be subdivided into various ideological trends and is widely supported by young people.

The peace movement's action mainly took the form of appeals for peace and a wide range of public compaigns including demonstrations and human chains. It helped to secure a better information of the general public in armament matters, and has shown that in a democratic state extra-parliamentary people's movements succeed in influencing politics. The peace movement is seen as an essential element of all effort to secure peace.

UK

Apart from the Campaign for Nuclear Disarmament (CND), only small local groups form a recognisable peace movement in the UK. Their purpose is to keep the issue of the arms race, particularly the nuclear arms race, in the public eye. The Campaign for Nuclear Disarmament (CND) campaigns for nuclear disarmament by the western nations. It is highly organised and mounts im-

durch die westlichen Länder ein. Sie ist gut organisiert und veranstaltet eindrucksvolle Demonstrationen. Da die Organisation politisch nicht gebunden ist, wird sie gleichermaßen von Jung und Alt unterstützt.

Führungsstile (m/pl)

D

Unter Führungsstil versteht man ein einheitliches Verhalten einer Person im Umgang mit anderen Personen, bzw. einer Gruppe.

Die ersten sozialpsychologischen Untersuchungen zum Führungsstil, bzw. Führungsverhalten, wurden in den 30er Jahren von Kurt Lewin und seinen Mitarbeitern durchgeführt. Lewin unterschied zwischen dem
a) autoritären
b) demokratischen und
c) laissez-faire Führungsstil.

Im deutschen Sprachgebrauch haben sich terminologisch Modifikationen durchgesetzt, ohne daß die inhaltliche Charakterisierung sich geändert hätte. Man spricht vom
a) autokratischen
b) sozialintegrativen/partnerschaftlichen und vom
c) laissez-faire Stil.

Die Grundannahme Lewins, daß sich das Verhalten und Einstellungen von Gruppen*führern* auf die Gruppen*mitglieder* übertragen, ist heute noch maßgeblich. Vor allem in der Schulpädagogik sind die Ergebnisse von Lewin stark beachtet worden und haben im Zuge der Demokratisierung des Bildungswesens die Diskussion um Erziehungsstile/Unterrichtsstile nachhaltig beeinflußt.

In der Sozialarbeit/Sozialpädagogik gewinnt die Frage nach dem angemessenen Führungsstil im Rahmen sozialer Gruppenarbeit an Bedeutung. Es wird diskutiert, inwieweit die soziale Gruppenarbeit führerorientiert, bzw. mitarbeiterorientiert, sein sollte. Über diesen Beziehungsaspekt hinaus erhebt sich die Frage, welchen Einfluß die Führungsstile auf die Arbeitsorientierung einer sozialen Gruppe hat.

Bei neueren Untersuchungen versucht man anhand bestimmter Merkmale im Verhalten einer Person (Zuwendung, Aktivität, Kontrolle, Beteiligung etc.) ein Führungsprofil zu ermitteln. Situationsfaktoren (Besonderheiten der Aufgabe, Motivationsstruktur, Gruppengröße) werden dabei mitberücksichtigt.

VK

Die Auffassungen über Führungsstile sind im Vereinigten Königreich und in der Bundesrepublik Deutschland sowie allgemein in der westlichen Welt im wesentlichen identisch.

pressive demonstrations. Purporting to be apolitical, CND is supported by young and old alike.

Styles of Leadership

G

Style of leadership means the consistent pattern of behaviour of one person (the leader) when dealing with another person or group.

The first research into styles of leadership was carried but by Kurt Lewin and his colleagues in the early 30s. Lewin distinguished between three types of leader:
a) authoritarian
b) democratic and
c) liberal
Current German has seen changes in terminology. However, the essential nature of the categories stays the same. People talk now of
a) directive
b) democratic/participatory and
c) non-directive styles of leadership.

Lewin's basic hypothesis that behaviour patterns and attitudes of group leaders are transferred to the group members is still held today. Lewin's findings had strong repercussions on educational theory and were widely used in the debate on styles of education/teaching in the course of introducing democracy to the education system.

In social work and youth work the debates on the style of leadership most appropriate to social group work or the extent to which social group work should be leader or member orientated are gaining in importance. The latter raises the question as to what influence the styles of leadership have on the approach of a social group.

More recent research has aimed at creating a *leadership profile* based on behaviour patterns (warmth of approach, dynamism, control, participation, etc.), taking into account such factors as the nature of the work, incentives, and group size when relevant to the situation.

UK

The basic framework of styles of leadership in the UK is identical to that in Germany and in the Western World in general.

Fürsorge (f), öffentliche

D

ist ein zwar heute noch vorfindbarer Begriff (besonders in Wortverbindungen wie Jugendfürsorge, Familienfürsorge, Tuberkulosenfürsorge), der aber wegen seiner Bedeutung „für jemanden sorgen" im Konzept einer → *Sozialarbeit/* modernen *Sozialpädagogik* zunehmend ersetzt wird.

Das Grundgesetz verwendet in Art. 74 Nr. 7 noch immer den Terminus „öffentliche Fürsorge" als Kompetenztitel für die konkurrierende Gesetzgebungskompetenz des Bundes. Er ist die Grundlage für das Kinder- und Jugendhilfegesetz sowie für das Bundessozialhilfegesetz.

VK

Spezifisch deutsche Gegebenheit

Hilfe (f) zur Erziehung (f)

D

Der Begriff „Hilfe zur Erziehung" wird als Oberbegriff für verschiedene Hilfen im Einzelfall verwendet.

Nach dem Jugendhilfegesetz (→ *Jugendgesetze*) ist die öffentliche Jugendhilfe verpflichtet, Hilfen zur Erziehung sicherzustellen, soweit der Anspruch des Kindes auf Erziehung von den nach Art. 6 GG (→ *Elterliche Sorge)* in erster Linie verpflichteten Eltern oder der Familie nicht erfüllt wird. Die Angebote der Jugendhilfe können dabei die Familien unterstützen, ergänzen oder ersetzen. Im einzelnen unterscheiden wir folgende Formen der besonderen Hilfen:

1. ambulante (familienunterstützende) Erziehungshilfen
   Zu den ambulanten familienunterstützenden Hilfen zählen neben der klassischen Erziehungsbeistandschaft und der Erziehungsberatung die sozialpädagogische Familienhilfe und die soziale Gruppenarbeit mit Jugendlichen.

2. → *Pflegekinderwesen*
   In den letzten Jahren haben sich auch immer mehr Zwischenformen zur Heimerziehung entwickelt: Kleinheime (nur eine Gruppe von 10–15 Kindern), Großpflegestellen (Pflegefamilien mit 6–8 Kindern, bei denen ein Elternteil eine pädagogische Ausbildung haben muß), betreutes Einzelwohnen, betreute Jugendwohngemeinschaften, Tagesgruppen im Heim.

3. Heimerziehung
   Die Durchführung der Heimerziehung geschieht in der Regel in Heimen der „freien Träger" (→ *Wohlfahrtsverbände)* unter der Aufsicht des Landesjugendamtes.

Public Welfare

G

This is a term which is still in use, particularly in compound words such as *Jugendfürsorge* (welfare work for the young), *Familienfürsorge* (family welfare work), *Tuberkulosenfürsorge* (welfare work for those suffering from tuberculosis). Because of the welfare aspect of the German verb "für jemanden sorgen", the term *Fürsorge* is increasingly being replaced by the concept of social work and present-day youth and community work (→ *Sozialarbeit/Sozialpädagogik*).

Section 74, item 7, of the Basic Law still contains the term *öffentliche Fürsorge* providing an entitlement for the national government to enact concurrent legislation. It constitutes the basis of the Child and Youth Services Act as well as the Federal Social Assistance Act.

UK

Relevant only for the FRG

Statutory Socio-Educational Provision for Children with Problems

G

The term *Hilfe zur Erziehung* is used as a blanket term for various forms to help in individual cases.

According to the Child and Youth Services Act (→ *Jugendgesetze)* statutory youth work and youth welfare services must provide assistance when the child's rights to be brought up and educated by the parents or the family (first and foremost responsible under article 6 of the Basic Law) are not fulfilled. In such cases, youth work and youth welfare services can support, supplement or replace the family. The following forms of special help may be distinguished:

1. non-residential, socio-educational provision for children with social, personal and environmental problems (to support the family)
   In addition to the more traditional forms of provision, such as the supervision order and child guidance, these include socio-educational help for families and social group work with young people.

2. fostering and small-scale residential provision for children (→ *Pflegekinderwesen)*
   In recent years alternative forms to large-scale residential care have developed such as small residential homes (comprising only one group of 10–15 children), large fostering units (foster families with 6–8 children where one of the foster parents must have a relevant qualification), living alone or communal living with social worker support, residential homes providing day care for groups of children.

4. Betreutes Jugendwohnen

Unter diesem Begriff sind in den letzten Jahren verschiedene Formen pädagogischer Betreuung von einzelnen Jugendlichen oder von Gruppen Jugendlicher (Jugendwohngemeinschaften) entstanden. Sie werden von Sozialarbeitern (meist ambulant) betreut.

VK

Im Vereinigten Königreich gibt es keine Entsprechung für das Kinder- und Jugendhilfegesetz. Britische Gerichte können jedoch verschiedene Maßnahmen für Kinder mit besonderen Schwierigkeiten treffen (→ *Jugendgesetze;* → *Jugendschutz;* → *Jugendstrafrecht, Maßnahmen des*).

Dabei soll möglichst verhindert werden, daß Kinder vor Gericht erscheinen müssen. Das Schwergewicht liegt auf der partnerschaftlichen Zusammenarbeit mit den Eltern bei der Erfüllung ihrer elterlichen Pflichten *(Children Act 1989)*.

Internationale Jugendarbeit (f)

D

Internationale Jugendarbeit soll die persönliche Begegnung junger Menschen aus verschiedenen Ländern, ihr gemeinsames Lernen und Arbeiten, den Erfahrungsaustausch von Führungskräften der Jugendarbeit sowie die Zusammenarbeit der Träger der Jugendhilfe über die Grenzen hinweg ermöglichen.

Internationale Jugendarbeit soll jungen Menschen helfen, andere Kulturen und Gesellschaftsordnungen sowie internationale Zusammenhänge kennenzulernen, sich mit ihnen auseinanderzusetzen und die eigene Situation besser zu erkennen (interkulturelles Lernen). Sie soll ihnen darüber hinaus bewußtmachen, daß sie für die Sicherung und demokratische Ausgestaltung des Friedens und für mehr Freiheit und soziale Gerechtigkeit in der Welt mitverantwortlich sind.

Internationale Jugendarbeit erstreckt sich auf alle Felder der Jugendarbeit.

Zur Erreichung dieser Zielsetzung wird von Bund, Ländern und Gemeinden der pädagogisch begleitete internationale Jugendaustausch finanziell gefördert. Um für diese Zwecke Mittel aus dem → *Bundesjugendplan* sowie den Jugendplänen der Länder und Kommunen zu erhalten, muß der Veranstalter nachweisen, daß bestimmte Bedingungen erfüllt sind: Die Maßnahme muß inhaltlich sowie organisatorisch gut vorbereitet, durchgeführt und nachbereitet werden. Ein anerkannter ausländischer Partner ist erforderlich. Das Programm muß Begegnungscharakter haben, auf Gegenseitigkeit angelegt sein und eine angemessene sprachliche Kommunikation (ggfs. durch Sprachmittler) muß gewährleistet sein. In Abgrenzung zum Jugendtourismus (→ *Jugend-*

3. residential care
Residential care is, as a rule, provided in community homes run by voluntary organisations (→ *Wohlfahrtsverbände*) under the supervision of the *Land* youth offices.

4. Young people living with socio-educational support in the community
In recent years, various forms of socio-educational support of individuals and groups of young people living together have developed. They are looked after by social workers who, for the most part, provide field support.

UK

In the UK there is no equivalent to the Child and Youth Services Act. However, British courts may take a variety of actions in respect of children with problems (→ *Jugendgesetze;* → *Jugendschutz;* → *Jugendstrafrecht, Maßnahmen des*).

The emphasis is on preventing children needing to appear before a court and on partnership with parents in fulfilling their responsibilities towards their children (Children Act 1989).

International Youth Work

G
International youth work aims to establish a personal contact among young people from different countries by learning and working together. It also comprises the exchange of experience amongst youth leaders and youth work specialists. The main objective is to contribute to a better understanding and cooperation across frontiers.

Young people are helped to develop the ability to put themselves in the place of those who carry the imprints of another language, culture and society (intercultural learning). International youth work aims to make the young concern themselves more deeply with international interaction and, by doing so, help them to get a better understanding of their own situation. Another objective is to develop amongst young people an awareness of shared responsibility for the safeguarding of peace according to the principles of democracy. The younger generation must realize that they are also called upon to secure freedom and social justice throughout the world.

All areas of youth work may serve as a basis for international contact.

In order to fulfill these aims, the Federation, the *Länder* and local authorities may give financial support for international youth exchanges accompanied by qualified staff. In order to be able to claim funds under the Federal Youth Plan (→ *Bundesjugendplan*) or the youth plans of the *Länder* and the local authorities, the organiser must prove that his project fulfils certain conditions: exchange programmes have to be well organised in advance with a clearly defined educational objective. They must be carried out according to plan, and an

reisen) wird besonderer Wert auf eine gemeinsame strukturierte Lernerfahrung gelegt.

Internationale Jugendbegegnung im In- und Ausland umfaßt ein breites Spektrum von Maßnahmetypen in allen Bereichen der Jugendarbeit, z.B. internationale Jugendgemeinschaftsdienste, *work camps,* Fachprogramme mit in- und ausländischen Mitarbeitern der Jugendarbeit und sonstigen Führungskräften, Kurse der Mitarbeiterfortbildung, jugendpolitische Maßnahmen mit Entwicklungsländern, Projekte zur Weiterentwicklung von Inhalten, Formen und Methoden internationaler Jugendarbeit, europäische Jugendlager, internationale Begegnungen der sozio-kulturellen und der politischen Bildung, internationale Maßnahmen der sportlichen Bildung.

Die internationale Jugendarbeit ist ein wichtiger Bestandteil der Aktivitäten der Träger der Jugendarbeit, insbesondere der → *Jugendverbände.* Der Deutsche Bundesjugendring (DBJR, → *Jugendringe)* bildet zusammen mit dem Ring Politischer Jugend das Deutsche Nationalkomitee für internationale Jugendarbeit (DNK). Das DNK beteiligt sich als Vertretung der wichtigen Jugendorganisationen in der Bundesrepublik Deutschland direkt an der Mitgestaltung europäischer Jugendstrukturen; insbesondere wirkt es im Europäischen Jugendrat (CENYC) sowie bei der WFDY (World Federation of Democratic Youth) mit.

VK

Internationale Jugendarbeit wird als wichtige Komponente der sozialen Erziehung und persönlichen Entwicklung junger Menschen angesehen. Sie soll Jugendlichen nicht nur zur Begegnung mit Altersgenossen anderer Länder verhelfen, sondern auch zum besseren Verhältnis der Probleme der Entwicklungsländer, zum interkulturellen Lernen, zum Abbau von Rassenvorurteilen und zur Friedenserziehung beitragen.

Der Jugendaustausch und auch der Austausch von Fachkräften der Jugendarbeit, jungen Werktätigen, Vertretern der kirchlichen, kulturellen und sportlichen Jugendarbeit sowie behinderten Jugendlichen besteht schon seit langem. In vielen Fällen wurden hierfür öffentliche Mittel bereitgestellt.

Die wichtigste Dienststelle zur Förderung des Austausches von Jugendlichen und Fachkräften der Jugendarbeit ist das → *Youth Exchange Centre* (YEC). Der Austausch mit dem Commonwealth ist jedoch weiterhin Aufgabe des *Commonwealth Youth Exchange Council.*

Im Bereich des Jugendaustausches bleibt die Bundesrepublik Deutschland der bedeutendste Partner des Vereinigten Königreiches, gefolgt von Frankreich und den anderen Mitgliedsländern der Europäischen Gemeinschaft. Es besteht ein geregeltes Austauschprogramm mit Osteuropa und den USA. Die

adequate follow-up must be part of the concept. A recognised foreign partner has to be found. The programme must also focus on mixing and mingling and provide for a return visit. The organiser has to make sure that linguistic communication (if necessary, with the help of interpreters) is achieved. As compared to youth tourism (→ *Jugendreisen*), emphasis is on a joint and structured learning experience.

International youth work meetings at home and abroad comprise a wide spectrum of types of programmes in all fields of youth work such as international youth community services, work camps, specialist programmes for national and foreign youth work staff and other leaders, further training courses for youth workers, youth projects for the benefit of developing countries, projects to help develop the contents, forms and methods of international youth work, European youth camps, international meetings devoted to socio-cultural and political education, international programmes of education in sports.

International youth work is an essential part of the activities organised by the bodies responsible for youth work, in particular the youth organisations. The *Deutscher Bundesjugendring* (DBJR, → *Jugendringe*) together with the *Ring Politischer Jugend* (Council of Political Youth Organisations) forms the German National Committee for International Youth Work (DNK). The DNK advocates the interests of the important German youth organisations in the Federal Republic of Germany. It is directly involved in the shaping of European youth structures. It is also a member of the CENYC and the WFDY (World Federation of Democratic Youth).

UK

International youth work is recognised as an important aspect of the social education and personal development of young people. Apart from contacts with the young of other countries, young people should be given an understanding of the problems of developing countries, as well as such questions as multi-cultural education, racism and peace education.

There is a long history of youth exchanges and visits between professional, vocational, religious, cultural and sports groups as well as young people with special needs, often with the assistance of government grants.

The principal support agency for youth and youth worker exchanges and visits is the → *Youth Exchange Centre* (YEC). Exchanges with the Commonwealth continue to be administered by the Commonwealth Youth Exchange Council.

Germany remains the most important partner for the UK in youth exchanges, followed by France and the other European Community member states. There is a regular programme of exchanges with East Europe and the USA. Apart from the central government funds for youth exchange administered by the YEC, many local authorities have small budgets for international youth activity. The major part of any costs are usually raised by the organisers themselves.

öffentlichen, auf nationaler Ebene für den Jugendaustausch bereitgestellten Mittel verwaltet das YEC. Daneben haben viele Kommunen einen kleinen Etat für internationale Aktivitäten. Der größere Teil der Kosten für Jugendaustauschprogramme wird im allgemeinen vom Veranstalter selbst aufgebracht.

Einige freie Träger, von denen in erster Linie *Oxfam* zu nennen ist, konzentrieren sich in ihrer Jugendarbeit vor allem auf die Belange der Entwicklungshilfe.

Die Förderungsbedingungen und Programmformen entsprechen in etwa denen der Bundesrepublik Deutschland.

Internationaler Jugendaustausch- und Besucherdienst der Bundesrepublik Deutschland (IJAB) e.V.

D
Der Internationale Jugendaustausch- und Besucherdienst der Bundesrepublik Deutschland (IJAB) e.V. ist eine bundeszentrale Einrichtung für die internationale Jugendarbeit. Er wurde 1967 gegründet. Ziel der Aktivitäten des IJAB ist es, das Verständnis der Jugend aus europäischen und außereuropäischen Ländern füreinander zu verbessern, die Beziehungen untereinander zu festigen und einen Beitrag zur Fortentwicklung der internationalen Jugendarbeit zu leisten. Zu den Aufgaben des IJAB gehören die Vorbereitung und Durchführung von qualifizierten Austauschprogrammen für Fachkräfte der Jugendarbeit, die er im Rahmen der bilateralen Beziehungen der Bundesrepublik Deutschland im Auftrag ausführt, die Förderung der sprachlichen Verständigung durch Terminologiearbeit, Sprachkurse für ausländische Mitarbeiter der Jugendhilfe, Übersetzungshilfen und Dolmetschen sowie ein breites Angebot an Informationsmöglichkeiten über die internationale Jugendarbeit. Auftraggeber für den IJAB können das Bundesministerium für Frauen und Jugend, die Mitgliedsverbände des IJAB e.V. und andere zentrale Träger der Jugendarbeit sein.

1989 wurde das Deutsche Büro „Jugend für Europa" beim IJAB angesiedelt. Es ist das nationale Büro zur Durchführung des 1988 vom Rat der Europäischen Gemeinschaften beschlossenen Jugendaustauschprogramms innerhalb der EG.

VK
Youth Exchange Centre (YEC)
Das *Youth Exchange Centre* wurde am 1. April 1985 von der britischen Regierung geschaffen, um den internationalen Jugendaustausch zwischen dem VK und anderen Ländern zu fördern. Seine Aufgaben sind die Entwicklung, Durchführung und Auswertung der Jugendaustauschpolitik der Regierung und deren Beratung in allen damit verbundenen Fragen.

There are some voluntary organisations which concentrate on youth education issues in Overseas Development, the most important being Oxfam.

Requirements for funding and the types of programmes provided are roughly the same as in the Federal Republic of Germany.

International Youth Exchange and Visitors' Service of the Federal Republic of Germany (IJAB)

G

The International Youth Exchange and Visitors' Service of the Federal Republic of Germany (IJAB) is a central agency for international youth work and was founded in 1967. The purpose of its activities is to help young people in Europe and from outside Europe to get to know each other better, to strengthen their ties with each other, and to contribute to the further development of international youth work. IJAB's tasks include the planning and realization of qualified exchange programmes for youth work specialists – undertaken in the framework of the Federal Republic's bilateral agreements – the promotion of international linguistic communication through terminology research, language courses for foreign youth workers, translating and interpreting services, in addition to a wide range of information on international youth work. Requests for its services come from the Federal Ministry for Women and Youth, the member organisations of IJAB, or other central organisations concerned with youth work.

In 1989, the German National Agency for the "Youth for Europe" scheme was attached to IJAB. Its remit is to implement the programme of youth exchanges within the EC countries which was adopted by the Council of the European Community in 1988.

UK
Youth Exchange Centre (YEC)
The Youth Exchange Centre was established on 1 April 1985 by the British Government to promote youth exchanges between the UK and other countries. It has responsibility for the development, implementation and evaluation of policy governing youth exchanges and for advice on this to the Government.

Das YEC ist Teil des *British Council.* Das Büro des *Youth Exchange Centre* befindet sich beim *Central Bureau for Educational Visits and Exchanges.* Seine Mittel erhält das *Youth Exchange Centre* teils vom britischen Außenministerium und teils vom Ministerium für Erziehung und Wissenschaft.

Die Aufgaben des YEC sind in vier Hauptbereiche untergliedert:

1. Förderungsmittel

Das YEC gibt Zuschüsse zu den Reisekosten britischer Jugendgruppen bei Auslandsbesuchen sowie für den Aufenthalt ausländischer Gruppen im VK. Das YEC bemüht sich um eine gerechte Verteilung der Förderungsmittel, wobei benachteiligte Gruppen, insbesondere arbeitslose und behinderte Jugendliche, bevorzugt berücksichtigt werden.

2. Information und Beratung

Der vom YEC vierteljährlich herausgegebene Rundbrief „Youth Exchange News" informiert über internationale Angebote für Jugendgruppen und Fachkräfte der Jugendarbeit. „HELP?", ein regelmäßig aktualisiertes Nachschlagewerk, enthält Informationen zum internationalen Jugendaustausch. Das YEC hilft bei der Suche nach Partnerorganisationen im Ausland und berät bei der Planung von Austauschprogrammen.

3. Aus- und Fortbildung der Mitarbeiter der Jugendarbeit

Zur Verbesserung des internationalen Jugendaustausches führt das YEC für britische Fachkräfte der Jugendarbeit verschiedene Bildungsmaßnahmen zur internationalen Dimension der Jugendarbeit durch. Zu bestimmten Themen werden Ausbildungsprogramme und Studienreisen im Ausland veranstaltet.

4. Projekte

Auf nationaler Ebene bietet das YEC verschiedene Modellprojekte für junge Menschen an. Es arbeitet mit dem *Commonwealth Youth Exchange Council* zusammen und gewährt finanzielle Hilfen für den Jugendaustausch zwischen dem VK und den anderen Commonwealth-Ländern.

5. Dezentralisierung/Regionalisierung

Mitte 1986 wurde mit der Gründung von zwölf Regionalkomitees begonnen, die alle inzwischen ihrer Arbeit aufgenommen haben. Die Mitglieder der Komitees – Vertreter der behördlichen wie der freien Träger der Jugendarbeit, auch der ethnischen Minderheiten – sind repräsentativ für die Region, in der sie arbeiten.

Aufgabe der Komitees ist es, Auskünfte zu erteilen sowie den internationalen Jugendaustausch zu fördern und zu unterstützen. Sie können selbständig über die Vergabe von Mitteln für den Austausch zwischen ihren Regionen und den westeuropäischen Ländern, den USA, sowie Polen und Jugoslawien entscheiden.

Ebenso wie der IJAB fungiert das *Youth Exchange Centre* als nationales Büro zur Durchführung des Programms „Jugend für Europa".

The Youth Exchange Centre is a part of the British Council, located with the Central Bureau for Educational Visits and Exchanges and funded by the Foreign and Commonwealth Office and the Department of Education and Science.

The activities of the YEC fall into four main categories:

1. Grants

Grants for youth exchanges are available to British groups to assist with the cost, not only of travelling abroad, but also of hosting visiting groups to the UK. The YEC is striving to employ an Equal Opportunities policy in its grant awards, paying particular regard to disadvantaged groups of young people such as the unemployed and the handicapped.

2. Information and Advice

The YEC produces a quarterly newsletter "Youth Exchange News", which draws attention to international opportunities for youth groups and youth leaders. "HELP?", which is regularly updated, is a guideline on international youth exchange. The YEC can help find partner agencies abroad and give advice on planning an exchange programme.

3. Training of Youth Workers

The YEC seeks to improve the quality of international exchanges through a range of training programmes on the international dimension of youth work. Training courses and study visits are organised in other countries around particular topics.

4. Projects

The YEC is responsible for running a certain number of national innovatory projects for young people. It cooperates with, and helps fund, the Commonwealth Youth Exchange Council which promotes youth exchanges between the UK and other members of the Commonwealth.

5. Regionalisation

Since mid-1986 the YEC has established twelve Regional Committees throughout the UK, all of which have been meeting regularly. On each Committee there are representatives of voluntary and statutory organisations, including ethnic minority bodies.

These committees have a threefold role in promoting, funding and providing information about youth exchanges. Their members make grant decisions on youth exchanges with West Europe, USA, Poland and Yougoslavia in their region.

The Youth Exchange Centre, like IJAB, acts as the National Agent for the Youth for Europe scheme.

Jugendamt (n)

D

Die öffentlichen Aufgaben im Bereich der → *Jugendhilfe* werden auf der Ebene der Landkreise und der kreisfreien Städte (→ *Kommunale Selbstverwaltung*) von den Jugendämtern wahrgenommen. Ihr Aufbau und ihre Aufgaben sind durch das Kinder- und Jugendhilfegesetz (KJHG) (→ *Jugendgesetze*) festgelegt. Gemäß diesem Gesetz besteht das Jugendamt aus Jugendhilfeausschuß (JHA) und Verwaltung.

Dem Jugendhilfeausschuß gehören neben Mitgliedern der Vertretungskörperschaft und der Verwaltung auch sachkundige Bürger und Vertreter der Jugendverbände und andere im Bereich der Jugendhilfe tätige Organisationen an. Die Aufgaben des Jugendhilfeausschusses umfassen alle Fragen der örtlichen Jugendhilfe. Dazu gehören die Anregung und Förderung von Maßnahmen sowie die Verteilung der vom Rat für dieser Zwecke bereitgestellten Mittel, von denen ein Teil auf bestimmte Verantwortlichkeiten der Jugendverbände entfällt. Die Verwaltung des Jugendamtes ist entsprechend der Größe der einzelnen Gebietskörperschaften sehr unterschiedlich aufgebaut.

Die Aufgaben des Jugendamtes gliedern sich nach dem KJHG in zwei größere Komplexe. Zu dem primär fürsorgerischen Aufgabenbereich (Jugendfürsorge) gehören vor allem die Angebote für Kinder, Jugendliche und Eltern in schwierigen Erziehungssituationen (Erziehungsberatung, sozialpädagogische Familienhilfe, (teilstationäre) Heimerziehung, Pflegekinder). Zu dem anderen stärker vorbeugenden und jugendpflegerischen Aufgabenbereich (Jugendpflege) gehören die Kinder- und Jugenderholung, Freizeithilfen, politische Bildung und internationale Begegnungen. Aufgabe des Jugendamtes ist es, für diese Zwecke Einrichtungen und Veranstaltungen zu initiieren, zu unterstützen und gegebenenfalls zu schaffen und die notwendigen Hilfen im Einzelfall zu leisten.

Das Jugendamt beschäftigt in seiner Verwaltung qualifizierte hauptamtliche Kräfte. Lediglich in seinen Einrichtungen der Jugendpflege wird auf nebenamtliche Mitarbeiter zurückgegriffen. Ehrenamtliche Kräfte findet man in diesem Bereich im wesentlichen nur bei freien Trägern. Die Fachkräfte der Jugendämter unterstützen die Aktivitäten der in der Jugendarbeit tätigen Verbände. So stellen die Jugendämter z.B. den freien Trägern in ihren Einrichtungen Räume für ihre Aktivitäten zur Verfügung.

Die Mitarbeiter der Jugendämter im vorbeugenden Bereich tragen die Bezeichnung Jugendpfleger (Stadt-/Kreisjugendpfleger).

Die Bezeichnung Jugendamt wird auch von nicht-staatlichen Organisationen verwandt, z.B. für Dienststellen der katholischen und evangelischen Kirche, die Jugendhilfeaufgaben übernehmen.

Zur Unterstützung und Koordinierung der Arbeit der Jugendämter sind auf überörtlicher Ebene in allen Bundesländern Landesjugendämter errichtet

Youth Welfare and Youth Service Office

G

The statutory responsibilities in the field of youth work and youth welfare services attributed to the local authorities at the level of the *Landkreise* and *kreisfreie Städte (→ Kommunale Selbstverwaltung)* are carried out by the youth welfare and youth service offices (hereinafter referred to as "youth office"). Their structure and tasks are laid down in the Child and Youth Service Act *(→ Jugendgesetze)*. According to this Act, the youth office comprises the Youth Services Committee and an administration section.

The members of the Youth Services Committee are representatives of the local council and administration as well as citizens with expertise in the youth field, representatives of the youth organisations and other associations concerned with *→ Jugendhilfe*. The responsibilities of the Youth Services Committee encompass all aspects of youth work and youth welfare services at the local level. Thus, it is the prerogative of the Youth Services Committee to initiate and support youth work and youth welfare services and to decide on the distribution of the funds made available by the local council. A proportion of such funds is set aside for certain responsibilities taken on by the youth organisations. The administration of the youth office may have a varying number of subsections and staff depending on the size of the respective local authority.

According to the Child and Youth Services Act, the responsibilities of the youth office are subdivided into those with an emphasis on welfare (welfare work for the young) and those mainly concerned with leisure time provision. The former include guidance and counselling for children, young persons and parents in cases involving educational problems (child guidance, socio-educational help for families, (part-time) residential care, foster children). The latter include holiday schemes for children and young people, help with leisure time, political education and international contacts. The youth office is called upon to give incentives to, promote or, if necessary, set up establishments and events devoted to these purposes. It also provides help in individual cases. The staff of the youth offices who do such preventive work are referred to as youth officers (municipal youth officer/*Stadtjugendpfleger* - *Kreis* youth officer/*Kreisjugendpfleger).*

The administrative section of the youth office works with full-time qualified staff whereas its youth work establishments may also employ part-time workers. For the most part, the voluntary organisations are the only bodies who work with volunteers. The youth office staff support the activities of the organisations concerned with youth work. The youth organisations, for instance, may use the premises of the establishments maintained by the youth office free of charge.

The term *Jugendamt* is also used by non-statutory organisations and agencies, e.g. for offices established by the Catholic and the Protestant Church with the aim of providing youth work and youth welfare services under their respective umbrellas.

worden. Sie geben Empfehlungen für die Tätigkeit der Jugendämter, schaffen und unterhalten Einrichtungen für den überörtlichen Bedarf (z.B. für die Fortbildung der Mitarbeiter der Jugendhilfe). Sie führen die Aufsicht über Heime und andere Einrichtungen (Heimaufsichtsbehörde), in denen Minderjährige wohnen oder betreut werden mit dem Ziel, das leibliche, seelische und geistige Wohl der Jugendlichen sicherzustellen. Die Landesjugendämter bestehen wie die Jugendämter aus Verwaltung und Jugendhilfeausschuß (→ *Jugendbehörden).*

VK

Im Vereinigten Königreich werden die vielfältigen Aufgaben in der Arbeit mit jungen Menschen nicht wie in der Bundesrepublik Deutschland von einem Jugendamt übernommen, sondern von unterschiedlichen Trägern. So ist der *youth service* für die Belange der Freizeit und der sozialen Erziehung Jugendlicher verantwortlich; andere Aufgaben, wie die fürsorgerischen Aspekte, Pflegekinderwesen, Adoption, Sorgerechtsanordnungen usw., fallen in die Zuständigkeit der Sozialen Dienste, der Jugendgerichte und *Magistrates' Courts* sowie der Bewährungshilfe.

In England und Wales hat jede kommunale Erziehungsbehörde einen *youth service* oder *youth and community service.* In Nordirland bestehen entsprechende Dienststellen bei den *education and library boards.* In Schottland sind Jugendarbeit und Erwachsenenbildung in einem *community education service* zusammengefaßt (→ *Jugendarbeit,* VK).

Die *youth services* der kommunalen Erziehungsbehörden sind autonom und unterschiedlich strukturiert. Ihre Angebote differieren. Im allgemeinen wird der *youth service* von einem *principal youth officer* geleitet. Ihm stehen mehrere Jugendpfleger für verschiedene administrative Bereiche zur Seite, die ihrerseits mit hauptamtlichen Fachkräften für Clubs und Projektarbeit sowie Teilzeitkräften und ehrenamtlichen Helfern zusammenarbeiten. Das Engagement und das umfangreiche Fachwissen letzterer ist eines der wesentlichen Merkmale der britischen Jugendarbeit.

Die vorstehend beschriebene administrative Seite des *youth service* wird ergänzt durch einen Ausschuß von Mitgliedern des Stadt- und Gemeinderates. Dem Ausschuß für Erziehung und Bildung der kommunalen Erziehungsbehörde untersteht ein Ausschuß für Weiterbildung. Einer seiner Unterausschüsse befaßt sich mit Fragen der Jugend- und Gemeinwesenarbeit. Seine Aufgaben umfassen die Festlegung von Richtlinien, die Verwirklichung der politischen Ziele der Kommunalvertretung und die Entscheidung über die Verwendung der verfügbaren Mittel.

Viele Kommunen haben *youth committees,* in denen die öffentlichen und die freien Träger vertreten sind. Ihnen unmittelbar unterstehende Jugendpfleger sind mit der Koordinierung der Jugendprogramme und der Durchfüh-

At the regional level, *Land* youth offices have been set up in all *Länder* and their task is to support and coordinate the work of the youth office. They make recommendations for the work of the latter and set up and run establishments for services needed at their administrative level (e.g. further education programmes for workers in youth work and youth welfare services). They are responsible for the supervision of homes and other establishments (supervisory authority for homes) where young people live or are cared for. The aim of such supervision is to safeguard the physical, emotional and mental welfare of young people. Like the local youth offices, the *Land* youth offices comprise a Youth Services Committee and an administration section (→ *Jugendbehörden*).

UK

Work with young people in the UK, unlike the multiple function of a *Jugendamt* in Germany, is carried out by a number of bodies. For example, the youth service deals with questions relating to the use of leisure time and the social education of young people; other matters, e.g. young peoples' welfare, fostering, adoption, care orders, etc., are the responsibility of the social services, the Juvenile and Magistrates Courts and the probation service.

In England and Wales, each local education authority (LEA), has a youth service or youth and community service. In Northern Ireland this is provided by the education and library boards. In Scotland most education authorities combine the youth service and adult education to form a community education service (→ *Jugendarbeit,* UK).

LEA youth services are autonomous and different from each other in the way they are organised and the services they provide. Generally speaking, the youth service is headed by a principal youth officer. There are several assistant or area youth officers who, in turn, work with full-time staff responsible for clubs and projects as well as part-time staff and volunteers. The commitment and various skills contributed by the latter are one of the essential characteristics of British youth services.

The above administrative side of the youth service is complemented by committees of elected representatives designated by the local council. Under the auspices of the LEA education committee there is a further education committee, a sub-committee of which deals with youth and community services. Their frame of reference is to set guidelines, implement the policies laid down by the council and decide on the spending of available funds.

Many authorities have youth committees on which official and voluntary bodies are represented. They employ youth officers to coordinate youth work and to arrange in-service training.

The authorities maintain and run their own centres and clubs. They also provide the bulk of financial support to local voluntary organisations by lending premises and equipment and contributing to costs. (Voluntary organisations meet a considerable part of their costs themselves from fund-raising activities and members' subscriptions.)

rung von Fortbildungsmaßnahmen für die Mitarbeiter der Jugendarbeit beauftragt.

Die Behörden unterhalten eigene Jugendzentren und -clubs; sie übernehmen auch den größten Teil der finanziellen Lasten der örtlichen freien Träger, indem sie ihnen Räume und Ausrüstungsgegenstände zur Verfügung stellen und Zuschüsse zu den laufenden Kosten gewähren. (Die freien Träger kommen für einen beträchtlichen Prozentsatz ihrer Kosten selbst auf, indem sie Veranstaltungen durchführen, die Geld einbringen, und Mitgliedsbeiträge erheben.)

Der öffentliche *youth and community service* arbeitet meist partnerschaftlich mit den freien Trägern zusammen.

Jugendarbeit (f)

D
Jugendarbeit ist gleichbedeutend mit außerschulischer Jugendbildung. Als eigenes Lernfeld ergänzt sie das Angebot des übrigen Bildungswesens und ist Teil der → *Jugendhilfe*.

Die öffentliche Jugendhilfe hat darauf hinzuwirken, daß die zur Förderung der Entwicklung junger Menschen erforderlichen Angebote der Jugendarbeit zur Verfügung stehen. Die Jugendarbeit soll durch die Vielfalt von Trägern unterschiedlicher Wertorientierungen und die Vielfalt von Inhalten, Methoden und Arbeitsformen wirken. Sie wird angeboten von Verbänden, Gruppen und Initiativen der Jugend, von anderen Trägern der Jugendarbeit und den Trägern der öffentlichen Jugendhilfe. Sie umfaßt die offene Jugendarbeit sowie verbandsgebundene Angebote.

Jugendarbeit ist geprägt durch Freiwilligkeit der Teilnahme und Verzicht auf Leistungsbewertungen. Sie soll an die Bedürfnisse und Interessen junger Menschen anknüpfen und von ihnen mitbestimmt und mitgestaltet werden. Jugendarbeit soll zu Selbstbestimmung, zu gesellschaftlicher Mitverantwortung und zu sozialem Engagement anregen und befähigen. Sie dient dem sozialen Lernen sowie der Freizeitgestaltung junger Menschen.

Zu den Schwerpunkten der Jugendarbeit gehören:

1. allgemeine, politische, soziale, gesundheitliche, kulturelle, naturkundliche und technische Bildung;
2. arbeitswelt- und familienbezogene Jugendarbeit;
3. → *internationale Jugendarbeit;*
4. Jugendarbeit in Geselligkeit, Spiel und Sport;
5. → *Kinder- und Jugenderholung;*
6. Jugendberatung (→ *Beratungsdienste*).

Jugendarbeit schließt ethische, religiöse, wirtschaftliche, ökologische und medienkundliche Gesichtspunkte ein.

The statutory youth and community service often works in partnership with the voluntary sector.

Youth Work/Youth and Community Work

G

Youth work is the out-of-school education of young people. It is a separate field of learning which supplements the provisions of the school system and forms part of the complex of youth work and youth welfare services (→ *Jugendhilfe*).

The statutory youth services are required to further the development of young people by making the necessary provision. Youth work should operate through a wide variety of organisers advocating different sets of values, dealing with a wide range of subjects, using different methods and types of work. Youth work is provided by associations, groups, young people's initiatives, and other voluntary as well as statutory bodies responsible for youth work and youth welfare services. It comprises activities for members of youth clubs or organisations and provision for unattached young people.

Youth work is distinguished by the concept of voluntary participation and the idea of non-competitive achievement. Provision must concentrate on the real needs and interests of young people, and they should take an active part in its organisation and participate in decision-making. Youth work is to promote self-determination, to enable the young to share social responsibility and to give incentives for community involvement. Moreover, opportunities are provided for social learning and leisure time activities.

Main areas of concern are:

1. the general, political, social, health and cultural education of the young as well as informal educational programmes in the fields of biology and technology;
2. youth work relative to the world of work and the family;
3. international youth work (→ *Internationale Jugendarbeit*);
4. youth work in social activities, play and sports;
5. recreational programmes for children and young people (→ *Kinder- und Jugenderholung*);
6. counselling services (→ *Beratungsdienste*).

Zur Jugendarbeit gehören auch Bildungsangebote für ehren- und nebenamtliche Mitarbeiter, die Mitarbeiterfortbildung sowie die Errichtung und Unterhaltung von Jugendfreizeit- und Jugendbildungsstätten.

Die nichtstaatlichen Träger erhalten für ihre Jugendarbeit Förderungsmittel des Bundesjugendplanes, der Landesjugendpläne und der Kommunen.

Soweit nicht an anderer Stelle erläutert (Querverweise), umfassen die Teilbereiche der außerschulischen Jugendbildung folgende Aktivitäten und Zielsetzungen:

— Kulturelle Bildung
(auch sozio-kulturelle Jugendbildung; früher: musische Bildung) ist Teil der sozio-kulturellen Jugendarbeit mit den Mitteln der Kunst (Musik, Tanz, Theater, Literatur, bildende Kunst). Impulse für die inhaltliche und methodische Fortentwicklung der kulturellen Jugendarbeit gehen insbesondere aus von den kulturellen Fachverbänden, von der Akademie Remscheid für musische Bildung und Medienerziehung (u.a. durch Fortbildungskurse für die Mitarbeiter der Jugendhilfe) und von der Bundesakademie für musikalische Jugendbildung in Trossingen.

— Politische Bildung
soll jungen Menschen durch Vermittlung von Kenntnissen über Gesellschaft und Staat die Urteilsbildung über politische Vorgänge und Konflikte ermöglichen, zur Wahrnehmung der eigenen Rechte und Interessen ebenso wie der Pflichten und Verantwortlichkeit gegenüber der Gesellschaft befähigen sowie zur Mitwirkung an der Gestaltung einer freiheitlich-demokratischen Lebens- und Staatsordnung anregen. Träger sind nichtstaatliche Verbände und Jugendbildungsstätten.

— Sportliche Jugendbildung
soll neben der Anleitung zur Ausübung des Sports als Teil der Jugendarbeit in umfassendem Sinne unter pädagogischen, sozialen und gesundheitlichen Gesichtspunkten zur Bildung junger Menschen beitragen. Führend für die inhaltliche Entwicklung und Mitarbeiterschulung der sportlichen Jugendbildung (Sportjugendleiter) sind die Deutsche Sportjugend im DSB und andere Jugendverbände.

Schwerpunkte der Jugendarbeit waren in den letzten Jahren auch die Entwicklung von Hilfen für benachteiligte Jugendliche, Jugendberatungsdienste und die Schaffung von arbeitsweltbezogenen Programmen für junge Arbeitslose. Träger sind überwiegend nichtstaatliche Verbände und Initiativen sowie die örtlichen Jugendämter (kommunale Jugendpflege).

VK

Der *Education Act* von 1944 verpflichtet die Kommunen, für die Bildungsbedürfnisse Jugendlicher in ihrer Freizeit Sorge zu tragen. Heute wird diese Aufgabe von den kommunalen Erziehungsbehörden (öffentliche Träger; → *Ju-*

Youth work also covers ethical and religious concepts and deals with economic, ecological and mass-media issues.

Responsibilities for youth work include educational provision for voluntary and part-time leaders, further education programmes for full-time staff – and the construction and maintenance of leisure time and educational centres for the young.

The voluntary organisations responsible for this type of youth work are grant-aided from Federal Youth Plan funds, the *Land* youth plans and the local authorities.

Except for those areas which are explained under the respective headings (cross references), the various sectors of out-of-school education comprise the following objectives and activities:

– cultural education
   (also referred to as socio-cultural education of the young, formerly called
   musische Bildung, i.e. education in music and the arts) is part of socio-cultural youth work in which the arts are used as a medium (music, dancing, drama, literature, visual arts). The development of the contents and methods of cultural youth work comes mainly from the organisations specialising in cultural work, the *Akademie Remscheid für musische Bildung und Medienerziehung* (Remscheid Academy for Education in Music, the Arts and Media, which provides, amongst other things, further education courses for youth workers) and the *Bundesakademie für musikalische Jugendbildung* (Federal Academy for Musical Youth Education) located in Trossingen.

– political education (active citizenship)
   aims to inform young people about society and the State and thereby enable them to assess political processes and conflicts, to represent their own rights and interests, and to fulfil their duties and responsibilities towards the society. It should, moreover, give incentives towards the formation of the individual in a democratic life-style within an ordered society. Political education is mainly provided by non-statutory organisations and educational centres for the young.

– sports education
   aims to promote the general education (including social and health aspects) of young people through participation in sport. The development of programmes as well as the staff training for youth (sports) leaders lies mainly with the *Deutsche Sportjugend* (German Sports Youth) of the German Sports Federation.

In recent years, a priority has been the development of programmes for disadvantaged young people, counselling services and schemes for the young unemployed relative to the world of work. The responsibility for such provision lies mainly with voluntary organisations, action groups and the → *Jugendpflege* section of local youth offices *(→ Jugendamt).*

gendbehörden, VK) zusammen mit mehr als 70 nationalen freien Jugendorganisationen (freie Träger) übernommen.

Die öffentliche und freie Jugendarbeit wird aus dem nationalen und kommunalen Steueraufkommen finanziert, wobei die freien Träger zusätzlich Mittel aus verschiedenen anderen Quellen erhalten. In den letzten zehn Jahren ist eine Zunahme der freien Träger auf Nachbarschaftsebene oder auf der kommunalen Ebene zu verzeichnen gewesen. Während dieser neue Wachstumsbereich der Jugendarbeit vielfach Förderungsmittel der kommunalen Erziehungsbehörden erhält, können weitere Gelder bei anderen Ministerien und Trägern beantragt werden, wobei oft auf die fachlichen Aspekte abgestellt wird.

Die Verwaltungsstrukturen und organisatorischen Schwerpunkte sind sehr unterschiedlich. In vielen Kommunen besteht ein *community education service,* in den die Jugendarbeit zusammen mit anderen Bildungsangeboten (z.B. Erwachsenenbildung) mehr oder weniger integriert ist. Andere Kommunen haben einen völlig getrennten *youth service,* vornehmlich für die Altersgruppe der 14- bis 21jährigen. In der Jugend- und Gemeinwesenarbeit kann das Schwergewicht auf der Arbeit mit jungen Menschen und Gruppen von Erwachsenen oder auf der Kinderarbeit liegen. Die Unterschiede sind oft geringfügig und spiegeln sich nicht notwendigerweise im Namen der Einrichtung wider. In anderen Fällen ist die Jugendarbeit bei der Freizeitbehörde angesiedelt. Während über die zentrale Zielsetzung der Jugendarbeit weitgehend Konsens besteht — Bereitstellung von Angeboten der informellen sozialen Erziehung und politischen Bildung für junge Menschen — differieren die Prioritäten und Arbeitsstile beträchtlich. In den letzten Jahren verlagerte sich das Schwergewicht immer mehr auf Maßnahmen zur Bekämpfung von Ausländer- und Frauenfeindlichkeit, auf die Arbeit mit arbeitslosen Jugendlichen, Mädchen- und Frauenprogramme, Hilfen für junge Männer und Frauen aus ethnischen Minderheiten und auf Behindertenarbeit. In jüngster Zeit sind die Aufgaben der Drogenerziehung und der Arbeit mit Drogenbenutzern noch hinzugekommen. Die Verlagerung der Schwerpunkte war oft eine Folge des Regierungsberichtes *Experience and Participation — The Thompson Report,* 1982. In vielen Fällen versucht die Zentralregierung, mit Hilfe des Ministeriums für Erziehung und Wissenschaft oder dessen Entsprechungen in Wales, Schottland und Nordirland die Schwerpunkte der Jugendarbeit der Kommunen durch die Veröffentlichung von Berichten und durch zweckgebundene Förderungsmittel für diese Ebene zu beeinflussen. Der *Education Reform Act* von 1988 wird wohl diesen Trend noch verstärken (→ *Jugendgesetze).*

Hauptmerkmal der Jugendarbeit ist die Freiwilligkeit der Beziehungen mit jungen Leuten und das Bemühen, ihre Mitwirkung bei den Angeboten zu fördern. In dieser Hinsicht ist Jugendarbeit für alle Jugendlichen da, selbst wenn die Prioritäten einzelner Behörden oder Organisationen besondere Zielgruppen, auch in fachlicher Hinsicht, bedingen.

UK

The 1944 Education Act requires local education authorities to provide for the educational needs of young people in their leisure time. Today, such provision is made through the local authorities (the statutory sector; → *Jugendbehörden,* UK) together with more than 70 national voluntary youth organisations (the voluntary sector).

Funding for both sectors is provided through local and national taxation, although the voluntary sector is often funded through a variety of other sources. In addition, the last ten years has seen a growth in local voluntary organisations at neighbourhood or municipal level. Whilst this latter sector, the "emerging" youth service, is often supported by local education authority grants, funds may also be sought from other departments and bodies, often reflecting the specialist nature of the work undertaken.

Administrative structures and organisational priorities vary widely. Many authorities operate a community education service, with youth work integrated to a greater or lesser extent with other forms of education provision (e.g. Adult Education). Others provide an entirely separate youth service, working mainly with the 14–21 age range. In youth and community services, there may be an emphasis upon work with young people and adult groups, or with young children. Differences are often subtle, and are not necessarily reflected in the title used. In some cases, provision is made through the Leisure Services Department of the local authority. Whilst there is broad consensus about the core aims and objectives of the service — to provide informal social and political education for young people — priorities and styles of work vary considerably. In recent years there has been an increasing emphasis upon work to combat racism and sexism; on work with unemployed young people; on specialist provision for girls and young women, and with young men and women from ethnic minorities; and on work with the handicapped. Even more recently, drugs education and work with drug users has become important. Many of these priorities emerged from the government report Experience and Participation — The Thompson Report, 1982. Frequently, central government, through the Department of Education and Science (DES), or its equivalent in Wales, Scotland and Northern Ireland, seeks to influence local priorities through the publication of reports and by specifically directed funding to local authorities. The Education Reform Act of 1988 may well increase this trend (→ *Jugendgesetze).*

The service is characterised by its voluntary relationships with young people, and the attempt to encourage their participation in provision. To this extent it is available to all young people, although priorities from one authority or organisation to another may dictate particular and specialist target groups.

Jugendarbeit (f), mobile

D
Jugendarbeit und Sozialarbeit sind nur sinnvoll, wenn man das weitere soziale Umfeld (Familie, Schule, *peer-groups*) nicht unberücksichtigt läßt. Mobile Jugendarbeit ist eine notwendige Reaktion auf die Tatsache, daß die „traditionelle" Jugendarbeit gerade gefährdete Jugendliche kaum erreicht oder sogar ausgrenzt. Mobile Jugendarbeit versteht sich auch als Kritik an der traditionellen Jugendarbeit. Sie richtet sich an Jugendliche, die häufig keiner mehr haben will, die das Netz der Jugendhilfe nicht auffangen konnte.

Am bekanntesten ist mobile Jugendarbeit in der Form von *street work* geworden. Straßensozialarbeit entwickelte sich Ende der 20er Jahre in den USA als professionelle Arbeitsweise von Sozialarbeitern im Zusammenhang mit der ständig wachsenden Jugendkriminalität. In der Bundesrepublik wird *street work* etwa seit Ende der 60er Jahre praktiziert und zielt keineswegs ausschließlich auf delinquente Jugendliche. Soziale Probleme *(→ Drogenmißbrauch, → Jugendarbeitslosigkeit)* erweitern dieses Arbeitsfeld, so daß man auch von „ambulanten Beratungsformen" sprechen kann.

Eine sinnvolle Konzeption mobiler Jugendarbeit wird aber über Einzel- und Gruppenberatung gefährdeter Jugendlicher hinausgehen und auch die Familien und das Gemeinwesen mit einbeziehen.

Wesentliches Kennzeichen mobiler Jugendarbeit ist ihr präventiver Charakter und ihre Absage an alle obrigkeitlichen Kontrollaufgaben. Letzteres vor allem, damit eine Vertrauensbasis zwischen Sozialarbeiter und Klientel überhaupt entstehen kann.

Zu den Aufgaben mobiler Jugendarbeit gehört z.B., die Entstehung von jugendlichen Randgruppen möglichst frühzeitig zu erkennen, Bedürfnisse und besondere Probleme von Straßengruppen festzustellen und ggfs. Lösungswege aufzuzeigen, bzw. Lösungsansätze zu unterstützen sowie die Aufnahme von besonders gefährdeten Jugendlichen in sozialpädagogisch betreute Jugendwohngruppen.

Insgesamt ist festzuhalten, daß es sich bei mobiler Jugendarbeit um einen lebensfeldbezogenen Ansatz handelt, der die Problem- und Bedürfnislagen der Jugendlichen und damit auch eines Gemeinwesens aufgreift.

VK
Mobile Jugendarbeit in Großbritannien bedeutet, daß der *youth worker* vor Ort auf den Jugendlichen zugeht. Er schaltet sich unmittelbar in die Aktivitäten einzelner oder bestimmter Gruppen ein. Er ist in Cafés anzutreffen, in *pubs,* in Diskotheken, auf Spielplätzen, in Kinos und Spielhallen; er arbeitet in Schulen und Fabriken. Der *youth worker* schafft eine Vertrauensbasis, durch die er Jugendlichen Informationen über Arbeitsplätze, die Schule, gesetzliche Bestimmungen, Freizeitaktivitäten, familiäre Beziehungen, Arbeitgeber und

Detached Youth Work

G

Youth work and youth welfare work are only valid if exercised within the wider social context (family, school, peer groups). Detached youth work is a recognition of the fact that the "traditional" forms of youth work fail to reach many if not a majority of young people. Detached youth work complements traditional youth work. It focuses on young people who have slipped through the youth work and youth welfare work net.

The best known form of detached youth work is street work. This was developed in the USA at the end of the 20s as a professional approach by social workers to combat the rise in juvenile delinquency. In the Federal Republic of Germany, where street work has been practised since the end of the 60s, it embraces more than work with juvenile delinquents. It covers other social problems such as drug abuse (→ *Drogenmißbrauch),* youth unemployment (→ *Jugendarbeitslosigkeit)* etc. as part of its programme so that it becomes a "mobile advice and counselling service".

This concept of detached youth work requires that counselling of individuals or groups of young people at risk is extended to include their families and the local community.

Essential characteristics of detached youth work are its preventive nature and the way in which it distances itself from authority controls in order that a relationship of confidence may be developed between the social worker and his client.

The main tasks of detached youth work are to identify as soon as possible emerging marginal groups of youngsters, to determine the particular needs of young people and the special problems of street gangs, to give advice and suggest solutions where necessary and appropriate. Additionally, young people particularly at risk may be accommodated in groups under the supervision of a youth worker.

It must be emphasized again that detached youth work takes account of the whole human environment and therefore aims to solve the problems and needs not only of young people but also those of the community at large.

UK

In the detached youth work situation, the worker goes out to the young person. He gets involved directly with various activities which the individual and groups undertake; he is around in coffee bars, pubs, discos, playing fields, cinemas, amusement arcades; he works in schools and factories; he offers a relationship in which a young person can be given information on jobs, schools, the law and recreation, family relationships, employers, etc. He works with friendship groups and interest groups as well as with various associations; ten-

vieles mehr vermitteln kann. Er arbeitet mit Freundschafts- und Interessengruppen zusammen, ebenso wie mit unterschiedlichen Organisationen: Mieterverbänden, Zusammenschlüssen ausländischer Arbeitnehmer, Trägern des sozialen Wohnungsbaus (→ *Sozialer Wohnungsbau,* VK), Hilfsorganisationen für die Inanspruchnahme wohlfahrtsrechtlicher Leistungen und sonstigen örtlichen Gruppierungen.

Jugendarbeitslosigkeit (f)

D

Zu den jugendlichen Arbeitslosen rechnen in erster Linie diejenigen Jugendlichen, die noch keine 20 Jahre alt sind. Zu den jungen Arbeitslosen zählt die Altersgruppe der 20- bis 25jährigen. Arbeitslos im Sinne des Gesetzes ist, wer vorübergehend nicht in einem Beschäftigungsverhältnis steht oder beim Arbeitsamt arbeitslos gemeldet ist.

Die Arbeitslosigkeit Jugendlicher ist seit 1988 deutlich rückläufig. Probleme auf dem Arbeitsmarkt haben hauptsächlich beruflich nicht qualifizierte Jugendliche. Daher ist es das Ziel der Bundesregierung, durch verstärkte Qualifizierung die Eingliederung Jugendlicher in den Ausbildungs- und Arbeitsmarkt zu erleichtern und ihre Berufschancen zu verbessern.

So kann z.B. Auszubildenden, die nicht zu Hause wohnen, unter bestimmten Voraussetzungen eine Berufsausbildungsbeihilfe für die berufliche Ausbildung in Betrieben oder überbetrieblichen Ausbildungsstätten sowie für die Teilnahme an berufsvorbereitenden Bildungsmaßnahmen gewährt werden.

Für Sonderschüler, Hauptschulabgänger ohne Abschluß, junge Ausländer und sozial benachteiligte Jugendliche (ehemalige Drogenabhängige, Strafentlassene, verhaltensgestörte Jugendliche), die auch nach Teilnahme an einer berufsvorbereitenden Bildungsmaßnahme ohne weitere Förderung nicht in eine Ausbildungsstelle in einem Betrieb vermittelt werden können, sind spezielle Förderungsinstrumente vorgesehen.

Zu den Hilfen für Arbeitslose gehören auch die Arbeitsbeschaffungsmaßnahmen, die von den Arbeitsämtern in Zusammenarbeit mit öffentlichen und privaten Trägern durchgeführt werden. Junge Arbeitslose werden insbesondere in Maßnahmen gefördert, bei denen Beschäftigung und Unterricht kombiniert sind. Die Förderung dauert in der Regel bis zu einem Jahr. Ziel ist, ihnen eine sinnvolle Tätigkeit, z.B im Bereich des Umweltschutzes, der Sanierung von Bauwerken und Betreuung von hilfsbedürftigen Menschen, anzubieten und sie wieder in einen geregelten Tätigkeitsbereich zu integrieren. Die Erfahrung zeigt, daß die Aussichten auf eine feste Stellung oder eine Ausbildung größer sind für jeden, der in einer Arbeitsbeschaffungsmaßnahme durchgehalten und dabei neue Fähigkeiten, u.a. auch den Hauptschulabschluß, erworben hat. Auch die Jugendämter und Einrichtungen der Jugendarbeit bieten zunehmend Beratung und arbeitsbezogene Bildungs- und Beschäftigungsmöglichkeiten für arbeitslose Jugendliche an.

ants, immigrants, housing (→ *Sozialer Wohnungsbau*, UK), welfare rights and community associations.

Youth Unemployment

G

Amongst the young unemployed are mainly ranked those who are not yet 20 years of age. Unemployed young adults belonging to the 20–25 age range are also included in this category in a wider sense. For legal purposes, to be unemployed means to be temporarily out of a job and registered with the employment office.

Unemployment figures have shown a marked decrease since 1988. Those who still have major difficulties in finding a job are unqualified young people. By promoting achievement of better qualifications, the Federal Government aims to assist the young in finding a training position as well as employment and to help them get on in their careers.

Apprentices who do not live with their parents, for instance, may, providing they fulfil certain requirements, receive a vocational training grant for serving their apprenticeship with a firm or attending the schemes provided by inter-firm training centres. Grants are also available for participating in vocational training preparatory schemes.

Special promotional programmes were instituted in order to assist special school pupils, drop-outs from the *Hauptschule* (→ *Bildungswesen)*, foreigners and socially disadvantaged young people (e.g. former drug-addicts, ex-prisoners, and the socially mal-adjusted) who, even after having taken part in a vocational training preparatory scheme, cannot be placed with a firm and require additional help.

Statutory provision for the young unemployed includes the Job Creation Scheme which is implemented by the employment office in cooperation with public and voluntary bodies. Especially the young unemployed are assisted through occupational and educational programmes of up to one year's duration. The programmes aim to give them an opportunity to take part in a useful activity such as environmental projects, reconstructing buildings and helping the needy. By assuming such responsibilities participants in the scheme will readapt to the demands of regular employment. Experience shows that those who have completed a Job Creation Scheme or have obtained the *Hauptschule* leaving certificate have a much better chance of finding a regular job or training place. The youth offices and youth work establishments increasingly provide advisory services as well as educational and occupational programmes for unemployed young people.

Besondere Förderungsangebote von Bund und Ländern kommen Mädchen und jungen Frauen, sozial benachteiligten, ausländischen und behinderten Jugendlichen zugute, da diese Personengruppen nach wie vor geringere Chancen auf dem Ausbildungs- und Arbeitsmarkt haben.

Weitere Maßnahmen zur beruflichen Qualifizierung sind die Einrichtung eines 10. Schuljahres an Hauptschulen auf freiwilliger Basis oder als Plichtschuljahr sowie von Berufsvorbereitungs- oder Berufsgrundbildungsjahren mit dem Ziel, sie auf die Ausbildung anzurechnen.

Abschließend ist noch auf die Selbsthilfegruppen Jugendlicher hinzuweisen. Junge Menschen schaffen sich selbstverwaltete Produktionseinheiten (Kfz-Werkstätten, ökologische Bäckereien, etc.), um eine minimale Existenzgrundlage zu finden.

Langfristig bleibt es das Bestreben der Bundesregierung, möglichst allen Jugendlichen zu einer abgeschlossenen Berufsausbildung zu verhelfen. Eine abgeschlossene Berufsausbildung wird für Jugendliche immer wichtiger, da angesichts der Entwicklung der Technologie der Bedarf an ungelernten Arbeitskräften auch in Zukunft weiter zurückgeht.

VK

Die Arbeitslosigkeit im Vereinigten Königreich war in den letzten Jahren generell rückläufig. Die Regierung ist der Überzeugung, daß es langfristig nicht im Interesse der 16- und 17jährigen oder das Landes überhaupt liegt, wenn Jugendliche ihr Arbeitsleben ohne fachliche Ausbildung oder als Arbeitslose und Empfänger von sozialen Leistungen beginnen, während positive Alternativen der Fortsetzung der Schul- und Berufsausbildung oder der Vermittlung eines Arbeitsplatzes durchaus vorhanden sind.

Das Problem der Arbeitslosigkeit allgemein, einschließlich der Jugendarbeitslosigkeit, fällt in die Zuständigkeit des Arbeitsministeriums, das gemeinsam mit seinen *Training and Enterprise Councils (TEC)* und der Arbeitsvermittlung (→ *Bundesanstalt für Arbeit, VK*) verschiedene großangelegte Initiativen für Jugendliche von 16 bis 17 Jahren sowie langfristig Arbeitslose ab 18 Jahren ins Leben gerufen hat.

— Berufsbildende Maßnahmen für Jugendliche im Rahmen des *Youth Training/YT,* das anstelle des *Youth Training Scheme* getreten ist, bieten eine anspruchsvolle Berufsausbildung und strukturierte praktische Erfahrung mit dem Ziel, Jugendliche besser für die Anforderungen des Arbeitsmarktes auszurüsten. Die geplante Neugestaltung des *Youth Training* wird eine größere Flexibilität der Dauer, Anlage, Teilnahmeberechtigung und Förderungspraxis einschließen.
  Allen Jugendlichen, die nicht mehr die Schule besuchen oder die nicht vollzeitbeschäftigt sind, garantiert die Regierung einen Ausbildungsplatz im Rahmen des YT. Das Angebot gilt bis zur Erreichung des 18. Lebensjahres nicht nur für Schulabgänger von 16 und 17 Jahren, sondern auch für junge Menschen, die aus den unterschiedlichsten Gründen aus einem Arbeitsverhältnis oder einem YT-Programm ausscheiden.

Other promotional programmes were instituted by the Federation and the *Länder* in order to assist girls and young women, the socially disadvantaged, the handicapped and young foreigners, as these groups are most affected by the lack of training places and jobs.

Moreover, the introduction of a 10th form at the *Hauptschule*, the attendance of which in some places is voluntary, and in others compulsory, also forms part of the measures to promote vocational qualification. Other devices are the Vocational Training Preparatory Year or the Basic Vocational Training Year, the completion of which counts as part of a vocational training course.

In conclusion, mention must be made of the self-help groups formed by the young. Young people set up self-administered production units (car repair workshops, organic bakeries, etc.) in order to eke out an existence.

The long-term policy of the Federal Republic is to help the maximum number of young people to obtain a vocational qualification. This will be increasingly important, as it is expected that there will be a diminishing need for unskilled labour in view of the development of high technology.

UK

The employment situation in the UK has generally improved over the past few years. The Government do not believe that it is in the long-term interests of 16 and 17-year-olds or the country as a whole for them to start their working lives unskilled and unemployed, supported by social security benefits when the positive choices of remaining in full-time education, vocational training, or finding employment are available.

Youth unemployment and unemployment amongst the population as a whole is the concern of the Employment Department which together with its Training and Enterprise Councils (TEC) and Employment Service (→ *Bundesanstalt für Arbeit, UK)* has taken a number of major initiatives directed at young people between the ages of 16 and 17 as well as the long-term unemployed aged 18 and over.

— Youth Training (YT), formerly the Youth Training Scheme (YTS), provides high quality training and planned work experience, aiming to better suit young people for the jobs market. New arrangements under YT will include greater flexibility in training design, duration, eligibility and funding.
   The Government has guaranteed an offer of a YT place to all young people who are not in full-time education or employment. The guarantee covers not only 16 to 17-year-old school-leavers but also young people who leave a job or YT, for whatever reason, and remains in force until the person's eighteenth birthday.

— An intensive Restart Interview is provided every six months to all the unemployed. The purpose of this Restart counselling is to ensure that they are either helped to find employment or get a place on a government scheme.

– Jedem Arbeitslosen wird alle sechs Monate ein intensives Beratungsgespräch angeboten, das darauf abzielt, ihm zu einem neuen Anlauf in das
Berufsleben oder einem Ausbildungsplatz in einer der von der Regierung
eingeleiteten Maßnahmen zu verhelfen *(Restart Interview)*.

– *Restart*-Kurse bieten Hilfen für Jugendliche, die sechs Monate oder länger
arbeitslos waren und dadurch mit besonderen Härten zu kämpfen haben.
Bei Arbeitslosigkeit von zwei Monaten und darüber und mangelnder Bereitschaft, die Hilfsangebote des *Restart*-Beratungsgespräches anzuneh-
men, muß ein *Restart*-Kurs besucht werden. Diese Kurse stellen eine Brük-
ke zwischen Beratungsgespräch und Ausbildungs- bzw. Beschäftigungs-
programm oder Arbeitsverhältnis dar. Sie ermöglichen es den Teilnehmern, Selbstvertrauen und Motivation wiederzugewinnen, ihre Stärken
und Fähigkeiten besser einzuschätzen, differenzierte Zukunftsperspekti-
ven zu entwickeln und selbst zu entscheiden, welche Schritte zu unternehmen sind, um zu einem festen Arbeitsverhältnis zurückzufinden.

– *Jobclubs* bieten einen zweiwöchigen Teilzeitkurs in Techniken der Stel-
lungssuche für Personen, die sechs Monate oder mehr arbeitslos waren.
Nach dem Kurs besuchen die Teilnehmer regelmäßig ein Zentrum für Arbeitssuchende, das Zeitungen, Zeitschriften, Briefmarken und Briefpapier,
Telefone, Kopiergeräte usw. kostenlos bereitstellt. Ein Netz von etwa 900
jobclubs kann 145.000 Ratsuchende betreuen.

– Für junge Erwachsene zwischen 18 und 24 Jahren besteht nach sechs- bis
zwölfmonatiger Arbeitslosigkeit die Möglichkeit, an berufsqualifizierenden Beschäftigungsmaßnahmen *(Employment Training)* oder am Unter-
stützungsprogramm für Unternehmensgründungen *(Enterprise Allowance
Scheme)* teilzunehmen *(→ Bundesanstalt für Arbeit, VK)*.

– Der Aufbau einer selbständigen Existenz oder die Schaffung von Arbeitsplätzen wird durch eine breite Palette von Ausbildungs-, Beschäftigungs-
und Unternehmenshilfeprogrammen gefördert. Weitere Maßnahmen sind
Deregulierung und Verbesserung der Beziehungen zwischen Arbeitgebern und Arbeitnehmern sowie der Absprachen über Löhne und Gehälter.
Zur Förderung der unternehmerischen Initiative stehen Mittel für Unternehmensgründungen, den Tourismus sowie Firmenerweiterungen zur Verfügung. Kleine Betriebe können Beratungsdienste in Anspruch nehmen.

– Alle Programme und Angebote des Arbeitsministeriums stehen, oft mit
leichter zu erfüllenden Zugangsvoraussetzungen, auch Behinderten offen.
Außerdem besteht eine große Palette von Hilfen und Sonderprogrammen
für diesen Personenkreis.

Den spezifischen Bedürfnissen von Behinderten und ethnischen Minderheiten wird durch die Bereitstellung von Zuschüssen Rechnung getragen. So gibt
es z.B. Hilfen für die Einstellung behinderter oder benachteiligter Personen,
finanzielle Unterstützung für die geschützte Beschäftigung, Anpassungshil-
fen für Ausstattung und bauliche Maßnahmen sowie einführende und fachbe-
zogene Sprachkurse für Englisch als Zweitsprache.

— Restart Courses are designed to help those people who have been out of work for six months or longer and have been hardest hit by unemployment. Those who have been out of work for two years or more and who refuse all offers to help at a Restart Interview will be required to attend a Restart Course. Restart Courses provide a bridge between an advisory interview and either a training or employment programme or a job. They help participants to rebuild confidence and motivation, reassess their strengths and skills, consider options for their future in more detail and decide what next action to take to get back to work.

— Jobclubs provide a two-week, part-time course in job-hunting skills for people who have been unemployed for six months or more, followed by regular attendance at a resource centre where newspapers, journals, stamps and stationery, telephones, photocopying etc. are available free of charge. There is a network of about 900 jobclubs with a capacity for 145,000 participants.

— All young adults who are aged 18 to 24 and have been unemployed for between six and twelve months may receive a place on Employment Training or the Enterprise Allowance Scheme (→ *Bundesanstalt für Arbeit, UK*).

— Enterprise and job creation are encouraged through the provision of a wide range of training, employment and business help schemes, deregulation, improved industrial relations and pay arrangements. To promote enterprise, funding is available to stimulate self-employment, tourism and business expansion, and to finance counselling services for small firms.

— All Employment Department programmes and services are open to people with disabilities, often with relaxed entry conditions. In addition, there is a wide range of services and schemes for those who need special help.

The needs of the disabled and ethnic minorities are met by funding for, for example, special aids to employment, sheltered employment, equipment and premises adaptation, as well as preparatory and skills-linked English as a Second Language courses.

Jugendbehörden (f/pl)
(Träger (m/pl) der öffentlichen Jugendhilfe (f))

D

Dies sind die Behörden (Verwaltungseinheiten), die die gesetzlichen Aufgaben der → *Jugendhilfe* auf den verschiedenen Verwaltungsebenen durchführen, d.h. die Jugendämter, Landesjugendämter, obersten Landesjugendbehörden und das Bundesministerium für Frauen und Jugend.

Die obersten Landesjugendbehörden erfüllen nach Landesrecht unterschiedliche Jugendhilfeaufgaben im Rahmen des Art. 1 § 82 KJHG (→ *Jugendgesetze).* In einzelnen Ländern wurden alle Jugendfragen an einer Stelle zusammengefaßt, in anderen Ländern sind sie verschiedenen Ministerien zugeordnet. Zu den Aufgaben der obersten Landesjugendbehörden zählt z.B die Unterstützung landesweiter Programme in den einzelnen Bereichen der Jugendhilfe, insbesondere die finanzielle Förderung. Sie sollen ihre Erfahrungen den Trägern der freien und öffentlichen Jugendhilfe übermitteln sowie die gesammelten Erfahrungen auswerten.

Die Landesjugendämter stellen eine mittlere Ebene zwischen den örtlichen Jugendämtern und den obersten Landesjugendbehörden dar. Sie sind in einzelnen Bundesländern als staatliche (Landes-)behörden organisiert (Bayern, Hessen, Saarland, Niedersachsen, Schleswig-Holstein), in anderen Bundesländern als kommunale Behörden (Behörden von Kommunalverbänden wie Landschaftsverbände und Landeswohlfahrtsverbände, so in Baden-Württemberg und Nordrhein-Westfalen). In den Stadtstaaten fallen oberste Landesjugendbehörden und Landesjugendämter weitgehend zusammen.

Die Aufgaben des Landesjugendamtes (LJA) werden durch den Landesjugendhilfeausschuß und durch die Verwaltung des Landesjugendamtes im Rahmen der Satzung und der dem LJA zur Verfügung gestellten Mittel wahrgenommen. Der Leiter des Landesjugendamtes ist an die Beschlüsse des Landesjugendhilfeausschusses, in dem die freien → *Träger der Jugendhilfe* zwei Fünftel der Stimmen besitzen, gebunden.

Im Gegensatz zu den Landesjugendämtern (→ *Jugendamt),* die einen nach Art. 1 § 89 Abs. 2 KJHG festen Pflichtkatalog haben und daher eher eine ausführende Tätigkeit ausüben, ist die Aufgabe der obersten Landesjugendbehörden nach Art. 1 § 89 Abs. 2 KJHG in erster Linie die fachlich-politische Unterstützung und Anregung von Bestrebungen der Jugendhilfe, soweit sie über die Verpflichtungen der Jugendämter und Landesjugendämter hinausgehen. Sie sind aufgerufen, die Voraussetzungen für die Weiterentwicklung der Jugendhilfe zu schaffen oder Schritte zur Behebung von Notständen einzuleiten.

Youth Authorities
(bodies responsible for the statutory youth services)

G

These are the authorities (administrative units) in which the responsibilities for youth work and youth welfare services are vested at the various administrative levels as laid down by law, i.e. the youth offices, the *Land* youth offices, the youth authorities of the *Land* governments and the Federal Ministry for Women and Youth.

The youth authorities of the *Land* governments have been given various responsibilities for youth work and youth welfare services under article 1, section 82, of the Child and Youth Services Act (→ *Jugendgesetze*). In some *Länder* all youth matters are collectively dealt with within one department whilst in others several ministries may be involved. One of the functions of the youth authorities of the *Land* governments is to assist programmes organised at *Land* level in the various areas of → *Jugendhilfe* and, in particular, to provide financial support. They are also required to make available their experience to voluntary and statutory bodies of youth work and youth welfare services and to evaluate progress in the above fields.

The *Land* youth offices constitute a medium – level situated between the local youth offices and the youth authorities of the *Land* governments. In some of the Federal *Länder* (Bavaria, Hesse, Saarland, Lower Saxony, Schleswig-Holstein) they are set up as state *(Land)* authorities, in others, such as Baden-Wuerttemberg and North Rhine-Westphalia, as local authorities. (In the latter case they are statutory bodies established by associations of local authorities, e.g. *Landschaftsverbände* (→ *Kommunale Selbstverwaltung*) and *Land* level welfare organisations.) In the city states, the functions of the youth authority of the *Land* government and *Land* youth office are, for the most part, vested in the same body.

The duties of the *Land* youth office are a responsibility of the Youth Services Committee at *Land* level and carried out by the administration department of the *Land* youth office according to its statutes and the funds made available to it. The head of the *Land* youth office is governed by the decisions of the Youth Services Committee at *Land* level, in which the voluntary bodies of youth work and youth welfare services (→ *Träger der Jugendhilfe*) have two fifths of the votes.

The *Land* youth offices (→ *Jugendamt*) have been assigned a catalogue of duties by article 1, section 89, subsection 2, of the Child and Youth Services Act and thus have an executive function. The rôle of the youth authority of the *Land* government is primarily to introduce and support, professionally as well as politically, initiatives in the youth field under article 1, section 89, subsection 2, of the Child and Youth Services Act (in so far as these extend beyond the duties and responsibilities of the youth offices and *Land* youth offices). They are required to create the necessary prerequisites for the proper development of youth work and youth welfare services or to take necessary steps to deal with emergency situations.

VK

Administrativ gehört der *youth service* im Vereinigten Königreich zum Bildungswesen. Er wird zentral durch die Erziehungsministerien finanziert *(Department of Education and Science, Welsh Office, Scottish Education Department, Northern Ireland Department of Education).*

Auf kommunaler Ebene ist der *youth service* meist Teil der 104 Erziehungsbehörden in England und Wales. In Nordirland sind die fünf *education and library boards* zuständig. In Schottland ist bei den meisten Erziehungsbehörden der *youth service* mit der Erwachsenenbildung zu den *community education services* zusammengefaßt und den zehn *regional councils* zugeordnet.

Die Gemeinden sichern die Finanzierung ihrer eigenen Jugendeinrichtungen und fördern die freien Träger auf der kommunalen Ebene (→ *Jugendamt,* VK). Jedoch sind sie dazu nicht ausdrücklich verpflichtet, und so differiert der Umfang der bereitgestellten Mittel von einer Behörde zur anderen.

Für bestimmte Bereiche der Jugendarbeit sind andere Ministerien zuständig:

- das Ministerium für Gesundheit und Soziale Sicherheit *(Welsh Office, Scottish Home and Health Department, Northern Ireland Department of Health and Social Services)* für die vorbeugende Sozialarbeit mit gefährdeten Jugendlichen (Heimerziehung, Vormundschaft, Adoption usw.) und die Behindertenarbeit;

- das Innenministerium für die Arbeit mit jugendlichen Straffälligen und den freiwilligen sozialen Einsatz;

- das Arbeitsministerium durch die *Training Agency* für Maßnahmen für arbeitslose Jugendliche;

- das Umweltministerium gewährt Zuschüsse an Kommunen zur Unterstützung der Arbeit freier Träger in Innenstadtbezirken mit besonderen sozialen Problemen;

- das Verteidigungsministerium gewährt Mittel für die *cadet forces* (Kadetten-Einheiten);

- das Außenministerium fördert über das *Youth Exchange Centre* den internationalen Jugendaustausch.

Jugendbericht (m)

D

In jeder Legislaturperiode hat die Bundesregierung nach dem Kinder- und Jugendhilfegesetz dem deutschen Parlament einen Bericht über die Leistungen der → *Jugendhilfe* vorzulegen und in jedem dritten Bericht einen Gesamtüberblick über diesen Bereich zu vermitteln. Die Berichte sollen Innovationen, Ergebnisse und Mängel darlegen. Sie werden von unabhängigen Sachverständigen seit 1965 erstellt.

UK

For administrative purposes the youth service in the UK is part of the education system and is supported centrally by the education departments (the Department of Education and Science, the Welsh Office, the Scottish Education Department, the Northern Ireland Department of Education).

At local level it is, in the main, provided by the 104 local education authorities in England and Wales and by the five education and library boards in Northern Ireland. In Scotland most education authorities combine the youth service and adult education to form the community education services of the ten regional councils.

The local authorities maintain their own youth establishments and also provide financial support to local voluntary youth organisations (→ Jugendamt, UK). However, this support is not a mandatory requirement and its extent varies between authorities.

For specific aspects of youth work, other government departments are responsible:

— the Department of Health and Social Security (the Welsh Office, the Scottish Home and Health Department, the Northern Ireland Department of Health and Social Services) for preventive social work for young people at risk (child care, guardianship, adoption, etc.) and the handicapped;

— the Home Office for work connected with young offenders and voluntary action;

— the Employment Department, through the Training Agency, for projects involving young unemployed;

— the Department of the Environment makes grants to local authorities to support voluntary youth work in inner city areas with special social needs;

— the Ministry of Defence gives support to the cadet forces;

— the Foreign and Commonwealth Office, through the Youth Exchange Centre, provides grants for international youth exchange.

National Youth Report

G

In accordance with the Child and Youth Services Act the Federal Government is required to submit to the German Parliament a report on youth work and youth welfare services (→ Jugendhilfe) in every legislative period and to give a general survey of this field in every third report. The reports provide information on innovations, results and deficiencies. They are compiled by independent experts.

Bis 1989 sind insgesamt acht Jugendberichte vorgelegt worden. Der Fünfte und der Achte Jugendbericht gaben Gesamtdarstellungen der Entwicklung der Jugendhilfe mit entsprechenden Empfehlungen. Der Sechste Jugendbericht galt der Verbesserung der Chancengleichheit von Mädchen. Der Siebte Jugendbericht befaßte sich mit dem Thema „Familienunterstützende Leistungen der Jugendhilfe".

VK
Keine Entsprechung im VK

Jugendförderung (f)

D/VK
Gewährung von öffentlichen Zuschüssen für die Zwecke und auf den gesetzlichen Grundlagen der → *Jugendhilfe,* insbesondere für die außerschulische Jugendbildung (→ *Jugendarbeit),* Aus- und Fortbildung von Mitarbeitern der Jugendhilfe, internationale Jugendbegegnungen, sowie Bau und Einrichtung von Stätten der Jugendhilfe.

Insoweit findet sich dieses Konzept in der Praxis der britischen Jugendarbeit wieder. Außerdem ist Jugendförderung in der Bundesrepublik Deutschland im Zusammenhang damit ein moderner Ausdruck für Jugendpflege, in der Bedeutung entsprechend etwa dem britischen *youth service (→ Jugendfürsorge/ Jugendpflege).*

Jugendforschung (f)

D
Die Gesamtheit der wissenschaftlichen Untersuchungen der Probleme und Verhaltensweisen Jugendlicher durch verschiedene Disziplinen. Eine spezielle Forschungseinrichtung, das Deutsche Jugendinstitut, das vom Bundesministerium für Frauen und Jugend gefördert wird, befaßt sich mit der Erforschung der Sozialisation in Kindheit und Jugend sowie mit Fragen der Jugendhilfe und Jugendpolitik. Einer seiner Schwerpunkte ist die Bereitstellung von Materialien und Dokumentationen mit Modellcharakter. Das Institut bietet den Trägern der Jugendhilfe, Studenten und Wissenschaftlern Informationen und Beratung an.

Das Bundesministerium für Frauen und Jugend vergibt daneben Forschungsaufträge, wie z.B zu den Ursachen selbstschädigenden Verhaltens von Jugendlichen. Jugendforschung wird aber auch von privaten Sponsoren unterstützt. Besonders bekannt geworden sind die beiden „Shell-Studien" mit den Titeln „Jugend 81" und „Jugend und Erwachsene 1985".

Between 1965 and 1989 eight reports were published. The fifth and the eighth report examined the overall development of youth work and youth welfare services and made recommendations for improvement. The sixth report dealt with the need to create better opportunities for girls. The seventh report looked into supportive provision for the family as part of youth work and youth welfare services.

UK
No UK equivalent

Supportive Measures for the Youth Service

G/UK
These include public grant-aid for the support of youth work and youth welfare services (→ *Jugendhilfe*) as required by law. In particular, such grant-aid is available for the out-of-school education of the young (→ *Jugendarbeit*), the training and further education of youth workers, international youth meetings, the construction and equipment of youth work and youth welfare service facilities.

This is reflected in the British system. In Germany, moreover, *Jugendförderung* meaning overall support for young people and their activities is, to some extent, replacing the term *Jugendpflege* (→ *Jugendfürsorge/Jugendpflege*).

Youth Research

G
This covers the whole spectrum of scientific research undertaken by different specialists on the problems and behavioural patterns of young people. A special research institute, the *Deutsches Jugendinstitut,* which is grant-aided by the Federal Ministry for Women and Youth, is concerned with research projects to study the social education of children and young people, problems relating to youth work and youth welfare services, as well as youth policy. It emphasizes the provision of material and documentation of a pilot nature. The Institute also provides information and advice to youth work establishments and organisations, students, and scientists.

Moreover, the Federal Ministry for Women and Youth initiates research projects in the youth field. One of these studies looked into the causes of self-detrimental behaviour of young people. Funds for youth research are also made available by private sponsors. The two "Shell Studies" entitled *Youth 81* and *Young People and Adults 1985* have acquired particular renown.

VK

Jugendforschung wird an verschiedenen Universitäten des Vereinigten Königreiches betrieben, aber nicht auf nationaler Ebene koordiniert. Untersuchungen werden von Fall zu Fall veröffentlicht.

Die Sorge um die Effektivität des *youth service* hat schon mehrere Regierungen nacheinander veranlaßt, Studien in Auftrag zu geben, die dann unter dem Namen des Vorsitzenden der jeweiligen Untersuchungskommission bekannt wurden. Der 1960 veröffentlichte *Albemarle Report* hatte erhebliche Verbesserungen im Personalbereich sowie in der Ausstattung mit Räumlichkeiten zur Folge und führte zur Ausbildung von 1.000 Jugendarbeitern in neuen nationalen Colleges. Anstelle der Fortentwicklung der Freizeitangebote lag nunmehr das Schwergewicht auf der experimentellen Arbeit im Bereich der Jugendberatung und der Hilfen für Jugendliche mit sozialen Problemen.

Der *Milsom-Fairbairn Report* der 70er Jahre untersuchte die Probleme benachteiligter Jugendlicher.

Im *Thompson Report* 1982 wurde u.a. die Aufgabe des *youth service* bei der Erweiterung des Erfahrungshorizontes der Jugendlichen und deren Einbeziehung in die Entscheidungsfindung auf allen Ebenen erörtert, da diese Faktoren als entscheidend für die persönliche und soziale Entwicklung junger Menschen anzusehen sind. Der *Thompson Report* stellte fest, daß rigorose Maßnahmen notwendig seien, um der Benachteiligung Jugendlicher in Ballungsgebieten, der ländlichen Isolation und dem Rassismus entgegenzuwirken, um die Ausbildungsmöglichkeiten für junge Arbeitnehmer und arbeitslose Jugendliche zu verbessern, mehr Chancengleichheit für Mädchen zu schaffen und die Behinderten zu integrieren. Arbeitslosigkeit, Rassismus und Obdachlosigkeit sieht der Report als die größten Probleme der Jugend an.

Das *National Youth Bureau* in Leicester, das ein breites Angebot von Dienstleistungen für Mitarbeiter der Jugendarbeit bereitstellte, zu dem curriculare Materialien, Konferenzen, Seminare sowie Ausbildungsberatung zählten, besteht nicht mehr als selbständige Einrichtung. Diese Aufgaben sowie das Zusammentragen, die Auswertung und Veröffentlichung von Informationen zu Jugendfragen, ein Bereich, in dem das *National Youth Bureau* in Großbritannien führend war, wurden von der *National Youth Agency (NYA) (→ Outline of the Youth Service in Britain,* Teil I) übernommen.

Um die Entwicklung der Jugendarbeit in England und Wales zu fördern, gründete die Regierung 1982 den *Council for Education and Training in Youth and Community Work* und 1985 die *Wales Youth Work Partnership.*

Der einmal jährlich stattfindende Wettbewerb *Youth Scientists of the Year* förderte die eigenständige Forschung junger Leute. Viele der dort eingebrachten Ideen Jugendlicher werden von der Industrie übernommen.

UK

Research into various aspects of youth takes place in different universities in the UK but is not co-ordinated nationally; works are published on a random basis.

Concern about the youth service has provoked successive governments to commission reviews which become known by the names of their chairmen. Thus the Albemarle Report was published in 1960; it prompted major improvements in staffing and premises and led to 1000 youth workers being trained in new national colleges. Experimental work in counselling or help with social problems was developed rather than provision of leisure activities.

The Milsom-Fairbairn Report of the 70s highlighted the problems of the disadvantaged.

The Thompson Report published in 1982 discussed, amongst other issues, the role of the youth service in extending and enlarging the experience of young people and in allowing them to participate in decision-taking at all levels as crucial parts of their personal and social development. Radical approaches were recognised as a means of countering urban deprivation, rural isolation and racism, influencing training for employed and unemployed young people, creating more opportunities for girls, and integrating the handicapped. It recognised unemployment, racism and homelessness as the most pressing concerns of the young.

The National Youth Bureau in Leicester, which provided a wide range of professional services for youth workers such as curriculum materials, conferences, seminars and consultation on training, no longer exists as an independent agency. These functions as well as the collection of information, analysis and publication of information on youth problems in which the National Youth Bureau held a leading position in the UK, have been taken over by the National Youth Agency (NYA) (→ *Outline of the Youth Service in Britain,* Part I).

To promote the development of youth work in England and Wales the Government set up the Council for Education and Training in Youth and Community Work in 1982 and, in 1985, the Wales Youth Work Partnership.

The annual "Young Scientists of the Year" competition promotes scientific research by young people, many of the ideas being adopted by industry.

Jugendfreizeitstätten (f/pl)

D

Jugendfreizeitstätten ist ein Sammelbegriff. Er bezeichnet die unterschiedlichsten Einrichtungen, die Kindern und Jugendlichen die Möglichkeit bieten sollen, ihre Freizeit sinnvoll zu gestalten. Die Angebote richten sich vorrangig an Kinder und Jugendliche, die nicht in Vereinen oder Verbänden organisiert sind (mit Ausnahme der Jugendheime), jedoch schließt die Mitgliedschaft in einer Organisation die Teilnahme an den „offenen" Programmen der Freizeitstätten nicht aus. Die Teilnahme an den Aktivitäten ist freiwillig und kostenlos. Die Einrichtungen werden von den Kommunen oder von freien Trägern unterhalten und in der unterschiedlichsten Weise von den Kommunen und Ländern bezuschußt.

Man unterscheidet dabei zwischen:
Haus der offenen Tür (OT) (auch: Haus der Jugend, Jugendhaus, Jugendzentrum). Hier sind die Angebote voll für die nicht verbandsgebundenen Jugendlichen konzipiert, um ihnen eine sinnvolle Freizeit, Unterhaltung, Entspannung und Bildung zu ermöglichen. OTs sind an mindestens fünf Tagen in der Woche geöffnet, meist von 14.00 bis 22.00 Uhr; sie werden von hauptamtlichen pädagogischen Fachkräften geleitet und betreut. OTs bieten ein breites Freizeit-, Bildungs- und Beratungsangebot (zunehmend auch tagsüber für arbeitslose Jugendliche).

Haus der teiloffenen Tür (TOT) in freier oder kommunaler Trägerschaft, mit ähnlichen Angeboten wie die OTs, jedoch zeitlich und räumlich begrenzt. Sie sind an mindestens vier Tagen in der Woche geöffnet (davon mindestens zwei für die offene Arbeit; die übrige Zeit ist geschlossenen Angeboten des Trägers vorbehalten) und werden ebenfalls von hauptamtlichen und pädagogischen Fachkräften betreut.

Haus der kleinen offenen Tür (KOT)
Jugendheime, die für bestimmte Zeiten ausschließlich offene Jugendarbeit leisten, an mindestens drei Tagen in der Woche für diese Arbeit zur Verfügung stehen und eine hauptamtliche pädagogische Fachkraft beschäftigen.

Jugendheime in freier Trägerschaft von Organisationen oder Kirchengemeinden, die ein Haus oder entsprechende Räume ihren Mitgliedern zur Nutzung zur Verfügung stellen.

Selbstverwaltete Jugendzentren entstanden Ende der 60er Jahre im Zusammenhang mit den Protestbewegungen. Sie wurden meist von jugendlichen Basisinitiativen gegründet, die ihre Forderung nach mehr Selbstverwaltung durch Jugendliche in den traditionellen Freizeitstätten nicht genügend berücksichtigt fanden.

VK

Der am häufigsten anzutreffende Typ der Jugendfreizeitstätte ist der örtliche Jugendclub, in dem sich junge Leute treffen und ihre Freizeit verbringen können. Die meisten Clubs sind Einrichtungen freier Träger, viele sind eng mit

Leisure Time Centres for Young People

G

This is a blanket term for the various forms of establishments which provide an opportunity for children and young people to make purposeful use of their leisure time. Programmes mainly cater for those who are not members of a youth organisation or association with the exception of the youth clubs listed below. But membership in an organisation does not exclude a young person form taking part in the "open" programmes offered by the leisure time centres. Joining in activities is voluntary and free to charge. The establishments are run by the local authorities or by voluntary organisations. They are supported by the local authorities or the *Länder* in many different ways.

The following forms of provision may be distinguished:
Open-door youth centre (Haus der Jugend, Jugendhaus, Jugendzentrum). Here the programmes exclusively cater for unattached young people in order to enable them to take part in purposeful leisure time activities, entertainment, recreational and educational pursuits. Open-door youth centres open at least five days per week, in most cases from 14.00 hrs to 22.00 hrs. Qualified full-time socio-educational workers are responsible for planning and running the programme. The centres offer a wide range of leisure time, educational and counselling activities, increasingly also for the young unemployed during the day.

Partially open youth centre run by a voluntary organisation or a local authority. It provides programmes similar to those of the open-door youth centres, but during limited hours only and with a limited number of rooms. They open for at least four days per week, of which two are devoted to open youth work, the rest to activities reserved for members only. The centres are also staffed with qualified full-time socio-educational workers.

"Small door" open youth centres are youth clubs which provide open youth work exclusively during certain periods, i.e. at least three days per week, and employ one full-time qualified socio-educational worker.

Youth clubs are establishments of voluntary organisations or church communities, who provide a house or appropriate rooms for the use of their members.

Self-programming youth centres sprang up towards the end of the 60s in connection with protest movements. They were mostly founded at the grass roots level by young people's initiatives, who felt that their demand for more participation was not being sufficiently met in the traditional leisure time centres.

UK
Youth Centre / Youth Club
The most usual type of youth centre is a local club as a place where young people can meet and spend their leisure time. Most of them are voluntary, many

den Kirchen verbunden. Die Kommunen haben zahlreiche eigene Zentren. Alle diese Freizeitstätten sind in der Regel am Abend und vielfach auch am Wochenende geöffnet. Manche arbeiten mit einer breiten Altersspanne, andere mit einer kleinen Altersgruppe, oder aber bestimmte Abende sind besonderen Altersgruppen, bzw. nur Jugendlichen desselben Geschlechts vorbehalten. Die Einrichtungen bieten im allgemeinen Musik, Spiele und Erfrischungen sowie sportliche und kulturelle Aktivitäten, Ausflüge und gemeinnützige Arbeit an. Zur Durchführung der Programme arbeiten gewöhnlich in den Clubs ein qualifizierter Jugendarbeiter, einige Teilzeitkräfte sowie viele ehrenamtliche Helfer.

In Jugendzentren, die sich innerhalb der Schulgebäude oder auch in der Nähe der Schulen befinden, liegt das Schwergewicht mehr auf Freizeitaktivitäten und weniger auf dem offenen Bereich. Das Angebot umfaßt Sport, Spiele, Werkarbeiten, Musik und Theater. Diese Jugendzentren werden meistens von einem *warden* geleitet, der durch Tutoren für die Freizeitaktivitäten unterstützt wird.

Jugendclubs erheben einen kleinen Mitgliedsbeitrag und stellen eine Mitgliedskarte aus.

Angesichts der fortbestehenden Jugendarbeitslosigkeit haben viele kommunale und freie Jugendclubs und -zentren auch tagsüber geöffnet. Neben den traditionellen Freizeitaktivitäten bieten sie den jungen Besuchern allgemeine Beratung, Berufsberatung und vielfache Hilfestellung an.

Zusätzlich zu den örtlichen Jugendfreizeitstätten haben die Kommunalbehörden und auch freie Träger Jugend- und Freizeitheime eingerichtet, von denen einige Programme der Erlebnispädagogik (→ *Erlebnispädagogik, VK)* durchführen.

Jugendfürsorge (f)/Jugendpflege (f)

D
Historisch hat sich die → *Jugendhilfe* aus den beiden Teilbereichen Jugendpflege und Jugendfürsorge entwickelt. Jugendfürsorge umfaßt den Teil der öffentlichen Jugendhilfe, der mit individuellen Erziehungshilfen konkreten Erziehungsschwierigkeiten oder Entwicklungsproblemen begegnen will. Jugendpflege ist mit → *Jugendarbeit* und außerschulischer Jugendbildung gleichzusetzen. In der behördlichen Jugendarbeit wird der Begriff Jugendpflege überwiegend für den sozialpädagogischen Aufgabenkatalog der Jugendämter verwandt.

In der Praxis der Jugendhilfe läßt sich die strikte Trennung von Jugendpflege und Jugendfürsorge nicht mehr aufrechterhalten, da beide Bereiche vielfach ineinander übergreifen. Die Fachkräfte der Jugendämter, die im Bereich der Jugendpflege auf kommunaler und regionaler Ebene tätig sind, werden als Jugendpfleger bezeichnet (Stadt-, Kreis-, Bezirks-, Landesjugendpfleger). Sie

are associated with churches, and a large number are provided by local authorities. All of them normally open in the evening with many extending their programmes into the weekend. They may cater for a broad or narrow age-range and certain evenings may be reserved for particular age groups or one sex. Music, games and refreshments are generally provided and there may also be sports, cultural activities, outings and involvements in community services. The clubs usually have one professional youth worker, several part-time and many voluntary workers to run the programmes.

In youth centres which are located in or near a school, greater emphasis is placed on activities and less on informal social pursuits. Sports, games, crafts, music and drama are offered. Such centres are usually run by a warden with tutors for the various activities.

Youth clubs are operated on the basis of membership, a nominal fee and a membership card.

In response to continuing youth unemployment a number of youth clubs and centres, both statutory and voluntary, now open in the day time. As well as the traditional club activities, they provide counselling, careers advice and general support.

In addition to the local clubs and youth centres, both local authorities and voluntary organisations provide residential centres, including centres for outdoor pursuits (→ *Erlebnispädagogik,* UK).

Welfare Work for the Young/Leisure Time Provision for the Young

G

Historically, → *Jugendhilfe* developed from its two constituent elements which are welfare work and leisure time provision for the young. Welfare work for young people *(Jugendfürsorge)* covers that part of statutory youth services which aims to counteract specific socio-educational difficulties or developmental problems with individual provision. Leisure time provision for the young *(Jugendpflege;* → *Jugendarbeit)* comprises youth work and out-of-school education. In statutory youth work, the term leisure time provision for the young is mainly defined by the socio-educational responsibilities of the youth office.

In general practice, however, the clear distinction between *Jugendpflege* and *Jugendfürsorge* is no longer made as both fields are correlated in many respects. The qualified youth workers employed by the youth offices in order to perform the above socio-educational duties at local or regional level are referred to as

haben eine Ausbildung zum → *Sozialarbeiter/Sozialpädagogen*. Der Begriff Jugendpfleger wird auch in anderen Bereichen für eine ähnliche Funktion verwandt.

VK

Der *youth service* in Großbritannien hat hauptsächlich erzieherische Aufgaben zu erfüllen. Die Notwendigkeit, die umfassenden Ziele der außerschulischen Bildung zusammen mit den Maßnahmen für sozial benachteiligte und unangepaßte Jugendliche in einer mit erweiterter Zuständigkeit ausgestatteten Behörde anzusiedeln, wird zwar allgemein anerkannt, doch waren Vorstöße, die darauf abzielten, diese Aufgaben in einem eigenen Jugendministerium zu koordinieren, bis jetzt erfolglos.

Der *youth service* im herkömmlichen Sinne umfaßt von den Kommunen unterhaltene Clubs und freie Träger, die soziale Aktivitäten anbieten, Jugendheime, Zentren der Erlebnispädagogik usw.

In den letzten zehn Jahren sind jedoch eine Reihe von sozialen und wirtschaftlichen Problemen immer dringlicher geworden. So stellen unter anderem Jugendarbeitslosigkeit, Obdachlosigkeit, Unangepaßtheit bei Jugendlichen weißer und schwarzer Hautfarbe sowie Drogenmißbrauch große Anforderungen an die Gesellschaft im allgemeinen und den *youth service* im besonderen. Zur gleichen Zeit ist auch die Erkenntnis gewachsen, daß der *youth service* effektiver auf aktuelle Jugendprobleme reagieren und beispielsweise zur Förderung der Chancengleichheit für Mädchen, ethnischer Minderheiten, behinderter Jugendlicher sowie zur Bekämpfung der ländlichen Isolation beitragen muß. Heute spielt der *youth service* eine bedeutende Rolle bei berufsfördernden Maßnahmen für Jugendliche (→ *Jugendarbeitslosigkeit*, VK), sowohl durch finanzielle Unterstützung als auch durch Beratung und Anleitung für die Teilnehmer. Daneben hat er ganztags geöffnete Jugendcafés eingerichtet und organisiert Beschäftigungsmaßnahmen für junge Leute, so z.B. Einsätze bei der Renovierung alter Gebäude, um sie für die Gemeinschaft nutzbar zu machen. Daneben besteht ein allgemeiner Beratungsdienst in Wohnungs-und Geldangelegenheiten sowie bei Problemen in Verbindung mit dem Ausfüllen von Formularen. Rat und Unterstützung gibt es auch für obdachlose oder von Obdachlosigkeit bedrohte Jugendliche.

Die Fachkräfte der Jugendarbeit sind mit den Problemen vertraut, die aus gestörten familiären Beziehungen, durch Drogenmißbrauch oder strafbares Verhalten Jugendlicher entstehen können. Sie treten oft als Vermittler zwischen mit dem Gesetz in Konflikt geratenen Jugendlichen und Bewährungshelfern oder der Polizei auf. In gewissem Umfang ist der *youth service* auch am *Intermediate Treatment Programme* für gefährdete oder in Schwierigkeiten geratene Jugendliche beteiligt (→ *Jugendstrafrecht, Maßnahmen des*, VK).

youth officers *(Stadt-, Kreis-, Bezirks-, Landesjugendpfleger)*. They must have completed a training course for → *Sozialarbeiter/Sozialpädagogen*. The term *Jugendpfleger* is also used by voluntary organisations, e.g. the churches to describe persons with similar functions.

UK

The primary role of the youth service in Britain is an educational one. The need for a more comprehensive service combining broad educational aims and those of a service connected with the disadvantaged and alienated was recognized, but plans to coordinate services by establishing a minister or department responsible for youth have not yet met with success.

Traditionally, the youth service comprises local clubs or organisations offering facilities for social activities, residential centres, outdoor centres etc.

However, over the last decade a number of social and economic issues have become more pressing and such questions as youth unemployment, homelessness, alienation of young people both white and black and drug misuse have posed major challenges to society and particularly to the youth service. At the same time there has been a growing awareness of the necessity for the youth service to respond more effectively to present-day youth problems such as equal opportunities for girls, provision for ethnic minorities, the needs of handicapped young people and rural isolation. Today the youth service plays an important part in the Youth Training schemes (→ *Jugendarbeitslosigkeit, UK*), either as sponsors or in providing advice and guidance to the participants. The youth service has also established "drop-in" centres which are open all day, and organise activities e.g. renovating an old building for community use. At the same time general advice is offered on such matters as housing, form-filling and budgeting. The service gives advice and help to young people who are homeless or in danger of becoming so.

Youth workers are familiar with problems that may result from difficult family relationships, with drug misuse, and forms of delinquent behaviour that might bring young people into conflict with the law, and often act as intermediaries with probation officers or the police. To some extent the youth service has also been involved in the Intermediate Treatment Programme (for young people in trouble or at risk) (→ *Jugendstrafrecht, Maßnahmen des, UK*).

The growth of drug and solvent abuse, especially among young people, has made it necessary for the youth service to develop special programmes contributing to the prevention of drug and solvent misuse.

Other areas, in which the youth service is active nowadays are special programmes for girls, for ethnic minority groups, for the handicapped and also for young people living in isolated rural areas where youth service provision is sparse.

Der wachsende Mißbrauch von Drogen und Lösungsmitteln besonders bei jungen Leuten hat die Entwicklung von speziellen Programmen zur Aufklärung und Vorbeugung notwendig gemacht.

In jüngster Zeit hat der *youth service* seine Tätigkeit erweitert, indem Sonderprogramme für Mädchen, ethnische Minderheiten, Behinderte und Jugendliche, die in isolierten ländlichen Gebieten leben, in denen es kaum Angebote der Jugendarbeit gibt, entwickelt wurden.

Jugendgesetze (n/pl)

D
Viele allgemeine Gesetze wie das Bürgerliche Gesetzbuch, das Strafgesetzbuch, das Bundessozialhilfegesetz und das Arbeitsförderungsgesetz haben besondere Bedeutung für junge Menschen. Daneben gibt es spezielle Gesetze, die sich ausschließlich mit Problemlagen Jugendlicher befassen.

1. *Kinder- und Jugendhilfegesetz (KJHG)*
Das Kinder- und Jugendhilfegesetz vom 26.6.1990 ist die Rechtsgrundlage für die Tätigkeit der Jugendämter, Landesjugendämter, obersten Landesjugendbehörden und den Bund im Bereich der Jugendhilfe. Es regelt eine Vielzahl von Leistungen mit dem Ziel, die Entwicklung junger Menschen zu fördern und die Erziehungsverantwortung der Eltern zu unterstützen. Das Gesetz ist auch die Grundlage für die Förderung freier Träger.

Zu den einzelnen Leistungen gehören insbesondere:

— Angebote der Jugendarbeit, der Jugendsozialarbeit und des erzieherischen Kinder- und Jugendschutzes;
— Angebote zur Förderung der Erziehung in der Familie;
— Angebote zur Förderung von Kindern in Tageseinrichtungen und Tagespflege;
— Hilfe zur Erziehung und ergänzende Leistungen;
— Hilfe für junge Volljährige und Nachbetreuung.

2. *Gesetz zum Schutze der Jugend in der Öffentlichkeit (JÖSchG)*
Das Jugendschutzgesetz in der Fassung vom 25.2.1985 verbietet Kindern oder Jugendlichen bis 18 Jahren den Aufenthalt an Orten, die sie gefährden können (sog. jugendgefährdende Orte). Eine weitere Gefahrenquelle sieht es im Genuß von Tabak und Alkohol in der Öffentlichkeit (grundsätzlich Verbot bis 16 Jahre). Außerdem werden Altersgrenzen für den Besuch von Gaststätten und Tanzveranstaltungen (Einschränkung vor allem für unter 16jährige), Spielhallen (Verbot für unter 18jährige) und den Filmbesuch (Freigabestufen: frei für alle, ab 6, 12, 16 und 18 Jahren) festgelegt und die Abgabe bespielter Videokassetten geregelt. Diese dürfen Kindern und Jugendlichen nur zugänglich gemacht werden, wenn sie für deren Alter von den obersten Landesjugendbehörden freigegeben sind. Das Gesetz wendet sich vor allem an Veranstalter und Gewerbetreibende. Es stellt Zuwiderhandlungen unter Strafe, bzw. Geldbuße.

Laws Relating to Young People

G

Many laws applying to all such as the German Civil Code, the Federal Social Assistance Act, and the Promotion of Employment Act contain provisions concerning the young. These Acts are supplemented by specific laws dealing particularly with problems related to young people.

1. Child and Youth Services Act

The Child and Youth Services Act, dated 26 June 1990, is the legal basis of all youth work and youth welfare provision made by the youth offices, *Land* youth offices, youth offices of the *Länder* governments and the Federal Government. It regulates a wide range of services aiming to promote the development of young people and to assist parents in meeting their educational responsibility. This Act is also the basis of public support available to voluntary organisations.

Such services include:

— youth work provision, socio-educational provision for young people, educational provision for the protection of children and young people;
— provision to support the upbringing of children and young people in the family;
— provision to promote the educational and personal development of children in day care establishments and to expand child minding services;
— statutory socio-educational provision for children with problems and supplementary services;
— provision for young adults and after-care.

2. Act concerning the Protection of Young People in Public

The Act concerning the Protection of Young People in Public in its wording of 25 February 1985 prohibits the presence of children or young people under 18 years of age in places where they may be at risk. A further danger is seen in smoking and drinking in public (generally prohibited for persons under 16). Age limits are fixed for access of young people to restaurants and at public dances (limited access for persons under 16), in gambling halls (prohibited for persons under 18) and in cinemas (classifications: films open to all, open to those over 6 years, 12, 16, and 18 years). There is also a ruling concerning the sale of video films to young persons. These may only be made available to children and young persons if the youth authorities of the *Land* governments (→ *Jugendbehörden*) have authorized access to them for the respective age. The Act is mainly directed at organisers and tradespeople. Infringements are punishable at law and subject to fines.

3. Protection of Young Persons at Work Act

This Act, as amended on 15 October 1984, bans the employment of children. Young people may not work at night nor may they do piece work or be employed on the assembly line. The Act lays down the working hours and periods

3. *Jugendarbeitsschutzgesetz (JASchG)*
Das JASchG, zuletzt geändert durch Gesetz vom 15.10.1984, verbietet Kinderarbeit sowie die Nacht-, Akkord- und Fließbandarbeit von Jugendlichen, regelt die Arbeitszeit und Ruhepausen der 14- bis 18jährigen und sieht einen Jahresurlaub von mindestens 25 Werktagen sowie eine gesundheitliche Überwachung vor.

4. *Jugendgerichtsgesetz (JGG)*
Gesetz in der Fassung der Bekanntmachung vom 11.12.1974, das Maßnahmen bei Verfehlungen Jugendlicher (14–18 Jahre) und Heranwachsender (18–21 Jahre), den Aufbau der Jugendgerichte und die Jugendgerichtshilfe regelt.

Es ergänzt das Strafgesetzbuch (StGB).

5. *Gesetz über die Verbreitung jugendgefährdender Schriften (GjS)*
Das GjS, zuletzt geändert durch das Gesetz zur Neuregelung des Jugendschutzes in der Öffentlichkeit vom 25.2.1985, verbietet den Verkauf von unsittlichen, verrohenden, zu Gewalttätigkeiten, Verbrechen oder Rassenhaß anreizenden und den Krieg verherrlichenden Schriften an Kinder und Jugendliche bis zu 18 Jahren, sofern diese auf Antrag einer Jugendbehörde von der Bundesprüfstelle für jugendgefährdende Schriften auf die Liste der jugendgefährdenden Schriften (Index) gesetzt wurden. Es sieht außerdem allgemeine Werbe-, Vertriebs- und Weitergabeverbote zum Schutz der Jugend vor. Für bestimmte, schwer jugendgefährdende Schriften, wie etwa Pornographie, gelten die Beschränkungen und Verbote des GjS, ohne daß es einer Indizierung bedarf.

6. *Bundesausbildungsförderungsgesetz (BAFöG)*
Das BAFöG (letzte Änderung 1990) gewährt einen Rechtsanspruch auf Ausbildungsförderung. Der Anspruch setzt allerdings Eignung und Bedürftigkeit voraus. Die Durchführung des Gesetzes ist den Ausbildungsförderungsämtern übertragen. Gefördert werden kann der Besuch von weiterführenden allgemein- und berufsbildenden Schulen, sofern der Schüler ausbildungsbedingt auswärts untergebracht ist, im übrigen von Abendschulen, Kollegs und Hochschulen. Die Lage des Einzelfalles entscheidet über eine Teil- oder Vollförderung (→ *Ausbildungsförderung).*

VK
1. Gesetzliche Grundlage für den *youth service:*
– Der *Education Act 1944* übertrug den kommunalen Erziehungsbehörden die Aufgabe, Einrichtungen und Angebote des *youth service* in ihrem Verantwortungsbereich sicherzustellen, mit den freien Trägern zusammenzuarbeiten, wo es zweckmäßig erscheint, und für ausreichende Möglichkeiten der sozialen und sportlichen Betätigung Sorge zu tragen.

– Der *Education Reform Act 1988,* der einschneidende Reformen für die Lehrpläne der Schulen sowie die Finanzierung der Schulen und Colleges brach-

of rest for the 14–18 age range. It provides for a yearly holiday of at least 25 working days and for their health welfare.

4. *Juvenile Court Act*
This Act, in its wording of the official announcement dated 11 December 1974, defines the measures to be taken when young people (14–18 years) and young adults (18–21) have committed an offence. It lays down the structure of the juvenile courts as well as a department responsible for social enquiry necessary in juvenile cases.

The Act supplements the Penal Code.

5. *Act concerning the Distribution of Publications Harmful to Young Persons*
This Act as amended on 25 February 1985 prohibits the sale of specified categories of publications to children and young people under 18 years. Immoral and brutalizing publications are banned as is printed material highlighting violence, crime, or racialism, or glorifying war. The youth authorities may submit an application to the Federal Board for the Review of Publications Harmful to Young Persons and ask for inclusion of writings, fitting into the above categories, in the list or index of harmful printed material. In order to protect young people, the Act also provides for a general injunction against the promotion, sale and distribution of the publications entered on the list. Certain types of severely harmful printed material such as pornography are banned without having to be indexed.

6. *Federal Educational Grants Act*
The Federal Educational Grants Act, as amended in 1990, gives young people legal claim to educational grants. This claim is based on aptitude and need. The implementation of the Act is carried out by special educational grants offices. Those eligible for educational grants are pupils who have to be boarded out in order to attend a formal secondary or vocational school. Students attending evening classes, special educational provision to reach university entrance qualification or a university are also entitled to receive an educational grant. The amount allotted is determined on the basis of the individual financial situation, whereby students may draw from a certain percentage up to the full amount of a set maximum rate *(→ Ausbildungsförderung)*.

UK
1. Legal basis of the youth service:
— The *Education Act 1944* placed upon local education authorities the duty to make provision for the youth service in their area, cooperating with voluntary bodies where appropriate and ensuring that facilities for social and physical activities were adequate.

— The *Education Reform Act 1988* which mainly focussed on introducing some major reforms in the curriculum of schools as well as the financial government of schools and colleges, left the youth service itself untouched

te, berührte den *youth service* nicht unmittelbar. Er hatte jedoch Auswirkungen auf die Aus- und Fortbildung der Fachkräfte der Jugend- und Gemeinwesenarbeit.

2. In den nachstehend aufgeführten *Children and Young Persons Acts* werden u.a. folgende Regelungen getroffen:

Children and Young Persons Act 1933: Nach diesem Gesetz ist die Verabreichung von Alkohol an Kinder unter fünf Jahren gesetzwidrig, es sei denn, sie ist aus medizinischen Gründen erforderlich. Das Rauchen wird ab 16 Jahren erlaubt. Weiterhin regelt das Gesetz die Beschäftigung von Minderjährigen zwischen 13 und 17 Jahren (geändert 1963 und 1972).

Der *Children and Young Persons (Harmful Publications) Act 1955* trifft Maßnahmen zum Schutz von Jugendlichen vor unsittlichen Schriften. Auch Teile des *Obscene Publications Act 1959* finden Anwendung.

Der *Children and Young Persons Act 1963* legt den Beginn der bedingten Strafmündigkeit bei 10 bzw. 14 Jahren fest (→ *Jugendstrafrecht, VK*).

Der *Children and Young Persons Act 1969* enthält Bestimmungen über die Anordnung der Hilfe zur Erziehung durch die Jugendgerichte.

Der neue *Children Act 1989* tritt voraussichtlich Ende 1991 in Kraft und wird einen Teil der bisherigen Regelungen ersetzen.

3. Weitere für den Bereich der Jugendarbeit relevante Altersgrenzen finden sich in folgenden Gesetzen (s. auch *Anhang, Tabelle Altersgrenzen):*

– *Sexual Offences Acts 1956, 1965* und *1967:* Enthalten Bestimmungen über Sexualvergehen an Mädchen und Jungen unter 16 sowie die Entführung von Mädchen unter 18.

– *DHSS Family Planning Service Memorandum of Guidance HSC May 1974:* Gestattet die Vergabe von empfängnisverhütenden Mitteln an Mädchen unter 16 Jahren.

– *Marriage Act 1949:* Eheschließungen unter 16 sind ungültig; zwischen 16 und 18 Jahren mit Zustimmung der Eltern oder des Gerichts möglich.

– *Licensing Act 1964:* Der Zutritt zu einem Lokal mit Schankkonzession ist ab 14 Jahren gestattet; ab 16 Jahren der Konsum von Bier und Apfelwein beim Essen in einem Restaurant. Wer als Minderjähriger Alkohol kauft, macht sich strafbar. Es ist auch eine strafbare Handlung, Personen unter 18 Jahren alkoholische Getränke zu kaufen oder zu verkaufen.

– *Armed Forces Act 1971:* Mit Zustimmung der Eltern können Jungen ab 16 und Mädchen ab 17 Jahren den Dienst in den Streitkräften aufnehmen; andernfalls erst ab 18 Jahren.

– *Shops Act 1950:* Verbietet die Beschäftigung von Minderjährigen unter 18 Jahren über 48 Stunden pro Woche.

– *Judges Rules:* Enthalten Bestimmungen über die Behandlung von Jugendlichen unter 17 Jahren durch die Polizei (→ *Jugendstrafrecht, Maßnahmen des, VK*).

but affected training and further education programmes for youth and community workers.

2. The following describe the most relevant Children and Young Persons Acts:
Children and Young Persons Act 1933: According to this Act the use of alcohol is illegal for children under age five except on medical grounds; smoking is permitted at age 16. The Act also makes provision for the employment of those aged between 13 and 17 (amended in 1963 and 1972).

The *Children and Young Persons (Harmful Publications) Act 1955* deals with young people and obscene publications. Sections under the Obscene Publications Act 1959 also apply.

The *Children and Young Persons Act 1963* defines criminality at age 10 and 14 (→ *Jugendstrafrecht*, UK).

The *Children and Young Persons Act 1969* lays down conditions applying to juvenile courts in committing a child or young person into the care of a local authority.

The new *Children Act 1989* is expected to come into force towards the end of 1991 and will then replace some of the earlier legislation.

3. Other age limits relevant in youth and youth welfare services are embodied in the following Acts (cf. *Appendices, Age Limits):*

— *Sexual Offences Acts 1956, 1965, and 1967:* Sexual offences relating to girls and boys under age 16 and abduction of girls under 18.

— *DHSS Family Planning Service Memorandum of Guidance HSC May 1974:* Contraceptives for girls under 16.

— *Marriage Act 1949:* Marriage under 16 is void. Under 18 the consent of parent or court is required.

— *Licensing Act 1964:* Entry to a licensed bar at 14; at age 16 beer and cider may be purchased with a meal in a restaurant, otherwise it is an offence to buy, buy for or sell alcohol to under 18s.

— *Armed Forces Act 1971:* With parental permission boys at 16, girls at 17, may join the Armed Forces; otherwise not until age 18.

— *Shops Act 1950:* Under 18-year-olds may not work more than 48 hours per week.

— *Judges Rules:* Deal with the handling of under 17-year-olds by the police (→ *Jugendstrafrecht, Maßnahmen des*, UK).

Jugendhilfe (f)

D

Die Jugendhilfe umfaßt in Ergänzung zu Elternhaus und Schule alle gezielten Maßnahmen zur Förderung des Wohles junger Menschen. Sie werden von öffentlichen Trägern, insbesondere dem → *Jugendamt,* und freien Vereinigungen geleistet. Über die im KJHG vorgesehenen Maßnahmen und Leistungen hinaus enthalten auch andere Gesetze Bestimmungen zugunsten junger Menschen, z.B. Jugendschutzgesetz, Bundesausbildungsförderungsgesetz, Bundessozialhilfegesetz (→ *Jugendgesetze).*

Jugendhilfe soll Eltern und andere Erziehungsberechtigte bei der Erziehung beraten, unterstützen und fördern. In Ergänzung der Erziehung in Familie, Schule und Berufsausbildung schafft sie eigene Angebote. Sie ersetzt die Erziehung in der eigenen Familie, wenn die eigene Familie bei der Erziehung versagt.

Zur Erfüllung dieser Aufgaben bestehen zahlreiche Leistungen, Einrichtungen und Angebote:

— Familienhilfe für Familien, die mit ihren Problemen nicht allein fertig werden
— Tageseinrichtungen für Kinder (Krippen, Kindergärten und Horte/Erziehung in Tagespflegestellen)
— Spielplätze, Erholungsmaßnahmen
— Familien- und Elternbildung
— Erziehungsberatung
— Gemeinwesenarbeit für benachteiligte Gruppen
— Jugendarbeit (Jugendpflege)
— Adoptionsvermittlung
— Unterbringung in Pflegestellen und Heimen
— Vormundschaftswesen
— Jugendgerichtshilfe
— Jugendschutz.

Die Maßnahmen der Jugendhilfe werden zu etwa 70 % aus kommunalen Mitteln, zu über 25 % aus Mitteln der Länder, im übrigen durch den Bund finanziert. Die Bundesregierung fördert durch den → *Bundesjugendplan* zentrale Einrichtungen, Verbände und die internationale Jugendarbeit. Die freien Träger (vor allem Wohlfahrtsverbände und Jugendverbände) erhalten für ihre Jugendhilfearbeit öffentliche Mittel. Im Bereich der Jugendhilfe sind bei öffentlichen und freien Trägern zahlreiche hauptamtliche und nebenamtliche Mitarbeiter tätig. Die Mehrzahl von ihnen arbeitet in Kindergärten und Heimen.

VK

Im Vereinigten Königreich sind die verschiedenen Teilbereiche der Jugendhilfe nicht in einem Ministerium zusammengefaßt. Näheres siehe *Teil I, Überblick über den Youth Service im Vereinigten Königreich,* und → *Jugendbehörden.*

Youth Work and Youth Welfare Services (Child and Youth Services)

G

The welfare of young people is the concern of the home and the school, supplemented by youth work and youth welfare services, as provided by the statutory bodies (→ *Träger der Jugendhilfe)*, in particular the youth work and youth welfare office (→ *Jugendamt)*, and the voluntary organisations. In addition to the Child and Youth Services Act, there are other laws specifically enacted for the benefit of young people, e.g. the Protection of Young People in Public Act, the Federal Educational Grants Act and the Federal Public Assistance Act (→ *Jugendgesetze)*.

Youth work and youth welfare services advise, support and encourage parents and other persons having parental authority in their task of bringing up children. In addition to the education provided by the family, school, and vocational training, *Jugendhilfe* offers supplementary facilities whenever the family alone cannot cope.

For these purposes, the following provision is made by the bodies responsible for youth work and youth welfare services:

— help for families who cannot cope with their problems on their own
— day care centres for children (crêches, nursery schools, day care centres for school-age children, placement with a child minder)
— play grounds, recuperative health schemes
— family and parental counselling
— child guidance
— community work for disadvantaged groups
— youth work (leisure time provision for the young)
— adoption procedures and implementation
— accommodation in/referral to, foster homes and other homes
— guardianship
— social enquiry in juvenile cases
— protection of young persons in public.

Youth and youth welfare services receive about 70 % of their funding from local authorities and about 25 % from the respective *Länder* budgets. The remainder is covered by the Federal Government, which supports central establishments, associations and international youth work from the Federal Youth Plan funds (→ *Bundesjugendplan)*. The voluntary bodies (in particular the welfare organisations and youth welfare services. The statutory and voluntary bodies involved in this field employ many full-time and part-time youth workers, most of whom work in nursery schools and homes.

UK

There is no unification of the various facets of *Jugendhilfe* under one ministry in the UK. For details see Part I, *Outline of the Youth Service in Britain,* and →*Jugendbehörden.*

Jugendkultur (f)

D

Jugend als besondere Form der Vergesellschaftung ist eine Begleiterscheinung der industriellen Entwicklung. Schon zu Beginn dieses Jahrhunderts gab es in Deutschland eine Jugendbewegung, deren Ziel es war, eigene Lebensformen zu entwickeln. Diese wandten sich gegen Intellektualismus und Zwang in der Erziehung und gegen die Instrumentalisierung des Menschen durch Organisationen und Institutionen. Die Jugendbewegung war bewußt unkonventionell. Die Jugend wollte ihr Leben selbst gestalten und damit eine eigene Jugendkultur schaffen, die aber unorganisiert und unpolitisch blieb. Dies änderte sich auch nicht, als sich die vielen kleinen Gruppierungen und Bünde 1913 auf dem Hohen Meißner bei Kassel zur „Freideutschen Jugend" zusammenschlossen. Im Manifest hieß es: „Die Freideutsche Jugend will aus eigener Bestimmung, vor eigener Verantwortung, mit innerer Wahrhaftigkeit ihr Leben gestalten. Für diese innere Freiheit tritt sie unter allen Umständen geschlossen ein. Alle Veranstaltungen der Freideutschen Jugend sind alkohol- und nikotinfrei".

Ein Teil der Ideen der Jugendbewegung (z.B. Kindheit und Jugend als zu fördernde, eigenständige Lebensweisen) fand Eingang in die Reformpädagogik des beginnenden 20. Jahrhunderts.

Das Phänomen einer eigenständigen Jugendkultur ist bis heute erhalten geblieben. Die Jugendkultur ist Identifikationsraum und Bezugsgruppe im Sozialisationsprozeß und hinsichtlich der Wert- und Symbolmuster weitgehend von der übrigen Gesellschaft unterschieden. Der Soziologe Tenbruck spricht von „Sozialisierung in eigener Regie" und stellt fest, daß die wachsende Selbständigkeit der Jugendlichen sie in den Rang einer dominanten Teilkultur erhebt. Die Konzentration der Werbung auf Jugend, auf jugendliches Lebensgefühl unterstreicht dies. Kennzeichen der Jugendkultur sind auf der einen Seite Gruppenbildungen, die einem bestimmten Modetrend folgen oder ihn kreiren (Teds, Popper, Punks, Heavies, Funkies, New Wave etc.) und dabei auch gruppentypische Sprachcodes entwickeln. Die jugendkulturelle Eigenständigkeit drückt sich insbesondere in der in den vergangenen Jahrzehnten sprunghaft gewachsenen Zahl informeller Gleichaltrigengruppen und -beziehungen aus. Als latente gesellschaftspolitische Funktion tragen sie zu einer wachsenden Separation und Fragmentierung der Gesellschaft entlang der Altergrenzen und Generationen bei. Darüberhinaus existiert auch eine bewußt gesellschaftspolitisch motivierte Jugendkultur, die sich als Impulsgeber für notwendige gesellschaftliche Änderungen versteht (z.B. Jugendgruppen einiger Wohlfahrtsverbände, Parteijugend, Die Falken, Pfadfinder).

Insgesamt ist festzuhalten, daß sich die Jugendphase im Zuge der Verlängerung von Ausbildungszeiten immer weiter ausdehnt. Sie umfaßt weit mehr als die gesetzliche Bestimmung des Jugendlichen (14–18 Jahre), die z.B. Auswirkungen auf das Strafrecht hat, und reicht bei einer zunehmenden Zahl junger Menschen weit bis ins dritte Lebensjahrzehnt hinein.

Youth Subculture

G

The phenomenon of youth forming a separate social group is a special characteristic of industrial development. At the very beginning of this century a youth movement sprang up with the aim of developing specific modes of life. These were directed against intellectualism and constraint in education and against the manipulation of man by organisations and institutions. The youth movement's aim was to be free of conventions. Young people wanted to shape their own lives and to create their own youth movement which, however, remained unorganised and apolitical. This did not change when the many small groupings and *Bünde* (associations) joined together to form the *Freideutsche Jugend* (Free German Youth) in 1913 at a meeting on the *Hoher Meißner* neer Kassel. The manifesto read: "The *Freideutsche Jugend* want to run their lives according to their own free will, assuming their own responsibility with inner truthfulness. They will stand up jointly for this inner freedom in all circumstances. For events organised by the *Freideutsche Jugend* there is a ban on alcohol and nicotine".

Some of the ideas of the youth movement, (e.g. the concept of childhood and youth as separate phases of life which must be fostered, were taken up by the reform educationalists of the early 20th century.

The phenomenon of an independent youth has remained with us until today. Youth is a sphere of identification and a reference group within the process of socialisation. Its pattern of values and symbols differ widely from the rest of society. The sociologist Tenbruck speaks about a "socialisation managed on young people's own account" and points out that the increasing independence of the youth subculture turns it into a dominant feature of our culture in general. This is enhanced by the fact that publicity is very much geared to the young and to feeling young. Characteristics of the youth subculture are, on the one hand, groups who follow a certain trend in fashion or who create one themselves (Teds, Poppers, Punks, Heavies, Funkies, New Wave, etc.) developing specific language codes typical of a given group. The separate identity of the youth sebculture is very much reflected in the number of informal peer groups and relationships which have shown a marked increase over the last decades. The strong affinity with the peer groups has a latent socio-political function, as it contributes to a growing fragmentation of society which is based on age brackets and generations. Moreover, there is a youth subculture with a socio-political motivation. The latter want to initiate the social change which they consider essential (e.g. youth groups of some of the welfare organisations, party-politically orientated youth groups, The Falcons, Scouts).

On the whole, it must be noted that the time span of "youth" is becoming increasingly longer as training programmes and education are extended. It goes far beyond the legal definition of a young person (14–18 years) and for an increasing number of young people extends well into their thirties.

VK
In Großbritannien gibt es ähnliche Jugendkulturen, die vorübergehende Phasen im Leben junger Menschen darstellen.

Jugendleiter (m)/Jugendleiterin (f)

D
Bezeichnet hauptsächlich den Gruppenleiter/Gruppenführer in der Jugendarbeit der → *Jugendverbände,* anderer freier Träger der → *Jugendhilfe* sowie der Kirchen. „Jugendleiter" ist keine Berufsbezeichnung mehr, da eine fachliche Ausbildung nicht Voraussetzung für die Wahrnehmung ihrer Aufgaben ist. Es handelt sich meistens um ehrenamtlich tätige Personen mit pädagogischen und organisatorischen Fähigkeiten. Jugendverbände, soziale Ausbildungsstätten, Jugendleiterschulen bieten Grund- und Aufbaukurse zur Vorbereitung auf die Aufgaben der Jugendleiter an.

In Deutschland trifft man in bestimmten Kontexten der internationalen Jugendarbeit für diese Tätigkeit die Begriffe „Animateur" und „Teamer" an, für die es bei uns ebenfalls keine Ausbildung gibt.

VK
Im Vereinigten Königreich übernehmen ehrenamtliche Jugendleiter der freien Träger den größten Teil der Jugendarbeit. Ihr Wirkungsbereich sind die sogenannten uniformierten Jugendgruppen, z.b. die Pfadfinder und Pfadfinderinnen, *Boys' Brigade* und *Girls' Brigade,* die Jugendorganisation des Roten Kreuzes und die *St. John Ambulance cadets,* ebenso wie kirchliche oder nicht konfessionell gebundene Jugendclubs in der Stadt und auf dem Land. Sie üben ihre Tätigkeit in Gemeinschaftszentren, Kirchen und Bürgerhäusern aus. Für die Kadetteneinheiten der Streitkräfte werden sie als Teilzeitkräfte beschäftigt. Die ehrenamtlichen Jugendleiter haben oft keine spezielle Ausbildung und kommen aus allen Lebens- und Berufsbereichen. Sie bringen ihre pädagogischen und sozialen Fähigkeiten sowie ihre Führungsqualitäten in die Arbeit für junge Menschen ein.

Zur Sicherung eines gewissen fachlichen Niveaus bieten alle uniformierten Organisationen ihren Jugendleitern besondere Ausbildungsmöglichkeiten an. Für diejenigen, die eine Tätigkeit in der Jugendarbeit anstreben oder bereits als Jugendleiter arbeiten und sich fortbilden wollen, bieten die kommunalen Träger der Jugendarbeit Teilzeitlehrgänge auf verschiedenen Ebenen an.

UK
Roughly similar youth subcultures are to be found in the UK which form transient phases in young people's lives.

Youth Leader

G
The term *Jugendleiter* (youth leader) mainly describes the group leader engaged in youth work with a youth organisation (→ *Jugendverbände*), other voluntary bodies responsible for youth work and youth welfare services (→ *Jugendhilfe*) as well as with the churches. *Jugendleiter* is no longer the designation for a profession since special training is not required for this kind of work. For the most part, youth leaders are unpaid workers with educational and organisational skills. Youth organisations, social training centres, and youth leader schools offer basic and continuation courses to prepare youth leaders for their responsibilities.

In the context of international youth work the terms *Animateur* and *Teamer* are also used in the Federal Republic to describe youth leaders. There is no specific training course for such work in Germany.

UK
Voluntary Youth Leader
The greater part of youth work in the UK is done by voluntary youth leaders in the non-statutory sector. They are to be found in the uniformed organisations, e.g. Scouts, Guides, Boys Brigade, Girls Brigade, Red Cross cadets, St. John Ambulance cadets, as well as church and non-denominational youth clubs in urban und rural settings using local community centres, church and village halls. Adult workers in the cadet forces of the armed services are usually part-time paid leaders. Often unqualified, these voluntary leaders come from all walks of life and have educational, social and leadership skills to offer in the service for young people.

In order to maintain standards all the uniformed organisations offer training for their leaders. For others aspiring to or already in the youth work field who wish to improve their skills, local authority youth and community services offer part-time training courses at appropriate levels.

Jugendmarke (f)

D

Einmal jährlich bringt die Deutsche Bundespost eine Serie von Sondermarken heraus, deren Zuschlagerlös (ca. 70 Millionen DM) in bestimmte Bereiche der Jugendhilfe fließt. Über die Verwendung der Mittel entscheidet die Stiftung Deutsche Jugendmarke e.V., in der alle → *Träger der Jugendhilfe* vertreten sind.

VK

Keine Entsprechung im VK

Jugendprotest (m)

D

Jugendprotest, wie er sich vor allem Ende der 70er und zu Beginn der 80er Jahre artikulierte, war im wesentlichen eine Reaktion auf ungelöste (sozial-)politische Probleme. Dabei muß man jedoch beachten, daß nie *die* Jugend protestiert hat, sondern immer nur *Gruppen* von Jugendlichen, wobei die Aktionsziele von Jugendprotest unterschiedlich sind: Neben politischen Gruppen, die gesellschaftliche Veränderungen anstreben, existieren auch solche, die eher „aussteigen" als laut zu protestieren (Hippies, Therapie- und Meditationsgruppen, Punks). Aber auch bei gesellschaftspolitisch aktiven Gruppen ist heute — anders als bei der Studentenbewegung Ende der 60er Jahre — keine durchgängige theoretische Fundierung auszumachen: Spontaneität und aktuelle Betroffenheit beeinflussen wesentlich den Protest.

Auffallend ist auch, daß viele Themen, die Jugendprotest verursachten (Zukunftsangst, die Folgen der technischen Entwicklung, Mangel an emotionaler Zuwendung, Unpersönlichkeit der Gesellschaft, Wertewandel, Konsumorientierung, Leistungsgesellschaft, Erwartungen an den Staat, Kritik am Staat etc.) keine jugendspezifischen Fragen waren, sondern genausogut erwachsene Bürger betrafen. Die Probleme wurden von Jugendlichen nur sensibler wahrgenommen.

VK

Die Protestbewegungen im Vereinigten Königreich sind ähnlich. Ein wesentlicher Unterschied besteht darin, daß sie sich nur sehr selten auf Jugendliche beschränken.

Jugendreisen (f/pl)

D

Unter Jugendreisen versteht man ein besonderes Reiseangebot für junge Leute.

Mit einer aus der Jugendbewegung herrührenden Tradition besteht ein umfangreiches Angebot durch Jugendverbände, das Jugendherbergswerk sowie

Youth Stamp

G

Once a year, the German Federal Postal Service issues a set of special stamps. The proceeds from the surcharge (roughly DM 70 mill.) are spent on certain fields of youth work. The *Stiftung Deutsche Jugendmarke e.V.,* in which all bodies responsible for youth work and youth welfare services are represented *(→ Träger der Jugendhilfe),* decides on how the funds are spent.

UK

No UK equivalent

Political Protest by the Young

G

Youth protests as they manifested themselves towards the end of the 70s and the beginning of the 80s were essentially a reaction to unsolved political or socio-political problems. One must bear in mind, though, that political protest never came nor comes from the young as such. It was initiated by groups of young people who were trying to reach different aims. In addition to political groups wishing to achieve social change there are others who prefer "opting out" to blatant protest, such as hippies, therapy and meditation groups, and punks. In contrast to the student movement at the end of the 60s, however, it is impossible to distinguish any uniformity in theory also amongst today's socio-politically active groups. Spontaneity and emotional involvement are important factors in protest movements.

It is conspicuous that many of the phenomena contributing to such reactions amongst young people were never specific youth problems, but matters of general concern: fear of the future, the consequences of technological development, lack of emotional responses, the impersonal face of society, changing values, consumerism, the rat race society, expectations from and criticisms of the State. Young people were merely more deeply affected by these phenomena than adults.

UK

Protest movements in the UK follow a similar pattern. There is, however, a major difference: They are very rarely restricted to young people.

Youth Travel/Youth Tours

G

The term youth travel indicates special travel provision for young people.

There is a wide range of programmes provided by youth organisations, the Youth Hostel Association, and non-profitmaking youth travel organisations

gemeinnützige Jugendreiseorganisationen, die Ferien- und Bildungsreisen für Jugendliche veranstalten und deren Tätigkeit nicht auf Gewinnerzielung ausgerichtet, sondern als Dienstleistung für die Jugend anzusehen sind.

Diese Form der Jugendreisen ist in der Regel mit pädagogischen Zielsetzungen verbunden; entsprechende Bedeutung haben Jugendreiseleiter. Die Ausbildung der Jugendreiseleiter wird aus dem → *Bundesjugendplan* gefördert.

Jugendreisen kommerzieller Reiseveranstalter (Jugendtourismus) sind zwar auch auf Jugendliche abgestimmt, gehören jedoch zum allgemeinen Reiseangebot.

Die Erfahrungen der gemeinnützigen Jugendreiseveranstalter und diejenigen der Jugendlichen mit dem Reisen haben das Angebot der kommerziellen Veranstalter beeinflußt. Außerdem ist die Zahl der auf eigene Faust reisenden Jugendlichen ständig gestiegen, für die neuerdings auch sogenannte alternative Reiseunternehmen Angebote machen. Daher haben sich die gemeinnützigen Jugendreiseorganisationen einerseits auf besondere Zielgruppen, z.B Reiseunsichere, sozial Benachteiligte, andererseits auf besondere Angebotsformen und Inhalte (interkulturelle Bildung, Gemeinschaftserleben, Sportprogramme, Erlebnispädagogik) spezialisiert.

VK

Der weitaus größte Teil der Reiseveranstalter, die Jugendreisen anbieten, arbeitet kommerziell. Selbst die traditionellen Angebote des Jugendherbergswerkes wurden auf einer gesunden kommerziellen Basis neugestaltet, obschon sie weiterhin preisgünstig bleiben.

Die neben dem Jugendherbergswerk bestehenden gemeinnützigen Jugendreiseveranstalter konzentrieren sich auf Schülerreisen und Sprachkursangebote. Einer der ältesten Träger dieser Art ist *Educational Travel Limited.* Viele Veranstalter bieten attraktive Pauschalreisen und gestaffelte Tarife für Schulklassen, Jugend- und Studentengruppen an, die durchaus mit dem übrigen Markt konkurrieren können. Sie gewähren jedoch keine besonderen Zuschüsse und arbeiten gewinnorientiert.

Im Vereinigten Königreich gibt es keine spezifische Ausbildung der Jugendreiseleiter.

Größere Reisedienste mit speziellen Angeboten für benachteiligte Jugendliche fehlen, aber eine Reihe von freien Trägern und sozialen Diensten der Kommunalbehörden organisieren Ferienprogramme für besonders benachteiligte Kinder, Behinderte und gelegentlich auch alleinerziehende Familien. Diese Programme finden meist in den Oster- und Sommerferien vor allem innerhalb des Vereinigten Königreiches statt.

Beispiele freier Träger mit einem umfangreichen Programmangebot innerhalb und außerhalb des Vereinigten Königreiches sind: *PHAB (Physically Handicapped and Able Bodied); British Red Cross Society; Camping for the Disabled; Holiday Care Service; Gingerbread Holidays* (für alleinerziehende Familien).

derived from the traditions of the youth movement. These organisations offer holiday trips and educational tours for young people. They are not geared to financial gain but must be considered as a service to the young.

Special travel provision for the young is characterized by educational objectives. The importance of training for those leading groups is recognised by the provision of programmes for them subsidized from Federal Youth Plan funds (→ *Bundesjugendplan*).

Although commercial travel agencies also cater for young people, they do this as part of general tourism.

The experience of non-profitmaking youth travel organisations and that of young people themselves has had an influence on the programmes of commercial agencies. Increasingly, young people are travelling on their own initiative and alternative travel establishments have emerged specifically catering for them. Consequently, non-profitmaking youth travel organisations are increasingly making special provision for specific target groups, e.g. those without clear plans of their own and the socially disadvantaged. These establishments offer special programmes whose content covers intercultural learning, community experience, sports programmes, out-door pursuits.

UK
The vast majority of travel agencies which offer a service to young people are commercial operations. Even the traditional facilities of the Youth Hostel Association have been restructured on a sound commercial basis while still offering low costs.

Those non-profit travel agencies other than the YHA focus mostly on the schools market and language learning, Educational Travel Limited being one of the oldest. There are a large number of agencies which offer packages, or specially structured fares, for youth, student and school groups which are attractive for youth and competitive with the ordinary travel market. However, they offer no specific subsidy and aim to make a profit.

There is no special system of training for "youth travel" guides in the UK.

There are no major specialist travel services for disadvantaged youth, but a number of voluntary organisations and local authority social services departments arrange holidays, usually in summer and Easter, most often in the UK, for children from severely disadvantaged backgrounds, those with special needs and, occasionally, single-parent families.

Examples of voluntary organisations who operate a programme on quite a wide scale both within the UK and to other countries are: PHAB (Physically Handicapped and Able Bodied); British Red Cross Society; Camping for the Disabled; Holiday Care Service; Gingerbread Holidays (for one-parent families).

Jugendreligionen (f/pl)

D

Vor allem seit Ende der 60er Jahre treten Gruppen in Erscheinung, die sich selbst als Religionsgemeinschaften bezeichnen und besonders unter jungen Menschen werben, ohne auf diese Zielgruppe festgelegt zu sein. Die Jugendreligionen haben verschiedene Wurzeln und stammen aus unterschiedlichen Kulturkreisen. Häufig sind folgende Merkmale: hierarchische Gliederung, hoher Konformitätsdruck gegenüber den Gruppenmitgliedern (auch bei der Kleidung), vollkommene Identifikation mit den Zielen der Gemeinschaft, Tabuisierung kritischen Verhaltens der eigenen Gruppe gegenüber, Ausbeutung der Mitglieder.

In der Regel sind diese Gruppen straff organisierte Wirtschaftsunternehmen, die ihre Anhänger zu unentgeltlicher Arbeit anhalten, Bücher und Schallplatten und teure Einführungskurse in die jeweilige Lehre anbieten.

In einigen Fällen (z.B. der Moon-Sekte) konnte bei den Gruppierungen kriminelles Verhalten festgestellt werden (Nötigung, Bettelbetrug, unlautere Werbemethoden). Die bekanntesten Jugendreligionen in der Bundesrepublik Deutschland sind: Bagwan-Sekte, Hare Krishna, Vereinigungskirche, Die Kinder Gottes, Transzendentale Meditation.

VK

Die Situation im Vereinigten Königreich ist ähnliche.

Jugendringe (m/pl)

D

Freiwillige Zusammenschlüsse von Jugendverbänden (Dachverbände) meist auf drei Ebenen:
— Kommunal- und Regionalebene: Orts-/Stadt-/Kreis-/Bezirksjugendring
— Landesebene: Landesjugendring
— Bundesebene: Deutscher Bundesjugendring.

Ihre Rechtsform ist in der Regel der eingetragene → *Verein* mit dem Charakter einer Arbeitsgemeinschaft. Sie nehmen jugendpolitische Aufgaben wahr und vertreten die Interessen der Jugend in allen politischen Bereichen und auf allen Ebenen. Die Jugendringe wirken auch in den Jugendhilfeausschüssen der Städte und Gemeinden mit.

Der wichtigste Zusammenschluß der Jugendverbände in der Bundesrepublik Deutschland ist der Deutsche Bundesjugendring (DBJR), dem 20 Jugendverbände, vier Anschlußverbände sowie die Landesjugendringe als Mitglieder angehören. Die parteipolitischen Jugendorganisationen arbeiten im Ring Politischer Jugend (RPJ) zusammen. Die Deutsche Sportjugend (DSJ) ist ein eigenständiger Verband, jedoch auf Kommunal- und Landesebene teilweise in den Jugendringen vertreten.

Youth Religions

G

Since the end of the 60s groups have been making their appearance calling themselves religious communities and canvassing mainly, but not exclusively, young people. The youth religions have diverse roots and come from different cultural backgrounds. Many of them show the following characteristics: a hierarchical structure, strong pressure to conform with the other members of the group (even in respect of clothing), full identification with the aims of the community, shunning criticism towards the group, exploitation of the members.

As a rule, these groups are well organised economic ventures. They make their followers work without pay, but present books and records and provide expensive initiation courses for the respective doctrine.

In some cases (e.g. the Moon Sect), criminal acts have been discovered (duress, fraudulent begging, unfair publicity methods). The most well-known groups in the Federal Republic are: Bagwan Sect, Hare Krishna, Church of the Unification, Children of God, Transcendental Meditation.

UK

The situation is reflected in the United Kingdom.

Standing Conferences of Youth Organisations

G

Voluntary associations of youth organisations (umbrella organisations) existing, in most cases, at three levels:
- the local and above-local level: local/municipal standing conference of youth organisations; standing conference of youth organisations at the level of a *Kreis* or *Bezirk* (→ *kommunale Selbstverwaltung*)
- *Land* level: standing conference of youth organisations at the *Land* level
- Federal level: German Federal Youth Council.

Their legal status is generally that of a registered association (→ *Verein*) in the form of a standing conference. They have the role of political representation of young people and defence of youth interests in all political spheres and levels. The standing conferences of youth organisations also participate in the work of Youth Services Committees of the towns and communities.

The most important association of youth organisations in the Federal Republic of Germany is the German Federal Youth Council *(Deutscher Bundesjugendring/DBJR)*. It consists of 20 youth organisations, four affiliated organisations and the standing conferences of youth organisations at the *Land* level. Party political youth organisations are brought together in the Council of Poli-

Die vordringliche Aufgabe des DBJR ist es, die Bereitschaft der Jugend zur Zusammenarbeit über alle politischen und weltanschaulichen Grenzen hinweg zu vertiefen, die Jugend für die Verwirklichung einer demokratischen Ordnung zu gewinnen und auf dieser Grundlage die gemeinsamen Interessen der Jugendverbände und der gesamten Jugend gegenüber der Öffentlichkeit, dem Parlament und der Regierung zu vertreten, gemeinsame Aktionen und Veranstaltungen durchzuführen, sowie das Aufleben militaristischer, nationalistischer und totalitärer Tendenzen zu verhindern. Darüber hinaus ist der DBJR ein wichtiges Kommunikations- und Informationsorgan für seine Mitgliedsverbände zur Abstimmung von jugendpolitisch relevanten Fragen.

DBJR und RPJ bilden das Deutsche Nationalkomitee für internationale Jugendarbeit (DNK), das an der Mitwirkung und Mitgestaltung europäischer Jugendstrukturen beteiligt ist und im Europäischen Jugendrat (CENYC) mitarbeitet.

VK

Es besteht ein beträchtlicher Unterschied zwischen dem strukturellen Aufbau der Dachverbände der Jugendarbeit im Vereinigten Königreich und in der Bundesrepublik Deutschland. Die mittlere oder regionale Ebene fehlt, und in vielen Fällen arbeiten nationale Verbände und kommunale Jugendringe auf derselben Ebene zusammen. Folgende Träger existieren nebeneinander:

National Youth Agency (NYA)
Bis April 1991 bestand in England ein Zusammenschluß der nationalen freien Träger der Jugendarbeit im *National Council for Voluntary Youth Services (NCVYS)*. Er war das Vertretungsgremium von etwa 60 nationalen freien Jugendorganisationen und über 40 örtlichen Jugendringen mit dem Ziel, die partnerschaftliche Zusammenarbeit zwischen freien und öffentlichen Trägern auf nationaler Ebene zu fördern. Die unlängst gegründete *National Youth Agency (NYA)* übernimmt die Aufgaben des NCVYS (→ *Überblick über den Youth Service im Vereinigten Königreich).*

Ähnliche Funktionen und Ziele haben der *Council for Wales of Voluntary Youth Services,* die *Scottish Standing Conference of Voluntary Youth Organisations (SSCVYO)* und die *Standing Conference of Youth Organisations in Northern Ireland (SCOYO).*

British Youth Council (BYC)
Der BYC wurde 1948 mit der Aufgabe ins Leben gerufen, britische Jugendorganisationen und die nicht-organisierte Jugend auf internationaler Ebene zu

tical Youth Organisations *(Ring Politischer Jugend/RPJ)*. The German Sport Youth *(Deutsche Sportjugend/DSJ)* is not a member of the DBJR, but is often represented in the standing conferences of youth organisations at local and Land level.

The most important task of the DBJR is to encourage young Germans to develop cooperatively, irrespective of political and ideological frontiers, and to involve themselves actively in the creation of a true democracy. Therefore it represents the common interests of youth organisations and indeed of all young people before the general public, Parliament and the Government. It arranges joint programmes and activities for its constituent members and fights the revival of militaristic, nationalist, or totalitarian tendencies. The German Federal Youth Council is, moreover, a vital organ of communication and information for its member organisations as a basis for discussion and agreement on important matters of youth policy.

The German Federal Youth Council together with the Council of Political Youth Organisations constitute the German National Committee for International Youth Work *(Deutsches Nationalkomitee für internationale Jugendarbeit/ DNK)*. It is therefore directly involved in cooperating with and in the shaping of the European youth structures, especially through its work within the Council of European National Youth Committees (CENYC).

UK
Youth Councils
The structural set-up of umbrella organisations advocating the interests of young people in the UK is different from that in the FRG. There is no medium or regional level and in many cases national organisations and local councils come together on an equal footing. The following exist side by side:

National Youth Agency (NYA)
Until April 1991, the national voluntary youth organisations in England came together in the National Council for Voluntary Youth Services (NCVYS) as a representative body of some 60 national voluntary youth organisations and more than 40 local youth councils in order to develop the partnership between voluntary bodies and statutory authorities at national and local level. The recently formed National Youth Agency (NYA) will take over the rôle of NCVYS in its new duties (→ *Outline of the Youth Service in Britain)*.

The Council for Wales of Voluntary Youth Services, the Scottish Standing Conference of Voluntary Youth Organisations (SSCVYO) and the Standing Conference of Youth Organisations in Northern Ireland (SCOYO) have similar aims and functions.

British Youth Council (BYC)
BYC was established in 1948 to represent British youth organisations and young people on an international level, receiving support from the Foreign and Commonwealth Office for these purposes. Since 1977 BYC has also been

vertreten. Für diese Zwecke wird der Britische Jugendrat vom *Foreign and Commonwealth Office* gefördert. Seit 1977 arbeitet der BYC auch auf nationaler und örtlicher Ebene. Heute ist er ein eigenständiger freier Träger der Jugendarbeit.

Der Britische Jugendrat bildet das Britische Nationalkomitee für internationale Jugendarbeit, d.h. er vertritt England, Schottland und Wales. Sein Sitz befindet sich in London. Er unterhält enge Beziehungen zum Walisischen *(Wales Youth Forum/WYF)* und zum Nordirischen Jugendforum *(Northern Ireland Youth Forum/NIYF)*, die beide Vertreter in das Exekutivkomitee des Britischen Jugendrates entsenden. Zur Zeit besteht kein Jugendrat für Schottland. TANGENT ist eine neue Initiative mit dem Ziel, eine Jugendvertretung in Schottland zu schaffen.

Dem BYC gehören 70 Mitgliedsverbände an. Diese lassen sich im wesentlichen in sechs Kategorien einteilen: örtliche Jugendgruppen, nationale Jugendverbände, konfessionell oder parteipolitisch gebundene Organisationen, Jugendabteilungen der Gewerkschaften und „uniformierte" Organisationen wie die Pfadfinderinnen und Pfadfinder. Der größte Mitgliedsverband ist die *National Union of Students* mit über einer Million Mitgliedern.

Seit einigen Jahren ist das Hauptanliegen des BYC die größtmögliche Mitwirkung junger Menschen in allen Bereichen der Gesellschaft, unabhängig von Geschlecht, Rasse, Konfession, geschlechtlicher Orientierung, Behinderung oder Nicht-Behinderung. Chancengleichheit für alle wird als wichtiges Ziel angesehen.

Der BYC ist Mitglied des CENYC und des Jugendforums der Europäischen Gemeinschaft. Auch bei anderen internationalen und europäischen Jugendkonferenzen, die in bestimmten Zeitabständen veranstaltet werden, wirkt er aktiv mit. Des weiteren unterhält er bilaterale Kontakte mit Entwicklungsländern des Commonwealth, verschiedenen Ländern West- und Osteuropas sowie mit außereuropäischen Staaten.

Youth Council for Northern Ireland (YCNI)
Aufgrund der *Youth Service (Northern Ireland) Order 1989* wurde im April 1990 der Nordirische Jugendrat geschaffen. Er ist ein halb-öffentlicher Träger, der sowohl Förderungsmittel als auch Direktiven von der Regierung erhält. Zu seinen Aufgaben zählt u.a. die Vergabe zentraler Mittel an die freien Jugendorganisationen, die Entwicklung der internationalen Jugendarbeit sowie die verantwortliche Mitwirkung bei der Erarbeitung des geplanten Kernstudiums für die Ausbildung der Fachkräfte der Jugendarbeit. Der Nordirische Jugendrat und das Nordirische Jugendforum bestehen nebeneinander.

Local Youth Councils
Local youth councils stellen ein Forum für junge Leute dar, die in örtlichen Jugendverbänden organisiert sind. Ihre Mitglieder sind freie Jugendgruppen, Jugendclubs, Schülervertretungen, politische Parteien, Bürgerinitiativen und auch Jugendliche, die keiner Gruppierung angehören. In ihnen arbeiten junge

involved in work on a national and local level. Today, it functions as an independent voluntary youth organisation.

BYC is the National Youth Committee of Britain, covering England, Scotland and Wales. BYC is based in London and has close links with the Wales Youth Forum (WYF) and the Northern Ireland Youth Forum (NIYF), both of which have representatives on the BYC Executive Committee. There is currently no Scottish Youth Council. TANGENT is a new initiative to set up a representation of young people in Scotland.

BYC represents 70 member organisations. The latter fall mainly into six categories: local youth groups, national young people's organisations, religious organisations, party political youth organisations, youth sections of trade unions and uniformed organisations such as the Guides and Scouts. The largest member organisation is the National Union of Students which has over a million members.

For several years BYC has pursued policies aimed at maximising participation of young people in all aspects of society, whatever their gender, race, creed, sexual orientation or physical ability. Equal opportunities for all are seen as a key issue.

BYC is a member of the Council of European National Youth Committees (CENYC) and the European Communities Youth Forum (ECYF). It also takes an active part in other world or European youth conferences which occur from time to time. The organisation maintains bilateral contacts with nations of the developing Commonwealth, Western, Eastern European and non-European Countries.

Youth Council for Northern Ireland (YCNI)
In April 1990 the Youth Council for Northern Ireland was established on the basis of the Youth Service (Northern Ireland) Order 1989. It is a non-departmental public body which receives funding from and is subject to directives from the Government. YCNI will have such functions as e.g. the payment of HQ grants to the voluntary youth organisations, the development of international work, and the monitoring and development of the youth service curriculum. The Council will exist side by side with the Northern Ireland Youth Forum.

Local Youth Councils
These are forums of young people organised locally, which involve young people from voluntary youth groups, youth clubs, school councils, political parties, community action groups and also young people helping them to discuss issues, develop ideas and thus increase their influence in the area where they live. There are not many local youth councils in the UK.

Local youth councils may not be considered as the exact counterpart to the German *Kreisjugendringe* or *Stadtjugendringe.*

Leute für junge Leute, um ihnen bei der Auseinandersetzung mit aktuellen Themen sowie bei der Entwicklung eigener Vorstellungen zu helfen und den Einfluß auf ihr Lebensumfeld zu verstärken. Die Zahl dieser Zusammenschlüsse auf örtlicher Ebene ist nicht groß.

Die örtlichen Jugendringe stellen keine genaue Entsprechung zu den deutschen Kreisjugendringen oder Stadtjugendringen dar.

Jugendschutz (m)

D

Der Staat trifft gesetzliche und erzieherische Maßnahmen zur Bekämpfung von jugendgefährdenden Einflüssen, um die körperliche und seelische Gesundheit der Kinder und Jugendlichen zu schützen.

Dieser gesetzliche Jugendschutz umfaßt insbesondere folgende (unter → *Jugendgesetze* näher zu erläuternde) Bestimmungen: das Gesetz zum Schutz der Jugend in der Öffentlichkeit (JöSchG), das Gesetz über die Verbreitung jugendgefährdender Schriften (GjS), und das Jugendarbeitsschutzgesetz (JASchG).

Die Durchführung obliegt nicht nur den Jugendämtern und Jugendwohlfahrtsorganisationen, sondern auch der Polizei. So werden aufgegriffene Jugendliche in Jugendschutzstellen, Auffangheimen oder Auffangstellen dieser Träger vorübergehend untergebracht. Auch führt die Polizei Jugendschutzstreifen durch, zumeist mit Beteiligung von Bediensteten des Jugendamtes oder des Gewerbeaufsichtsamtes, um die Einhaltung des gesetzlichen und gewerberechtlichen Jugendschutzes zu überwachen, insbesondere um Kinder und Jugendliche von gefährdenden Orten fernzuhalten.

Nach § 42 KJHG ist das Jugendamt zur Inobhutnahme verpflichtet, wenn ein Kind oder Jugendlicher um Obhut bittet oder eine dringende Gefahr für sein Wohl besteht. Die vorläufige Aufnahme von Kindern und Jugendlichen in Krisensituationen durch geeignete Einrichtungen und Bereitschaftspflegestellen ist bundeseinheitlich geregelt. Dabei wird vor allem der pädagogische Auftrag im Rahmen der Krisenintervention herausgestellt und den notwendigen personensorgerechtlichen Erfordernissen Rechnung getragen.

Immer größere Bedeutung erhält der Jugendmedienschutz (Ergänzung des Jugendschutzgesetzes 1985). Danach ist ein Kennzeichnungssystem geschaffen worden, nach dem kommerzielle Einrichtungen Videokassetten, Bildplatten, etc. nur dann an Kinder und Jugendliche abgeben dürfen, wenn sie von der obersten Jugendbehörde für diese Gruppe als geeignet erklärt worden sind. Der Verkauf von bespielten Bildträgern in Automaten ist verboten.

Die Durchführung des GjS liegt bei einer dem Bundesministerium für Frauen und Jugend nachgeordneten Behörde, der Bundesprüfstelle für jugendgefährdende Schriften. Sie wird nur auf Antrag der Jugendbehörden tätig. Ergibt die

Protection of Young Persons in Public

G

In order to safeguard the physical and emotional well-being of children and young persons from the risks to which they are exposed, legal and educational measures have been enacted by the State.

The statutory protection of young persons in public is embodied in the following acts (explained in detail under → *Jugendgesetze):* The Act Concerning the Protection of Young Persons in Public *(Gesetz zum Schutz der Jugend in der Öffentlichkeit/*JöSchG), the Act Concerning the Distribution of Publications Harmful to Young Persons *(Gesetz über die Verbreitung jugendgefährdender Schriften/*GjS), and the Protection of Young Persons at Work Act *(Jugendarbeitsschutzgesetz/*JASchG).

Implementation of these acts is not only a responsibility of the youth offices and the youth welfare organisations, but also of the police. Temporary accommodation hostels are provided by these bodies to house young people detained as being at risk. The police organise protection squads which include, in most cases, a representative of the youth office and the trade supervisory authority. The aim of these patrols is to check compliance with the provisions of the above acts and trade law and, in particular, to keep children and young people away from places where they may be at risk.

Under Section 42 of the Child and Youth Services Act the youth office must provide a place of safety if a child or young person requests shelter and protection or his/her welfare is seriously at risk. Measures to be taken for those found in a situation of crisis are now laid down nationwide. Such persons will be accommodated provisionally in suitable establishments or short-stay foster families. The weight of effort hereby lies on assuming a caring responsibility within the framework of crisis intervention. Allowance must be made for the statutory requirements governing the care and custody of a child.

It is also felt that young people need to be more and better protected from the harmful influences of the media. This development was taken into consideration when the Act Concerning the Protection of Young Persons in Public was amended in 1985. According to this amendment, a system of classification is to be introduced under which commercial establishments may only sell video cassettes, video discs, etc. to children and young people if marked as suitable for persons under 18 by the Youth Authority of the *Land* Government. The sale of video cassette and video disc material through publicly accessible vending machines is forbidden.

Compliance with the Act Concerning the Distribution of Publications Harmful to Young Persons is ensured by an authority, the Federal Board for the Review of Publications Harmful to Young Persons, set up within the Ministry for Women and Youth. This body may only act on request of the youth authorities existing at various levels. If after careful examination of the publications in question (audio-visual materials, pictures and other pictorial representations) they are

Prüfung, daß die bedenkliche Schrift (hierzu gehören auch Ton- und Bildträger, Abbildungen und andere Darstellungen) jugendgefährdend ist, nimmt sie diese in eine Liste auf. Für die auf der Liste stehenden Schriften bestehen umfassende Werbebeschränkungen; sie dürfen auch nicht an Kinder und Jugendliche verkauft werden.

Der erzieherische Jugendschutz ist sozialpädagogisch (präventiv) ausgerichtet. Die Aufklärungsarbeit ist Aufgabe der Jugendämter (Art. 1 § 14 KJHG), die mit Eltern und Erziehern zusammenarbeiten. Manche Städte arbeiten auch an polizeilichen Präventionsmodellen (z.B. Jugendpolizist).

Zur Förderung der Aufgaben des erzieherischen und gesetzlichen Jugendschutzes haben sich 64 auf Bundesebene tätige Organisationen, die Landesarbeitsgemeinschaften Aktion Jugendschutz sowie freie Mitarbeiter 1951 zur Bundesarbeitsgemeinschaft Aktion Jugendschutz (BAJ) zusammengeschlossen.

VK

Es ist Aufgabe der Öffentlichkeit im allgemeinen sowie der Polizei, der sozialen Einrichtungen und der kommunalen Erziehungsbehörden im besonderen, dafür zu sorgen, daß junge Menschen während ihrer Erziehung durch Elternhaus und Schule gegen schädigende Einflüsse geschützt werden, wobei der Schutz der Jugend, falls erforderlich, mit Unterstützung der Gerichte sicherzustellen ist. Die Gesetzgebung zielt darauf ab, den jungen Menschen vor körperlicher und seelischer Mißhandlung in der Öffentlichkeit (und im Privatleben) zu bewahren. Nicht alle gesetzlichen Bestimmungen, die Jugendliche betreffen, sind in eigenen Gesetzen enthalten. Das Erwachsenenstrafrecht trifft auch zahlreiche Maßnahmen für Jugendliche.

Die Durchsetzung des Rechts durch die Gerichte geschieht auf Antrag der Betroffenen. Die Einschaltung der Gerichte kann ein einzelner Bürger, ein Inspektor der *National Society for the Prevention of Cruelty to Children*/NSPCC (Nationale Gesellschaft zur Verhinderung von Grausamkeit gegenüber Kindern), eine kommunale Sozialbehörde, die Polizei oder ein Bewährungshelfer veranlassen.

Befindet sich ein Kind oder Jugendlicher in einer Krisensituation, wird in der Regel durch einen Mitarbeiter der Sozialen Arbeit Inobhutnahme beantragt (Anordnung meist für 72 Stunden). Falls Anlaß zur weiteren Sorge um das Wohl des Kindes besteht, kann ein Antrag auf Anordnung der vorläufigen Hilfe zur Erziehung (28 Tage) gestellt werden.

Der *Children and Young Person Act 1969* gibt den Gerichten die Möglichkeit, Hilfe zur Erziehung anzuordnen, wenn ein junger Mensch als gefährdet anzusehen ist (→ *Jugendstrafrecht, Maßnahmen des,* VK).

Wird für einen Minderjährigen Hilfe zur Erziehung gefordert, überträgt das Gericht der zuständigen Kommunalbehörde die Entscheidung darüber, wo das Kind oder der Jugendliche untergebracht und die Schule besuchen wird.

judged to be harmful, they will be proscribed. Proscribed publications may not be generally advertised or sold to young people.

The educational measures for the protection of young people have a mainly preventive slant. This work is the responsibility of the youth offices (Art. 1, section 14, KJHG) in cooperation with parents and educationalists. Some cities are setting up model preventive schemes, e.g. allocation of special officers, to deal with young people at risk.

To further promote the educational and statutory protection of young people, 64 organisations working at the Federal level, the Standing Conferences for the Protection of Young Persons in Public at *Land* level as well as independent workers in this field came together in 1951 to form the Federal Association for the Protection of Young People.

UK

It is the concern of the public in general, the police, social services and the local education authority in particular, if necessary acting through the courts, to ensure that young people are brought up and educated protected from harmful risks to which they are exposed. Legislation seeks to protect the young person from physical and mental abuse in public (and in private). Not all law relating to young people is specific legislation; much is under sections of adult criminal law.

The implementation of the law through the courts is at the request of any concerned body; it could be an individual, it can be an inspector of the National Society for the Prevention of Cruelty to Children (NSPCC), the local social services department, the police, or a probation officer.

When a child or young person is found in a situation of crisis, the usual procedure is for a social worker to apply for a place of safety order (usually valid for 72 hours). If there continues to be concern about the welfare of the young person, an interim care order (28 days) may be applied for at the juvenile court.

The Children and Young Persons Act 1969 allows the courts to make a care order where the young person is considered at risk (→ *Jugendstrafrecht, Maßnahmen des,* UK).

In committing a child to care, the court is saying that the local authority will then decide where and with whom the child will live and go to school.

Once the new Children Act is in force, "to be put in care" will be restricted to an order imposed by the court, and parents will come to a voluntary arrangement with the local authority. This will be known as children "in accommodation".

The Sexual Offences Acts 1956, 1965 and 1967 define offences and by age of the victim the seriousness of the offence. These Acts also cover incest.

Wenn der neue *Children Act* in Kraft getreten ist, wird die Hilfe zur Erziehung nur noch auf Anweisung des Gerichts verfügt. Die Eltern haben dann die Möglichkeit, mit der zuständigen Kommunalbehörde eine freiwillige Vereinbarung zu treffen. Diese Regelung trägt die Bezeichnung *children in accomodation.*

Die *Sexual Offences Acts 1956, 1965 und 1967* definieren den Tatbestand sexuellen Mißbrauchs von Minderjährigen und setzen Altersgrenzen fest, innerhalb derer die strafbare Handlung als unterschiedlich schwer anzusehen ist. Diese Gesetze enthalten auch Bestimmungen über den Inzest.

Der *Children and Young Persons (Harmful Publications) Act 1955* verbietet die Verbreitung von Publikationen, die in erzählender oder bildlicher Form Verbrechen, Gewalt und Grausamkeit darstellen oder angsterregende Vorfälle behandeln, die bei Kindern und Jugendlichen, in deren Hände sie fallen, zu seelischen Schäden führen können.

Der Alkoholgenuß Jugendlicher wird durch den *Children and Young Persons Act 1933* und durch den *Licensing Act 1964* geregelt. (→ *Alkoholmißbrauch,* → *Jugendgesetze, VK).*

Jugendsozialarbeit (f)

D

Jugendsozialarbeit gibt benachteiligten Jugendlichen sozialpädagogische und berufsbezogene Hilfen, um ihre berufliche Ausbildung, Eingliederung in die Arbeitswelt und soziale Integration zu fördern. Sie richtet sich auch an junge Aussiedler, Zuwanderer, Ausländer und ausländische Flüchtlinge sowie an junge Menschen, die außerhalb der Familie in Jugendwohnheimen untergebracht sind.

Die Angebote der Träger von Jugendsozialarbeit umfassen insbesondere Maßnahmen der Berufshinführung, Berufsvorbereitung, Berufsausbildung und Sprachförderung. Lern- und leistungsbeeinträchtigten sowie arbeitslosen jungen Menschen bieten sie sozialpädagogische Beratung und berufsbezogene Hilfen an. Weitere Aufgaben sind die Schulung und Fortbildung von Mitarbeitern sowie die Entwicklung von wissenschaftlich begleiteten Modellprojekten des Bundes.

Die Erfüllung dieser Aufgaben nehmen jene Trägergruppen (evangelische, katholische, freie, sozialistische und kommunal-staatliche) wahr, die in der Bundesarbeitsgemeinschaft Jugendsozialarbeit — Jugendaufbauwerk — zusammengeschlossen sind. Sie erhalten Förderungsmittel aus dem Bundesjugendplan und den Landesjugendplänen, von der Arbeitsverwaltung gemäß Arbeitsförderungsgesetz, aber auch aus Sonder- und Länderprogrammen, die der Förderung beruflicher Bildung sowie der Bekämpfung von Jugendarbeitslosigkeit dienen, sowie von den örtlichen Jugendämtern, die auch eigene Angebote der Jugendsozialarbeit entwickelt haben.

The Children and Young Persons (Harmful Publications) Act 1955 prohibits the provision, in any form, by stories or pictures of works which wholly or partially portray:
— the commission of crime
— acts of violence or cruelty
— incidents of an horrific nature that would tend to corrupt a child or young person into whose hands it fell.

The use of alcohol by young persons is covered by the Children and Young Persons Act 1933 and the Licensing Act 1964 (→ *Alkoholmißbrauch*, → *Jugendgesetze*, UK).

Socio-educational Provision for Young People

G

The aim of socio-educational provision for young people is to promote their vocational training, integration into the world of work and social integration through socio-educational and job-related measures. These are also available to young resettled persons and immigrants, to foreigners and young people living in homes away from their families.

Socio-educational provision for young people includes vocational training preparatory schemes, vocational training as such, and language classes. Slow learners and persons whose achievement is impaired, as well as unemployed young people, may turn to the above organisations and bodies for socio-pedagogical counselling and job-related assistance. Furthermore, the above organisers run training and further education courses for workers involved in socio-educational programmes and develop scientifically evaluated pilot projects in their respective field on behalf of the Federation.

Socio-educational provision for young people is arranged by those groups of organisations (Protestants, Catholic, voluntary, socialist and local authority) which are associated in the Federal Association of Socio-educational Programmes for the Young *(Bundesarbeitsgemeinschaft Jugendsozialarbeit — Jugendaufbauwerk)*. They are funded under the Federal Youth Plan and the *Land* youth plans. They also receive grant-aid from the manpower administration under the Promotion of Employment Act, and under special schemes and *Land* level programmes aiming to further vocational training and to combat youth unemployment. Moreover, grant-aid may be provided to them by the

VK
Keine genaue Entsprechung im VK

Jugendsport (m)

D
Jeder dritte Einwohner in der Bundesrepublik Deutschland ist Mitglied in einem Sportverband. Der Sport ist auch eine der beliebtesten Aktivitäten deutscher Jugendlicher. Die Sportart mit der längsten Tradition in Deutschland ist das Turnen, die beliebteste Sportart ist das Schwimmen.

Jugendliche betreiben Sport in der Schule, in Sportvereinen, in Jugendeinrichtungen und im privaten Bereich. Der Sport ist freiwillige Sache des einzelnen; er soll vor allem Freude machen. Zwar gibt es eine öffentliche Sportverwaltung auf Bundes-, Landes- und kommunaler Ebene, doch nimmt sie keinen Einfluß auf fachliche oder organisatorische Entscheidungen der sportlichen Selbstverwaltung. Die Vereine sind in Landessportbünden und zahlreichen Fachverbänden zusammengefaßt. Die Dachorganisation ist der Deutsche Sportbund (DSB). Die Jugendorganisation des DSB ist die Deutsche Sportjugend (DSJ).

Die Lehrpläne der Schulen sehen regelmäßigen Sportunterricht sowie Neigungs- und Leistungsgruppen vor, durch die die Schüler die für sie geeigneten Sportarten selbst entdecken und ein sinnvolles Freizeitverhalten erlernen sollen. Der Schulsport wird ergänzt durch den Breitensport für Menschen, die nicht nach Höchstleistungen streben. Ihm dienen auch die vom DSB ins Leben gerufenen Aktionen „Trimm Dich" und „Sport für alle", in deren Rahmen Volkswettbewerbe im Laufen, Schwimmen, Radfahren u.a. veranstaltet werden.

Einmal jährlich wird, unterstützt durch Mittel des Bundesjugendplans, ein breitensportlicher Wettbewerb, die Bundesjugendspiele, in allen Schulen durchgeführt, an denen jeweils ca. 4 Millionen Jugendliche teilnehmen. Spitzensportler haben zahlreiche Möglichkeiten der fachlichen Ausbildung und finanziellen Förderung durch den modernen Hochleistungssport (Deutsche Sportförderung).

Die Deutsche Sportjugend, deren Mitglieder den örtlichen Turn- und Sportvereinen angehören, hat sich nicht nur die Ausbildung der sportlichen Fähigkeiten zum Ziel gesetzt, sie betreibt Jugendarbeit als außerschulische Bildungsarbeit mit jungen Menschen (sportliche Jugendbildung; → *Jugendarbeit).*

VK
Nach dem *Education Act 1944* ist Sport ein integrierter Bestandteil der Lehrpläne der Grund- wie auch der weiterführenden Schulen.

local youth offices. These, in turn, have developed socio-educational provision for young people on their own initiative.

UK
No exact UK equivalent

Sport for Young People

G

Every third inhabitant of the Federal Republic of Germany is a member of a sports organisation. Sports, in particular, are a great favourite of the younger generation. The sport with the longest tradition in Germany is gymnastics, the most popular sport is swimming.

Young people practice sports at school, in sports organisations, in youth establishments and privately. Participation is a matter of individual choice, its primary aim being to provide enjoyment. Although there are statutory sport administrations at Federal, *Land* and local authority level, they exercise no influence on sporting or organisational decisions of the self-governing sport bodies. The sports associations are grouped in *Land* Sports Federations and many specialised organisations. Their umbrella organisation is the German Federation of Sport *(Deutscher Sportbund/*DSB), its youth organisation being the German Sport Youth *(Deutsche Sportjugend/*DSJ).

Modern school curricula provide for regular sports lessons as well as extra voluntary groups based on preference and ability, which should enable the pupils to discover on their own for which kinds of sport they are suited and help them to develop a useful leisure time activity. School sport is supplemented by popular sport for those who are not out to achieve top competitive results. Also serving popular sport are the "Keep-Fit" and "Sport for All" campaigns set up and run by the DSB. They include popular competitions in running, swimming, cycling, etc.

Grant-aided from the Federal Youth Plan, a popular sport competition, the Federal Youth Games *(Bundesjugendspiele),* is arranged annually in all schools. About 4 million young people take part every year. The elite athletes have numerous opportunities to undergo specialist training and may benefit from the generous financial support which is available for high-level competitive sport (Promotion of German Sport).

The German Sport Youth whose members are registered with the local associations for gymnastics and sports, not only sets itself the task of developing the sporting abilities of the young, but also of providing youth work *(sportliche Jugendbildung;* → *Jugendarbeit)* as an out-of-school educational activity.

UK
Under the Education Act 1944 sport is an integral part of both the primary and secondary schools curriculum.

Das Konzept der Ausweitung des Lehrplanes auf den sportlichen Wettbewerb innerhalb der Schulen und zwischen verschiedenen Schulen war jahrzehntelang vom Geist der Privatschulen geprägt. Sport galt als wesentliches Element in der Persönlichkeitsentwicklung junger Leute. In den 60er und 70er Jahren wurde darüber diskutiert, ob die Durchführung von Wettkämpfen überhaupt wünschenswert sei. Infolge langanhaltender Kontroversen zwischen Lehrergewerkschaften und Anstellungsträgern Ende der 70er und Anfang der 80er Jahre hat der Sport an den öffentlichen Schulen an Bedeutung verloren. Diese Kontroversen wirkten sich negativ auf die bis dahin bestehende große Einsatzbereitschaft aus, die zur Durchführung von Sportveranstaltungen außerhalb der Unterrichtsstunden erforderlich ist. Das Schwergewicht der sportlichen Arbeit liegt heute auf der Einführung eines breiten Spektrums sportlicher Aktivitäten, so daß junge Leute während der Schulzeit und nach dem Schulabschluß eine gezielte Auswahl unter den Möglichkeiten körperlicher Betätigung treffen können.

Außerhalb der Schulen unterhalten Erwachsene auf freiwilliger Basis Sportklubs für junge Leute, die je nach Sportart schon in sehr jungen Jahren eintreten und an auf der Ebene der Kommunen und der *counties (→ Kommunale Selbstverwaltung,* VK) veranstalteten Wettkämpfen teilnehmen können. Außerdem haben verschiedene Erwachsenensportvereine Juniorengruppen, die sich auch an diesen Wettkämpfen beteiligen können. Da die Kommunalbehörden den Sport nur durch die subventionierte Benutzung von Sporteinrichtungen unterstützen, weil es keine öffentliche Direktförderung gibt, verwenden die ehrenamtlichen Sportveranstalter einen großen Teil ihrer Arbeit darauf, die Finanzierung ihrer Aktivitäten aus anderen Quellen sicherzustellen.

Für die wichtigsten Sportarten besteht ein übergeordnetes nationales Gremium, das die Teilnahme- und Wettkampfbedingungen von der örtlichen bis zur nationalen Ebene festlegt und auch die Auswahl für internationale Veranstaltungen trifft. Es gibt keinen der Deutschen Sportjugend vergleichbaren Dachverband für den Jugendsport; der *Sports Council* ist die dem Deutschen Sportbund annähernd entsprechende britische Organisation.

Jugendstrafrecht (n)

D

Vornehmlich im Jugendgerichtsgesetz (JGG) *(→ Jugendgesetze)* kodifizierte Sonderregelungen des allgemeinen Strafrechts zur Bearbeitung von Straftaten Jugendlicher und Heranwachsender *(→ Altersgrenzen).* Im Jugendstrafrecht steht der Erziehungsgedanke im Vordergrund.

Der Jugendliche ist nur dann verantwortlich, wenn er zur Zeit der Tat reif genug ist, das begangene Unrecht einzusehen und danach zu handeln. Heranwachsende werden nach Jugendstrafrecht behandelt, wenn sie zur Tatzeit einem Jugendlichen gleichstanden (Entwicklungsretardierung) und bei typischen Jugendverfehlungen.

For decades the concept of extending curricula sport to competition in intra- and inter-school games followed the ethos of the "public" (private) schools and was regarded as a vital element in a young person's development. In the 60s and 70s the desirability of competition as such came into question which, combined with long-running disputes between teachers' unions and employing authorities in the late 70s and the 80s which greatly affected the amount of goodwill available and necessary to organise extra-curricular activities, sports in state schools have diminished in importance. The emphasis now is on an introduction to a broad spectrum of activities that will enable young persons to make an educated choice of physical activity both at and after leaving school.

Outside the schools adults working voluntarily organise clubs for young people from, depending on the activity, sometimes very young ages, to take part in local and county leagues; voluntary adult sports organisations have junior sections which would also take part in these organised competitions. Although help may be given by local authorities in the form of subsidised use of sports facilities, since no financial assistance is available from any statutory bodies, fund raising is an important part of the work done by the volunteer adult organisers.

Most major sports have a national regulating body that provides a framework for participation and competition from local to national level, and selection for international events. There is no national body comparable to the *Deutsche Sportjugend,* but the British organisation closest to the *Deutscher Sportbund* is the Sports Council.

Penal Law Relating to Young Offenders

G

Special provision for young offenders supplementing general penal law is embodied mainly in the Juvenile Court Act (→ *Jugendgesetze),* which applies to offences committed by those under 18 and those in the 18–21 age group (→ *Altersgrenzen).* In penal law relating to young offenders educational considerations are a major concern.

A young person may only be held responsible if he was mature enough to understand the wrong he did and to act accordingly at the time when the offence was committed. The 18–21 age group *(Heranwachsende)* are dealt with under the penal law relating to young offenders if their behaviour was like that of a

Über strafbare Handlungen Jugendlicher entscheiden nach dem JGG die Jugendgerichte. Jugendgerichte sind der Jugendrichter, das Jugendschöffengericht, das aus einem Jugendrichter und zwei Jugendschöffen (Laien) besteht, sowie die Jugendkammer (Landgericht). Vor der Jugendkammer werden insbesondere schwere Straftaten verhandelt. Jugendgerichtsverhandlungen sind nicht öffentlich.

Im Verfahren vor den Jugendgerichten erhält der Angeklagte die Unterstützung der Jugendgerichtshilfe, die die erzieherischen, sozialen und fürsorgerischen Gesichtspunkte zur Geltung zu bringen hat und von einem spezialisierten Mitarbeiter des Jugendamts (Sozialarbeiter) beim Jugendgericht (Jugendgerichtshelfer) ausgeübt wird. Nach der Erforschung der Persönlichkeit, des sozialen Umfeldes und der Entwicklung des Jugendlichen erstellt der Jugendgerichtshelfer einen Bericht, nimmt an der Hauptverhandlung teil und betreut den Delinquenten fürsorgerisch.

VK

In England und Wales können Kinder unter zehn Jahren nicht für strafbare Handlungen schuldig gesprochen werden. Bei Kindern zwischen 10 und 14 Jahren geht man davon aus, daß sie nicht in der Lage sind, begangenes Unrecht einzusehen. Sofern nicht das Gegenteil bewiesen ist, wird angenommen, daß Personen über 14 Jahren ein ausreichendes Maß an Einsicht besitzen, um sie für ein Verbrechen verantwortlich zu machen. (Als „Kinder" gelten Personen unter 14 Jahren und als „Jugendliche" Personen von 14 bis 17 Jahren).

In England, Wales und Nordirland kommen Verfahren gegen Personen zwischen 10 und 17 Jahren, die im Verdacht stehen, eine strafbare Handlung begangen zu haben, in der Regel vor ein Jugendgericht, es sei denn, es handelt sich um ein schweres Vergehen oder um Fälle, in denen Personen dieser Altersgruppe zusammen mit Erwachsenen angeklagt werden. Die Verhandlung erfolgt dann vor einem *Magistrates Court* oder einem *Crown Court.* Nach britischem Recht gibt es die gesonderte Altersgruppe der 18- bis 21jährigen, die im deutschen Gesetz als „Heranwachsende" bezeichnet werden, nicht. Im Vereinigten Königreich sind Personen der Altersspanne von 17–25 Jahren nach dem Gesetz junge Erwachsene.

Im Strafverfahren ist das Gericht in der Regel ein besonderes Jugendgericht. Bei Verfahren zur Anordnung der Hilfe zur Erziehung *(care order)* muß ein Jugendgericht entscheiden. Das Jugendgericht besteht in der Regel aus drei Laienrichtern, zu denen mindestens ein Mann und eine Frau gehören müssen, es sei denn, es liegen besondere Umstände vor. Jugendgerichtsverhandlungen sind nicht öffentlich.

In Schottland wird die Straffähigkeit mit 8 Jahren erreicht. Die gerichtliche Strafverfolgung von Kindern unter 16 Jahren ist jedoch selten und nur auf An-

young person at the time of the offence (retarded development) or if the misdemeanour concerned was typical of a young person.

According to the Juvenile Court Act, offences committed by young persons are dealt with by the Juvenile Courts. Juvenile Courts are the juvenile court judge (one legally qualified local court judge), the *Jugendschöffengericht* where the bench consists of one juvenile court judge and two lay magistrates, and the Youth Chamber (regional court). Very serious offences are heard before the Youth Chamber. Hearings of the Juvenile Court are not open to the public.

During juvenile court proceedings the defendant is assisted by a specially trained social worker whose task is to prepare a case history. Social enquiry into the case is designed to draw the court's attention to educational, social and welfare aspects. These social workers are attached to the Youth Office. The character, social environment and development of the young person are looked into and a report is submitted to the court. The social worker is present at the trial and looks after the welfare of the offender.

UK

In England and Wales no child under the age of 10 can be held guilty of an offence. It is assumed that a child between the ages of 10 and 14 does not possess sufficient capacity to know what he is doing wrong unless proved otherwise. A person over 14 is presumed to have a degree of reason sufficient to make him responsible for his crimes. (A "child" is under 14 years old and a "young person" aged from 14 to 17).

In England, Wales and Northern Ireland persons aged between 10 and 17 who are alleged to have committed an offence would normally be tried by a Juvenile Court, except in the case of a serious offence or if charged together with an adult, when they would be brought before a Magistrates Court or a Crown Court. British law makes no provision for an 18–21 age group which German law calls *Heranwachsende*. In the UK, the 17–25 age group are young adults in the eye of the law.

In criminal proceedings the court is usually a special Juvenile Court and in care proceedings it must be such a court. A Juvenile Court is normally composed of three lay justices, who must, except in special circumstances, include both a man and a woman. Juvenile Court hearings are not open to the public.

In Scotland the age of criminal responsibility is 8, but prosecution of children under 16 in court is rare and can take place only as instructed by the Lord Advocate (the head of the legal administration), usually where the case is of a serious nature or the child is prosecuted together with an adult. Normally a special children's hearing is held in an informal setting. The bench is composed of three lay justices drawn from a panel.

A child or young person must either be legally represented or must be assisted in his defence by his parent or guardian. If he is found guilty of an offence the

ordnung des *Lord Advocate* (des Leiters der Rechtsverwaltung) möglich. Sie erfolgt in der Regel in schweren Fällen oder bei gemeinsamer Anklage mit Erwachsenen. Normalerweise findet ein besonderes Jugendverfahren statt, das einen weniger formalen Charakter hat. Das Gericht besteht aus drei Laienrichtern, die aus einer Liste ausgewählt werden.

Kinder oder Jugendliche müssen einen Rechtsbeistand haben oder bei ihrer Verteidigung von einem Elternteil oder Vormund unterstützt werden. Wenn sie einer Straftat für schuldig befunden werden, muß das Gericht das allgemeine Verhalten, das häusliche Umfeld, die schulischen Leistungen und den Gesundheitszustand des Angeklagten berücksichtigen, wobei es einen Bericht eines Sozialarbeiters, der Bewährungshilfe oder der Jugendbehörde und ggfs. ein medizinisches Gutachten einbeziehen kann. Jedes Gericht muß im Verfahren gegen Personen unter 17 Jahren auf deren Wohl bedacht sein, Maßnahmen zu ihrer Entfernung aus einer schädlichen Umgebung treffen und sicherstellen, daß sie eine angemessene Bildung oder Ausbildung erhalten.

Jugendstrafrecht (n), Maßnahmen (f/pl) des

D

I. Als Folgen der Jugendstraftat können vom Jugendgericht verhängt werden:

(1) Erziehungsmaßregeln

(a) Erziehungsbeistandschaft (EB)
wird angeordnet, um die leibliche, geistige oder seelische Entwicklung eines Minderjährigen vor Gefährdung zu schützen oder eine bereits eingetretene Schädigung zu beseitigen. Sie ist eine offene erzieherische Hilfe. Auf Antrag des Personensorgeberechtigten oder auf Anordnung des Vormundschaftsgerichtes wird vom Jugendamt ein Erziehungsbeistand bestellt, der die Eltern des Jugendlichen berät.

(b) Weisungen
Das Gesetz nennt beispielhaft die Weisung, am Verkehrsunterricht teilzunehmen oder den Umgang mit bestimmten Personen zu meiden. Der Richter hat auch die Möglichkeit freier Weisungen, die z.B. den Umgang mit Geld betreffen.

(c) Hilfe zur Erziehung/HzE
(§ 27 Sozialgesetzbuch VIII)
Wenn Weisungen und EB nicht ausreichen und öffentliche Erziehung durch Fachkräfte unumgänglich ist, kann Hilfe zur Erziehung (HzE) angeordnet werden. HzE wird in einer geeigneten Familie oder in Heimen durchgeführt.

(2) Zuchtmittel
sind die im Jugendstrafrecht am häufigsten verhängten Maßnahmen. Sie sind juristisch nicht als Strafe anzusehen.

court must take into account his general conduct, home surroundings, school record and medical history, and may receive a report from a social worker, the probation service, the local authority or the medical services. Every court, in dealing with a person under the age of 17, must have regard to his welfare and may take steps to remove him from undesirable surroundings and to ensure that he is properly educated or trained.

Measures under Penal Law Relating to Young Offenders

G

I. Following an offence committed by a young person the Juvenile Court may decide to take the measures listed below:

(1) *Erziehungsmaßregeln* (socio-educational court orders)

    (a) *Erziehungsbeistandschaft/EB*
    (socio-educational provision similar to a supervision order)
    to protect the physical, mental or emotional development of a minor at risk or to make good damage already done. This is a home-based provision. A person is designated by the youth office to advise the parents on request of those exercising the right of care and custody or following an order made by the guardianship court.

    (b) *Weisungen* (directions)
    Examples cited under penal law cover compulsory attendance at police traffic tuition courses, restrictions on contact with certain persons or broader directions, e.g. limitations on the spending of money.

    (c) *Hilfe zur Erziehung/HzE* (reception into care)
    The court may issue a care order where directions or socio-educational provisions are considered inadequate and the only alternative is imposed education. The young person may either be placed in the care of a suitable family or in a residential establishment.

    (d) Educational therapy

(2) *Zuchtmittel* (correctional treatment)
describe the measures most frequently ordered under penal law for young offenders. Legally, they are not to be seen as sentences.

(a) Verwarnungen
allein sind relativ wirkungslos. Als effektiver haben sich

(b) Auflagen
erwiesen, z.B. die Zahlung eines Geldbetrages zur Wiedergutmachung des Schadens.

(c) Jugendarrest
ist die stärkste Form der Zuchtmittel, angeordnet bei nicht mehr geringfügigen Delikten. Es handelt sich um Freizeitarrest für mindestens ein, höchstens vier Wochenenden oder um Dauerarrest für mindestens eine, höchstens vier Wochen. Auch Kurzarrest von zwei bis sechs Tagen ist möglich.

(3) Jugendstrafe
ist unumgänglich, wenn die Tat „schädliche Neigungen" offenbart oder wegen der „Schwere der Schuld" im Einzelfall. Sie beträgt sechs Monate bis fünf Jahre bei Jugendlichen, bei schweren Verbrechen bis zu zehn Jahren.

Auf Jugendstrafe von unbestimmter Dauer (sechs Monate bis vier Jahre) wird erkannt, wenn die Erfolge einer erzieherischen Einwirkung nicht abzusehen sind. Nach Ablauf der Mindeststrafe wird geprüft, ob eine Entlassung zur Bewährung oder ein neuer Prüfungstermin angezeigt ist. Die Jugendstrafe ist juristisch eine Kriminalstrafe und gilt als Vorstrafe. Der Strafmakel kann jedoch bei günstiger Prognose beseitigt werden. Bei der Strafzumessung steht immer der Resozialisierungsgedanke im Vordergrund.

II. Der Vollzug der Maßnahmen geschieht für Jugendliche und Heranwachsende (→ *Jugendstrafrecht*) in folgenden Einrichtungen:

– Jugendarrestanstalt
für den Vollzug des Arrests unter Aufsicht des Jugendrichters. Heute werden nach einer kurzen Besinnungsphase erzieherische Kurse, Sport und gemeinsame Freizeit angeboten. In vielen Fällen wird eine Nachbetreuung verwirklicht. Die Jugendlichen werden von qualifizierten Fachkräften betreut.

– Erziehungsheim
für die Durchführung der Hilfe zur Erziehung. Die HzE wird aufgehoben, wenn die Volljährigkeit oder der Erziehungszweck erreicht sind. Die Fachkräfte dieser Einrichtungen sind überwiegend Erzieher (Heimerzieher) und Sozialarbeiter/Sozialpädagogen. Die HzE wird auch in Pflegestellen und Wohngemeinschaften durchgeführt, um den schädlichen Auswirkungen der Heimunterbringung vorzubeugen.

– Jugendstrafanstalt
für den Vollzug der Jugendstrafe. Sie soll zu einer geregelten Lebensführung erziehen und bietet hierzu die Hilfen des Schulunterrichts, der

(a) *Verwarnungen* (cautions)
by themselves are relatively ineffective.

(b) *Auflagen* (directions/conditions)
e.g. the payment of a fine to make good damage done seem to be more effective than (a) above.

(c) *Jugendarrest* (treatment of young offenders at attendance centres)
is the strongest form of correctional treatment. It is ordered when the offence can no longer be considered minor. It takes the form of *Freizeitarrest* (attendance during leisure time) for at least one and a maximum of four weekends, *Dauerarrest* (long-term attendance) for at least one and a maximum of four weeks or *Kurzarrest* (short-term attendance) ranging from two to six days.

(3) *Jugendstrafe* (committal order/custodial sentence)
is compulsory if, in a given case, the offence shows "harmful inclinations" or a "serious guilt" has been incurred. Committal orders range from six months to five years for young persons, and may cover as much as ten years in case of a serious crime.

An indeterminate committal order (six months to four years) is used where the outcome of educational treatment cannot be predetermined. After the offender has served the minimum sentence the court decides either to release him/her on probation or sets a further hearing date. Legally, a committal order is a penalty for a criminal offence. It ranks as a previous conviction. Where there is a favourable expectation as to the future conduct of the offender, the taint of a previous conviction may be removed. When the type of sentence is determined, the court's major concern is always the offender's social rehabilitation.

II. Establishments for the treatment of young offenders under 18 years, and, where appropriate, the 18–21 age group *(→ Jugendstrafrecht)* are:

— *Jugendarrestanstalt* (attendance centre)
This is where treatment of young offenders is provided under the supervision of a juvenile court judge. Nowadays a short period for reflexion and adjustment is followed by educational courses, sports, and joint leisure activities. The young people are looked after by qualified specialist personnel. In many cases after-care is provided.

— *Erziehungsheim* (community home)
for those placed under a care order. Care orders are terminated when the age of majority is reached or when the aim of the educational training has been achieved. The majority of the staff working in these establishments are residential child care workers *(→ Erzieher)* and qualified social or youth and community workers *(→ Sozialarbeiter/Sozialpädagoge)*. Socio-educational provision under a care order may also take place in a foster home or a "supervised" commune in order to avoid the harmful effects of placement in a residential establishment.

beruflichen Ausbildung, Arbeit, Sport und sinnvolle Beschäftigung in der Freizeit. Der Vollzug in freien Formen (Urlaub mit den Eltern, Ausgang, Freigang zur Arbeit, Ausbildung in freien Betrieben außerhalb) ist in den meisten Anstalten möglich. Die Beamten sollen für die Erziehungsaufgabe des Vollzugs ausgebildet sein.

Die für 1991 geplanten Änderungen des Jugendgerichtsgesetzes werden zu Neuerungen in diesem Bereich führen, die bei Redaktionsschluß noch nicht absehbar waren.

VK

I. Der *Children and Young Persons Act 1969,* ergänzt durch den *Criminal Justice Act 1982,* führte zu Änderungen hinsichtlich der Vollmachten der Gerichte sowie der gerichtlichen Maßnahmen für Minderjährige. Danach hat das Gericht im Jugendhilfe- und Strafverfahren bei Personen bis zum 17. Lebensjahr grundsätzlich drei Alternativen: Die *order binding over the parents* (Anordnung an die Eltern), die *supervision order* (Aufsichtsanordnung) und die *care order* (Anordnung der Hilfe zur Erziehung).

In England und Wales bestehen bei der Anordnung an die Eltern zwei Formen, für die es offenbar im deutschen Recht keine genaue Entsprechung gibt. Es sind dies die *matrimonial supervision order* im Falle der Eheschließung (Zivilverfahren) mit dem Ziel, Hilfen für die Erziehung eines Kindes bereitzustellen, und eine weitere Anordnung, die die Eltern oder den Vormund des Kindes verpflichten, es angemessen zu betreuen und ordnungsgemäß zu beaufsichtigen. (Bei dieser Anordnung ist die Zustimmung der Eltern oder des Vormundes erforderlich.)

Ein Vergleich zwischen den deutschen Erziehungsmaßregeln und den Maßnahmen, die britische Gerichte für Kinder treffen können, die Betreuung, Schutz oder Kontrolle benötigen, ist schwierig, da die Interventionskriterien oft divergieren. Daher sollen hier nur die Interventionsformen aufgelistet und die zweite und dritte der vorgenannten Alternativen erläutert werden, die letzten Endes darauf abzielen, vergleichbare Probleme zu lösen.

Anordnung der Hilfe zur Erziehung/Aufsichtsanordnung im Jugendhilfeverfahren
Im Falle der körperlichen und seelischen Vernachlässigung, des sexuellen Mißbrauchs oder der Körperverletzung (gefährdetes Kind) kann die Kommunalbehörde oder die *National Society for the Prevention of Cruelty to Children* (NSPCC) ein Jugendhilfeverfahren beantragen. Lehrer, Freunde, Nachbarn, die Polizei oder die Kinder selbst haben die Möglichkeit, sich an diese Stellen zu wenden.

— *Jugendstrafanstalt* (youth custody centre/youth prison)
for treatment of young offenders under a committal order. Its aim is to teach the young people to lead a disciplined life. For this purpose, it provides school education, vocational training, work, sports and purposeful leisure-time activities. Freer forms of custodial treatment (being allowed out on holiday to stay with parents, leave, permission to work on a job outside the establishment, training provided outside with a private firm) are possible in most establishments. The prison officers should be trained in the educational responsibilities of custodial treatment.

The amendment of the Juvenile Court Act which is planned for 1991 will lead to certain changes in the above field that could not be foreseen in detail when this Glossary went to the printer's.

UK

I. The Children and Young Persons Act 1969, as amended by the Criminal Justice Act 1982, made changes in the powers of courts and in the treatment of children brought before courts. The Act gives the court three basic options in care and criminal proceedings alike for all persons up to age 17. These are an order binding over the parents, a supervision and a care order.

In England and Wales there are two types of orders under the first option mentioned above which seem to have no exact counterpart in German law. These are the matrimonial supervision order in divorce cases to provide educational help to bring up a child (civil proceedings) and another form of order which requires the child's parent or guardian to agree to take proper care of him and exercise proper control over him (the consent of the parent or guardian to such an order is required).

It is difficult to compare the German socio-educational court orders to the forms of action British courts may take in respect of children in need of care, protection or control, as the criteria for intervention often differ. It is therefore only possible to list the forms of intervention, which, in essence, aim to resolve comparable problems, i.e. the second and third options referred to above.

Care Order/Supervision Order — Care Proceedings
In cases of neglect, sexual and physical abuse or emotional deprivation (Child At Risk), the local authority or the National Society for the Prevention of Cruelty to Children (NSPCC), may apply for care proceedings. Care cases are signalled to these bodies by teachers, friends, neighbours, police or the children themselves.

In all cases a specialist social worker (guardian *ad litem*), and a solicitor are appointed by the court to act on behalf of the child. Such applications are heard before a Magistrates Juvenile Court, where the bench consists of three lay magistrates, one of which must be a woman. These magistrates must have 2 to 3 years experience and specialist training before being allowed to sit on a juvenile court hearing.

In allen diesen Fällen bestellt das Gericht zur Vertretung der Interessen des Kindes einen fachlich speziell für diesen Bereich qualifizierten Sozialarbeiter *(guardian at litem)* sowie einen Anwalt. Zuständig ist der *Magistrates Juvenile Court,* der aus drei Laienrichtern besteht, zu denen eine Frau gehören muß. Für die Ausübung dieses Amtes beim Jugendgericht benötigen die Laienrichter zwei bis drei Jahre Erfahrung sowie eine einschlägige Schulung.

Wenn eine Anordnung der Hilfe zur Erziehung ergeht, werden alle elterlichen Rechte dem örtlichen Sozialamt übertragen. Das Kind kann zu Hause wohnen, in einem Heim untergebracht werden oder bei einer geeigneten Familie leben.

Wird Aufsicht angeordnet, behalten die Eltern das Sorgerecht, und die Rechte der Aufsichtsführung gehen an die Kommunalbehörde über, die die Aufgabe hat, dem Kind Unterstützung und Hilfe zuteil werden zu lassen. Es bleibt in der Regel im Hause der Eltern.

Anordnung der Hilfe zur Erziehung im Jugendstrafverfahren
Wenn ein Kind mehrere Straftaten begangen hat und die Richter in seiner häuslichen Umgebung eine Gefährdung sehen, kann Hilfe zur Erziehung angeordnet werden. Diese Anordnung entspricht der des Zivilverfahrens. Sie wird aufgehoben, wenn der Jugendliche das 18. oder 19. Lebensjahr erreicht. Bei Personen über 17 Jahren wird sie nicht ausgesprochen.

Aufsichtsanordnung – Jugendstrafverfahren
Diese Aufsichtsanordnung ist der des Zivilverfahrens sehr ähnlich, mit dem Unterschied, daß bestimmte Auflagen einbezogen sind. Auflagen bedürfen der Zustimmung der Eltern, des Minderjährigen und des *social worker*/Bewährungshelfers.

Der Zeitraum, über den sich eine Aufsichtsanordnung erstreckt, liegt zwischen sechs Monaten und höchstens drei Jahren. Die zuständige Kommunalbehörde hat jedoch die Möglichkeit, Änderung (d.h. Streichung oder Verhängung von Auflagen) oder Aufhebung zu beantragen.

Weisungen/Auflagen im Rahmen einer Aufsichtsanordnung
Für die deutsche Form der Weisungen gibt es keine genaue Entsprechung. Weisungen im Rahmen einer Aufsichtsanordnung können Auflagen hinsichtlich des Aufenthaltes enthalten, das Verbot aussprechen, bestimmte Orte oder Veranstaltungen wie Fußballspiele zu besuchen oder die Teilnahme am Programm eines *intermediate treatment (IT) centre* vorschreiben.

Diese Programme schließen regelmäßig stattfindende Wochenendveranstaltungen ein. Wie bei allen Auflagen müssen sich Eltern und Kind mit der jeweiligen Anordnung einverstanden erklären. Wenn der Minderjährige nicht an dem vorgeschriebenen Programm teilnimmt, kann eine Geldstrafe und/oder der Besuch eines *attendance centre* verfügt werden (s. unter II). Für Jugendliche, bei denen eine krankhafte Störung der Geistestätigkeit festgestellt wird, besteht die Möglichkeit der Anordnung des ambulanten Besuchs einer

If a care order is made, all parental rights are transferred to the local authority social services department and the child may remain at home or be placed in a community home or with an approved family.

If a supervision order is made, the parents retain their parental rights and the supervision rights are transferred to the local authority whose duty is to befriend and assist the child who normally remains at home.

Care Order — Criminal Proceedings
If a child has committed a series of offences and the magistrates are concerned about the child's home environment, a care order can be made. This care order is the same as a care order made under civil proceedings. Care orders terminate when the young person reaches 18 or 19 years and are not made above the age of 17 years.

Supervision Order — Criminal Proceedings
This supervision order is very similar to that made in civil proceedings except that a number of conditions can be included. These conditions can only be applied if the parents, the child and the social worker/probation officer agree to them.

The period of supervision can range from 6 months to a maximum of 3 years. However, the local authority can apply to have such an order changed (i.e. the deletion or imposing of conditions) or discharged.

Directions/Conditions under a Supervision Order
There is no exact counterpart for the German directions *(Weisungen)*. The directions under a supervision order can range from directions as to residence, directions to attend certain approved activities, to directions not to attend certain places or activities, e.g. football matches. In addition, the magistrates can direct that a child must attend an intermediate treatment (IT) centre programme.

These programmes involve regular residential weekends. As in all conditions the parents and the child must agree to such an order being made. Should the child fail to attend a fine and/or attendance centre order could be made. Young persons diagnosed as suffering from a mental illness may be directed to attend as an outpatient at a suitable treatment centre. They cannot be directed to stay in an (approved) mental health hospital.

Secure Accommodation Orders —Civil Proceedings
If a young person is proved to be too unruly, at risk to himself or to others, a secure accommodation order may be made under civil proceedings. The young person may have committed offences but those matters are not dealt with in this hearing.

Forms of correctional treatment are:
1) Cautions:
    a) The instant caution, i.e. a verbal warning on the spot, given by a policeman. The policeman makes a note of it and reports it to the Social Services.

Therapieeinrichtung. Sie dürfen jedoch nicht in ein (anerkanntes) psychiatrisches Krankenhaus eingewiesen werden.

Anordnung zur Unterbringung in einer geschlossenen Einrichtung – Zivilverfahren
Bei Jugendlichen, die aufsässig sind oder für sich selbst oder andere eine Gefährdung darstellen, kann auch im Zivilverfahren eine *secure accomodation order* (Anordnung zur Unterbringung in einer geschlossenen Einrichtung) ausgesprochen werden. Falls der Jugendliche Straftaten begangen hat, sind sie nicht Gegenstand dieses Verfahrens.

Es bestehen folgende Formen der Zuchtmittel:
1) Verwarnung
   a) die sofortige Verwarnung, d.h. eine mündliche Verwarnung vor Ort, die durch einen Polizisten ausgesprochen wird. Der Polizeibeamte nimmt sie zu Protokoll und informiert das Sozialamt.

   b) die formale Verwarnung, die voraussetzt, daß das betreffende Kind und seine Eltern in der Polizeiwache erscheinen, worauf ein Polizeiinspektor die Verwarnung erteilt.

2) Auflagen
   a) Wiedergutmachung des Schadens
   b) Übernahme der Gerichtskosten
   c) Geldstrafen
   In der Regel ordnet das Gericht an, daß die Geldstrafe von den Eltern oder dem Vormund, nicht aber von dem Kind selbst zu zahlen ist.

3) Anordnung gemeinnütziger Arbeit
   Straffällige im Alter von 16 Jahren und darüber können angewiesen werden, zwischen 20 und 240 Stunden unbezahlte gemeinnützige Dienste zu leisten (bzw. maximal 120 Stunden bei Straffälligen unter 17 Jahren). Die angeordnete Stundenzahl ist innerhalb von 12 Monaten abzuleisten. Gemeinnützige Arbeiten sind bespielsweise die Renovierung des Hauses älterer oder behinderter Menschen oder die Mitwirkung beim Bau eines Abenteuerspielplatzes.

4) Freizeitarrest in einem *attendance centre* (s. unter II)
   Das Gericht kann Freizeitarrest von insgesamt 24 Stunden (aufgeteilt in Zeiträume von jeweils bis zu drei Stunden) anordnen, der an Samstagen in einem *attendance centre* abzuleisten ist.

Grundsätzlich gibt es für Personen unter 21 Jahren keine Gefängnisstrafe, und auf Jugendstrafe darf bei diesem Personenkreis nur erkannt werden, wenn das Gericht der Meinung ist, daß andere Maßnahmen nicht zum Erfolg führen. Jugendstafen können umfassen

a) *Detention*
   Freiheitsentzug von mindestens drei Wochen bis maximal vier Monaten für männliche Straffällige, die eine Gefängnisstrafe erhalten hätten, wenn sie über 21 Jahre gewesen wären.

b) The formal caution, which means that the child and his parents attend the police station, where an inspector gives a warning.

2) Conditions
   a) compensation for damage done
   b) court costs
   c) fines
   The court normally orders that the parents or guardian, not the child himself, must pay.

3) Community service orders: Offenders aged 16 or over may be ordered to complete between 20 and 240 hours unpaid service (or a maximum of 120 hours for offenders under 17), to be completed within 12 months. Community service may consist, for example, in decorating the houses of old or disabled persons or building adventure playgrounds.

4) Attendance at attendance centre: The court may order that a total of up to 24 hours (in spells of up to 3 hours) shall be spent at an attendance centre on Saturdays.

On principle, no person under the age of 21 may be sent to prison, and the court may not pass a custodial sentence on a person under 21 unless it is of the opinion that no other method of dealing with him is appropriate. If a custodial sentence is passed it may provide for:

a) Detention for at least 3 weeks up to 4 months for a male offender which would have been punishable by imprisonment had he been over 21.

b) Youth custody for a period of more than four months for offenders of either sex aged between 15 and 21. This is the equivalent of the former borstal order. Sentences for a maximum of one year are made by a Magistrates Court. Sentences extending over one year have to be confirmed by a Crown Court presided over by a judge. Youth custody orders rarely provide for custody over two years.

c) Custody for life, upon conviction for an offence which would be punishable by life imprisonment if committed by a person over 21. The case is heard before a Crown Court. If the young person is found guilty, he/she is detained "at Her Majesty's pleasure" and may only be released by the Home Office.

II. Establishments for the treatment of young offenders are:
   − The attendance centre which is run by the police. The centres provide physical education and instruction in practical subjects and are designed for those found guilty of offences for which older people could be sent to prison. There are special junior attendance centres for boys aged 14 to 16.
   − Community home. This establishment provides for those children and young people who are either "in care" by parental request (voluntary care), or who are subject to a care order.

b) *Youth custody*
Freiheitsentzug für einen Zeitraum von mehr als vier Monaten für Straffällige beiderlei Geschlechts im Alter von 15 bis 21 Jahren. Dies entspricht der früheren *borstal order*. Strafen von bis zu einem Jahr werden von einem *Magistrates Court* verhängt. Darüber hinausgehende Strafzumessungen müssen von einem *Crown Court*, in dem ein Richter den Vorsitz führt, bestätigt werden. Die Anordnung einer Jugendstrafe erstreckt sich selten über einen längeren Zeitraum als zwei Jahre.

c) *Custody for life*
Jugendstrafe von unbestimmter Dauer nach Verurteilung für eine Straftat, auf die bei einer Person von über 21 Jahren eine lebenslängliche Gefängnisstrafe stünde. Die Verhandlung findet vor einem *Crown Court* statt. Wenn der/die Jugendliche schuldig gesprochen wird, folgt eine Inhaftierung *at Her Majesty's pleasure* (auf unbestimmte Dauer). Eine Entlassung ist nur durch das Innenministerium möglich.

II. Der Vollzug der Maßnahmen für junge Straffällige geschieht in folgenden Einrichtungen:
   — Das von der Polizei geleitete *attendance centre* (Zentrum für Freizeitarrest). Sein Programm umfaßt Sportunterricht sowie Unterweisung in praktischen Fächern. Die Zentren sind für Straffällige bestimmt, die Delikte begangen haben, für die ältere Personen eine Gefängnisstrafe erhielten. Es bestehen besondere *junior attendance centres* für Jungen von 14 bis 16 Jahren.
   — *Community home* (Erziehungsheim). Diese Einrichtung ist für Kinder und Jugendliche bestimmt, die entweder auf Antrag der Eltern (freiwillige) Erziehungshilfen erhalten oder für die eine Anordnung der Hilfe zur Erziehung besteht.
   — *Intermediate treatment centre* (Einrichtung für offene Erziehungshilfen). Diese Einrichtungen arbeiten mit straffälligen Kindern und Jugendlichen. Die Mehrzahl der Einrichtungen führt vom *Magistrates Court* als Vollzugsmaßnahmen für junge Straffällige anerkannte Programme durch. Dies sind im allgemeinen sehr intensive Maßnahmen, die eine „Alternative zur Jugendstrafanstalt" darstellen, und/oder Programme mit einer spezifischen Zielsetzung wie die Behandlung des Mißbrauchs von Lösungsmitteln, Sozialisationsschwierigkeiten usw. durchführen. Die Jugendlichen wohnen in der Regel zu Hause, wobei die Eltern mit den Mitarbeitern des Zentrums in regelmäßiger Verbindung stehen. Die Dauer der Programme beträgt gewöhnlich sechs Monate, bzw. 30, 60 oder 90 Tage je nach Anordnung des Gerichts. Es gibt keine deutsche Entsprechung zum *intermediate treatment centre*.
   — Das *detention centre* für den Vollzug von Jugendstrafen von drei Wochen bis zu vier Monaten, für das es wohl ebenfalls keine deutsche Entsprechung gibt. Es soll einen kurzen und harten, aber heilsamen Schock vermitteln.

- Intermediate treatment centres: These resources are designed to work with those children and young people involved in criminal activities. Most IT centres run programmes which are approved by the magistrates for the treatment of young offenders. These could be highly intensive "alternative to custody" programmes and/or programmes specifically designed to look at solvent abuse, relationship difficulties etc. The young people normally reside at home and parents are in regular contact with IT officers. The programmes usually last six months or 30, 60 and 90 days if directed by the court. There is no German equivalent.
- The detention centre covers periods from three weeks to four months. There seems to be no exact German equivalent. It aims to give a "short, sharp shock".
- The youth custody centre covering periods of four months to three years. For all practical purposes, the youth custody centre is the equivalent of borstal training which has been abolished. (In very serious cases young persons may also be sent to prison.)

In Scotland children under 16 are rarely brought to court but may be required to attend a children's hearing before a panel of three lay people, which determines whether compulsory measures are required and, if so, what form they should take. In Northern Ireland children under the age of 17 charged with committing a criminal offence may be brought before a juvenile court, which may order the child to be sent to a training school, placed in the care of a fit person, or put under supervision. The court may also order attendance at an attendance centre or remand home, impose a fine or compensation, or require the parents to ensure the child's good behaviour.

The new Children Act which is expected to come into force towards the end of 1991 will bring about some changes in the above provision.

– Das *youth custody centre* (Jugendstrafanstalt) dient dem Vollzug von Jugendstrafen von vier Monaten bis zu drei Jahren. Es ersetzt weitgehend das frühere *borstal*. (In sehr schwierigen Fällen können Jugendliche auch Gefängnisstrafen erhalten.)

In Schottland werden Minderjährige unter 16 Jahren nur selten vor Gericht gestellt. Es findet vielmehr ein *children's hearing* vor einem Gremium von drei Laien statt. Dieses Gremium entscheidet, ob Zwangsmaßnahmen erforderlich und in welcher Form sie gegebenenfalls zu treffen sind. In Irland ist für minderjährige Straffällige unter 17 Jahren in der Regel ein Jugendgericht zuständig, das die Einweisung in ein Erziehungsheim, die Bestellung eines Erziehungsbeistandes oder Erziehungshilfe unter einer Aufsichtsanordnung verfügen kann. Das Gericht hat weiterhin die Möglichkeit, die Teilnahme am Programm eines *attendance centres,* die Einweisung in ein *remand home* (Jugendarrestanstalt), eine Geldstrafe, die Wiedergutmachung des Schadens oder die Einwirkung der Eltern auf das Wohlverhalten des Kindes anzuordnen.

Der neue *Children Act,* der Ende 1991 in Kraft treten soll, wird zu einigen Änderungen bei den hier beschriebenen Maßnahmen führen.

Jugendverbände (m/pl)

D
In Jugendverbänden und Jugendgruppen wird → *Jugendarbeit* von jungen Menschen selbst organisiert, gemeinschaftlich gestaltet und mitverantwortet. Ihre Arbeit ist in der Regel als Angebot zu dauerhafter und verbindlicher Mitarbeit auf die eigenen Mitglieder ausgerichtet, kann aber auch Angebote der offenen Jugendarbeit einschließen. Durch Jugendverbände und ihre Zusammenschlüsse können Anliegen und Interessen junger Menschen zum Ausdruck gebracht und vertreten werden.

Jugendverbände sind freiwillige Zusammenschlüsse mit einer Satzung und ehrenamtlichen Leitungskräften. Als freie Träger der Jugendhilfe sind sie in der Regel auf Orts-, Kreis-, Landes- und Bundesebene gegliedert und Mitglied des jeweiligen → *Jugendringes.*

Die öffentliche Jugendhilfe hat die eigenverantwortliche Tätigkeit der Jugendverbände und Jugendgruppen unter Wahrung ihres satzungsgemäßen Eigenlebens zu fördern, sofern diese nach Zielsetzung und Organisation der freiheitlich-demokratischen Grundordnung entsprechen (*nicht* z.B. rechtsradikale Gruppierungen). Diese Gelder für bestimmte Bereiche ihrer Tätigkeit werden aus dem → *Bundesjugendplan* oder entsprechenden Fördermitteln der Länder und Gemeinden bereitgestellt.

Je nach ihrer Zielsetzung können die Jugendverbände grob eingeteilt werden in konfessionelle (z.B. Bund der Deutschen Katholischen Jugend), politische (z.B. Jungsozialisten), gewerkschaftliche (z.B. Gewerkschaftsjugend, DGB) und freizeitbezogene Organisationen (z.B Deutsche Sportjugend).

Youth Organisations

G

In youth organisations and youth groups youth work (→ *Jugendarbeit*) is organised by young People for young people. Activities are carried out jointly on the basis of shared responsibility, and are, as a rule, provided for the group members who, by taking an active part, are given an opportunity for long-term commitment and regular involvement. Some of the activities are open to non-members. Youth organisations and their central associations constitute a platform for discussing the issues young people are concerned with and serve as a forum to advocate their interests.

Youth organisations are voluntary groupings who operate on the basis of their respective statutes and work with voluntary leaders. As voluntary bodies responsible for youth work and youth welfare services they are, as a rule, organised at the local, *Kreis, Land* and Federal level and are members of the standing conferences of youth organisations existing at these levels (→ *Jugendringe)*.

As long as the aims and organisational structure of the youth organisations are in keeping with the basic principles of democracy, the statutory sector is required to support them financially while respecting the responsibility for their own work and the independence vested in their statutes. Under this proviso some groups such as the right-wing extremists are debarred from receiving grant-aid. For certain areas of activity, youth organisations are given public support from the Federal Youth Plan funds (→ *Bundesjugendplan)* or from the appropriate funds available at *Land* or local level.

Depending on their aims, the youth organisations may be roughly divided into denominational organisations (e.g. Federation of German Catholic Youth), political organisations (e.g. Young Socialists), trade union organisations (e.g. Trade Union Youth in the German Trade Union Congress) and organisations mainly devoted to leisure-time activities (e.g. German Sports Youth).

The youth organisations are bodies responsible for out-of-school education of the young or youth work generally covering leisure time provision for young people. Moreover, youth organisations strive to promote the political and social commitment of their members and also of those who do not belong to any youth organisation. Their attention is increasingly focussed on the latter group. Political action (demonstrations, campaigns to inform the general public) aimed at removing social injustice have been one of their main areas of learning in recent years.

Die Jugendverbände sind Träger der außerschulischen Jugendbildung/Jugendarbeit. Sie dienen der Freizeitgestaltung der Jugend. Darüber hinaus fördern sie das politische und soziale Engagement ihrer Mitglieder und der nicht-organisierten Jugend, die sie zunehmend ansprechen wollen. Politische Aktionen zur Abschaffung gesellschaftlicher Mißstände gehören seit einigen Jahren zu den bevorzugten Lernfeldern (Demonstrationen, Aufklärungskampagnen).

VK
Die freien Jugendverbände haben in Großbritannien eine lange Tradition. Der YMCA (CVJM) wurde bereits 1844 gegründet, die *Boys Brigade* 1883. Wie in der Bundesrepublik Deutschland sind die Jugendorganisationen freiwillige Zusammenschlüsse junger Menschen zur Verfolgung gemeinsamer Ziele.

Obwohl in Großbritannien eine Vielzahl unterschiedlicher Jugendverbände besteht, lassen sich die meisten in folgende Gruppen einordnen:

— Die *uniformierten Jugendorganisationen* umfassen die Pfadfinder und Pfadfinderinnen, die *Girls Brigade* und die *Boys Brigade.*

— Zu den *konfessionell gebundenen Jugendverbänden* gehören die *Church of England Youth Assembly,* die *Association of Jewish Youth* und viele andere.

— Die auf der Basis der *Jugendclubs* bestehenden Organisationen sind in der *National Association of Youth Clubs,* bzw. der *National Association of Boys Clubs* zusammengefaßt.

— Die *parteipolitischen Jugendorganisationen* umfassen Jugend- und Studentengruppen, die den großen politischen Parteien angeschlossen sind, wenn auch ihre Ziele im einzelnen oft von denen der jeweiligen Mutterpartei abweichen.

— Die *örtlichen youth councils* sind Arbeitsforen für junge Menschen bestimmter Gebiete. Sie werden ebenfalls zu den freien Jugendverbänden gezählt und sind nicht mit den deutschen Jugendringen vergleichbar.

Außerdem gibt es die *Young Farmers Clubs,* die Organisation der *Physically Handicapped and Able Bodied* (PHAB) und sonstige Träger wie die *Welsh League of Youth,* die nur in einem Teil des Vereinigten Königreiches bestehen.

Die nationalen freien Jugendverbände werden von den Erziehungsbehörden der Landesteile gefördert. Sie erhalten Zuschüsse zu den Kosten für ihre zentrale Geschäftsstelle, Innovationen und experimentelle Projekte sowie nationale bauliche Maßnahmen.

Kinder- und Jugenderholung (f)

D
Für Kinder und Jugendliche besteht vor allem bei gesundheitlicher Gefährdung die Möglichkeit eines mehrere Wochen oder Monate andauernden Aufenthaltes in Erholungsheimen, Ferienlagern oder auch örtlichen, nur tagsüber besuchten Erholungseinrichtungen.

UK

Voluntary youth organisations have a long tradition in Britain; the YMCA was founded as early as 1844, the Boys Brigade dates from 1883. Like in the FRG they are voluntary groupings of young people to pursue a common aim.

Although youth organisations in Britain are very varied, there are certain groups in which most of them can be placed:

— *Uniformed organisations* include the Scouts and Guides, the Girls Brigade and the Boys Brigade.

— *Religious/church-based organisations* comprise the Church of England Youth Assembly, the Association of Jewish Youth and many more.

— *Club-based youth organisations* cover the member organisations of the National Association of Youth Clubs and the National Association of Boys Clubs.

— *Party political youth organisations* are youth and student groups attached to the main political parties, although their detailed policies often differ from the main party.

— *Local youth councils* are forums of young people from a particular area. They are also considered voluntary youth organisations and must not be compared with the German *Jugendringe* (→ *Jugendringe*).

Other categories include the Young Farmers Clubs, the Physically Handicapped and Able Bodied (PHAB) and organisations which exist only in one part of the UK such as the Welsh League of Youth.

The national voluntary youth organisations receive grants from the central education departments for headquarters expenses, innovatory developments, experimental projects, and for national building projects.

Holiday Schemes for Children and Young People

G

Children and young people, particularly those whose health is at risk, may be placed in convalescent homes, rest centres, holiday camps or with local daytime recreational schemes for periods of weeks or even months.

Die Erholungskuren werden von sozialpädagogischen Fachkräften geleitet. Falls erforderlich, ist eine ärztliche Betreuung damit verbunden. Die Einrichtungen stehen unter der Aufsicht der Jugend- und Gesundheitsbehörden. Die Kinder und Jugendlichen erhalten ein zielgruppenorientiertes Freizeitangebot (Wandern, Spiel, Sport u.a.) und können an musischen Aktivitäten teilnehmen. Träger der Einrichtungen sind die freie und öffentliche Jugend- und Sozialhilfe, Sozialversicherungsanstalten, Kirchen und gelegentlich auch Privatpersonen. Die Kosten der Erholungsmaßnahmen tragen grundsätzlich die Erziehungsberechtigten. In bestimmten Fällen können Leistungen von Versicherungsträgern oder gesetzlich vorgesehene Hilfen in Anspruch genommen werden.

Zahlreiche Kommunen unterhalten Einrichtungen der Stadtranderholung und bieten während der Schulferien von Fachkräften angeleitete Erholungs- und Freizeitaktivitäten für Kinder und Jugendliche an. Außerhalb der Ferienzeit können sie der örtlichen Erholung für Kleinkinder oder Erwachsene dienen.

VK
Im Vereinigten Königreich bestehen ähnliche Einrichtungen mit der Bezeichnung Sommerspielzentren, Sommerprojekte usw.

Kommunale Selbstverwaltung (f)

D
Den Gemeinden muß nach Art. 28 (2) GG das Recht gewährleistet sein, alle Angelegenheiten der örtlichen Gemeinschaft im Rahmen der Gesetze in eigener Verantwortung zu regeln. Hinzu kommt die Befugnis, in einem von Bundes- und Landesnormen weitgehend freien Bereich kommunaler Aufgaben Recht (Satzungen) zu setzen. Gesetzgebungsorgane sind der Gemeinde- oder Stadtrat und der Kreistag. Die staatliche Aufsicht ist auf die Prüfung der Rechtmäßigkeit kommunalen Handelns beschränkt (Rechtsaufsicht) und umfaßt nicht die Prüfung der Zweckmäßigkeit der jeweiligen Tätigkeit (Fachaufsicht).

Die Träger der kommunalen Selbstverwaltung sind die Gemeinden und Städte, die Landkreise und kreisfreien Städte sowie die Regierungsbezirke. Die kommunale Organisation ist in den einzelnen Ländern sehr unterschiedlich; teilweise gibt es eine vierte Ebene: Landschaftsverband (Nordrhein-Westfalen), Bezirkstag (Pfalz). Nach den Kommunalreformen der 60er Jahre sind häufig die Gemeinden zu Verbandsgemeinden, Gemeindeverbänden u.a. zusammengefaßt worden.

Art. 28 (2) garantiert nicht den Bestand der einzelnen Gemeinden. Es gibt nicht einmal eine Bestandsgarantie ihrer Aufgaben. Allerdings ist ein Kernbestand unantastbar.

Zu den örtlichen Angelegenheiten gehören der örtliche öffentliche Nahverkehr, der örtliche Straßenbau, die Elektrizitäts-, Wasser- und Gasversorgung,

The convalescent treatment is supervised by socio-educational specialists and may include medical attention. These establishments are controlled by the youth and health authorities. Children and young people in such centres take part in leisure-time activities (hiking, games, sports, etc.) appropriate to their abilities. Other activities include music and the arts. The centres and schemes are run by statutory bodies, the voluntary youth and social services, social insurance agencies, the churches and occasionally by private persons. Costs of holiday schemes are in general borne by those having parental authority over the respective child. In certain cases, however, benefits may be claimed from social insurance agencies or appropriate legal funds.

Many local authorities provide for children and young people suburban rest centres and suburban holiday play schemes staffed by youth work specialists. During term time, these facilities are available to pre-school children and also adults.

UK
Roughly similar provision exists in the UK under the title of summer play centres, summer projects etc.

Local Self-Government

G
According to article 28 (2), The Basic Law, the right to govern themselves in all local affairs within statutory limits is guaranteed to the communities. They also are entitled to make laws (statutes) within this frame of reference. The legislative bodies are the community or town council and the *Kreistag* (district council). State supervision is limited to assessing the legality (legal supervision) of action taken at the local level and does not involve the examination of the suitability of a given activity (substantive supervisory power).

Responsibility for local self-government rests with the communities and towns, the *Landkreise (~* districts) and *kreisfreie Städte (~* municipal districts) as well as the *Regierungsbezirke* (see below). The organisation of local government varies considerably from one *Land* to the next. In some *Länder* there is a fourth level, the *Landschaftsverband* (North Rhine-Westphalia), the *Bezirkstag* (Palatinate). Following the reorganisation of local government in the sixties, the communities were often grouped together to form bigger units such as *Verbandsgemeinden* or *Gemeindeverbände*.

Article 28 (2) does not provide a guaranty for the continued existence of the individual communities, not even for the inviolability of their duties. But a nucleus of duties must always continue to exist.

The local authorities are responsible for short-distance public transport, local road-building, electricity, water and gas supplies, housing construction, building and maintenance of elementary and secondary schools, theatres and mu-

der Wohnungsbau, der Bau und die Unterhaltung von Grund-, Haupt- und Realschulen, von Theatern und Museen, Krankenhäusern, Sportstätten und öffentlichen Bädern sowie die Erwachsenenbildung und die Jugendhilfe.

Kommunalwahlen finden alle vier Jahre statt. Der Zeitpunkt der Wahlen ist von Land zu Land unterschiedlich.

(Die nachstehenden Begriffe sind in alphabetischer Reihenfolge aufgeführt.)

Bezirksregierung
Verwaltung des Regierungsbezirkes. Übt die staatliche (Rechts-) Aufsicht über die Kreise und kreisfreien Städte aus.

Gemeindeverband
In den meisten Ländern sind die kleinen Gemeinden zu solchen Verbänden zusammengeschlossen. Die Bezeichnungen variieren, z.B. „Verbandsgemeinde", „Samtgemeinde", „Amt".

Gemeinderat, Verbandsgemeinderat
Gemeindeparlament (Gemeinderat ist auch die Bezeichnung für das gewählte Ratsmitglied.)

Kommunale Spitzenverbände
Informelle Zusammenschlüsse von kommunalen Einheiten; ohne eigene Rechtspersönlichkeit und staatliche Kompetenz (z.B. „Deutscher Städtetag", „Landkreistag", „Gemeindetag") Sie haben jedoch erheblichen politischen Einfluß auf die Bundesregierung, bzw. die jeweiligen Landesregierungen.

Kreis/Landkreis
Zweite Ebene der kommunalen Selbstverwaltung; Aufsicht über die Gemeinden.

Kreisfreie Stadt
Große Städte gehören keinem Landkreis an. Sie nehmen neben ihren Aufgaben als Gemeinde gleichzeitig die eines Kreises für ihren Bereich wahr.

Kreistag
Parlament des (Land-)Kreises

Landrat
In einigen Ländern ist der Landrat Vorsitzender des Kreisrates *und* der Kreisverwaltung. In Ländern, in denen diese Funktionen geteilt sind, ist der Landrat nur Vorsitzender des Kreisrates. Der Leiter der Kreisverwaltung ist dann der Kreisdirektor.

(Ober-)Bürgermeister
Gemeinde- und Stadtvorstand; Stellung nach Ländern unterschiedlich (Nordrhein-Westfalen: Vorsitzender des Gemeinde-/Stadtrates; Rheinland-Pfalz: gleichzeitig Leiter der Verwaltung)

Oberkreisdirektor
Leiter der Kreisverwaltung in manchen Ländern (z.B. Nordrhein-Westfalen). Der (Ober-)Bürgermeister, bzw. der Landrat ist dann Vorsitzender des Kreistages.

seums, hospitals, sports facilities and public baths, adult education, youth work and youth welfare services.

Elections for the council are held every four years. Election dates vary from *Land* to *Land*.

(The following terms are listed in alphabetical order.)

Bezirksregierung
The administrative department of the *Regierungsbezirk* which exercises governmental (legal) supervision over *Kreise* and *kreisfreie Städte*.

Gemeindeverband
In most *Länder* the smaller communities group together to form associations, e.g. *Verbandsgemeinde, Samtgemeinde, Amt.*

Gemeinderat, Verbandsgemeinderat
Council of a community. (*Gemeinderat* is also the title of a member of the council.)

Kommunale Spitzenverbände
Informal associations of communal units; not endowed with a juridical personality of their own nor governmental competence (e.g. *Deutscher Städtetag –* Association of German Cities and Towns; *Landkreistag –* Association of Country Districts; *Gemeindetag –* Association of Communities). They do, however, have considerable political influence on the Federal Government and/or the respective *Länder* governments.

Kreis/Landkreis (metropolitan or county district)
Secondary level of local self-government; exercising a supervisory rôle over its constituent communities.

Kreisfreie Stadt (metropolitan authority)
Big cities do not form part of a *Landkreis*. In addition to their communal responsibilities they also assume the functions of a *Kreis*.

Kreistag
Council of the *(Land-)Kreis*

Landrat
In some *Länder* where the function of Leader of the Council and Chief Administrative Officer are combined, this is the title given to the holder of the joint post. In other *Länder,* where the functions are split, the title *Landrat* is given to the Leader of the Council. The Chief Administrative Officer then holds the title of *Kreisdirektor*.

(Ober-)Bürgermeister (Chief Burgomaster)
Head of a community or town. Functions vary according to the individual *Land*. In North Rhine-Westphalia e.g. he/she is only the chairman of the community or town council, in Rhineland-Palatinate the *(Ober-)Bürgermeister* is also the head of the administration.

Oberstadtdirektor
Leiter der Stadtverwaltung in manchen Ländern. Der Bürgermeister ist dann nur Vorsitzender des Stadtrates.

Regierungsbezirk
Verwaltungseinheit zwischen Land und kommunaler Selbstverwaltung.

Regierungspräsident
Leiter der Bezirksregierung

Stadtrat
Parlament der Stadt

VK

Die kommunale Selbstverwaltung fällt in Großbritannien in den Verantwortungsbereich der gewählten *local authorities,* die kraft ihrer vom Parlament verliehenen Vollmachten die demokratische Vertretung ihres Zuständigkeitsbereiches wahrnehmen und kommunale Einrichtungen unterhalten.

Die Rahmenbedingungen der kommunalen Verwaltungsstruktur wurden festgelegt im *Local Government Act 1972,* im *Local Government, Planning and Land Act 1980* (für England und Wales), im *Local Government (Scotland) Act 1973* (für Schottland) und im *Local Government Act (Northern Ireland) 1972* (für Nordirland).

Den *county, district, parish* und *community councils* gehören direkt gewählte, ehrenamtliche Ratsmitglieder an. Kommunalwahlen finden jeweils im Abstand von vier Jahren statt. Alle während eines Jahres fälligen Wahlen werden am selben Tag, üblicherweise am ersten Donnerstag im Mai, abgehalten. Die Ratsmitglieder wählen jedes Jahr aus ihren Reihen einen Vorsitzenden, der das Amt des Leiters der Verwaltung übernimmt (*mayor*/Bürgermeister), während das politische Oberhaupt (*leader of the council*/Vorsitzender des Rates) nur von den dem Rat angehörenden Mitgliedern der Mehrheitspartei gewählt wird.

Das Konzept eines umfassenden Systems von örtlich gewählten Vertretungskörperschaften, die zum Nutzen des Gemeinwesens die kommunalen Angelegenheiten regeln, ist erstmalig in Gesetzen des späten 19. Jahrhunderts niedergelegt worden, als die Aufgaben der Gemeinde in erster Linie das öffentliche Gesundheitswesen, den Straßenbau, die Polizei und ordnungsrechtliche Belange umfaßten. Später wurden den Kommunen auch die Verantwortung für das Bildungswesen, den Wohnungsbau, große Teile des Umweltschutzes, die sozialen Dienste, das Verkehrswesen, die Feuerwehr, die Bibliotheken

Oberkreisdirektor
Head of the administration of a *Kreis* in some *Länder* (e.g. North Rhine-West-phalia). In such cases the chairman of the *Kreistag* is the *(Ober-)Bürgermeister* or the *Landrat* respectively.

Oberstadtdirektor (~ Town Clerk)
In some *Länder,* head of the municipal administration. In such cases, the *Bür-germeister* is only the chairman of the *Stadtrat.*

Regierungsbezirk
Administrative unit at a level in-between the *Land* and local self-government.

Regierungspräsident
Head of the *Bezirksregierung*

Stadtrat
Parliament (council) of a town

UK
Local Government
Local government in Britain is the responsibility of elected local authorities which are the democratic representatives of their areas and provide local serv-ices under specific powers conferred by Parliament.

The basic framework of local government structure is set out in the Local Gov-ernment Act 1972 and the Local Government, Planning and Land Act 1980 (for England and Wales), the Local Government (Scotland) Act 1973 (for Scot-land) and the Local Government Act (Northern Ireland) 1972 (for Northern Ireland).

County, district, parish and community councils consist of directly elected un-paid councillors. Elections for any form of local government take place every four years; all local elections due in any one year are held on the same day, nor-mally the first Thursday in May. The councillors annually elect one of their members as chairman who acts as the civil head of the authority (mayor), while the members of the majority political party elect a leader who is the authority's political head (leader of the council).

The concept of a comprehensive system of councils locally elected to manage various services provided for the benefit of the community was first incorpora-ted in statute law in the late nineteenth century, when local authorities' func-tions were centred on public health, highways, the police and regulatory du-ties. The authorities have since also become responsible for education, hous-ing and most of the environmental health and personal social services, traffic administration, planning, fire services, libraries and many other functions. Some of the functions are mandatory, that is the local authority must do what is required by the statute; others are purely optional, enabling an authority to provide services if it so wishes.

und vieles andere mehr übertragen. Einige dieser Aufgaben sind zwingend vorgeschrieben, andere sind freigestellt, d.h. ihre Erfüllung liegt im Ermessen der Kommunen.

Der Haushalt der Kommunen wird überwiegend aus drei Quellen gespeist: Zuwendungen der Regierung, die Kommunalsteuer, die ab 1990 für Erwachsene „pro Kopf" erhoben wird, sowie andere Einnahmen, einschließlich der Mieterträge für Häuser und Wohnungen, die der Kommune gehören.

Mädchenarbeit (f)

D

Eine Unterscheidung der Jugendarbeit mit Mädchen und Jungen wird in weiten Teilen der → *Jugendhilfe* bisher abgelehnt; die Folge davon ist, daß Mädchen in zahlreichen Feldern der Jugendarbeit unterrepräsentiert sind und damit die ohnehin knappen öffentlichen Mittel Mädchen nicht in gleichem Maße zugute kommen wie Jungen. Zu diesem Ergebnis kommt die Kommission des Sechsten → *Jugendberichts* (1984). Sie stellte die folgenden Forderungen und Empfehlungen zur Mädchenarbeit in der Jugendhilfe auf, die im wesentlichen darauf abzielen, „Aktivitäten öffentlich anzuerkennen und zu fördern, die versuchen, Mädchen bei der Entwicklung und Verteidigung eines eigenen Lebensentwurfs zu unterstützen":

— in → *Tageseinrichtungen für Kinder* sollen → *Erzieher/Erzieherinnen* und Eltern intensiv daran arbeiten, daß bewußte oder unbewußte geschlechtsspezifische Festlegungen abgebaut werden. (In diese Elternarbeit sind zunehmend auch die Väter einzubeziehen.)

— in Einrichtungen der → *Jugendarbeit,* Jugendförderung und Jugendbildung sollen eigene Freiräume für Mädchen geschaffen werden, in denen sie lernen können, ihre Gefühle, Wünsche und Bedürfnisse festzustellen, zu besprechen und durchzusetzen. (Jungen reagieren zumeist auf eine eigenständige Mädchenarbeit außerordentlich heftig, da sie stark verunsichert sind. Mädchenarbeit kann also für emanzipatorische Lernprozesse nur dann erfolgreich sein, wenn gleichzeitig eine entsprechende Jungenarbeit begonnen wird.)

— in der Erziehungsberatung (→ *Beratungsdienste)* sollen stärker als bisher die „spezifischen Reaktions- und Verarbeitungsweisen von Mädchen gegenüber Problemen ihrer Lebenssituation innerhalb der Familie, insbesondere aber in der Schule und im Prozeß des Heranwachsens" Berücksichtigung finden.

— offene Angebote und Maßnahmen, die den Mädchen in Konflikt- und Krisensituationen Hilfestellung geben (Erzieherische Einzelhilfe, Heime und Wohngemeinschaften), sollen ausgebaut werden.

Neben diesen Forderungen im Bereich der Jugendhilfe gibt die Kommission auch Empfehlungen für zentrale Politikbereiche sowie zu Wissenschaft/Forschung, für Aus-/Fortbildung und Kooperation von Institutionen, die sämt-

Local government expenditure is financed from three main sources: central government grants, the community charge, a "head tax" levied on all adults from 1990, and other income, including rents from houses and flats owned by the authority.

Work with Girls

G

In many areas of youth work and youth welfare services a distinction between boys and girls has been rejected until now. This practice resulted in girls being underrepresented in many sectors of youth work. Public funds, which are often scarce, are not equally divided between boys and girls. This was pointed out by the Commission for the Sixth Youth Report of the Federal Government 1984 (→ *Jugendbericht*). A need was recognised to "acknowledge and support from public funds those activities that attempt to help girls develop and defend their own life-styles". The report makes the following requirements and recommendations for youth work with girls and youth welfare services:

— in day care establishments (→ *Tageseinrichtungen für Kinder*) the staff (→ *Erzieher/Erzieherin*) and the parents must aim to break down conscious or unconscious sex-stereotypes, involving to a greater extent the fathers;

— in youth work establishments (→ *Jugendarbeit*) supportive measures for the youth service and in educational establishments for the young, room for personal development should be created for girls so that they may learn how to identify, discuss and assert their feelings, wishes and needs. Boys, on the other hand, frequently react very strongly to separate work with girls as it trends to shake their confidence considerably. For the purposes of emancipatory learning processes, work with girls can only be successful if similar work with boys is initiated at the same time;

— in child guidance (→ *Beratungsdienste*) the way in which girls react to and assimilate problems arising within the family, at school and while growing up must be given more consideration than has been the practice until now;

— a more open provision should be made to help girls cope with situations of conflict and crisis, such as individual counselling and help, homes and communal living.

In addition to these requirements for youth work and youth welfare services, the Commission also makes recommendations for major aspects of policy, education, research, training, further education and cooperation amongst institutions. In all these recommendations the need is recognised for girls and women to achieve equal opportunities, partnership and freedom of choice.

lich darauf abzielen, Gleichberechtigung, Partnerschaft und Wahlfreiheit der Frauen zu verbessern.

Die Empfehlungen im Sechsten → *Jugendbericht* sind mit großem Interesse aufgenommen und sowohl in der Fachöffentlichkeit als auch in politischen Gremien diskutiert worden. Die Jugendminister der Bundesländer haben entsprechende Empfehlungen an die Jugendbehörden gegeben.

Der Bericht der Arbeitsgemeinschaft der obersten Landesjugendbehörden über Ansätze zur Verbesserung der Situation von Mädchen in der Jugendhilfe wurde in der Konferenz der Jugendminister und -senatoren der Länder im Mai 1989 positiv bewertet.

Fortschritte wurden insbesondere in folgenden Bereichen erzielt:

— in der Jugendarbeit die Entwicklung spezieller Angebote für Mädchen und junge Frauen und die verstärkte Berücksichtigung von Mädchen in der verbandlichen Organisation,

— bei berufsqualifizierenden Maßnahmen die Bemühungen um eine Erweiterung des Berufsspektrums für Mädchen und junge Frauen sowie die entsprechenden berufsvorbereitenden Hilfen,

— hinsichtlich des sexuellen Mißbrauchs von Mädchen die verstärkte fachliche Auseinandersetzung mit der Problematik und die Entwicklung besonderer Beratungs- und Hilfsangebote.

VK
Die allgemeine Entwicklung in der Gesellschaft hin zu mehr Chancengleichheit für Frauen und der Aufstieg der Frauen in berufliche Positionen, die früher ausschließlich den Männern vorbehalten waren, veranlaßte auch den *youth service,* die Situation der Mädchen in seinen Einrichtungen zu überprüfen. Das führte zu der Erkenntnis, daß Schritte unternommen werden müßten, um ein besseres Gleichgewicht bei der Partizipation der Frauen und Mädchen sicherzustellen.

Der *Thompson Report 1982* erkannte die Bedeutung einer besonderen Förderung von Mädchen und jungen Frauen folgendermaßen an:

„Der *youth service* reflektiert unkritisch frauenfeindliche Einstellungen der Gesellschaft und hat sie auf einzelne Elemente seiner praktischen und konzeptionellen Arbeit übertragen. Es ist daher notwendig, daß der *youth service* gezielte Maßnahmen ergreift, um diesem Mißstand Abhilfe zu schaffen."

Darüber hinaus ist man der Meinung, daß in gemischten Clubs oder Verbänden Anstrengungen unternommen werden müssen, um bessere Möglichkeiten zur Förderung der persönlichen Entwicklung der Mädchen zu schaffen. Dies kann in Form von speziell für Mädchen und junge Frauen bestimmten abendlichen Treffen, Ausflügen und anderen Veranstaltungen geschehen, mit dem Ziel, ihnen zu helfen, die ihnen offenstehenden Auswahlmöglichkei-

The recommendations made in the Sixth National Youth Report (→ *Jugendbericht)* were taken up with great interest and discussed by youth work specialists and political bodies alike. The youth ministers of the *Länder* responded by working out recommendations for the youth authorities.

The Working Party of the Youth Authorities of the *Land* Governments compiled a report on how to improve the situation of girls in youth work and youth welfare services. The issues put forward in this report were seen as a positive contribution by the Conference of Youth Ministers and Youth Senators held in May 1989.

Notable progress was made in the following areas:

— Special youth work provision for girls and young women was developed and the problems encountered by girls were increasingly taken into account by the youth organisations,

— efforts were made to widen the spectrum of vocational training programmes in order to increase career opportunities for girls and young women and to provide schemes designed to help prepare girls for a career,

— the problem of the sexual abuse of girls was looked into more deeply by the appropriate experts, and the need was stressed to provide specific counselling services as well as adequate assistance.

UK

The general movement in society towards equal opportunities for women with women entering occupations previously filled exclusively by men has led the youth service to examine the position of girls within their organisations and to recognise the need for measures to secure greater equality of participation.

The Thompson Report 1982 recognised the significance of the provision for girls and young women:

"The youth service uncritically mirrors sexist attitudes in society and has carried these into elements of its practice and philosophy. It is necessary that the Service should take deliberate steps to put this situation right".

It is also considered that efforts should be made within mixed clubs or organisations to create greater opportunities to encourage the personal development of girls. This may be done through evenings, outings or activities arranged specially for girls and young women with the aim of helping them to understand the choices open to them and to develop their social confidence. The opportunities for participation, counselling, and community involvement within the youth service all provide scope for boys as well as girls to consider the status of girls and women in society so that ingrained attitudes and assumptions can be examined and challenged.

ten zu erkennen und ihr Selbstbewußtsein zu stärken. Die Möglichkeiten der Partizipation, der Beratung und des sozialen Engagements in der Jugendarbeit bieten sowohl Jungen als auch Mädchen genügend Spielraum, um den gesellschaftlichen Status der Mädchen und Frauen zu überdenken, so daß tief verwurzelte Einstellungen und Vorurteile untersucht und in Frage gestellt werden können.

Die *National Association of Youth and Community Education Officers* (NAYCEO) bekräftigte die Bestimmungen des *Equal Pay Act 1970* und des *Sex Discrimination Act 1985,* die die Bedeutung des gleichberechtigten Zugangs zu Bildungseinrichtungen und Arbeitsplätzen unterstreichen.

Trotz der positiven landesweiten und örtlichen Reaktionen auf diese Gesetze müssen die Mitglieder dieses Verbandes immer noch besondere Anstrengungen unternehmen, um die Chancengleichheit der Frauen in der Praxis zu verwirklichen. Eine passive Unterstützung der Gleichberechtigung reicht nicht aus, denn die grundlegende Ungleichbehandlung der Frauen in unserer Gesellschaft wird dadurch nicht beseitigt. Bestehende Benachteiligungen können nur durch die Bekämpfung geschlechtsspezifischer Einstellungen und Vorurteile ausgeglichen werden. Beide Geschlechter haben unter diesen Einstellungen zu leiden, aber Frauen und Mädchen sind am meisten benachteiligt, da sie in den politischen, sozialen und wirtschaftlichen Systemen, die unser Leben bestimmen, weniger Einfluß und Macht besitzen *(NAYCEO Policy Statement 1987).*

Management Committee

VK
Im Vereinigten Königreich hat fast jeder Club oder jede Jugendeinrichtung ein *management committee* bestehend aus erwachsenen Verantwortlichen, deren Aufgabe es ist, für die Bereitstellung und Unterhaltung von Räumlichkeiten sowie für die Mitwirkung geeigneter Leitungskräfte zu sorgen und ganz allgemein die rechtliche Verantwortung für den Club oder die Einrichtung zu tragen. In vielen Fällen sind im *management committee* auch Jugendliche als Delegierte der Mitglieder der Einrichtung vertreten.

Ein dem *management committee* entsprechendes Gremium gibt es in der Bundesrepublik Deutschland nicht.

Mitarbeiter (m/pl)/Mitarbeiterinnen (f/pl) der Jugendhilfe (f)

D
In der → *Jugendhilfe* in der Bundesrepublik finden wir heute eine Vielzahl von unterschiedlichen Mitarbeiter(n)/-innen. Diese Unterschiede ergeben sich

The National Association of Youth and Community Education Officers (NAYCEO) adopted the legislation contained in the Equal Pay Act 1970 and the Sex Discrimination Act 1985 which emphasise the importance of equal access to educational and employment opportunities.

In spite of national and local responses to this legislation, there is still a need for the members of the Association to ensure that women have access to the same opportunities as men. A passive support for equal opportunities is not sufficient as this does not achieve a change in the fundamental inequalities which exist in our society. These inequalities cannot be balanced until the sexist attitudes and assumptions which exist in our society are challenged. Both sexes are affected by these attitudes, but women and girls are most strongly disadvantaged as they have less influence and power in the political, social and economic systems which govern our lives (NAYCEO Policy Statement 1987).

Management Committee

UK

In the UK each club or youth service almost invariably has a management committee of responsible adults whose duty it is to provide and maintain premises, secure leadership, and generally accept legal responsibility for the club or unit. In many cases representatives of the membership will form part of this management committee.

There is no German equivalent.

Workers in Youth and Youth Welfare Services

G

Today in the Federal Republic of Germany there is a wide variety of workers in youth work and youth welfare services. This variety is a result of existing differences in training courses and forms of employment.

einmal aus den verschiedenen Ausbildungsgängen und zum anderen aus den Formen der Anstellungsverhältnisse:

– *Ausbildungsgänge (→ Bildungswesen/→ Berufsbildung)*

– Fachschule: Staatlich anerkannte(r) → *Erzieher/Erzieherin* oder Kinderpfleger/Kinderpflegerin *(→ Tageseinrichtungen für Kinder)*

– Fachhochschule/Gesamthochschule:
   Diplom- *(→) Sozialarbeiter/Sozialpädagoge* (FH) sowie staatliche Anerkennung, oder Dipl.-Heilpädagoge (FH)

– Berufsakademie: Staatlich anerkannter Diplom-Sozialpädagoge (BA)

– Wissenschaftliche Hochschule: Diplom-Pädagoge (mit Schwerpunkt Sozialarbeit/Sozialpädagogik oder Heil-(Sonder-)pädagogik)

– *Anstellungsverhältnisse*

– hauptberuflich tätige, professionelle Mitarbeiter mit entsprechender Ausbildung (s. oben)

– ehrenamtlich tätige Mitarbeiter (z.B. → *Jugendleiter),* die in eigenen Lehrgängen der Jugendverbände geschult werden.

Das Mit- und Nebeneinander der unterschiedlich ausgebildeten und hauptberuflichen oder ehrenamtlichen Mitarbeiter ist ein wesentliches Merkmal der Jugendhilfe in der Bundesrepublik, wobei die Mitarbeit der ehrenamtlichen Jugendleiter ein unverzichtbares Element der Jugendarbeit darstellt.

VK

Im Vereinigten Königreich gibt es wie in der Bundesrepublik Deutschland verschiedene Qualifikationen für diejenigen, die in den Bereichen beschäftigt sind, die in der Bundesrepublik Deutschland als Jugendhilfe bezeichnet werden. *Social workers* durchlaufen im Hinblick auf ihre spätere Tätigkeit in den sozialen Diensten eine getrennte Ausbildung. Folgende Ausbildungsgänge und Anstellungsverhältnisse bestehen:

Ausbildungsgänge (→ Bildungswesen, VK)
– Lehrerausbildung erfolgt an den Hochschulen. Studenten, die später in der Jugendarbeit tätig sein wollen, belegen spezielle Lehrveranstaltungen zur Jugendarbeit, die Bestandteil der Lehrerausbildung sind. Wenn sie die Abschlußprüfung bestanden haben, können sie sowohl an Schulen unterrichten als auch in der Jugendarbeit beschäftigt werden.

– Ausbildung in *youth and community work* erfolgt an bestimmten Universitäten und Colleges des Hochschulbereiches. Abschlüsse: *certificate, diploma, Bachelor of Arts (BA)* oder (seltener) *Master of Arts (MA) (→ Sozialarbeiter/ Sozialpädagoge,* VK).

Training courses (→ Bildungswesen/→ Berufsbildung)
— *Fachschule* (technical school): qualified youth or child care worker with state recognition *(→ Erzieher/Erzieherin)* or nursery assistant *(→ Tagesein-richtungen für Kinder)*

— *Fachhochschule (FH)/Gesamthochschule* (polytechnic-type institutions/ combined polytechnic and university): diploma course: *Diplom (→) Sozialarbeiter/Sozialpädagoge* (FH) with state recognition or diploma course: remedial teacher *(Diplom-Heilpäda-goge,* FH)

— *Berufsakademie* (BA) (polytechnic-tpye establishment): diploma course: *Diplom-Sozialpädagoge* (BA) with state recognition *(→ Sozialarbeiter/So-zialpädagoge)*

— *Wissenschaftliche Hochschule* (institute of higher education): diploma course: *Diplom-Pädagoge* (university-trained youth worker) with special emphasis on either → *Sozialarbeit/Sozialpädagogik* or remedial teaching.

Forms of employment
— full-time professional staff with one of the above qualifications
— voluntary workers (e.g. youth leaders → *Jugendleiter)* who follow specific training courses provided by youth organisations.

The co-existence and cooperation of differently trained full-time and voluntary workers is an essential characteristic of youth work and youth welfare services in the Federal Republic of Germany. The contribution of the voluntary youth leaders is an indispensable element of youth work.

UK
In the United Kingdom there is, as in Germany, a variety of qualifications for those employed in youth work and social services for the young. Social workers are trained separately with a view to moving into the social services. There are different forms of training and employment for youth workers:

Forms of training (→ Bildungswesen, UK)
— teacher training provided by institutes of higher education. Those wishing to become engaged in youth work opt for the youth work modules included in teacher training, graduates then being able to move into either teaching or youth work.

— youth and community work training provided by certain universities and colleges of higher education. Students may obtain a certificate, a diploma, a BA or (rarely) a MA (→ *Sozialarbeiter/Sozialpädagoge,* UK).

— social work training provided by universities, polytechnics and colleges of further education. Students may obtain a CSS, CQSW or DipSW (→ *Sozial-arbeiter/Sozialpädagoge,* UK). People holding certain social service qualifications are at present also recognised as qualified youth workers.

– Ausbildung in *social work* erfolgt an Universitäten, *polytechnics* und Colleges im Hochschulbereich. Abschlüsse: CSS, CQSW und DipSW (→ *Sozialarbeiter/Sozialpädagoge,* VK). Personen mit bestimmten Qualifikationen für die sozialen Dienste werden zur Zeit auch als qualifizierte Jugendarbeiter anerkannt.

– Für Kindergärtner/-innen und Spielgruppenleiter/-innen, die aber nicht als Jugendarbeiter angesehen werden, besteht ein kurzer, mehr praxisorientierter Ausbildungsgang in Vorschulpädagogik. Es gibt keinen anerkannten Ausbildungsberuf, der dem deutschen → *Erzieher* entspricht.

Anstellungsverhältnisse
– hauptberufliche, professionelle Mitarbeiter mit entsprechender Ausbildung

– teilzeitbeschäftigte und ehrenamtlich tätige Mitarbeiter. Es wird heute allgemein anerkannt, daß auch Teilzeitkräfte sich ausbilden lassen können. Viele Kommunalbehörden haben deshalb spezielle Jugendleiterkurse für Mitarbeiter der öffentlichen und freien Jugendarbeit eingerichtet. Zahlreiche freie Träger bieten eigene Kurse an.

Obwohl hauptberufliche, professionelle Mitarbeiter eine entscheidende Rolle in der öffentlichen und freien Jugendarbeit spielen, ist auch im Vereinigten Königreich die Beschäftigung von Teilzeitkräften und freiwilligen Helfern, die ihr umfangreiches Fachwissen und vielseitige Erfahrungen in die Jugendarbeit mit einbringen, ein wesentliches Merkmal des *youth service.*

Partizipation (f) Jugendlicher (pl)

D
Gesetzliche Grundlagen für die Mitwirkung junger Menschen an gesellschaftlichen Entscheidungsprozessen in der Bundesrepublik Deutschland sind für drei Lebensbereiche vorgegeben: die Schule, den Arbeitsplatz und die Jugendarbeit.

Nach der jeweiligen Landesgesetzgebung (Kulturhoheit der Länder, → *Föderalismus)* ist Ziel der schulischen Mitwirkung, die Eigenverantwortung in der Schule zu fördern und das Zusammenwirken aller Beteiligten (Lehrer, Eltern, Schüler) in der Bildungs- und Erziehungsarbeit durch eigens zu diesem Zweck zu schaffende Organe (z.B. Schülervertretung (SV), Klassenpflegschaft) zu stärken.

Die Interessenvertretung junger Berufstätiger ist bundeseinheitlich im Betriebsverfassungsgesetz *(*→ *Betriebsrat)* festgelegt.

Die Interessen junger Menschen außerhalb von Schule und Beruf werden in erster Linie von einer Vielzahl freier gesellschaftlicher Gruppierungen (freie → *Träger der Jugendhilfe)* wahrgenommen. Besondere Bedeutung haben dabei die Jugendverbände.

— nursery school teachers and play school leaders qualify after a short, more practice-orientated course in education. They are not considered as youth workers. No single recognised profession parallels the German → *Erzieher.*

Forms of employment
— full-time professional staff with adequate training

— part-time and volunteer staff. The need for part-time workers to undertake training is now generally recognised and many local authorities run leadership courses open to workers in the statutory and voluntary sectors. Many voluntary organisations provide their own courses.

Although full-time professional staff play a crucial part in both the statutory and the voluntary sectors, the youth service is characterized by the extensive use of part-time and volunteer staff who bring a variety of skills and experience to their work.

Participation of Young People in Decision-Making

G

In the Federal Republic of Germany participation of young people in social decision-making processes is based on statutory provision regarding three different spheres of their lives: school, the work place and youth work.

According to the respective Acts passed by the *Länder* (cultural sovereignty of the *Länder/→ Föderalismus)* participation in the school system aims to promote individual responsibility and to secure the cooperation of everyone involved in educational work. Various committees must be established for teachers, parents and pupils such as the *Schülervertretung* (SV) (pupils' council), the *Klassenpflegschaft* (consisting of parents, the form teacher and a non-voting SV representative), and other bodies.

The Works Constitution Act provides for the whole of the Federal Republic that young people at work may advocate their interests through elected youth representatives (→ *Betriebsrat).*

The views of young people outside of school and work are mainly represented by a wide variety of voluntary social groups responsible for youth work and

Die Mitwirkung von jungen Menschen in anderen gesellschaftlichen Entscheidungsprozessen wie Bürgerinitiativen zum Umweltschutz, gegen Kernkraftwerke, für die Abrüstung ist gesetzlich nicht geregelt.

VK

Der Regierungsbericht der Prüfungskommission für den *youth service* von 1982 (Thompson Report) stellte fest, daß die Partizipation Jugendlicher in allen Bereichen verstärkt werden müsse, so z.B. in Arbeits- und Freizeitgruppen, in Jugendclubs, kommunalen Angelegenheiten, nationalen Jugendorganisationen usw., sowie auf nationaler und internationaler Ebene.

Die Idee, junge Leute in Entscheidungsprozesse einzubeziehen, ist nicht neu. Mitgliederausschüsse, Jugendringe und Jugendparlamente bestehen schon seit geraumer Zeit (→ *Jugendringe)*. Partizipation heißt, bewußt an Entscheidungsprozessen teilzunehmen und diese zu beeinflussen. Sie bedeutet Meinungsfindung und Meinungsbildung, Teilnahme an Entscheidungsprozessen und auch Übernahme der Verantwortung für die Konsequenzen dieser Entscheidungen. Partizipation ermöglicht es den Jugendlichen, ihren Platz in der Gesellschaft einzunehmen als junge Menschen mit eigenem Status und Wertgefühlen, die bereit und in der Lage sind, Impulse im Sinne des Fortschritts für alle zu geben.

Pflegekinderbereich (m)/Pflegekinderwesen (n)

D

Für Kinder und Jugendliche, die auf Wunsch der Eltern *(→ Hilfe zur Erziehung)* oder aufgrund eines Gerichtsbeschlusses (Sorgerechtsentzug) nicht in der eigenen Familie leben können, besteht die Möglichkeit der Unterbringung in einer Pflegefamilie oder in einem Heim. Wegen der Nachteile der Heimerziehung insbesondere für Säuglinge und Kleinkinder wird heute, wenn möglich, die Unterbringung in einer Familie bevorzugt. Im allgemeinen wird das Kind vom → *Jugendamt* in eine geeignete Familie vermittelt, die für die Pflege einer Erlaubnis des Jugendamts bedarf. Die Begleitung der Pflege ist Aufgabe des Jugendamtes, das insbesondere auch für den Schutz der Kinder verantwortlich ist.

Bei Berufstätigkeit beider Elternteile bzw. der Erziehungsberechtigten können Kinder in Tagespflege („Tagesmutter") gegeben werden. Etwa die Hälfte der Tagespflegeverhältnisse werden dem Jugendamt gemeldet.

VK

Pflegekindschaftsverhältnisse bestehen entweder aufgrund einer privaten Absprache, nach der ein Kind auf Wunsch der Eltern von einer Pflegeperson auf-

youth welfare services (→ *Träger der Jugendhilfe)*, the youth organisations playing a particularly important part in this sphere.

There is no legal basis for the participation of young people in other decision-making processes such as community action groups who work for the protection of the environment, fight against nuclear power plants, or strive for disarmament.

UK

The 1982 Government Report of the Review Group on the Youth Service (Thompson Report) stated that "participation of young people should be strengthened at all levels, in activity groups, clubs, local affairs, national youth organisations and at the national and international level. It may follow a variety of patterns".

The idea of involving young people in decision-making is not a new concept. Members' committees, youth councils, and youth parliaments have existed for quite some time (→ *Jugendringe)*. Participation means opportunities to influence and share consciously in the decision-making process. Participation is a matter of finding out about and forming opinions, taking part in decision-making and taking responsibility for the consequences of these decisions. It will enable young people to take a place in society as a young person of standing and worth, willing and able, from personal conviction, to initiate progress for all.

Child Fostering

G

Those children and young people removed from their families either at parental request (→ *Hilfe zur Erziehung)* or on the basis of a court order (withdrawal of the right of custody) may be placed with a foster family or in a community home. Because of the dangers of institutionalization particularly for infants and small children, preference is nowadays given to placement with a family wherever possible. In general, the youth office (→ *Jugendamt)* arranges for placement with a family recognised for this purpose by the youth office. Supervision of foster children is a responsibility of the youth office, as is the protection of the children concerned.

When both parents or the persons holding parental authority are at work, children may be placed in the care of a child minder ("day mother"). About 50 % of such placements are registered with the youth office.

UK

Fostering is an arrangement whereby a child is placed either with a foster parent through a private placement by a parent or where the child is in

genommen wird oder aber bei Sorgerechtsübertragung auf die entsprechende Kommunalbehörde durch Unterbringung eines Kindes in einer von dieser bestellten Pflegefamilie.

Die besonderen Pflichten der Ämter oder der freien Träger bei der Fremdunterbringung von Kindern sind in den *Boarding Out of Children Regulations 1955* festgelegt. Diese Bestimmungen wurden seither ergänzt, um den Kommunalbehörden völlige Entscheidungsfreiheit bei der Auswahl von Pflegeeltern zu gewähren. Dadurch ist es heute möglich, daß ein alleinstehender Mann als Pflegevater und auch unverheiratete, zusammenlebende Paare als Pflegeeltern gewählt werden können. Beide gehören Gruppen an, die vorher vom Pflegekinderwesen ausgeschlossen waren.

Die Pflegeeltern entscheiden in allen Angelegenheiten der täglichen Sorge für das Kind. Wichtige Entscheidungen sind jedoch der Kontrolle der kommunalen Behörde unterworfen. Pflegeeltern müssen sich grundsätzlich darüber klar sein, daß das Pflegekindschaftsverhältnis jederzeit aufgehoben werden kann.

Sie können jedoch eine Anordnung auf *custodianship* (→ *Pflegschaft,* VK) erwirken, die ihnen das Sorgerecht für ihr Pflegekind überträgt. Wenn das Kind fünf Jahre bei Pflegeeltern gelebt hat, und diese bei Gericht einen Antrag auf Adoptionsbeschluß stellen oder die Kommunalbehörden benachrichtigen, daß sie beabsichtigen, innerhalb der nächsten drei Monate die Adoption zu beantragen, dann kann das Kind den Pflegeeltern nur noch durch einen Gerichtsbeschluß weggenommen werden.

Pflegschaft (f)

D

Der Pfleger hat — im Gegensatz zur Vormundschaft — nicht für alle Angelegenheiten des ihm anvertrauten minderjährigen Pfleglings zu sorgen, sondern nur für einen begrenzten Kreis.

Ergänzungspflegschaft kann angeordnet werden für Angelegenheiten, für die Eltern oder Vormund aus tatsächlichen oder rechtlichen Gründen nicht sorgen können (z.B. weil ihnen die elterliche Sorge wegen Kindesmißhandlung entzogen wurde).

Zur Wahrung ihrer künftigen Rechte kann ein Pfleger für eine Leibesfrucht bestellt werden, wenn die künftigen Sorgerechtsinhaber bestimmte Rechte nicht wahrnehmen können.

Außer der Ergänzungspflegschaft bestehen noch weitere Formen der Pflegschaft, die jedoch für den Themenkreis dieses Glossars nur selten Bedeutung haben und daher hier nicht erläutert werden.

VK

Den Begriff der Pflegschaft gibt es im englischen Recht nicht.

the care of a local authority and placed by them with a local authority foster parent.

The specific duties which a local authority or voluntary organisation boarding out a child has in relation to foster children are set out in the Boarding Out of Children Regulations 1955. These have since been amended to allow local authorities complete discretion over whom they approve as foster parents. Therefore nowadays it is possible for a single man to be a foster parent, as well as cohabiting couples; two groups which were previously barred from fostering.

Foster parents must make the normal day-to-day decisions; important decisions are subject to local authority control. Foster parents must remember that their care for a child may be terminated at any time.

Foster parents are able to apply for a custodianship order which would give them the legal custody of the child they are fostering. If the child has had his home with foster parents for five years, and they apply to the court for an adoption order or give notice to the local authorities that they intend to apply for an adoption and do so within three months, the child cannot then be removed from them except by a court order.

Curatorship/Custodianship

G
As opposed to guardianship, the curator does not care for all matters regarding the minor under curatorship for whom he has assumed responsibility, but only for a limited number.

Supplementary curatorship may be ordered in respect of matters for which the parents or guardian cannot provide for factual or legal reasons (e.g. in cases where the parental rights were withdrawn from them because of cruelty to children).

A curator may also be appointed for the unborn child in order to protect the baby's future rights. This applies when the prospective holders of parents' rights and responsibilities are not in a position to assume certain rights.

In addition to supplementary curatorship there are other forms of curatorship which are not listed here as they have little relevance to the subject of this glossary.

UK
There is no concept of curatorship in English law.

Aufgrund des *Children Act* von 1975 und späteren Änderungen können Personen, die ein Kind über einen längeren Zeitraum betreut haben (z.B. Pflegeeltern, Stiefvater/-mutter, Verwandte), beim Gericht eine Anordnung auf *custodianship* erwirken, die dem Antragsteller das Sorgerecht für das Kind überträgt.

Eine solche Sorgerechtsanordnung kann auf Antrag des *custodian,* der Eltern des Kindes, des Vormundes oder der Behörden rückgängig gemacht werden. (Bei einem Adoptionsbeschluß ist das nicht möglich).

Wenn das Gericht bei einem Antrag auf *custodianship* entscheidet, wer das Sorgerecht erhält oder über die Erziehung des Kindes zu bestimmen hat, muß es in erster Linie das Wohl des Minderjährigen im Auge haben.

Rechtsinstrumente (n/pl)

D
Oberste Rechtsquelle ist die Verfassung, das Grundgesetz von 1949. Gesetze, die mit ihr nicht übereinstimmen, können vom Bundesverfassungsgericht aufgehoben werden.

Das Gesetz ist abstrakt, es gilt für eine unbestimmte Zahl von Fällen; es ist generell, es gilt für eine unbestimmte Vielzahl von Personen; es ist bindend für und gegen den Bürger und für Verwaltung und Gerichte.

Die Rechtsverordnung ist ebenso wie das Gesetz eine materielle Rechtsnorm auf dem Gebiet des Verwaltungsrechts. Formell ist sie kein Gesetz, da sie von der Bundes- oder Landesregierung (mit der Möglichkeit weiterer Delegation) erlassen wird. Erforderlich ist eine gesetzliche Ermächtigung, die selbst Inhalt, Zweck und Ausmaß der Regelung nennt. Die Rechtsverordnung muß ihre Ermächtigungsgrundlage ausdrücklich zitieren. Sie muß sich auch im Rahmen der Ermächtigung halten. Gesetzesvertretende Verordnungen sind unzulässig.

Die Satzung ist das von einer autonomen, mit Selbstverwaltungskompetenz ausgestatteten Körperschaft gesetzte Recht. Städte, Gemeinden, Kreise (→ *Kommunale Selbstverwaltung),* Hochschulen, Rundfunkanstalten, Sozialversicherungsträger haben zum Beispiel diese Befugnis.

Der Tarifvertrag zwischen Gewerkschaft und Arbeitgeberorganisationen hat seine Stellung zwischen einem privatrechtlichen Vertrag und einer Rechtsnorm. Wird er für allgemeinverbindlich erklärt, hat er fast die Wirkung einer Norm, eines Gesetzes.

Die Verwaltungsvorschrift (Weisung, Erlaß, Anordnung, Richtlinien) ist — anders als die Rechtsverordnung — keine Rechtsnorm. Gerichte und Bürger sind nicht daran gebunden; der Bürger kann sich nicht darauf berufen. Innerhalb der Verwaltung sind sie zu beachten. Entweder regeln sie den internen Dienstbetrieb oder die nähere und gleichmäßige Durchführung von Gesetzen (z.B. als Ermessens-, Vereinfachungs-, interpretierende Richtlinien).

Since the Children Act of 1975 and subsequent amendments it has been possible for a person who has cared for a child for some time (e.g. a foster parent, step-parent or relative) to apply to the court for a custodianship order, which vests legal custody of the child in the applicant.

A custodianship order may be revoked by the court on the application of the custodian, the child's parent or guardian or any local authority. (An adoption order cannot be revoked).

In deciding any question as to the custody or upbringing of a child on an application for a custodianship order the court must regard the minor's welfare as the first and paramount consideration.

Legal Instruments

G
The primary source of law is the constitution, the Basic Law of 1949. Acts which are not in accordance with the constitution can be repealed by the Federal Constitutional Court.

An Act of the legislature is abstract and valid for an indefinite number of cases. It is universal and applies to an indefinite number of persons. It is binding for and against the citizen, for the administration and the courts.

The *Rechtsverordnung* (statutory order) is a material legal norm in the field of administrative law. Formally, it is not an Act, as it is made by the Federal or *Land* Government (with a possibility of further delegation). A legal authorization is required which states the content, purpose and extent of the ruling; a *Rechtsverordnung* must expressly quote the basis of the authorization. It must also stay within the scope of that authorization. *Rechtsverordnungen* standing in lieu of an Act are inadmissible.

The *Satzung* (statutes) is the law laid down by an autonomous corporate body entitled to self-administration. Towns, communities and districts (→ *Kommunale Selbstverwaltung),* establishments of higher education, broadcasting corporations, social insurance agencies may draw up their own statutes.

The collective agreement on salaries of wages concluded between trade unions and employers' organisations is halfway between a contract under civil law and a legal norm. If it is declared generally binding, it almost has the effect of a norm or law.

The *Verwaltungsvorschrift* (administrative provision: *Weisung* (direction), *Erlaß* (decree), *Anordnung* (instruction), *Richtlinien* (directives) unlike the *Rechtsverordnung* is not a legal norm. Courts and citizens are not bound by them nor can the citizen claim a right under them. They must be observed within the administration. Either they lay down internal administrative procedures or the details for and uniform execution of a given Act (e.g. providing directives to be applied at discretion or a simplification or interpretation).

VK

Die oberste Rechtsetzungsgewalt hat der Souverän im Parlament. Ein Parlamentsgesetz (oder *statute*), das vom Souverän gebilligt wurde, hat Vorrang vor jeder anderen Norm, einschließlich des *common law* (d.h. allgemeingültiges Gewohnheits- und Fallrecht), örtlicher Rechtsbräuche und der Bestimmungen früherer Gesetze, die damit unvereinbar sind. Da jedes Parlament die höchste Entscheidungsgewalt besitzt, kann es die Vollmachten eines späteren Parlaments nicht einschränken. Demzufolge darf auch ein *statute* nicht verfügen, daß es nicht außer Kraft gesetzt werden kann oder spätere Gesetze ungültig macht.

Es gibt keine geschriebene Verfassung. Vom Parlament geschaffene Gesetze können Teile der Verfassung ändern oder aufheben und wie bestehende Gesetze ändern. Es gibt kein Verfassungsgericht. Die Gültigkeit eines Parlementsgesetzes kann nicht von den Gerichten angefochten werden.

Parlamentsgesetze können Regelungen zur delegierten Gesetzgebung durch andere Organe als das Parlament treffen, etwa durch einen Minister oder eine Kommunalbehörde, eine Möglichkeit, von der oft Gebrauch gemacht wird. Die delegierte Gesetzgebung bedarf einer vom Parlament festgelegten Ermächtigungsgrundlage. Im Gegensatz zum Parlamentsgesetz kann delegierte Gesetzgebung von den Gerichten angefochten werden, zum Beispiel mit der Begründung, daß die vom Parlament übertragene Ermächtigung überschritten wurde.

Die delegierte Gesetzgebung umfaßt verschiedene Rechtsformen wie die Proklamation (amtliche Verkündung durch die Krone), *Orders in Council* (Verfügung der Krone auf Anraten des alle Kabinettsmitglieder umfassenden Kronrates/Regierungsverordnung), *Orders of Council* (Verfügungen des Kronrates ohne Mitwirkung der Krone), *rules* (von den Verwaltungsbehörden aufgrund gesetzlicher Ermächtigung erlassene Normen), *regulations* und *orders* (Formen der Rechtsverordnung), die beispielsweise von einem Minister erlassen werden, sowie von einer Kommunalbehörde niedergelegte *byelaws* (örtliche Satzungen).

Nach *common law* hat der Souverän die Befugnis, durch eine *royal charter* (Verleihungsurkunde) eine beliebige Zahl von Personen zu inkorporieren, die einen Zusammenschluß mit Rechtspersönlichkeit gründen wollen. Durch *royal charter* werden zum Beispiel Kommunalverwaltungen (*town* und *district,* → *Kommunale Selbstverwaltung, VK*), öffentliche Versorgungsbetriebe, berufsständische Zusammenschlüsse oder Rundfunkanstalten inkorporiert, die dann in ihrer Tätigkeit an die Bestimmungen ihrer *charter* gebunden sind. (Auch das Parlament ist zu diesem Rechtsakt befugt.)

Nach englischem Recht ist ein *collective agreement* ein Abkommen über Beschäftigungsbedingungen, das in der Regel zwischen Arbeitgebern oder Arbeitgeberverbänden und Arbeitnehmerorganisationen geschlossen wird. Es ist keine Rechtsnorm. Ein solches Abkommen gilt nur dann als einklagbar,

UK

The legislative authority of the Sovereign in Parliament is supreme. An Act of Parliament (or statute) to which the Sovereign has assented overrides all other law, including the common law, local custom and the provisions of earlier statutes which are inconsistent with it. Since every Parliament is supreme, one Parliament cannot limit the power of a later Parliament and it follows that a statute cannot provide that it is to be incapable of repeal or that it will prevail over subsequent legislation.

There is no written constitution and Acts of Parliament can amend or repeal constitutional rules in the same way that they can change any other existing law. There is no constitutional court and the validity of an Act of Parliament cannot be challenged in the courts.

Acts of Parliament may, and frequently do, provide for the making of subordinate legislation by a body other than Parliament, usually an executive authority such as a Secretary of State or a local authority. Subordinate legislation can be enacted only within the scope of the authority conferred by Parliament. Unlike Acts of Parliament, subordinate legislation can be challenged in the courts, for example on the ground that the authority conferred by Parliament has been exceeded.

Subordinate legislation may take a variety of forms including Orders in Council (made by the Crown with the advice of the Privy Council) rules, regulations and orders (made, for example, by a Secretary of State) and byelaws (made by a local authority).

The Sovereign has the power, at common law, to incorporate by royal charter any number of persons assenting to be incorporated. Royal charters have been used, for example, to incorporate town and district authorities, public utilities, professional bodies and broadcasting corporations, which are then obliged to function in accordance with the terms of their charter. (Corporations may also be set up by authority of Parliament.)

Under English law a "collective agreement" (an agreement as to terms and conditions of employment normally between employers or organisations of employers and organisations of employees) is not a "source of law". Such an agreement is presumed not to be legally enforceable unless it is in writing and contains a provision that the parties intended that the agreement, or some part of it, should be legally enforceable: at the most, a collective agreement could be considered as a binding contract.

Legal instruments may take other forms, such as codes of practice and rules of professional bodies, which may be taken into account by the courts but have no legislative force.

Circulars may be issued by Government Ministers but these are not to be regarded as a "source of law" except in rare instances. Usually they are issued for purposes of information, for example stating ministerial policy, explaining

wenn es schriftlich niedergelegt wird und eine Bestimmung enthält, in der die Vertragsparteien es für ganz oder teilweise einklagbar erklären. Ein *collective agreement* kann bestenfalls als rechtsverbindlicher Vertrag angesehen werden (Tarifvertrag).

Rechtsinstrumente können auch andere Formen haben wie *codes of practice* (Ausführungsvorschriften) und *rules* (Satzung) berufsständischer Zusammenschlüsse, die von den Gerichten berücksichtigt werden können, aber keine Rechtskraft haben.

Circulars (Erlasse) können von Ministern der Regierung herausgegeben werden, sind aber mit ganz wenigen Ausnahmen nicht als Rechtsnorm anzusehen. *Circulars* dienen in der Regel der Information, z.B. der Erklärung politischer Richtlinien des Ministers, der Erläuterung von Gesetzen oder der Bereitstellung von administrativen Instrumentarien. In der Praxis greift man nur in bestimmten Bereichen wie im Bildungswesen und der Städte- und Landschaftsplanung auf sie zurück.

Rehabilitation (f) Behinderter (m/f/pl)

D
Unter Rehabilitation werden alle Maßnahmen verstanden, die der Eingliederung eines Behinderten in die Gesellschaft dienen (→ *Behindertenhilfe*).

Entscheidend ist, daß im Sozialgesetzbuch SGB Erstes Buch (I) in § 10 ein Rechtsanspruch auf umfassende Hilfen zur Eingliederung in Beruf und Gesellschaft festgeschrieben ist. Dabei können in Anspruch genommen werden:
a) medizinische Leistungen
b) berufsfördernde Leistungen (→ *Berufsbildung*)
c) Leistungen zur allgemeinen sozialen Eingliederung.

Leistungsträger für alle Rehabilitationsmaßnahmen sind alle Gruppen im gegliederten System der → *sozialen Sicherung* (Kranken-, Renten-, Unfallversicherung, Arbeitsverwaltung, Kriegsopferversorgung, Sozialhilfeträger).

VK
Rehabilitation setzt zu Beginn einer Krankheit oder nach einer Verletzung ein und wird weitergeführt mit dem Ziel, kranken und behinderten Menschen dabei zu helfen, sich ihren veränderten Lebensbedingungen anzupassen, eine möglichst normale Existenz zu führen oder ihr Leben in der Gemeinschaft wiederaufzunehmen, soweit die Behinderung dies gestattet.

In Großbritannien gibt es eine Reihe von gesetzlichen Bestimmungen über monetäre Leistungen aus dem System der sozialen Sicherung, über Beschäftigungsrechte und die Integration der Behinderten im Bildungswesen. Auf nationaler Ebene liegen die Zuständigkeiten für die finanzielle Unterstützung von Behinderten sowie Maßnahmen zu ihrer Rehabilitation beim Ministe-

legislation or providing administrative machinery. In practice they are used only in certain areas of law, for example education and town and country planning.

Rehabilitation of the Handicapped

G

This is a cover term for schemes designed to help the integration of a disabled person into society (→ *Behindertenhilfe*).

The Social Code, Book I, section 10, guarantees a legal right to comprehensive help for occupational and social integration, such as:
a) medical services
b) employment promotional schemes (→ *Berufsbildung*)
c) services to further general social integration.

The bodies responsible for these rehabilitation schemes are all those groups within the social security system (e.g. Health Insurance, Retirement Pensions, Accident Insurance, Federal Institute of Labour, War Victims Welfare and those other bodies with a responsibility for social service organisations) (→ *Soziale Sicherung*).

UK

Rehabilitation begins at the outset of illness or injury and continues throughout with the aim of helping people to adjust to changes in lifestyle, to lead as normal a life as possible, or, if feasible, to resume life in the community.

In Great Britain there are a number of laws covering social security benefits, employment rights and integration in education. Schemes concerned with the benefits for and rehabilitation of disabled persons are the overall responsibility of the Department of Health and Social Security (benefits), the Department of Employment (provision of employment for the disabled through its Training Agency), and the Department of Education and Science (overall provision of special educational opportunities).

rium für Gesundheit und Soziale Sicherheit (monetäre Leistungen), beim Arbeitsministerium (Beschäftigungsmaßnahmen für Behinderte durch die *Training Agency)* und beim Ministerium für Erziehung und Wissenschaft (Bereitstellung spezieller Bildungsangebote).

Die personenbezogenen sozialen Dienste der Kommunalbehörden bieten eine breite Palette von Möglichkeiten für die soziale Rehabilitation von Behinderten sowie für die Anpassung an eine Behinderung. Diese Dienststellen sind verpflichtet, die Zahl der Behinderten in ihrem Verantwortungsbereich zu erfassen und Hilfen für Behinderte bei der breiten Öffentlichkeit bekanntzumachen. Die Leistungen umfassen z.b beschützende Werkstätten, Betreuung, Bildungs- und Freizeitangebote in Tagesstätten und anderen Einrichtungen. Die kommunalen Sozialbehörden gewähren zwar Zuschüsse für die Anpassung des Wohnraums an die Bedürfnisse Behinderter, sind aber, wie vorstehend angedeutet, nicht für die Auszahlung der finanziellen Unterstützung aus dem System der sozialen Sicherung zuständig (→ *Soziale Sicherung,* VK).

Schwangerschaftsabbruch (m)

D

Der Abbruch der Schwangerschaft (auch Abtreibung) ist nach dem 15. Strafrechtsänderungsgesetz (1976) unter bestimmten Voraussetzungen nicht strafbar. Nach dem Gesetz sind Gründe — genannt Indikationen —, die einen Eingriff rechtfertigen:

- medizinische Indikation: Gefahr für das Leben oder die Gesundheit der Schwangeren;

- eugenische Indikation: Gefahr einer körperlichen oder geistigen Schädigung des Kindes (Abbruch bis zur 22. Woche nach der Empfängnis);

- ethische Indikation: Vergewaltigung (Abbruch bis zur 12. Woche nach der Empfängnis);

- sog. soziale Indikation: Gefahr einer schwerwiegenden Notlage der Schwangeren (Abbruch bis zur 12. Woche nach der Empfängnis).

Jeder Eingriff setzt eine medizinische und eine soziale Betreuung der Schwangeren durch einen Arzt oder eine anerkannte Beratungsstelle voraus. Hinzu kommen muß die ärztliche Feststellung, ob eine Indikation vorliegt. Der Eingriff darf dann nur von einem anderen Arzt—im allgemeinen nur einer Klinik — vorgenommen werden. Die katholische Kirche bezeichnet jeden Schwangerschaftsabbruch als Tötung werdenden Lebens und wehrt sich u.a. dagegen, daß die Krankenkassen die Kosten des Abbruchs der Schwangerschaft bei sozialer Indikation übernehmen.

VK

Der Abbruch einer Schwangerschaft (Abtreibung) ist im Vereinigten Königreich strafbar, es sei denn, er wird rechtmäßig nach den Bestimmungen des

Local authority social services departments provide a wide range of personal social services for disabled people to assist with social rehabilitation and adjustment to disability. They are also required to establish the number of handicapped persons in their area and to publicise services, which may include sheltered employment, care, educational and recreational facilities either at day centres or elsewhere. They provide grants for adapting homes, but do not pay benefits as indicated above (→ *Soziale Sicherung,* UK).

Termination of Pregnancy

G

Termination of pregnancy (also referred to as abortion) is not punishable at law on certain conditions under the 15th Amendment of the Penal Code (1976). The Amendment specifies the grounds (called "indications") which justify a surgical intervention:

- medical grounds: risk to the life and health of the pregnant woman;

- eugenic grounds: risk to the physical or mental health of the child (termination until the 22nd week after conception);

- ethical grounds: rape (termination until the 12th week after conception);

- so-called social grounds: risk of a grave situation of need arising for the pregnant woman (termination until the 12th week after conception).

Any surgery must be preceded by medical and social counselling provided by a physician or a recognised counselling service. Moreover, the physician must determine whether one of the above indications is given. The operation may then only be performed by another physician — generally in a clinic. According to the Catholic Church, termination of pregnancy means killing life in the uterus. Amongst other things, this Church protests against the fact that the health insurance funds cover the cost of termination of pregnancy on social grounds.

UK

Termination of pregnancy (abortion) is an offence in the United Kingdom except when it is carried out lawfully under the provisions of the Abortion Act

Abortion Act aus dem Jahre 1967 durchgeführt. Nach diesem Gesetz ist der Schwangerschaftsabbruch nicht strafbar, wenn er von einem eingetragenen Arzt der Allgemeinmedizin vorgenommen wird und zwei praktische Ärzte in gutem Glauben erklären, daß

- die Fortsetzung der Schwangerschaft eine Gefahr für das Leben der Schwangeren darstellt oder die Schädigung der körperlichen oder geistigen Gesundheit der Schwangeren oder der Kinder in ihrer Familie schwerwiegender als der Schwangerschaftsabbruch wäre, oder

- ein beträchtliches Risiko einer körperlichen oder geistigen Anomalie des Kindes nach seiner Geburt besteht, die zu einer schweren Behinderung führen würde.

Es besteht keine Verpflichtung zur Mitwirkung bei einem Schwangerschaftsabbruch, wenn dies einen Gewissenskonflikt bedeutet, es sei denn, der Abbruch ist erforderlich, um das Leben einer schwangeren Frau zu retten oder eine schwere dauerhafte Schädigung ihrer körperlichen oder geistigen Gesundheit abzuwenden. Der *Abortion Act* von 1967 berührt die Bestimmungen des *Infant Life (Preservation) Act 1929* nicht, nach dem es strafbar ist, das Leben eines Kindes zu beenden, das lebendig geboren werden könnte (d.h. eines mehr als 28 Wochen alten Foetus). Der Schwangerschaftsabbruch muß in Krankenhäusern des Staatlichen Gesundheitsdienstes oder anderen vom Innenministerium anerkannten Einrichtungen vorgenommen werden.

Sozialarbeit (SA) (f)/Sozialpädagogik (SP) (f)

D

SA und SP bezeichnen gesellschaftliche Hilfen, die einen Theorie- und Praxisbereich umfassen. Sie entstanden aus den gleichen gesellschaftlichen Bedingungen, wobei jedoch unterschiedliche Ziele verfolgt wurden. Früher wollte die Sozialpädagogik eine Verhaltensänderung bewirken. Die Basis der Arbeit war das (individuelle) Lernen, und so war sie gesellschaftspolitisch im → *Bildungswesen* angesiedelt (Grundlage: Erziehungswissenschaft). Die Sozialarbeit zielte darauf ab, die Problemlagen des einzelnen und der Gesellschaft zu verändern. Das bedingte eine Zuordnung zum System → *sozialer Sicherung* (Grundlage: Sozialpolitikwissenschaft). Diese klare Trennung gilt heute als nicht mehr zeitgemäß.

Im Bereich der Sozialarbeit hat sich ein Wandel vom Konzept der → *Fürsorge* für Arme, also einer „caritativen" Motivation, zu psychosozialer Hilfe für alle vollzogen. Die Sozialpädagogik ist von der „Nothilfe" für Kinder und Jugendliche abgerückt. Sie will heute generell Hilfen für alle Altersgruppen leisten. Diese Umorientierung hat die Trennung zwischen Sozialarbeit und Sozialpädagogik aufgehoben. Hinzu kamen verstärkte Bemühungen um Wissenschaftlichkeit und Professionalisierung, die mit der Einführung des universitären Diplom-Studiengangs Erziehungswissenschaft mit Schwerpunkt SA/SP

1967. Under that Act no offence is committed when a pregnancy is terminated by a registered medical practioner if two medical practioners are of the opinion, formed in good faith, that

— continuance of the pregnancy would involve risk to the life of the pregnant women, or of injury to the physical or mental health of the pregnant woman or any existing children of her family greater than if the pregnancy were terminated; or

— there is a substantial risk that if the child were born it would suffer from such physical or mental abnormalities as to be seriously handicapped.

No person is under a duty to assist in the termination of a pregnancy to which he has a conscientious objection, unless the termination is necessary to save the life or to prevent grave permanent injury to the physical or mental health of a pregnant woman. The Abortion Act 1967 does not affect the provisions of the Infant Life (Preservation) Act 1929, under which it is an offence to take the life of a child capable of being born alive (i.e.: of a foetus more than 28 weeks old). Abortions must be carried out in National Health Service hospitals or other institutions approved by the Secretary of State.

≠
(social work/social help)
G

Sozialarbeit (SA) and *Sozialpädagogik* (SP) denote the theoretical and practical aspects of social help. Both developed from the same social conditions but had different objectives. Formerly, *Sozialpädagogik* aimed at changes in behaviour. The work was founded on individual learning and therefore was incorporated in the education system (→ *Bildungswesen)*, its basis being educational theory. *Sozialarbeit* wanted to transform the problems of the individual and society at large. Thus it came to form part of the system of social security (→ *Soziale Sicherung),* its foundation being the science of social policy. This distinct separation is now considered obsolete.

In social work there has been a change from the concept of welfare work for the needy, i.e. a "charitable" motivation, to psychosocial help for all. *Sozialarbeit* has moved away from the notion of "emergency help". It now aims to provide help in general for all age groups. This reorientation marked the end of the distinction between *Sozialarbeit* and *Sozialpädagogik.* At the same time efforts increased to secure a more scientific and more professional approach, which coincided with the introduction of a university level degree course *(Diplom)* in educational theory focussing on SA/SP in 1969, and from 1970 the introduc-

(1969) und der Einführung der Fachhochschulen für SA/SP (ab 1970) einhergingen. Gemeinsame Aufgabe von SA/SP — auch als „Soziale Arbeit" bezeichnet — ist die Befähigung von Individuen und Gruppen (im Gemeinwesen) zu selbstbestimmter, befriedigender Lebensweise. Mit Hilfe professioneller Interventionen sollen Änderungen sowohl des Sozialverhaltens als auch sozialer Verhältnisse bewirkt werden.

VK

Soziale Arbeit ist eine verantwortungsvolle professionelle Tätigkeit, die einzelne, Familien und Gruppen in die Lage versetzt, persönliche, soziale und milieubedingte Schwierigkeiten zu identifizieren. *Social work* hilft ihnen und befähigt sie, diese Schwierigkeiten durch unterstützende, rehabilitierende, beschützende und korrektive Maßnahmen zu bewältigen. Soziale Arbeit dient dem Wohl der Gesellschaft und reagiert auf umfassende soziale Bedürfnisse durch Förderung der Chancengleichheit für alle Altersgruppen, soziale Schichten, Formen der Behinderung, Rassen, Kulturen und Glaubensgemeinschaften.

Die Mitarbeiter der Sozialen Arbeit üben ihre Tätigkeit im umfassenden Netz der Wohlfahrtspflege, des Gesundheitswesens, der Strafgerichtsbarkeit und des Vollzugs strafrechtlicher Maßnahmen aus. Sie sind für die sachgemäße Nutzung der ihnen zur Verfügung stehenden Mittel verantwortlich. Das Parlament steckt den gesetzlichen Rahmen der Befugnisse der öffentlichen, freien und privaten Träger ab, die Mitarbeiter der Sozialarbeit beschäftigen. Ihre Aufgaben können je nach Einsatzbereich (Heime, Tagesstätten, Hauspflege, praktische Feldarbeit, Gemeinwesenarbeit) unterschiedlich sein, beruhen aber auf einer gemeinsamen Basis des Sachverstandes, der Fachkompetenzen und Wertvorstellungen.

Youth and community work (Jugend- und Gemeinwesenarbeit) wird unter → *Jugendarbeit,* VK näher erläutert.

Sozialarbeiter (m)/Sozialarbeiterin (f)
Sozialpädagoge (m)/Sozialpädagogin (f)

D

In der Bundesrepublik besteht aufgrund des → *Föderalismus* für die Ausbildung der Sozialarbeiter/Sozialpädagogen keine Einheitlichkeit der Ausbildung und der Berufsbezeichnung. So gibt es in einigen Bundesländern noch unterschiedliche Diplome (Sozialarbeiter oder Sozialpädagoge), in anderen Bundesländern dagegen nur ein Diplom (Sozialpädagoge). Für die Zukunft wird jedoch ein einheitliches Diplom (Sozialarbeiter) vorgeschlagen (Studienreformkommission).

Die Ausbildung zum Sozialarbeiter/Sozialpädagogen erfolgt in der Bundesrepublik normalerweise an der Fachhochschule/Gesamthochschule oder einer Wissenschaftlichen Hochschule (→ *Bildungswesen).*

tion of Fachhochschulen for SA/SP *(→ Bildungswesen)*. It is a common objective of SA/SP, also referred to as *Soziale Arbeit,* to enable individuals and groups within the community to find a satisfactory life-style of their own. Professional intervention is used to bring about changes in social behaviour and conditions.

UK

Social work is an accountable professional activity which enables individuals, families and communities to identify personal, social and environmental difficulties. It assists and empowers them to manage these difficulties through supportive, rehabilitative, protective or corrective action. Social work promotes social welfare and responds to wider social needs promoting equal opportunities for every age, class, disability, race, culture and creed.

Social workers are part of a network of welfare, health, criminal justice and penal provision. They have a responsibility to ensure proper use of the resources available to them. Parliament lays down the legal framework and delineates the powers of statutory, voluntary and private agencies within which social workers practice. Their role can vary in residential, day care, domiciliary, field work and community settings, but they share a common core of knowledge, skills and values.

For youth and community work see *Jugendarbeit,* UK.

≠
Social Worker (qualified)
Youth and Community Worker
Residential Care Worker
(depending on the respective work situation)

G

Because of Germany's federal structure *(→ Föderalismus)* there is no uniform course of training and no standard designation for *Sozialarbeiter/Sozialpädagogen.* In some *Länder* separate diplomas may still be found (*Sozialarbeiter* or *Sozialpädagoge),* in others there is only one *(Sozialpädagoge).* The Reform Commission on Higher Education has submitted a proposal to standardize the diploma and call it *Sozialarbeiter.*

Das Studium an der Fachhochschule/Gesamthochschule dauert drei Jahre. Zugangsvoraussetzung ist die Fachhochschulreife oder das Abitur plus Vorpraktikum. Nach einem dreisemestrigen, integrierten Grundstudium erfolgt im Hauptstudium eine Differenzierung in die Schwerpunkte:
– Sozialpädagogik
– Soziale Hilfen und Beratung
– Rehabilitation und Resozialisation.
Die Diplome werden mit der Zusatzbezeichnung FH (= Fachhochschule) geführt. In einigen Bundesländern schließt sich ein Berufspraktikum von einem Jahr an. Danach erfolgt die staatliche Anerkennung. In anderen Bundesländern ist das Anerkennungsjahr in das Studium integriert (daher vier Jahre). Dort werden das Diplom und die staatliche Anerkennung gleichzeitig verliehen.

In Baden-Württemberg wird die Ausbildung an der Berufsakademie angeboten. Zugangsvoraussetzung ist das Abitur. Das Studium dauert drei Jahre und unterscheidet sich wesentlich von den beiden anderen Studiengängen:

– die Studierenden sind gleichzeitig in einem Ausbildungsverhältnis bei Sozialeinrichtungen und wechseln regelmäßig zwischen Akademie und Ausbildungsstelle;
– nach zwei Jahren kann das Studium mit dem Abschluß → *Erzieher* (BA) beendet werden;
– im letzten Studienjahr werden fünf Schwerpunkte, darunter „Offene Jugendarbeit" angeboten;
– nach drei Jahren wird der Titel Diplom-Sozialpädagoge mit der Zusatzbezeichnung BA (= Berufsakademie) verliehen. Dieser Abschluß schließt die staatliche Anerkennung ein.

Das Studium an den Wissenschaftlichen Hochschulen fordert das Abitur als Eingangsvoraussetzung und dauert vier Jahre. Nach einem viersemestrigen Grundstudium in Allgemeiner Erziehungswissenschaft und Soziologie/Psychologie, bildet Sozialarbeit/Sozialpädagogik einen Schwerpunkt im Hauptstudium. Der Abschluß (Diplom-Pädagoge) berechtigt jedoch nicht zum Einstieg in das Berufspraktikum und führt auch daher nicht zur staatlichen Anerkennung.

Absolventen der o.a. Studiengänge können in den unterschiedlichsten Arbeitsfeldern der → *Sozialarbeit/Sozialpädagogik* tätig werden.

VK

Im Vereinigten Königreich besteht eine klare Trennung in der Ausbildung der Fachkräfte für Soziale Arbeit (im weitesten Sinne). Für *social worker* und *youth and community worker* gibt es unterschiedliche Ausbildungsgänge.

Training courses for *Sozialarbeiter/Sozialpädagogen* in the Federal Republic are normally provided at a *Fachhochschule/Gesamthochschule* (polytechnic-type institution/combined polytechnic and university) or an institution of higher education *(→ Bildungswesen)*.

A course of study at a *Fachhochschule/Gesamthochschule* normally lasts three years. Students must have the entrance qualification for a polytechnic or the general entrance qualification for university *(Abitur)* to be admitted to the *Fachhochschule*. Those who have successfully completed their *Abitur* must also do a practical placement before they can be accepted. Following an integrated basic course of three semesters (there are two semesters of four months each to an academic year), the main course has three specialisms:
— *Sozialpädagogik (→ Sozialarbeit/Sozialpädagogik)*
— social help and counselling
— rehabilitation and social reintegration.
Diplomas are specified by adding the letters FH (= *Fachhochschule*). The diploma is only awarded after completion of a probationary year, which in some *Länder* follows the theoretical studies and in others is part of the study course, which then extends over four years. In the latter case, state recognition is awarded at the same time as the diploma.

In Baden-Württemberg, training is provided by the *Berufsakademie* (polytechnic-type establishment), for which the *Abitur* is the entrance qualification. The course of study lasts three years. It is quite different from the other two courses in that
— students simultaneously work under a training contract with social establishments and alternate regularly between the *Berufsakademie* and their training post;
— after completing two years, students may finish their studies by obtaining their qualification as → *Erzieher* (BA);
— during the last year of studies five major subjects are offered, one of which is leisure time provision for the young;
— after completing the three year course students are awarded the title of *Diplom-Sozialpädagoge* (BA). This qualification includes state recognition.

For the four-year university course the *Abitur* is required as an entrance qualification. Following a four-semester basic course in General Education Theory and Sociology/Psychology, the main course focuses on → *Sozialarbeit/Sozialpädagogik*. The diploma *(Diplom-Pädagoge)* does not entitle the students to begin a probationary year nor does it lead to state recognition.

Those having successfully completed the above courses may then work in the various fields of → *Sozialarbeit/Sozialpädagogik*.

UK
In the UK, training programmes for Social Work in the widest sense of the term are clearly subdivided into those for social workers and those for youth and community workers.

Social Worker
Der *Central Council for Education and Training in Social Work (CCETSW)*, der 1970 geschaffen wurde, ist das einzige Gremium, das das Recht zur Verleihung von Abschlüssen in Sozialer Arbeit hat.

Es bestehen zwei auch von den Arbeitgebern anerkannte Basis-Berufsqualifikationen, das *Certificate in Social Service (CSS)* und das *Certificate of Qualification in Social Work (CQSW)*. Der CCETSW führt zur Zeit auf der Grundlage des CSS und des CQSW einen dritten Abschluß ein, der beide ersetzen soll, das *Diploma in Social Work (DipSW)*. Nach 1994/95 wird für das CSS und das CQSW keine Zulassung mehr erteilt. Beide Abschlüsse werden jedoch weiterhin anerkannt.

Zwei unterschiedliche Ausbildungswege führen zu den drei Abschlüssen. Man kann sie sowohl auf der Basis einer fachbezogenen Beschäftigung als auch durch ein Fachstudium erwerben. Für den DipSW werden zunehmend Ausbildungsmodule, offene Angebote und Fernunterricht eingeführt. Auch der Erwerb eines *Bachelor's* oder *Master's* ist möglich, aber für die Anerkennung als Fachkraft nicht erforderlich.

Die Ausbildungsformen (Ebenen im Bildungswesen, Länge des Studiums, Eingangsvoraussetzungen, etc.) sind sehr unterschiedlich, jedoch lassen sich drei Typen festmachen:

— *non graduate* Studiengänge:
Zugang ohne Hochschulreife, überwiegend an *polytechnics* in England und *central institutions* in Schottland, auch an einigen *colleges of further education*, z.T. auch an Universitäten. Das Studium dauert zwei Jahre.

— *undergraduate* Studiengänge:
Zugang mit Hochschulreife, an *polytechnics* und Universitäten, zumeist als *social work option* in einem vierjährigen Studium der Sozialwissenschaften.

— *graduate* Studiengänge:
Zugang nach Abschluß eines ersten Hochschulstudiums an einer Hochschule, überwiegend an Universitäten, aber auch an einigen *polytechnics*. Bei Vorliegen eines Abschlusses in Sozialwissenschaften dauert das Studium manchmal nur ein Jahr, ansonsten mindestens zwei Jahre.

Die Curricula für diese unterschiedlichen Studiengänge enthalten in der Regel die folgenden Elemente:

Vermittlung von Fach- und Sachkenntnissen sowie Wertmaßstäben in
— Praxis der sozialen Arbeit
— Sozialpolitik
— Rechtslehre
— Soziologie und Psychologie
— anderen Fächern (z.B. Psychiatrie, Sozialphilosophie, Kriminologie, usw.).

Ausbildungsstätten, Anstellungsträger sowie der CCETSW arbeiten eng zusammen und teilen sich in die Verantwortung für die Ausbildung. Der

Social Worker

The Central Council for Education and Training in Social Work (CCETSW) which was established in 1970 is the only body with statutory authority to award social work qualifications.

For social work staff employers recognise two basic qualifications which are currently available: the Certificate in Social Service (CSS) and the Certificate of Qualification in Social Work (CQSW). A third qualification, the Diploma in Social Work (DipSW) is being introduced by CCETSW. Based on the CSS and CQSW, it will eventually replace them both with a single award. There will be no more CSS and CQSW intakes after 1994/5. The CCS and CQSW will continue to be recognised as professional qualifications.

Two different training routes — employment-based and college-based — lead to the three social work qualifying awards. For the DipSW, modular, open and distance learning arrangements are being progressively introduced. It is also possible to obtain a Bachelor's or Master's degree, which, however, is not necessary for recognition as a specialist in social work.

Forms of training, education levels, duration of studies, entrance qualifications, etc. differ widely, but three major types may be distinguished:

- non-graduate courses,
  where admission is without a university entrance qualification mainly to polytechnics in England, central institutions in Scotland, and to a few colleges of further education, some courses also being provided by universities. These are two-year courses.

- undergraduate courses,
  where admission is mostly with a university entrance qualification, mainly as a social work option within a four-year course of social sciences at a polytechnic or university;

- graduate courses,
  where admission is to an institute of higher education (predominantly universities but also some polytechnics), upon completion of an undergraduate course. Persons having previously obtained a qualification in social sciences sometimes only need to take a one-year course, others must complete at least a two-year course.

As a rule, the curricula for these different training courses comprise the following elements:
Knowledge, skills and values relating to
- approaches to social work practice
- social policy and administration
- legal studies
- sociology and psychology
- other subjects (such as psychiatry, social philosophy, criminology, etc.).

There is close cooperation of educational institutions, employing bodies, and the CCETSW in sharing responsibility for training. The CCETSW has given

CCETSW hat sich für eine vorrangige Behandlung der Problematik der ethnischen Minderheiten ausgesprochen und empfiehlt ihre Einbeziehung in die Curricula aller Studiengänge. Praktika — unter Supervision — werden als wesentliche Bestandteile der Ausbildung (mindestens 50 v.H.) getrennt von den theoretischen Fächern *(academic work)* bewertet. Für den Erwerb des CQSW ist die erfolgreiche Bewertung beider Teile Voraussetzung.

Anstellungsträger der Fachkräfte des *social work* (einschließlich der Mitarbeiter des Nationalen Gesundheitsdienstes) sind hauptsächlich die kommunalen Sozialbehörden, die Bewährungshilfe sowie freie oder kommerzielle Träger.

Jugend- und Gemeinwesenarbeiter/-in

Die Ausbildung zum *youth and community worker* ist z.Z. noch weitaus uneinheitlicher als die zum *social worker,* jedoch sind eindeutige Trends in Richtung Vereinheitlichung und Professionalisierung auszumachen. So spielt z.B. der 1982 geschaffene *Council for Education and Training in Youth and Community Work (CETYCW)* eine zentrale Rolle bei der Standardisierung der Ausbildungsgänge und der Anerkennung der Abschlüsse für England und Wales sowie hinsichtlich der Grundausbildung und beruflichen Fortbildung auch für Nordirland (seit 1984). Für Schottland hat der *Scottish Community Education Council (SCEC)* eine beratende Funktion in Fragen der Ausbildung.

Trotz dieser zum Teil verworrenen Situation im Bereich der Ausbildung für *youth and community work* — in Schottland eher gebräuchlich *community education* — sind zwei bzw. drei Ausbildungstypen zu identifizieren, die in etwa denen für die Ausbildung in *social work* gleichen; so gibt es auch hier *non graduate, undergraduate* und *graduate* Studiengänge an den verschiedenen Bildungseinrichtungen im *further education* und *higher education* Bereich, wobei die *postgraduate* Kurse nur vereinzelt zu finden sind. Die Abschlüsse sind ebenfalls nicht einheitlich. So gibt es neben einem *Certificate in Youth and Community Work/Development* auch ein *Diploma.* Möglich sind zudem die akademischen Grade eines *Bachelor's* oder *Master's.* Die Ausbildung mit dem *Certificate* oder *Diploma* als Abschluß wird als Vollzeitstudium (meist zwei Jahre) und als Teilzeitstudium (meist drei Jahre) angeboten.

1989 hat der CETYCW für junge Berufstätige verschiedene Programme mit Ausbildungsverhältnis eingeführt. Der Abschluß gilt als Berufsqualifikation. Die Ausbildung wird aus öffentlichen Mitteln *(Education Support Grants/ESG)* gefördert. Die Auszubildenden leisten praktische Arbeit bei fachbezogenen Trägern. Während der Ausbildungszeit besuchen sie Teilzeitkurse an der *Open University (→ Bildungswesen, VK).*

Um mehr Fachkräfte zu gewinnen, ist eine beträchtliche Anzahl von berufsbegleitenden Ausbildungsgängen für bereits praktizierende (formal jedoch „nicht qualifizierte") Mitarbeiter eingerichtet worden. Einige Kommunalbehörden schaffen eigene Ausbildungsprogramme in partnerschaftlicher Zusammenarbeit mit *polytechnics.* Dazu zählt auch das *M-One Project,* eine Teilzeitausbildung mit Dienstbefreiung für die Unterrichtstage, die zu einem an-

high priority to the problem of ethnic minorities and recommends integrating this subject into the curriculum of all training courses. Practical placements under supervision are considered an essential element of social work training (at least 50 %) and are assessed alongside the academic work. In order to obtain the qualification of CQSW, successful completion of both elements is required.

Professional social workers (including those working in the National Health Service) are mainly employed by the social services departments of local authorities. Others work in the probation service, in voluntary or in private organisations.

Youth and Community Worker
Training for youth and community workers is at present even less standardized than programmes available for social workers. But there are distinct trends towards standardization and professionalization. Thus, for instance, the Council for Education and Training in Youth and Community Work (CE-TYCW), which was established in 1982, assumes a central role in the standardization of training courses and their recognition for England and Wales and, in respect of initial and in-service training, also for Northern Ireland (since 1984). In Scotland, the Scottish Community Educational Council (SCEC) has an advisory function for training programmes.

In spite of this complex situation in the field of training for youth and community work — in Scotland known as community education — two or rather three routes to qualification may be identified, which are roughly similar to those offered in social work training. Thus, in youth and community work there are also non-graduate, undergraduate and graduate courses provided by further and higher education establishments. However, postgraduate courses are rare. The various qualifications to be obtained at these establishments are also quite heterogenous. In addition to a Certificate in Youth and Community Work/Development there is a Diploma as well as academic degrees such as the BA and MA. Certificate and Diploma courses are provided on a full-time (mostly two years) and part-time basis (mostly three years).

In 1989, a number of two to three-year apprenticeship schemes for young workers were introduced by the Council. They lead to qualified status and will be funded by Education Support Grants (ESG). Recruits are placed in appropriate organisations for practical placement. During the same period, structured part-time courses are given at the Open University.

A considerable number of on-the-job training courses has been set up for practitioners (who are not formally qualified) in order to recruit and qualify professionals. Some local authorities are creating their own training programmes in partnership with polytechnics. One of these is the "M-One Project", a part-time qualifying course on a day-release basis for those who have already been in service for a substantial period.

The curricula for a wide range of courses normally include the following elements:

erkannten Abschluß führt. Sie ist für bereits Berufstätige gedacht, die über längere Berufserfahrung verfügen.

Die Curricula für die unterschiedlichen Kurse enthalten in der Regel folgende Elemente:
- Grundsätze und Praxis der Jugend- und Gemeinwesenarbeit
- Angewandte Sozialwissenschaften
- Professionale Techniken/Verfahren.

Als integrierte Bestandteile der Ausbildung werden die Praktika — unter Supervision (50 v.H.) — auch gesondert bewertet und sind zusammen mit dem erfolgreichen Bestehen der Prüfung des theoretischen Lehrangebots Voraussetzung für den Erwerb der Berufsqualifikation.

Es empfiehlt sich für Absolventen einer Fachausbildung, unmittelbar nach Erwerb ihres Abschlusses eine Stelle zu suchen, an der in den ersten Jahren der Beschäftigung ausreichende fachliche Unterstützung gewährt wird. Sie müssen ein berufspraktisches Jahr ableisten, bevor sie als voll qualifizierte Fachkräfte angesehen werden. Einige Kommunalbehörden und die größeren freien Träger haben einen Ausbildungsreferenten für Jugend- und Gemeinwesenarbeit, zu dessen Aufgaben oft auch Einstiegsbetreuung und berufsbegleitende Ausbildungsangebote für Berufsanfänger gehören.

Die Mehrzahl der Jugend- und Gemeinwesenarbeiter sind in Clubs oder Zentren tätig, entweder bei den kommunalen Erziehungsbehörden (gegebenenfalls auch bei Ämtern für Erholung und Freizeit) oder bei freien Trägern der Jugendarbeit, wobei oft die jeweilige kommunale Erziehungsbehörde einen Teil des Gehaltes übernimmt.

Immer mehr Jugend- und Gemeinwesenarbeiter werden in anderen Bereichen beschäftigt, z.B in der Nachbarschaftsarbeit, in der Jugendarbeit der Gemeinden oder in der mobilen Jugendarbeit. Sie finden auch ein Betätigungsfeld bei dörflichen und gemeindlichen Bildungseinrichtungen, bei Trägern, die im Rahmen von Gemeinschaftsdiensten das Engagement junger Menschen fördern, in der Leitung von Beratungsdiensten sowie in jüngster Zeit bei Projekten für junge Arbeitslose.

Soziale Sicherung (f)/Soziale Sicherheit (f)

D
Die deutsche Sozialversicherung entstand als erste umfassende Gesetzgebung der Welt zur Sicherung der Arbeitnehmer bereits vor Ende des 19. Jahrhunderts (Gesetz über die Krankenversicherung der Arbeiter, 1883; Unfallversicherungsgesetz, 1884; Gesetz über die Invaliditäts- und Altersversicherung, 1889). Nach der Jahrhundertwende folgte u.a. das Gesetz über die Arbeitsvermittlung und Arbeitslosenversicherung (1927). Damit waren die Grundsteine des „Systems sozialer Sicherung" gelegt.

– principles and practice of youth and community work
– applied social sciences
– professional techniques/procedures.

As an integral part of training, practical placements under supervision (50 %) are assessed separately. Along with the successful completion of theoretical training they are a requirement for obtaining a professional qualification.

Newly qualified workers are encouraged whenever possible to take posts where sufficient support is available in the first years of employment. They are required to serve a probationary year before they are regarded as fully qualified practitioners. Some local authorities and the larger voluntary organisations have a Youth and Community Service training officer who, in most cases, will have as part of his responsibility induction and in-service training provision for the newly qualified worker.

The majority of youth and community workers work in clubs or centres, either in the employ of local education departments (or, in some cases, recreation and leisure departments) or voluntary youth organisations, often with a percentage of their salaries provided by the local education authority.

However, youth and community workers are now increasingly employed in a range of other settings as neighbourhood youth and community workers or as community youth workers or detached workers. They may be employed with titles such as community educators within village and community colleges; in agencies encouraging community involvement by young people, often through community service; they may be responsible for counselling services; and in the past few years in projects for unemployed young people.

Social Security

G

By the end of the 19th century German social insurance was already developed as the world's first comprehensive legislation aiming to secure the welfare of workers (Act concerning the Health Insurance of Workers, 1883; Accident Insurance Act, 1884; Act Securing Maintenance during Invalidity and Old Age, 1889). After the turn of the century these laws were followed by others such as the Act concerning Job Placement and Unemployment Insurance (1927). Thus, the cornerstones of the "system of social security" were laid.

Seit Bestehen der Bundesrepublik Deutschland wurden diese Gesetze zum Teil novelliert, und es kamen weitere Gesetze hinzu, die die unterschiedlichsten Risiken absichern sollten. Heute verfügt die Bundesrepublik Deutschland über eines der leistungsfähigsten sozialen Sicherungssysteme der Welt.

So wurden 1988 etwa 30 % der von der Volkswirtschaft erzeugten Güter und Dienstleistungen für die soziale Sicherheit aufgewendet. Im Sozialgesetzbuch, Allgemeiner Teil (SGB I) wird ein Katalog sozialer Rechte, die der Verwirklichung sozialer Gerechtigkeit und sozialer Sicherung dienen, angeführt:
— Bildungs- und Arbeitsförderung
— Sozialversicherung
— Soziale Entschädigung bei Gesundheitsschäden
— Minderung des Familienaufwandes
— Zuschuß für eine angemessene Wohnung
— → *Jugendhilfe*
— → *Sozialhilfe*
— Eingliederung Behinderter, → *Behindertenhilfe.*

Zusätzlich zu diesen öffentlichen Sozialleistungen finden wir weitere Sicherungsinstitute, z.B :
— betriebliche Sozialleistungen
— Eigenvorsorge
— freie Wohlfahrtspflege, z.B. → *Wohlfahrtsverbände*
— Unterhaltsrecht
— Erbrecht
— Unterhaltspflichtrecht.

Im gegliederten Sozialleistungssystem gibt es drei Leistungstypen:
— Leistungen nach dem Versicherungsprinzip, bei denen ein Anspruch durch Beitragsleistung des Pflichtversicherten entsteht;

— Leistungen nach dem Versorgungsprinzip, die ohne selbstentrichtete Beiträge aus Rechtsansprüchen gegen den Staat realisiert werden;

— Leistungen aus öffentlichen Mitteln der → *Sozialhilfe,* bei denen lediglich Bedürftigkeit und Nachrangigkeit (→ *Subsidiaritätsprinzip)* zu prüfen sind.

Die Aufwendungen für sämtliche Sozialleistungen (soziale Sicherung, freiwillige Arbeitgeberleistungen, Entschädigungen, soziale Hilfen und Dienste sowie indirekte Leistungen) werden jährlich im Sozialbudget zusammengefaßt. Die Leistungen des Sozialbudgets werden zu knapp zwei Dritteln durch Beiträge und zu einem Teil durch Zuweisungen finanziert.

VK

Das Hauptanliegen des britischen Systems der sozialen Sicherung, für das die Regierung unmittelbar verantwortlich ist, besteht darin, ein leistungsfähiges

Since the Federal Republic of Germany was founded, these Acts have been partly amended. Others have been added to insure the population against a wider variety of risks. Today the Federal Republic of Germany has one of the most comprehensive systems of social security in the world.

In 1988, about 30 % of the gross national product was earmarked for social security. The Social Code, General Provisions (*Sozialgesetzbuch*/SGB I), contains a catalogue of social rights to promote social justice and social security. These cover the fields of
— education and labour
— social insurance
— social compensation for impairments resulting from ill health
— reduction of family expenditure
— grants towards adequate housing
— youth work and youth welfare services (→ *Jugendhilfe*)
— social assistance benefits (→ *Sozialhilfe*)
— integration of the handicapped (→ *Behindertenhilfe*)

Additional to statutory social security benefits, further provision is available through:
— work-based benefits
— individual providence
— voluntary welfare work (→ *Wohlfahrtsverbände*)
— the right to maintenance law
— the laws of inheritance
— maintenance liability law.

In this overall system of social security, there are three types of benefits:
— benefits under the insurance principle. They are paid on the basis of a claim acquired through the contributions/fees paid by the person subject to compulsory insurance;

— benefits under the pension scheme. These are granted on the basis of legal claims against the State whereby those eligible need not have paid contributions themselves;

— benefits from the statutory funds of social assistance (→ *Sozialhilfe*). Entitlement to these benefits follows a means test and is according to the → *Subsidiaritätsprinzip*.

Total expenditure on social benefits (social security, voluntary benefits granted by the employers, compensations, social help and services as well as indirect benefits) constitute the annual social budget. Benefits under the social budget are financed by slightly less than two thirds from contributions and one third from government subsidies.

UK
The general aim of the social security programme in the UK is to provide an efficient and responsible system of financial help for people who are elderly, sick,

und verantwortliches System finanzieller Unterstützung für alte Menschen, Kranke, Behinderte, Arbeitslose, Verwitwete und Personen, die für den Unterhalt von Kindern aufkommen, zu schaffen.

Der Anspruch auf eine große Anzahl von monetären Leistungen hängt von vorhergehender Beitragsentrichtung an die Sozialversicherung ab, während andere Leistungen ohne Beitragsverpflichtungen in Anspruch genommen werden können. Geldleistungen werden aus den Mitteln des *National Insurance Fund* gewährt, der sich aus den Beitragszahlungen der Arbeitnehmer und Arbeitgeber, der Selbständigen und der Regierung zusammensetzt. Die nichtbeitragspflichtigen Leistungen werden aus dem allgemeinen Steueraufkommen finanziert.

Der Anspruch auf Leistungen aus der Sozialversicherung, wie Altersruhegeld, Krankengeld, Invalidenrente, Arbeitslosengeld, Witwenrente, Erziehungsgeld, Mutterschaftsgeld, Sterbegeld und Kinderzuschuß bzw. -zulage hängt von der Erfüllung der Beitragspflicht ab. Für den Erhalt der meisten Sozialleistungen, die jährlich angehoben werden, sind zwei Bedingungen Voraussetzung: Erstens muß eine bestimmte Anzahl von Beiträgen eingezahlt worden sein, bevor ein Anspruch auf monetäre Leistungen besteht. Zweitens kann der volle Leistungssatz nur dann gewährt werden, wenn die Beitragszahlungen während eines festgelegten Zeitraumes erfolgt sind oder gutgeschrieben werden und einen bestimmten Richtwert erreicht haben.

Social Security stellt zusammen mit dem Nationalen Gesundheitsdienst und den personenbezogenen sozialen Diensten den Kernbereich der *statutory social services* dar. Dieser Begriff schließt im weitesten Sinne alle Hilfen der Gesellschaft ein, die in positiver Weise auf soziale Probleme einwirken.

Sozialer Wohnungsbau (m)

D

Staatliche Förderung des Baus von Wohnungen, die nach Größe, Ausstattung und Miete für die breiten Schichten der Bevölkerung bestimmt und geeignet sind. Die Förderung des sozialen Wohnungsbaues ist öffentliche Aufgabe von Bund, Ländern und Gemeinden. Sie erfolgt hauptsächlich durch den Einsatz öffentlicher Mittel (z.B zinsgünstiger Baudarlehen) an nicht-staatliche Wohnungsbauträger, u.a. gemeinnützige Wohnungsunternehmen. Die Sozialwohnungen werden preisgünstig an Haushalte mit geringem Einkommen vergeben; bevorzugt werden kinderreiche Familien, junge Ehepaare, alleinstehende Elternteile mit Kindern, ältere Menschen, Schwerbehinderte, Flüchtlinge und Zuwanderer gefördert.

Als Folge der öffentlichen Förderung gehen die Eigentümer der Wohnungen längerfristige gesetzliche Bindungen hinsichtlich Miete (kostendeckende Miete) und Belegung ein. Den Bindungen unterliegen z.Z. gut 3 Millionen Mietwohnungen.

disabled, unemployed, widowed or bringing up children. Central government is directly responsible for it.

The payment of many benefits depends on prior payment to the National Insurance scheme, while others are available without contribution conditions. The former are paid from the National Insurance Fund, which consists of contributions from employed persons and their employers, the self-employed and the Government. Non-contributory benefits are financed from general taxation revenue.

Entitlement to National Insurance benefits such as retirement pension, sickness and invalidity benefit, unemployment benefit, widow's benefit, maternity allowance, death grant and child's special allowance is dependent upon the payment of contributions. For most benefits there are two contribution conditions. First, before benefit can be drawn at all a certain number of contributions has to be paid; secondly, the full rate of benefit cannot be paid unless contributions have been made or credited up to a specific level over a specified period. Benefits are increased annually.

Social security, the National Health Service and personal social services constitute the nucleus of the statutory social services. These comprise, in the widest sense of the term, all types of help given by society in order to take positive action against social problems.

Subsidized Housing/Council Housing

G

This refers to the provision of public support for the construction of dwellings which in terms of size, equipment and rent, are intended and suitable for a broad cross-section of the population. The provision of such support is a statutory responsibility of the Federation, the *Länder* and local authorities. It is mainly provided by grants (e.g. low-interest loans) to non-statutory housing associations such as non-profitmaking housing cooperatives. These dwellings are allocated to low-income households at reasonable rates. Preferential treatment is given to large families, young couples, single-parent families, the elderly, the severely handicapped, refugees and persons moving in from the new *Länder*.

Public funding carries with it certain conditions. Owners of such dwellings must observe the statutory regulations as regards the level of rent and the categories of tenants. At present, more than 3 million rented flats are covered by these regulations.

VK

Die Bereitstellung von Wohnraum aus öffentlichen Mitteln, meist als *council housing* bezeichnet, ist in England, Wales und Schottland Aufgabe der kommunalen Wohnungsbehörden (d.h. der *district councils* sowie der *London borough councils*) und in Nordirland der *Northern Ireland Housing Executive*. Etwa sechs Millionen Häuser und Wohnungen befinden sich im Besitz kommunaler Wohnungsbehörden, die von der Regierung Zuschüsse zu den Kosten der Bereitstellung von Wohnraum erhalten und die Mieten der Bewohner einziehen.

Die Kommunalbehörden sind gesetzlich dazu verpflichtet, Wohnraum für Obdachlose zu schaffen. Priorität wird dabei Personen mit Kindern eingeräumt. Auch Obdachlose, die z.B. durch Flut- und Brandkatastrophen ihr Heim verloren haben, und andere Hilfsbedürftige wie ältere oder geistig und körperlich behinderte Menschen gehören zu dem vorrangig begünstigten Personenkreis.

Seit 1980 sind Mieter von Sozialwohnungen berechtigt, das Haus, in dem sie wohnen, zu kaufen; viele Bewohner (schätzungsweise mehr als eine Million) haben von dieser Möglichkeit Gebrauch gemacht.

Die Regierung gewährt nicht nur den kommunalen Wohnungsbehörden finanzielle Unterstützung; sie fördert auch die Gründung von Wohnungsbaugesellschaften, die durch Errichtung von Neubauten oder Renovierung alter Gebäude Wohnraum zum Kauf anbieten oder vermieten. Die Wohnungsbaugesellschaften richten sich an einen Personenkreis, der sich sonst wegen einer geeigneten Wohnung an die Kommune wenden würde. Sie berücksichtigen insbesondere die Bedürfnisse älterer, behinderter und alleinstehender Menschen. Als gemeinnützige Einrichtungen erhalten sie öffentliche Mittel von der Regierung, sofern sie bei der *Housing Corporation* registriert sind. Zur Zeit sind dort etwa 2.600 Gesellschaften eingetragen, die zusammen ungefähr 500.000 Häuser und Wohnungen besitzen.

Sozialhilfe (f)

D

Sozialhilfe ist ein Bereich des Systems sozialer Sicherung (→ *Soziale Sicherung/soziale Sicherheit*) in der Bundesrepublik Deutschland, in dem Leistungen zur Abwendung und Verhinderung individueller sozialer Notlagen gewährt und die dazu notwendigen Einrichtungen und Dienste bereitgestellt werden. Die Hilfe soll vor allem als „Hilfe zur Selbsthilfe" gegeben werden.

Rechtsgrundlage ist das Bundessozialhilfegesetz (BSHG) als Teil des Sozialgesetzbuches sowie die dazu erlassenen Rechtsverordnungen und Ausführungsgesetze der Länder.

Für die Durchführung dieser Gesetze sind im wesentlichen die kreisfreien Städte und Landkreise (→ *Kommunale Selbstverwaltung)*, für bestimmte Leistungen die überörtlichen Träger der Sozialhilfe in eigener Verantwortung zuständig.

UK

Public or "Council" housing is provided in England, Wales and Scotland by local housing authorities (i.e.: district councils and London borough councils) and in Northern Ireland by the Northern Ireland Housing Executive. Local housing authorities own about six million houses or flats. They receive subsidies from central government to assist them with housing costs and also collect rent from tenants.

Local authorities have a statutory obligation to provide housing for homeless people. Priority is given to persons with dependent children, those who have been made homeless as a result of an emergency, such as flood or fire, and those who are vulnerable as a result of old age, mental illness or other physical handicap.

Since 1980 persons living in council housing have been entitled to buy the homes in which they are living and many people (probably more than a million) have done so.

As well as giving financial assistance to local housing authorities the central government encourages the establishment of housing associations, which provide accommodation for rent or sale through new buildings or the renovation of older property. Housing associations normally cater for people who would otherwise look to a local authority for a home and provide particularly for the needs of elderly, disabled and single people. They are non-profitmaking and receive financial assistance from government if they are registered with the Housing Corporation. At present some 2,600 associations are registered and together own approximately 500,000 homes.

Social Assistance Benefits/Income Support

G

Social assistance benefits are that part of the system of social security (→ *Soziale Sicherung/soziale Sicherheit*) in the Federal Republic of Germany which provides benefits for individuals who find themselves in a position of financial need or for whom such situations must be averted, making available as necessary establishments and services. Above all, assistance is given to people to become self-sufficient.

The legal basis is the Federal Social Assistance Act *(Bundessozialhilfegesetz/ BSHG)* as embodied in the Social Code, pertinent statutory orders and implementing laws as enacted by the *Länder*.

Responsibility for the implementation of these acts is vested in the *kreisfreie Städte* and *Landkreise (→ kommunale Selbstverwaltung)*. Social

Auf alle Leistungen der Sozialhilfe besteht ein einklagbarer Rechtsanspruch. Nach dem Grundsatz der Individualisierung müssen die persönlichen und wirtschaftlichen Verhältnisse des Hilfesuchenden berücksichtigt werden.

Sozialhilfe kann in Form einer persönlichen Hilfe, Geldleistung oder Sachleistung gewährt werden. Sie umfaßt „Hilfe zum Lebensunterhalt" und „Hilfe in besonderen Lebenslagen".

Hilfe zum Lebensunterhalt wird als laufende Hilfe in der Regel bar (nach sogenannten Regelsätzen) zur Deckung des notwendigen Bedarfs für Ernährung, Kleidung in geringem Umfang, Körperpflege, Hausrat und andere Dinge des täglichen Bedarfs gewährt. Neben den Regelsätzen werden gesondert gewährt die laufenden Leistungen für die Unterkunft, einschließlich der Heizung, grundsätzlich in ihrer tatsächlichen Höhe, der sogenannte Mehrbedarf (u.a. für alte Menschen, Erwerbsunfähige, werdende Mütter, Erwerbstätige mit geringem Einkommen, Alleinerziehende, Behinderte) in Höhe von 20 bis 50 % der Regelsätze sowie die einmaligen Leistungen, insbesondere für Bekleidung und Hausrat.

Die Regelsätze werden der Entwicklung der Lebenshaltungskosten angepaßt. Sie staffeln sich für eine hilfebedürftige Familie nach Haushaltsvorstand und Zahl der Familienmitglieder unter Berücksichtigung des jeweiligen Alters. Bei dieser Hilfeart muß das eigene Einkommen grundsätzlich voll eingesetzt werden.

Bei der Hilfe in besonderen Lebenslagen bleibt das Einkommen unterhalb bestimmter Grenzen zumeist anrechnungsfrei. Im einzelnen werden folgende Hilfearten unterschieden:
– vorbeugende Gesundheitshilfe
– Krankenhilfe und sonstige medizinische Hilfen
– Hilfen für werdende Mütter und Wöchnerinnen
– Eingliederungshilfe für körperlich, geistig oder seelisch Behinderte
– Hilfe zur Pflege (zu Hause oder in einem Heim)
– Hilfe zur Weiterführung des Haushalts
– Hilfe zur Überwindung besonderer sozialer Schwierigkeiten
– zusätzliche Hilfen für ältere Menschen.

Die Sozialhilfe hebt nicht die allgemeine Unterhaltspflicht der Verwandten auf. Deshalb prüft das Sozialamt im Einzelfall, ob und in welchem Umfang die unterhaltspflichtigen Angehörigen ersten Grades oder der Ehegatte (auch der ständige Lebenspartner) zum Ersatz von Sozialhilfeaufwendungen herangezogen werden können.

VK

Income support (Sozialhilfe/bis 1988 als *supplementary benefit* bezeichnet) wird an Personen ab 16 Jahren gezahlt, die weder einer Vollzeitbeschäftigung nachgehen noch eine Schule besuchen und deren Einkommen unterhalb einer bestimmten Grenze liegt. Die zu zahlenden Beträge werden nach Richtwerten

assistance agencies at higher levels act on separate authority for certain benefits.

There is a legal entitlement to social assistance benefits. On the legal principle of individual entitlement the personal and economic situation of each claimant has to be judged in deciding the benefit.

Social assistance may take the form of personal help, cash benefits or help in kind and includes "help to meet the cost of living" and "help in special circumstances".

Assistance towards the cost of living is granted, as a rule, as a regular cash benefit (based on a graded scale) covering food, clothing on a small scale, personal hygiene, household equipment and other day-to-day living expenditure. On principle, benefits for accommodation and heating cover the actual expenditure. Persons with extra needs (such as the elderly, those unable to earn a living, pregnant women, gainfully employed persons with a low income, single-parent families and the disabled) are entitled to an extra allowance ranging from 20 to 50 % of the graded scales. Additionally, there are one-off allowances for major purchases, especially for clothing and household equipment.

The graded scales are linked to the cost of living index. Family benefits take into account the head of household, the number of family members and their respective ages. In this assessment, the family's own income has to be counted in full.

Below certain limits personal income is not taken into account when assessing special circumstance payments.
Assistance is available for:
- preventive health measures
- illness and other medical needs
- expectant mothers and women in childbed
- the integration of the physically, mentally or emotionally handicapped
- nursing at home or in residential care
- home helps
- coping with special social difficulties
- additional help for the elderly.

Social assistance benefits do not substitute for the general maintenance responsibilities of relatives. Consequently, the Social Services Department examines each individual case on its merits to determine if and to what extent first-degree relatives, the spouse (and also a common-law husband/wife) are liable to maintain the claimant. These relatives may be held responsible for restitution of social assistance payments already made.

UK

Income support (until 1988 called supplementary benefit) is payable to people of the age of 16 and over who are not in full-time work or at school and whose financial resources fall below a certain level. The amounts payable are based on weekly levels laid down for the requirements of married couples, single house-

bemessen, die den lebensnotwendigen wöchentlichen Bedürfnissen von verheirateten Paaren, Ein-Personen-Haushalten und sonstigen Anspruchsberechtigten entsprechen. Die gewährte Sozialhilfe gleicht die Differenz zwischen den eigenen Mitteln der Antragsteller und diesem Existenzminimum aus. Langfristige Zahlungen erhalten Personen über 60 Jahre, die Mehrzahl der Behinderten sowie Personen unter 60, die ein Jahr lang ohne Unterbrechung Sozialhilfe oder eine langfristige Erwerbsunfähigkeitshilfe bezogen haben, vorausgesetzt, daß die Mittel nicht mit der Bedingung gewährt wurden, der Arbeitsvermittlung zur Verfügung zu stehen.

Familien mit geringem Einkommen haben Anspruch auf eine Kinderzulage, wenn ein Elternteil einer Vollzeitbeschäftigung nachgeht und der Unterhalt für mindestens ein Kind aufzubringen ist. Die Kinderzulage wird gewährt, wenn das wöchentliche Bruttoeinkommen einer Familie bestimmte Richtwerte unterschreitet, die nach Anzahl der Kinder und deren Alter abgestuft sind. Zwischen Alleinerziehenden und Familien mit beiden Elternteilen wird kein Unterschied gemacht.

Familien, die *income support* erhalten, können eine Reihe zusätzlicher Leistungen in Anspruch nehmen, wie Wohngeld, kostenlose Brillen, Schulmahlzeiten und Versorgung mit Milch und Vitaminen für werdende Mütter sowie Kinder im Vorschulalter; Befreiung von Rezeptgebühren des *National Health Service* und kostenlose Zahnbehandlung. Auch bei besonderen Anschaffungen (z.B. Bekleidung, Möbel, Haushaltsgeräte) können Pauschalbeträge als Zuschuß gewährt werden.

Strafaussetzung (f) zur Bewährung (f)

D
Das deutsche Strafrecht kennt mehrere Voraussetzungen und Modalitäten für die Strafaussetzung zur Bewährung. Bei der Verurteilung nach Jugendstrafrecht werden überwiegend folgende Formen angewandt:

1. Die Strafaussetzung zur Bewährung wird grundsätzlich nur bei Jugendstrafe bis zu einem Jahr verfügt, wenn zu erwarten ist, daß der Täter nicht mehr straffällig wird. Die Bewährungszeit beträgt zwei bis drei Jahre. Nach Ablauf der Bewährungsfrist erläßt der Richter (Jugendrichter) die Jugendstrafe, wenn die Strafaussetzung nicht vorher — etwa wegen einer in der Bewährungszeit begangenen Straftat — widerrufen wurde.

2. Strafaussetzung zur Bewährung ist auch bei einem Strafrest zulässig, wenn bei günstiger Prognose über das Verhalten des Straffälligen ein bestimmter Teil der Strafe verbüßt ist.

3. Damit verwandt ist die Aussetzung der Verhängung der Jugendstrafe (isolierter Schuldausspruch). Kann nicht sicher festgestellt werden, ob in einer Jugendstraftat schädliche Neigungen zum Ausdruck kommen, die Jugendstrafe erforderlich machen, und ist diese nicht wegen der Schwere der

holders and others. The support payable amounts to the difference between a person's existing resources and these levels. Long-term rates apply to people aged 60 or over, most disabled people, and to those people aged less than 60 who have received income support or long-term incapacity benefit continuously for one year, provided that the award is not subject to the condition of being available for employment.

Families with low incomes where one of the parents is in full-time work and where there is at least one dependent child are entitled to a family credit. It is payable when the gross weekly income of a family falls below a prescribed amount which varies according to the number of children in the family but is the same for single- and two-parent families. The age of the children is also taken into account.

Families receiving income support are entitled to a number of other benefits including housing benefits, free spectacles, free school meals, milk and vitamins for expectant mothers and for children under school age, and exemption from National Health Service prescription charges and charges for dental treatment. Lump-sum payments may also be made for special needs such as clothing, furniture and domestic appliances.

Sentence Suspended whilst on Probation

G
German penal law provides for several forms of a sentence to be suspended during probation. Court orders made under penal law for young offenders make use in particular of the following alternatives:

1. Suspense of sentence whilst on probation is, in principle, only ordered when a young person is sentenced for up to one year and it may be expected that he or she will not reoffend. The probation order may last between two and three years. When the probation period has elapsed, the judge (juvenile court judge) will order the sentence to be remitted. Should the young person reoffend during the probation period, suspense of the sentence will be revoked before that time.

2. A sentence may also be suspended in cases where a given part of a sentence has been served and where there is a favourable expectation as to the future conduct of the offender.

3. Related to this alternative is a court order that a sentence will not be passed (isolated verdict of guilt). In cases where the judge cannot with certainty determine whether culpable tendencies can be detected in a juvenile offence

Schuld geboten, so kann der Richter den Strafausspruch für ein bis zwei Jahre zur Bewährung aussetzen. Für diese Zeit kann er Weisungen und Auflagen verhängen. Erweist sich, vor allem durch schlechte Führung in der Bewährungszeit, daß Jugendstrafe erforderlich ist, kann der Strafausspruch nachgeholt werden.

Der Jugendrichter soll für die Dauer der Bewährungszeit den Jugendlichen durch Weisungen oder Auflagen erzieherisch beeinflussen. Er kann z.b. den Einsatz in sozialen Diensten, gemeinnützige Spenden, ein Verbot des Aufenthalts an gefährdenden Orten verfügen.

Der Jugendliche steht in der Bewährungszeit unter der Aufsicht eines Bewährungshelfers (Bewährungshilfe). Dieser betreut den Probanden regelmäßig, überwacht seine Lebensführung sowie die Erfüllung der richterlichen Auflagen und versucht, ihn zu resozialisieren. Der unter Bewährungsfrist stehende Straffällige kann in seiner Familie leben oder in einem offenen Heim (Bewährungs-, Probandenheim) untergebracht werden. Neben hauptamtlichen Bewährungshelfern werden zunehmend auch ehrenamtliche Kräfte herangezogen.

VK

In England und Wales können die Gerichte eine Gefängnisstrafe von nicht unter sechs Monaten und nicht über zwei Jahren zur Bewährung aussetzen. Gleichzeitig kann eine *supervision order* (Aufsichtsanordnung) ergehen, wobei der Straffällige der Aufsicht eines Bewährungshelfers unterstellt wird. Personen unter 21 Jahren können jedoch nur bei schweren Verbrechen zu Gefängnis verurteilt werden.

In England gibt es keine Strafaussetzung zur Bewährung bei Minderjährigen unter 17 Jahren. In Schottland beträgt das Mindestalter 16 Jahre und in Nordirland 14 Jahre. Ansonsten sind die Bestimmungen im gesamten Vereinigten Königreich gleich.

Ein Gericht, das einen Straffälligen von über 17 Jahren wegen eines Delikts schuldig gesprochen hat, kann, anstatt eine Strafe zu verhängen, Bewährungsaufsicht anordnen und ihn für nicht weniger als sechs Monate und nicht mehr als zwei Jahre der Aufsicht eines Bewährungshelfers unterstellen. Der Zweck der Bewährungsaufsicht ist, die Gesellschaft durch die Resozialisierung des Straffälligen zu schützen, der in der Bewährungszeit ein normales Leben in der Gemeinschaft weiterführt. Bevor Bewährungsaufsicht angeordnet werden kann, muß das Gericht dem Täter die Auswirkungen der Anordnung in allgemeinverständlicher Sprache erklären. Der Straffällige muß auch verstehen, daß die Nichterfüllung der Bedingungen der Anordnung ihm eine Konventionalstrafe einträgt oder er wegen der ursprünglichen Straftat zur Verantwortung gezogen wird.

Die Anordnung der Bewährungsaufsicht kann auch eine Auflage über den Aufenthaltsort des unter Bewährungsfrist stehenden Straffälligen enthalten und

which require him to pass a juvenile court sentence or where such a sentence is not justified by the seriousness of guilt, he may order the sentence to be suspended for one or two years and give directions and conditions for that period in conjunction with a probation order. If the young offender's conduct during the probation period is such that a custodial sentence is deemed necessary, he will then be given a conviction.

The juvenile court judge must make sure that a positive educational influence is provided for the young offender during probation through his directions and conditions. He may order, for example, a period of community service, donations to be made to charities, or ban the young person from staying in places where he/she is at risk.

During probation, the young person is placed under the supervision of a probation officer (probation service). He looks after the probationer regularly, supervises his way of life, and makes sure the conditions of the court are observed. Moreover, he tries to rehabilitate him. The young person under probation may live with his family or in an open home (hostel for probationers). The probation service is mainly staffed with full-time probation officers, but increasingly also employs voluntary helpers.

UK

In England und Wales the courts may pass a suspended sentence of imprisonment for not less than six months and not more than two years and may at the same time make a supervision order, placing the offender under the supervision of a probation officer for a period not exceeding the operational period of the suspended sentence. However, on persons who are under 21 a sentence of imprisonment may only be passed in case of a serious crime.

In England there is no probation for the under 17 age group. In Scotland the minimum age is 16 years and in Northern Ireland 14. Otherwise, arrangements throughout the UK are the same.

A court before which a person over the age of 17 has been convicted of an offence may, instead of sentencing him, make a probation order requiring him to be under the supervision of a probation officer for a period of not less than six months and not more than three years. The purpose of probation is to protect society by the rehabilitation of the offender, who continues to live a normal life in the community while subject to supervision. Before making a probation order the court must explain to the offender in ordinary language the effect of the order being made. The offender must also understand that failure to comply with the requirements of the order will make him liable to a penalty or to be dealt with for the original offence.

A probation order may include a provision requiring the probationer to live in a particular place, such as an approved probation hostel or approved probation home, taking into consideration the probationer's home surroundings.

seine Unterbringung in einem Bewährungs- oder Probandenheim verfügen, wobei das familiäre Umfeld des Probanden zu berücksichtigen ist.

Gegebenenfalls verpflichtet das Gericht mit der Anordnung der Bewährungsaufsicht den Probanden auch zu einer medizinischen Behandlung während der gesamten oder eines Teils der Bewährungszeit mit dem Ziel, einer Beeinträchtigung seiner Geisteskräfte entgegenzuwirken.

Die Anordnung der Bewährungsaufsicht kann auch die Auflage enthalten, daß der Proband während der Bewährungszeit eine Tageseinrichtung besucht. Voraussetzung ist die vorherige Befragung eines Bewährungshelfers durch das Gericht sowie die Durchführbarkeit von Maßnahmen, die den regelmäßigen Besuch der Einrichtung durch den Probanden sicherstellen. Außerdem muß der Leiter der betreffenden Einrichtung der Auflage zustimmen.

Wenn ein Proband eine Auflage im Rahmen einer Anordnung der Bewährungshilfe nicht erfüllt, kann eine Geldstrafe oder eine weitere Auflage verfügt werden, z.B. die Anordnung gemeinnütziger Arbeit. Begeht der Proband im Laufe der Bewährungsfrist ein weiteres Delikt, kann der Strafausspruch für die ursprüngliche Strafe nachgeholt werden.

Subsidiaritätsprinzip (n)

D

Das Subsidiaritätsprinzip durchzieht die Gliederung und den Aufbau des gesamten Systems sozialer Sicherung in der Bundesrepublik Deutschland. Dieses Prinzip konvergiert in starkem Maße mit der liberal-bürgerlichen Gesellschafts- und Staatsauffassung.

Daraus werden für die Gestaltung des konkreten Systems sozialer Sicherheit zwei Ausprägungen abgeleitet: Beistands*grenzen* und Beistands*pflichten* des übergeordneten Systems gegenüber dem untergeordneten System; übertragen auf die Beziehung zwischen den freien Trägern (z.B. → *Wohlfahrtsverbände*) und den öffentlichen Trägern (z.B. Sozial- und → *Jugendamt)* bedeutet dies:

— unbedingte Vorrangigkeit der Selbsthilfe des Individuums vor der Fremdhilfe; kann es sich nicht helfen, tritt die nächsthöhere Gemeinschaft (Wohlfahrtsverbände und in den letzten Jahren Selbsthilfegruppen) ein und leistet Hilfe.

— Der Staat (und die Kommunen) hat als übergeordnete Instanz die im Verhältnis zu ihm untergeordneten Wohlfahrtsverbände und Selbsthilfegruppierungen anzuerkennen und bei der Wahrnehmung ihrer Aufgaben zu unterstützen.

Die kommunale Selbstverwaltung ist daher in ihrer Hilfeleistung nachrangig zu den Wohlfahrtsverbänden und Selbsthilfegruppen anzusehen, die sie vor allem mit Geldmitteln unterstützen muß. Erst wenn die freien Träger keine

In appropriate cases a probation order may make provision for the medical treatment of the probationer during all or part of the probation period, with a view to improving his mental condition.

A probation order may also include a requirement that the probationer must during the probation period attend at a day centre, provided that the court has consulted a probation officer and is satisfied that arrangements can be made for the probationer's attendance at a centre and that the person in charge of the centre agrees to the inclusion of the requirement.

If a probationer breaches a requirement of the probation order he may be fined or subjected to an additional requirement, such as a community service order. If the probationer commits a further offence while the probation order is in force the court may sentence him for his original offence.

≠
(Subsidiaritätsprinzip)

G

This principle permeates the structure and set-up of the entire system of social security of the Federal Republic of Germany. It is strongly related to the liberal middle-class view of society and the State.

Two facets of the very system of social security are derived from this view: *Limits of support* by and *obligation to support* of the higher-level system towards the subordinate system. When applied to the relationship between the voluntary organisations (e.g. welfare organisations → *Wohlfahrtsverbände)* and the statutory bodies (e.g. social services department, youth office → *Jugendamt)* this means:

— Without exception, the individual must first attempt to help himself before help is given by others. If the individual is not in a position to do so, the community placed at the next higher level (the welfare organisations and, in recent years, self-help groups) steps in and provides help.

— The State (and local authorities) must acknowledge the welfare organisations and self-help groups under their jurisdiction and assist them in fulfilling their responsibilities.

Thus, when help is required, local social services are a second resort in line to welfare organisations and self-help groups. The former must subsidize the latter as necessary. Only when the voluntary bodies are unable or unwilling to make provision, then the statutory body must intervene as having the final re-

Angebote machen können, muß als Letztverantwortlicher der öffentliche Träger einspringen; diese Verantwortung erstreckt sich auch auf die Planung und Anregung von Einrichtungen und Diensten zur Sicherstellung einer rechtzeitigen und ausreichenden Versorgung.

Durch dieses Prinzip wird hauptsächlich das Verhältnis der öffentlichen Träger zu den freien Trägern und zum einzelnen bestimmt.

VK
Zwar ist der Begriff der Subsidiarität in der britischen sozialpolitischen Diskussion nicht gängig, trotzdem aber ist der in diesem Prinzip enthaltene Grundgedanke der Sozialpolitik des VK nicht fremd (vgl. Beveridge-Plan 1942).

Tageseinrichtungen (f/pl) für Kinder (n/pl)

D
Oberbegriff für familienergänzende und familienunterstützende sozialpädagogische Einrichtungen, in denen Kinder ganztägig oder für einen Teil des Tages betreut werden. Zu den Tageseinrichtungen für Kinder gehören:

- Kinderkrippe (für Säuglinge bis zu einem Jahr)
- Krabbelstube (Kleinstkinder von 1 bis unter 3 Jahren)
- Kindergarten (3–6jährige Kleinkinder bis zum Beginn der Schulpflicht)
- Kinderhort/Schülerhort (Betreuung von 6–15jährigen Kindern nach Schulende bis zum Spätnachmittag).

Diese Einrichtungstypen bestehen sowohl als selbständige Einrichtungen als auch in verschiedener Kombination. Sie werden zumeist von Kommunen (Zuständigkeitsbereich des → *Jugendamtes),* Verbänden, Kirchen, Betrieben oder privaten Trägern unterhalten. Die Mitarbeiter sind qualifizierte Fachkräfte mit einer Ausbildung als Sozialpädagoge/in *(→ Sozialarbeiter/Sozialpädagoge)* und → *Erzieher/in* und Kinderpfleger/in *(→ Mitarbeiter der Jugendhilfe)* überwiegend in Helferfunktion.

Die Kindergärten werden nicht zum Schulwesen gerechnet, aber trotz ihrer Zuordnung zur Jugendhilfe als Einrichtungen der Elementarstufe des Bildungswesens angesehen. Ihr Besuch ist freiwillig. Im Mittelpunkt der erzieherischen Arbeit steht eine spielorientierte und lebensnahe Sozialerziehung, in die der Aufbau von Selbstvertrauen und der Erwerb von elementaren Sachkompetenzen eingebunden ist.

Ein Teil der Kindergärten wird als Kindertagesstätten geführt, in denen insbesondere Kinder erwerbstätiger Eltern ganztägig erzieherisch betreut und verpflegt werden.

Manche größeren Betriebe unterhalten Betriebskindergärten zur Betreuung der Kinder von Betriebsangehörigen.

sponsibility. This responsibility includes the planning of and timely proposals for adequate establishments and services.

The *Subsidiaritätsprinzip* primarily defines the relationship between the statutory and voluntary bodies and the individual.

UK

The concept of *Subsidiarität* is not a major aspect of British socio-political thinking in the UK, but the basic idea is not alien to British social policy (cf. Beveridge Plan 1942).

Day Care Establishments for Children and Young People

G

These comprise all socio-educational establishments designed to complement or assist the family. Such centres care for children throughout the day or part of the day. Day care establishments for children and young people include:

- the crêche (for infants under one)
- the toddlers' group (small children from 1 to under 3 years)
- the nursery school (children from 3–6 years, i.e. until the beginning of compulsory education)
- day care centre (for children from 6–15 years after school hours until late afternoon) (N.B. school hours in Germany end at lunch time.)

These types of establishments exist as independent units or in various combinations. In most cases they are run by the local authorities (i.e. under the competence of the youth office → *Jugendamt)*, voluntary organisations, churches, factories, institutions or private persons. Day care centre staff must be trained and qualified as → *Sozialarbeiter/Sozialpädagoge* and → Erzieher or nursery assistants (→ *Mitarbeiter der Jugendhilfe)*. The latter are mainly employed in an ancillary function.

Nursery schools are not generally considered as part of the school system. But despite of their position under the terms of reference of youth work and youth welfare services they continue to be seen as the lowest level of the education system. Attendance at nursery schools is voluntary. Teaching at these schools focuses on social education, which is based on play and the children's everyday life experience. The development of self-assurance and elementary skills is part of the educational concept.

Some of the nursery schools are run as day care centres catering escpecially for children of working mothers. The children attend during day-time and take their meals in the respective establishment.

In den Schulkindergärten (in Bremen und Hessen Vorklassen), die zumeist den Grundschulen zugeordnet sind, sollen Kinder, die nicht altersgemäß entwickelt sind, auf den Besuch der Schule vorbereitet werden.

Die Finanzierung dieser Einrichtungen erfolgt durch öffentliche Mittel, Eigenmittel der Träger und Beiträge der Eltern. Der Beitrag der Eltern richtet sich nach dem durch öffentliche Mittel oder eigene Mittel der Träger nicht abdeckbaren Defizit.

VK

In England bestehen für Kinder ab drei Jahren Kindergärten, separate Kinderklassen oder Kinderklassen in Grundschulen. Es gibt zudem die Möglichkeit der Teilnahme an informellen Vorschul-Spielgruppen, die von Eltern und freien Trägern organisiert werden.

Die Schulpflicht beginnt mit fünf Jahren. Von dieser Altersgrenze ab gehen Kinder in England und Wales in Kinderschulen oder Vorschulklassen. In Schottland bestehen an den Grundschulen normalerweise eigene Klassen für Kinder unter sieben Jahren; daneben gibt es in manchen Gegenden getrennte Kinderschulen.

In begrenztem Umfang bestehen Tageseinrichtungen für Kinder unter fünf Jahren, die die sozialen Dienste, mitunter auf Betreiben der Eltern, bereitstellen. Bei der Zuteilung von Plätzen in Tageseinrichtungen für Kinder und in anderen Angeboten, die die Kommunalbehörden selbst unterhalten, werden Kinder mit besonderen Bedürfnissen bevorzugt behandelt. Die Kommunalbehörden führen Register, gewähren finanzielle Unterstützung und unterhalten Beratungsdienste für Tagesmütter, private Kindertagesstätten und Spielgruppen in ihrem Zuständigkeitsbereich.

Die Mitarbeiter von Kindergärten und Tageseinrichtungen für Kinder durchlaufen eine zwei Jahre umfassende nicht akademische Ausbildung in der Betreuung und Berücksichtigung der spezifischen Bedürfnisse von Kindern im Vorschulalter (→ *Erzieher*, VK).

Träger (m/pl) der Jugendhilfe (f)

D

Öffentliche und freie Träger, die Aufgaben der → *Jugendhilfe* übernehmen. Öffentliche Träger der Jugendhilfe sind örtliche und überörtliche Behörden, denen das Jugendhilfegesetz (KJHG) (→ *Jugendgesetze)* bestimmte Jugendhilfeaufgaben überträgt (z.B. Jugendamt, Landesjugendamt). Freie Träger der Jugendhilfe sind nicht-öffentliche, gemeinnützige Zusammenschlüsse, die selbständig und freiwillig Jugendhilfeaufgaben leisten. Zu ihnen gehören die freien Vereinigungen der Jugendwohlfahrt, Wohlfahrtsverbände, die Jugend-

Some of the bigger factories and institutions run factory nurseries for the children of their employees.

School kindergartens (in Bremen and Hesse referred to as pre-school classes), which are mostly integrated into the primary school, cater for school-age children not yet mature enough for school but being prepared to meet the demands of school life.

These establishments are financed from public and/or private funds, and the fees paid by the parents. The latter depend on the remainder of cost which is left over after deducting the public funds allotted or the organisers' own means.

UK

In England, children from the age of three years onwards may attend nursery schools or classes or infants' classes in primary schools. In addition, many children attend informal pre-school play groups organised by parents and voluntary bodies.

Compulsory education begins at five when children in England and Wales go to infant schools or departments. In Scotland, the primary schools normally have infant classes for children under seven, although in a few areas there are separate infant schools.

Limited day care facilities for children under five are provided by social services sometimes on parents' initiative. In allocating places in day nurseries and other facilities that they themselves provide, local authorities give priority to children with special needs. They also register and provide support and advice services for childminders, private day nurseries and play groups operating in their areas.

The staff of nursery schools and day care facilities follow a non-graduate two-year training course in the care and needs of pre-school age children (→ *Erzieher*, UK).

Bodies Responsible for Youth Work and Youth Welfare Services

G

These are the statutory authorities and voluntary organisations with responsibilities in the field of youth work and youth welfare services (→ *Jugendhilfe*). The statutory authorities of youth work and youth welfare services at the local and above-local level derive their functions from the Child and Youth Services Act (→ *Jugendgesetze*/KJHG) (e.g. the youth work and youth welfare offices, the *Land* youth work and youth welfare offices). Voluntary organisations of

verbände, juristische Personen, deren Zweck es ist, das Wohl der Jugend zu fördern, insbesondere eingetragene → *Vereine,* sowie die Kirchen.

VK

Spezifisch deutsche Gegebenheit

Umweltschutz (m)

D

Der Schutz unserer Umwelt ist eine der wichtigsten Fragen unserer Zeit, und Fragen des Umweltschutzes und des umweltgerechten Verhaltens treten seit mehr als 15 Jahren immer mehr in den Vordergrund der öffentlichen Diskussion. In allen Bundesländern gibt es Umweltministerien, und 1986 wurde auch das Bundesministerium für Umwelt, Naturschutz und Reaktorsicherheit eingerichtet. Viele Umweltschutzbestimmungen wurden in den vergangenen Jahren neu erlassen. Außerdem wird der Umweltbildung und Umwelterziehung in allen Bildungsgängen vom Kindergarten über Schulen und Universitäten bis hin zu Einrichtungen der Erwachsenenbildung große Bedeutung beigemessen.

Gerade bei der Jugend wird ein zunehmendes Interesse an Umwelt- und Naturschutzfragen festgestellt. In den Jugendbildungsstätten ist Umweltpädagogik ein konzeptioneller Schwerpunkt; mehr und mehr jugendlichen Arbeitslosen wird durch aktive Mitarbeit bei Naturschutzprojekten eine Beschäftigungsmöglichkeit geboten. Auch bei den Jugendverbänden ist Umwelt- und Naturschutz immer mehr Bestandteil der Jugendarbeit. Die Jugendorganisationen leisten praktische Arbeitseinsätze zum Schutz der gefährdeten Natur, sie führen Naturschutzseminare, Umwelttage und Podiumsdiskussionen zum Thema durch und engagieren sich aktiv bei Demonstrationen in Sachen Naturschutz.

VK

In den letzten Jahren tritt sowohl bei Regierungsbehörden als auch bei privaten Organisationen die Sorge um den Umwelt- und Naturschutz immer mehr in den Vordergrund.

Auf Regierungsebene ist das *Department of the Environment* für die Belange des Umweltschutzes bei Landnutzungsplänen, Wohnungsbau und Städteplanung sowie für Landschaftspflege und den Schutz der Umwelt zuständig. Die unterschiedlichsten Gruppierungen, darunter viele freie Träger, engagieren sich aktiv in der Umweltbewegung. Die freien Träger haben sich auf nationaler Ebene im *National Council for Environmental Conservation* zusam-

youth work and youth welfare services are non-statutory and non-profitmaking associations which operate independently and on a voluntary basis. They include the voluntary associations of youth welfare, the welfare organisations, the youth organisations, corporate bodies aiming to promote the welfare of young people, particular registered associations (→ *Verband/Verein),* and the churches.

UK
Relevant only for the FRG

Environmental and Nature Conservation

G

The protection of the environment is one of the major concerns of our times and issues concerning the protection of the environment and environmental behaviour have focussed public discussion for more than 15 years. Each Federal *Land* has its own Ministry of the Environment. A Federal Ministry of the Environment, Nature Conservation and Reactor Safety was established in 1986. Many new directives dealing with environmental matters were launched in recent years. Emphasis is also put on environmental education at all levels, e.g. from kindergarten to schools, universities and further and adult education centres.

It is above all young people who show an increased interest in environmental and nature conservation. In the programmes of the youth educational training centres attention is also focussed on environmental education. Active participation in conservation projects provides more and more employed young people with job opportunities. Involvement in environmental issues has been integrated into the work of many youth organisations. They participate in practical conservation projects in order to protect our threatened nature, they arrange nature conservation seminars and panel discussions and also participate in demonstrations in favour of nature conservation.

UK
There has been increased concern by both government and other organisations in Britain about environmental and nature protection in recent years.

The official body responsible for the environment is the Department of the Environment, which brings together the major responsibilities for land-use planning, housing and construction, countryside policy and environmental protection. A wide range of groups, including many voluntary organisations, are active in the conservation movement. The National Council for Environmental Conservation is the national coalition of non-governmental organisations which focusses attention on major issues.

mengeschlossen, der das Interesse der Öffentlichkeit auf wichtige Fragen lenkt.

Auch viele Jugendorganisationen setzen sich tatkräftig für den Umweltschutz ein. Reinigungsarbeiten in Gestrüpp und Unterholz, das Fällen oder Pflanzen von Bäumen, das Anlegen von Hecken und Zäunen usw. sind typisch für diese Bewegung. Der *British Trust for Conservation Volunteers* bietet Jugendlichen über 16 Jahren die Möglichkeit, an Wochenenden oder während der Ferien ehrenamtlich Naturschutzarbeiten durchzuführen.

Der *Council for Environmental Education* ist die nationale Koordinierungsstelle zur Förderung der Umwelterziehung. Seine Jugendabteilung unterstützt und fördert die außerschulische Umwelterziehung besonders durch die freien und öffentlichen Träger der Jugendhilfe.

Verein (m)/Verband (m)

D

Verband (Organisationsform)
Eine Organisationsform für Fachvereinigungen der Jugendhilfe und insbesondere auch Jugendorganisationen ist die des Verbandes. Ein Verband ist ein Zusammenschluß von natürlichen oder juristischen Personen zur Förderung gemeinsamer Interessen, insbesondere wirtschaftlicher, sozialer, kultureller und politischer Art. Verbände haben vielfach die Rechtsform eines eingetragenen Vereins und können fachlich oder regional zu Landes- und Bundesverbänden zusammengeschlossen sein (Dach- oder Spitzenverbände).

Verein (Rechtsform)
In der Regel werden Träger der Jugendhilfe in der Rechtsform eines „eingetragenen Vereins" (e.V.) geführt. Ein eingetragener Verein ist ein körperschaftlicher Zusammenschluß von mindestens sieben Personen (auch freien und/oder öffentlichen Trägern), der einen einheitlichen Namen führt, auf Dauer eingerichtet und vom Wechsel seiner Mitglieder unabhängig ist.

Der rechtsfähige Verein setzt einen Gründungsvertrag zwischen den künftigen Mitgliedern, welcher die Satzung des zukünftigen Vereins enthalten muß, und die Eintragung in das Vereinsregister des zuständigen Amtsgerichtes voraus. Der Name des Vereins enthält dann den Zusatz „e.V." (eingetragener Verein).

Der e.V. besitzt zwei Organe:
a) die Mitgliederversammlung, die als oberstes Organ durch ihre Beschlußfassung die Angelegenheiten des Vereins erledigt,
b) den von ihr zu bestellenden Vorstand, welcher die Satzung eines gesetzlichen Vertreters innehat.

Zur Durchführung ihrer satzungsmäßigen Aufgaben besitzen Vereine oftmals eine Geschäftsstelle mit mehreren hauptamtlichen und/oder eh-

Many youth organisations actively participate in conservation work. Typical tasks include clearing scrub and undergrowth, felling and planting trees, fencing, hedging, etc. The British Trust for Conservation Volunteers provides facilities for young people over 16 who wish to do voluntary work in the countryside by organising parties at weekends and during holidays to carry out conservation work.

The Council for Environmental Education is the national coordinating body for the promotion of environmental education. Its Youth Unit promotes and encourages out-of-school environmental education particularly within the voluntary and statutory youth service.

Association/Society/Club

G

Association (organisational form)
The *Verband* is a structure for specialist groups concerned with youth work and youth welfare services and, in particular, for youth organisations. A *Verband* is an association of individuals or corporate bodies which promotes common interests, in particular economic, social, cultural and political interests. In many cases a *Verband* has the legal form of a registered association (→ *Verein*) and several may join together to form a larger organisation at the *Land* or Federal level depending on their specialism or on a regional umbrella organisation.

Association (legal form)
As a rule, the bodies responsible for youth work and youth welfare services take the legal form of a "registered association". A registered association is a body corporate of at least seven persons (which may also be voluntary or statutory bodies). It has a specific name, is not limited in its duration, and is not affected by changes in its membership.

In order to obtain full legal capacity for the registered association, the future members must agree on a memorandum of association which must contain the statutes of the association-to-be. It is then entered into the register of associations of the competent German local court *(Amtsgericht)*. The letters e.V. *(eingetragener Verein)* are added to the name.

The registered association comprises:
a) the assembly of members which is the supreme body whose function is to pass decisions on the association's business matters,
b) the executive committee which is elected by the assembly of members. The executive committee has the status of a legal representative.

renamtlichen Mitarbeitern unter Leitung eines Geschäftsführers oder Direktors.

Im Bereich der Jugendhilfe bestehen im wesentlichen eingetragene Vereine mit anerkannter Gemeinnützigkeit, d.h. sie leisten ihre auf das allgemeine Wohl gerichtete Arbeit ohne Gewinnerzielungsabsicht.

VK

Im allgemeinen stehen *associations, clubs* und *societies* in Großbritannien nicht auf einer festgefügten juristischen Basis. Die überwiegende Mehrzahl erlangt Anerkennung durch ihre Arbeit und die Solidität ihres Managements.

Das Management liegt in der Regel in den Händen der *officers* (des Vorstands) und des → *management committee,* die anläßlich der Jahres-Mitgliederversammlung des jeweiligen Trägers demokratisch gewählt werden. Die *officers,* die für die Führung der Geschäfte des Trägers verantwortlich sind und die Beschlüsse der Mitgliederversammlung durchführen, sind grundsätzlich ein Vorsitzender, ein *secretary* und ein Schatzmeister. Bei größeren Trägern können weitere Vorstandsmitglieder hinzukommen, z.B. ein stellvertretender Vorsitzender, ein *membership secretary* (Verantwortlicher für die Mitgliedschaft) usw. In manchen Fällen wird ein nicht gewählter hauptamtlicher Geschäftsführer beschäftigt, der dem gewählten *secretary* gegenüber weisungsgebunden ist. Träger mit dieser Organisationsstruktur sind die nächste britische Entsprechung zum deutschen Verband.

Wenn eine *association,* ein *club* oder eine *society* eine Rechtsform haben, bedeutet dies meist die Anerkennung der Gemeinnützigkeit. Das bedingt die Errichtung eines *trust* (Treuhandverhältnis) oder einer *company limited by guarantee* (Gesellschaft mit beschränkter Nachschußpflicht). Dies ist die nächste britische Entsprechung zum deutschen Verein. Bei einer als *trust* konstituierten *association* ist die schriftlich niedergelegte Grundordnung der *Trust Deed* (Treuhandvertrag). Die *company limited by guarantee* arbeitet aufgrund eines *Memorandum* (Gründungsurkunde) sowie der *Articles of Association* (Satzung), die im *Companies Registration Office* (Gesellschaftsregister) in Cardiff (England und Wales) eingetragen werden.

Von freien Trägern der Jugendarbeit, die die Zuschüsse, Dienste und Einrichtungen des *youth and community service* (→ *Jugendarbeit,* UK) der Kommunalbehörden in Anspruch nehmen wollen, wird erwartet, daß sie sich bei dieser Behörde eintragen lassen und ein solides Management nachweisen.

Oben beschriebene Organisationen, die ausschließlich gemeinnützige Arbeit leisten und die Bedingungen des *Charities Act 1960* erfüllen, müssen sich bei den *Charity Commissioners* in London oder Liverpool, beim *Home and Health Department* in Edinburgh oder beim *Department of Finance* in Belfast als *Charity* (Wohltätigkeitsorganisation) registrieren lassen, wenn sie Steuerbefreiung bei *Her Majesty's Inland Revenue Service* erlangen wollen.

In order to carry out the responsibilities laid down in the statutes, registered associations often have offices with several full-time staff and/or voluntary workers, headed by an executive secretary or director.

In youth work and youth welfare services, for the most part, there are registered associations whose work is recognised as non-profitmaking and as being in the public interest.

UK
Generally, associations, clubs and societies in Britain do not have a fundamental legal basis for their existence. The great majority of them achieve recognition by their activities and the soundness of their management.

The management would normally be in the hands of the officers and committee who are elected democratically by the members at the annual general meeting (AGM) of the organisation. The officers, who are responsible for the day-to-day running of the organisation, implementing policy as decided at the AGM, are basically a chairman, a secretary and a treasurer; in larger organisations there would be additional officers, e.g. a vice-chairman, a membership secretary, etc. In some instances a non-elected, full-time administrative secretary may be employed but he would be subservient to the elected secretary. Organisations so structured are the nearest UK equivalent to the German *Verband*.

Where an association, club or society has a legal basis often it will have charitable status and therefore be constituted as a trust or a company limited by guarantee, and is the closest VK equivalent to the German *Verein*. If an association was formed as a trust, the basic document would be the Trust Deed; in the case of a company limited by guarantee there would normally be a Memorandum and Articles of Association, and it would be recorded at the Companies Registration Office in Cardiff.

Non-statutory youth organisations wishing to make use of the grants, services and facilities offered by a local authority's youth and community service would be expected to register with that authority and provide evidence of a sound management structure.

Any organisation described above, engaged solely in charitable works under the terms of the Charities Act, 1960 and wishing to avoid taxation by Her Majesty's Inland Revenue Service, would register as a charity with the Charity Commissioners in London or Liverpool, the Home and Health Department in Edinburgh and the Department of Finance in Belfast.

Vormundschaft (f)

D

Ein Vormund kann bestellt werden, wenn ein Minderjähriger nicht (mehr) unter → *elterlicher Sorge* steht (z.B. Tod der Eltern, Entzug des Sorgerechts, mangelnde Eignung beider Elternteile nach der Scheidung) oder wenn Volljährige entmündigt sind. Ferner tritt sie kraft Gesetzes z.B. für ein Kind ein, dessen unverheiratete Mutter minderjährig ist.

Der Vormund wird vom Vormundschaftsgericht bestellt. Dabei sollen möglichst Verwandte und Verschwägerte berufen werden. Ansonsten sucht ihn das Vormundschaftsgericht nach Anhörung des → *Jugendamtes* nach seinem Ermessen aus. Ist keine geeignete Einzelperson vorhanden, kann es auch ein Verein sein. Letzte Möglichkeit ist die Amtsvormundschaft des Jugendamtes selbst.

Vormundschaft ist ein Amt, das man grundsätzlich zu übernehmen verpflichtet ist.

Der Vormund ist gesetzlicher Vertreter des Mündels. Seine Personensorge entspricht der elterlichen Sorge. Er braucht aber zu einer Reihe von Rechtsakten die Genehmigung des Vormundschaftsgerichts. Die Vermögenssorge unterliegt einer strengen Aufsicht des Vormundschaftsgerichts. Diesem hat der Vormund regelmäßig zu berichten.

VK

Nach englischem Recht haben Mutter oder Vater die Möglichkeit, durch Testament einen Vormund einzusetzen, um Vorsorge für die Betreuung des Kindes nach ihrem Tode zu treffen. Außerdem kann die Abteilung Familie des *High Court* (Oberster Gerichtshof für England und Wales) auf Antrag einen Vormund bestellen, wenn ein Kind keinen Verwandten oder Vormund besitzt und auch sonst niemand da ist, dem die elterliche Sorge übertragen wurde.

Bei Entscheidungen über eine Vormundschaft muß das Gericht in erster Linie das Wohl des Kindes berücksichtigen.

Die Vormundschaft kann sich auf die Person des Kindes, auf sein Vermögen oder aber auf beides beziehen. Der Vormund für die Person des Kindes besitzt keine Verfügungsgewalt über sein Vermögen, und der Vormund für das Vermögen eines Minderjährigen hat nicht über seine Person zu bestimmen. Ein Vormund mit beiden Vollmachten besitzt im großen und ganzen dieselben Rechte und Pflichten wie die natürlichen Eltern, wobei das Gericht die allgemeine Aufsicht führt. Die Beziehung zwischen Vormund und Mündel unterliegt stets dem anglo-amerikanischen Rechtsinstitut des Treuhandverhältnisses. Wenn nicht ein kürzerer Zeitraum festgesetzt wird, ein Fall, der eintreten kann, sofern ein Elternteil nur vorübergehend nicht in der Lage ist, für ein

Guardianship

G

A guardian may be appointed for a minor who is (no longer) in parental custody (→ *elterliche Sorge*) (e.g. his/her parents are dead; parental rights and responsibilities have been withdrawn; after divorce neither of the divorcees is suitable to be given all parental rights and responsibilities) or for adults who have been legally incapacitated. Guardianship for a child may also be established by force of law, e.g. as long as an unmarried mother is not of age.

The guardian is appointed by the Guardianship Court. If possible, relatives and in-laws should be appointed as guardians. Otherwise, after having consulted with the youth office (→ *Jugendamt)* the Guardianship Court selects a guardian as it sees fit. If there is no suitable individual guardianship may also be vested in an association. The final possibility is to entrust guardianship to the local authority, i.e. the youth office itself.

Guardianship is an office which one is under an obligation to take on as a matter of principle.

The guardian is the legal representative of the ward. He is given care and custody of the ward, which equal all parental rights and duties. However, he must obtain authorization from the Guardianship Court for a number of legal acts. The statutory duty of care for a minor's property is strictly supervised by the Guardianship Court. The guardian must report to this court at regular intervals.

UK

Under English law a guardian may be appointed by the father or mother of a child by will so as to make provision for care of the child after the parent's death. In addition, the Family Division of the High Court may appoint a guardian on application where a child has no parent or guardian or other person having parental rights with respect to him.

In making decisions about guardianship the court is obliged to regard the child's welfare as the first and paramount consideration.

Guardianship may be either of the minor's person or of his estate or both. A guardian of the person has no authority over the minor's property and a guardian of his estate has no authority over his person. A person who is guardian both of the minor's person and of the estate has broadly speaking the same rights and responsibilities with regard to the child as a natural parent has, subject to the general supervision of the court. The relationship between guardian and ward is in all cases that of trustee and beneficiary. Unless a shorter period is set, which may be the case when e.g. a parent's inability to care for the child is merely temporary, a guardian continues in office until the minor reaches the age of majority (18), or, if the minor is a female, until she marries.

Kind zu sorgen, behält der Vormund sein Amt, bis der Minderjährige volljährig wird (18 Jahre) oder bei Mädchen bis zur Verehelichung.

Neben der Bestellung eines Vormundes hat die Abteilung Familie des *High Court* die Möglichkeit, einen Amtspfleger zu ernennen, wenn es im Interesse des Kindes erforderlich ist.

Der Antrag auf Ernennung eines Amtspflegers an die Abteilung Familie des *High Court* muß nicht von einem Verwandten gestellt werden. Auch andere sind dazu berechtigt. Amtspflege wird vor allem dann beantragt, wenn ernsthafte Bedenken wegen des Verhaltens, einer Beeinflussung oder der Behandlung des Kindes bestehen.

Amtspflege bleibt bis zum 18. Lebensjahr des Minderjährigen bestehen. Anordnungen, die seinen Unterhalt oder seine Erziehung betreffen, können jedoch bis zum 21. Lebensjahr fortgesetzt werden.

Bei bedeutsamen Entscheidungen für das Leben des Mündels wie Eheschließung, Schulbesuch und Vermögensverwaltung besitzt das Gericht umfangreiche Vollmachten. Die Bestellung eines Vormundes soll gewährleisten, daß keine schwerwiegenden Schritte ohne die Zustimmung des Gerichts unternommen werden. In der Praxis ist es jedoch nicht möglich, das Verhalten eines Kindes im täglichen Lebensablauf durch ein Gericht zu regeln.

Wandern (n)

D

Das Wandern hat in Deutschland eine lange Tradition. Waren es früher Handwerker und Studenten, die den Lernort ständig wechselten, solange sie noch nicht ihre volle berufliche Qualifikation erlangt hatten, so bedeutet Wandern heute mehr eine Freizeitbeschäftigung. Sowohl Kinder als auch Erwachsene sollen durch das Wandern die Heimat, die Natur, die Landschaft, Pflanzen, Tiere und Menschen entdecken und beobachten. Insbesondere das Schulwandern ist seit der Jahrhundertwende hier Tradition geworden. Der Lehrer Richard Schirrmann, der mit seiner Klasse regelmäßig Wanderfahrten unternahm, gründete dann 1912 die erste Jugendherberge, um seinen Schülern eine feste Unterkunft zu garantieren. Daraus entwickelte sich das Deutsche Jugendherbergswerk (DJH), eine der wichtigsten Institutionen zur Förderung des Wanderns. Als eine seiner vorrangigsten Aufgaben betrachtet das DJH die Gesundheitspflege, für die es mit seinen Einrichtungen einen Rahmen für Jugendliche und Erwachsene bietet. Jugendliche, Familien, Einzelwanderer und Gruppen können in Jugendherbergen günstig übernachten. Diese stehen an vielen Wanderwegen und ermöglichen so Rund- oder Sternwanderungen.

Immer beliebter werden Volkswanderungen; das sind organisierte Unternehmungen, an denen sich oft Tausende von Wanderern beteiligen. Auch hier,

In addition to its powers to appoint a guardian, the Family Division of the High Court may make a child a ward of court if it is in the interests of the child's welfare to do so.

Anyone can apply to the Family Division of the High Court to have someone under 18 made a ward of court. The person does not have to be a relative. The application is most likely to be made where someone disapproves of the way the child is behaving or the way another person is influencing or treating the child.

Once made a ward of court, a juvenile remains so until the age of 18. Maintenance or education orders can, however, be continued until the ward is 21.

The court has extensive power over the major decisions of a ward's life such as marriage, education and control of property. An official guardian is appointed to ensure no major steps are taken without the court's agreement. In practice, however, the court cannot regulate the day-to-day behaviour of the ward.

Hiking

G

Hiking has a long tradition in Germany. In former times, craftsmen and students often changed their place of training or study until they obtained full qualification. Today, hiking is more of a leisure-time activity. On a walking tour children and grown-ups alike rediscover and observe their home country, nature, the countryside, plants, animals and human beings. School hikes, in particular, have become a standard practice since the turn of the century. The teacher Richard Schirrmann, who regularly went on hiking expeditions with his form, later founded the first youth hostel in 1912 in order to have fixed accommodation for his pupils. Out of this action grew the German Youth Hostel Association, one of the most important institutions to promote hiking. The German Youth Hostel Association considers a healthy way of life as one of its prime aims, its various establishments providing a suitable framework for this for young people and adults. Young persons, families, individual hikers and groups may stay at youth hostels overnight, finding accommodation at inexpensive rates. The hostels are situated along the many hiking trails and thus enable the hosteller to walk on a circular route or to follow different routes to the same eventual destination.

People's walking tours are becoming more and more popular. These are organised walks in which often thousands of hikers take part. Here, as for other walk-

wie bei allen anderen Wanderungen, muß die Strecke sorgfältig geplant werden; sie sollte 25 Kilometer pro Tag auf keinen Fall überschreiten.

Heimat- und Gebirgs- und Wandervereine sowie andere Institutionen haben in der Bundesrepublik ca. 160.000 km gekennzeichnete Wanderwege angelegt, die an das Netz der europäischen Wanderwege angeschlossen sind. Neben der Pflege des Wegenetzes betrachten sie, genau wie das Deutsche Jugendherbergswerk, es als eine ihrer wichtigsten Aufgaben, die Bevölkerung über Umweltrisiken in der bedrohten Natur aufzuklären.

VK

Wie in Deutschland liegen auch in Großbritannien die Ursprünge des Wanderns in den Reisen der Handwerkslehrlinge und Studenten, die durch die Lande zogen, um eine möglichst umfassende Ausbildung zu erwerben. Heute wird Wandern als eine gesunde und erholsame Freizeitbeschäftigung angesehen.

Rambling (to ramble: Spazierengehen/wandern zum Vergnügen, mit oder ohne festgelegte Route, Concise Oxford Dictionary, 6. Aufl.) ist eine sehr beliebte Version dieses Sports. Die *Ramblers' Association* zählt 40.000 Mitglieder in 220 Ortsgruppen. Sie organisiert Veranstaltungen und nimmt die Interessen ihrer Mitglieder in der Öffentlichkeit wahr, vor allem auch im Parlament und in *Whitehall,* wo sie auf die Minister einwirkt und den *Royal Commissions* (vom Parlament beauftragte Untersuchungskommissionen) Eingaben zuleitet, die darauf zielen, Natur und Landschaft zu schützen sowie den Menschen das Recht zu erhalten, das Land bei ihren Wanderungen zu durchqueren. Rechte dieser Art werden gesetzlich festgelegt und geschützt. Die *Ramblers' Association* macht ihren Einfluß geltend, um die Eintragung des Wegerechts für die Öffentlichkeit auf den Meßtischblättern der nationalen Landesvermessung sicherzustellen. Der Verein hat auch einen Beitrag zur Schaffung von Langstrecken-Wanderwegen geleistet. Ein herausragendes Beispiel einer solchen ausgedehnten Route ist der *Pennine Way.* Die *Long Distance Walking Association,* die Wanderungen von mehr als 20 Meilen organisiert, hat heute etwa 6.000 Mitglieder. Im jährlich erscheinenden *Bed and Breakfast Guide* werden Übernachtungsmöglichkeiten aufgeführt, die besonders für Wanderer geeignet sind.

Die *Youth Hostel Association of England and Wales,* die *Scottish Youth Hostel Association,* die *Youth Hostel Association of Northern Ireland* und die *Irish Youth Hostel Association* wurden nach dem Vorbild des Deutschen Jugendherbergwerkes (DJH) in den Jahren 1930–31 gegründet. Die Arbeit dieser Organisationen weist viele Parallelen zum DJH auf. 1932 wurde das Internationale Jugendherbergswerk gegründet, dem heute 60 Länder angehören.

(s.a. → *The Duke of Edinburgh's Award Scheme)*

ing tours, the route which should not exceed 25 km per day must be planned carefully.

German regional associations, mountain walking and hiking associations, as well as other establishments have set up about 160,000 km of hiking trails which link up with the network of European hiking trails. In addition to caring for this network, such organisations and the German Youth Hostel Association consider spreading information on environmental risks as being one of their prime purposes.

UK

As in Germany, hiking in Britain has its origins in the journeys of apprentice craftsmen and students in their search for a wide and complete education. Today it is seen as a healthy form of recreation.

Rambling (ramble: v.i. & n. – Walk for pleasure, with or without definite route. Concise Oxford Dictionary 6th ed.), one version of the sport, is very popular and the Ramblers' Association with a membership of 40,000 in 220 local groups organises events and looks after the interests of its members. It is also vigilant at Parliament and in Whitehall where it lobbies ministers and makes submissions to Royal Commissions to preserve the countryside and maintain the right of the people to walk through it. Rights are defined and preserved by legislation. The Rambling Association maintains pressure to have public rights of way marked on the national Ordnance Survey maps. It has also been instrumental in the creation of long-distance footpaths, a prime example being the Pennine Way. The Long Distance Walking Association, which organises walks of in excess of 20 miles, has membership of about 6,000. The annual Bed and Breakfast Guide lists accommodation that especially welcomes walkers.

The Youth Hostel Association of England and Wales, the Scottish Youth Hostel Association, the Youth Hostel Association of Northern Ireland, the Irish Youth Hostel Association, following in the footsteps of the *Deutsches Jugendherbergswerk (DJH)*, were founded in the period 1930–31, and today their work closely parallels that of the DJH. In 1932 the International Youth Hostel Federation was formed; today it has 60 member countries.

(See also → *Duke of Edinburgh's Award Scheme*)

Wehrpflicht (f), allgemeine

D

Jeder männliche wehrfähige deutsche Bürger ist gesetzlich verpflichtet, Wehrdienst zu leisten. Die Verpflichtung zum Dienst in den Streitkräften (Bundeswehr) oder in einem Zivilschutzverband besteht vom vollendeten 18. Lebensjahr bis zum 45. Lebensjahr (Offiziere und Unteroffiziere und im Verteidigungsfall alle bis zum 60. Lebensjahr). Der Grundwehrdienst beträgt 12 Monate.

Das Grundgesetz gewährleistet das Recht auf Kriegsdienstverweigerung aus Gewissensgründen. Wehrpflichtige, die von diesem Recht Gebrauch machen wollen, müssen einen entsprechenden schriftlichen Antrag stellen. Der anerkannte Kriegsdienstverweigerer hat eine zivilen Ersatzdienst (Zivildienst) außerhalb der Bundeswehr zu leisten, der 15 Monate dauert.

Für die Durchführung des Zivildienstes ist das Bundesamt für Zivildienst zuständig. Anerkannte Einrichtungen und Beschäftigungsstellen für Zivildienstpflichtige bestehen vor allem im sozialen Bereich, in der individuellen Betreuung von Alten, Kranken und Behinderten sowie in Heimen und Krankenhäusern. Zivildienstleistende (ZDL) werden auch in anderen, dem Allgemeinwohl dienenden Bereichen wie dem Natur- und Umweltschutz beschäftigt.

VK

Im Vereinigten Königreich wurde die allgemeine Wehrpflicht 1959 abgeschafft. Ab 16 Jahren können junge Männer mit der Einwilligung der Eltern eine berufliche Laufbahn in den Streitkräften einschlagen. Junge Mädchen werden unter derselben Voraussetzung ab 17 Jahren aufgenommen.

Weiterbildung (f)

D

Hierunter versteht man jede Form organisierten Lernens nach Abschluß der ersten Bildungsphase und Aufnahme der Berufstätigkeit.

Die berufliche Fortbildung umfaßt organisierte Lehr- und Lernprozesse auf der Grundlage eines Berufes mit dem Ziel der berufsspezifischen Kenntniserweiterung. Berufliche Weiterbildung zielt auf eine Höherqualifizierung für spezifische Funktionen ab (z.B leitender Mitarbeiter in der Jugendhilfe).

Die Zusatzausbildung ist eine gesetzlich geregelte Weiterbildung. Sie führt zu einer Höherqualifizierung für ein anerkanntes Berufsbild.

Maßnahmen der Weiterbildung werden von Bund, Ländern und Gemeinden sowie freien Trägern angeboten. Auf der kommunalen Ebene ist als Einrichtung der Erwachsenenbildung und der schulischen Weiterbildung vor allem die Volkshochschule zu nennen, die zu relativ günstigen Sätzen eine breite Palette von Kursen für alle Altersstufen anbietet.

Liability for Military Service

G

Every able-bodied male citizen is liable to serve in the Armed Forces *(Bundeswehr)* or with a non-military national service association. This liability begins when a young man of German nationality completes his 18th year and ends at 45 years (for officers as well as non-commissioned officers, and in the case of an armed conflict it extends to the 60th year). Basic military service covers a period of 12 months.

The right of conscientious objection to military service is embodied in the Basic Law (constitution). Those liable to serve who wish to claim this right must submit a written application. A person recognised as a conscientious objector is subject to compulsory non-military national service outside the *Bundeswehr,* which covers a period of 15 months.

Compulsory non-military national service is administered by the *Bundesamt für Zivildienst.* Persons on compulsory non-military national service may work in the social sector, look after senior citizens individually, care for the sick and the handicapped or work in residential establishments and hospitals on condition that these jobs are recognised for the purpose. Other types of occupation are community service, nature conservation and environmental protection.

UK

In the UK, national service was abolished in 1959. At the age of 16, boys may join the Armed Forces as a career with their parents' permission. Girls may join at 17 years of age, also on the same conditions.

Further Education

G

The term further education denotes any form of structured learning after completion of the first phase of education and after the beginning of gainful employment.

Vocational further education comprises the structured process of teaching and learning after vocational education. The aim is to develop specific vocational skills. The intention of vocational further education is to upgrade one's qualification for specific functions (e.g. senior staff in youth work).

Additional training is that form of further education which is defined by the respective legal provisions. It is directed towards obtaining a higher qualification for the official requirements of a trade or profession.

Further education programmes are provided by the Federation, the *Länder* and local authorities, as well as voluntary bodies. At local level there are adult education centres (offering a wide variety of courses for all age groups at fairly

In einigen Bundesländern wird für Maßnahmen der Weiterbildung vom Arbeitgeber Bildungsurlaub in Form von Freistellung von den beruflichen Pflichten bei Lohnfortzahlung gewährt.

VK

Im Vereinigten Königreich bezeichnet der Begriff *further education* alle Formen des organisierten Lernens nach Verlassen der Schule, jedoch mit Ausnahme der Universitäten: Er umfaßt die schulische Fortbildung auf der Ebene der Sekundarstufe (*A-level* oder darunter/→ *Bildungswesen*, VK) für Schulabgänger von 16 bis 19 Jahren. Kurse der Sekundarstufe und gelegentlich auch akademische Studiengänge findet man an den 740 Fortbildungs-Colleges, die fast alle unter der Aufsicht der kommunalen Erziehungsbehörden stehen. Auch die Einrichtungen der Erwachsenenbildung veranstalten Maßnahmen der schulischen Weiterbildung.

Die Bandbreite der Erwachsenenbildung und der *continuing education* (allgemeine und berufliche Weiterbildung) ist in den letzten Jahren größer geworden. Zusätzlich zur Entwicklung der Fähigkeiten des einzelnen durch kulturelle, sportliche und handwerkliche Aktivitäten gehören heute auch die Bereiche der elementaren Schulbildung (z.B. Lesen und Rechnen) dazu sowie Bildungsangebote für benachteiligte Gruppen und Gruppen mit besonderen Bedürfnissen. *Continuing education* schließt die berufliche Fortbildung für diejenigen ein, die bereits im Arbeitsleben stehen. Sie soll ihnen helfen, mit dem Fortgang der technologischen Entwicklung Schritt zu halten.

Neben von den Universitäten angebotenen Programmen des zweiten Bildungswegs gibt es Fortbildungsangebote der Kommunalbehörden, der Colleges mit Internatsunterbringung, der extramuralen, d.h. ausgegliederten Abteilungen von Universitäten, der Fernuniversitäten und verschiedener anderer Stellen einschließlich zahlreicher freier Träger. Die meisten Angebote machen die kommunalen Erziehungsbehörden in einer großen Palette von Einrichtungen. Zu diesen gehören die Abendschulen und in einigen Fällen die *community schools,* die Bildungsmöglichkeiten im schulischen, sozialen und kulturellen Bereich für alle Mitbürger bereitstellen.

Die extramuralen Abteilungen der Universitäten und die *Workers' Educational Association* (WEA), der größte anerkannte freie Träger, erhalten Förderungsmittel für die Durchführung von erweiterten Teilzeit-Kursen im Bereich der Allgemeinbildung sowie von Kurzlehrgängen für besondere (auch berufsspezifische) Interessen.

Das *National Institute of Adult Education* ist ein Informations-, Forschungs- und Publikationszentrum für die Erwachsenenbildung. Sein schottisches Gegenstück ist das *Scottish Institute of Adult Education.*

inexpensive rates) which also make provision for mature students wishing to obtain qualifications normally obtained during formal education.

In some *Länder* educational leave is granted to those wishing to take part in further education programmes. These people then get release from duties on full pay.

UK

In the UK, the term "further education" is used to define all post-school education outside the universities and includes non-advanced courses (of A-level standard or below (→ *Bildungswesen,* UK) for 16 to 19-year-olds who have left school. Non-advanced and some advanced courses are provided by 740 colleges of further education, almost all of them controlled by local education authorities. Non-advanced courses are also provided by adult education centres.

The scope of adult and continuing education has widened over recent years and now includes, in addition to the development of the individual through cultural, physical and craft pursuits, such subjects as basic education (for example, in literacy and numeracy); education for disadvantaged groups and those with special needs. Continuing education includes training for those in employment, to enable them to keep pace with technological change.

Besides university provision for mature students, courses are provided by local authorities, residential colleges, extramural departments of universities, the Open University and various other bodies including a number of voluntary organisations. Most of the provision is made by the local education authorities in a wide variety of establishments including schools used for adult evening classes and in some cases in "community schools" which provide educational, social and cultural opportunities for the wider community.

University extra-mural departments and the Workers' Educational Association (WEA), the largest recognised voluntary body, are grant-aided to provide extended part-time courses of liberal studies. They also run short courses for special (including vocational) interests.

The National Institute of Adult Education is a centre of information, research and publication for adult education. Its counterpart in Scotland is the Scottish Institute of Adult Education.

In Scotland the Scottish Community Education Council advises the Government on all community education matters and administers the Scottish Adult Education Unit.

In Norther Ireland the Council for Continuing Education advises the Department of Education on adult and continuing education matters.

In Schottland berät der *Scottish Community Education Council* die Regierung in allen Fragen der Gemeinwesenarbeit und verwaltet die *Scottish Adult Education Unit.*

In Nordirland obliegt die Beratung des Erziehungsministeriums im Bereich der Erwachsenenbildung, der allgemeinen Weiterbildung und der beruflichen Fortbildung dem *Council for Continuing Education.*

Wohlfahrtsverände (m/pl), freie

D

Private Träger, die neben den öffentlichen Trägern selbständig in der freien Wohlfahrtspflege tätig sind. Ihre Aufgabe ist die Sorge um notleidende oder gefährdete Mitmenschen. Sie arbeiten eng mit den Sozialhilfeträgern zusammmen. Die anerkannten Wohlfahrtsverbände, die auch Jugendhilfeaufgaben übernehmen (z.B. im Jugendhilfeausschuß, → *Jugendamt)* sind: Arbeiterwohlfahrt, Deutscher Caritasverband, Diakonisches Werk der Evangelischen Kirche in Deutschland, Deutscher Paritätischer Wohlfahrtsverband, Deutsches Rotes Kreuz, Zentralwohlfahrtsstelle der Juden in Deutschland.

VK

In Großbritannien übernehmen die freien Träger wichtige Aufgaben im Gesundheitswesen und in der Wohlfahrtspflege. Die Mehrzahl widmet sich der Arbeit mit besonderen Gruppen hilfsbedürftiger Menschen, z.B. Personen mit persönlichen und familiären Problemen, Kranken und Behinderten, Senioren usw. Die kommunalen Behörden und die Zentralregierung fördern ihre Zusammenarbeit mit den öffentlichen Trägern und gewähren den freien Trägern der Wohlfahrtspflege finanzielle Unterstützung.

Das bedeutendste Koordinierungsgremium in England ist der *National Council for Voluntary Organisations,* dessen Ziel es ist, die Arbeit der freien und öffentlichen Wohlfahrtsverbände zentral zu verknüpfen. (Ähnliche Aufgaben haben der *Scottish Council for Community and Voluntary Organisations* und der *Wales* bzw. der *Northern Ireland Council for Voluntary Action.)* Für die Koordinierung der Regierungsinteressen im Bereich der freien Wohlfahrtspflege in ganz Großbritannien ist ein *Home Office Voluntary Service Unit* zuständig.

Zu den großen nationalen Wohlfahrtsorganisationen gehören, um nur wenige Beispiele herauszugreifen, folgende Träger: *Family Welfare Association, British Red Cross Society, Women's Royal Voluntary Service, Church of England Council for Social Aid, Committee on Social Services of the Church of Scotland, Salvation Army.*

Welfare Organisations, Voluntary

G

These are private organisations engaged in voluntary welfare work additional to the statutory bodies. Their task is to care for the needy or persons at risk, and to work in close cooperation with bodies responsible for the discharge of social services. The recognised welfare organisations which also take on youth work and youth welfare responsibilities (e.g. within the Youth Services Committee, → *Jugendamt)* are the National Association for Workers' Welfare, the German Caritas Association, the Service Agency of the Protestant Church in Germany, the German Non-denominational Welfare Association, the German Red Cross Society, the Central Welfare Office of Jews in Germany.

UK

Voluntary organisations play an important role in health and social welfare in Britain. However, most of them specialize in working with one particular group of needy persons, e.g. people with personal and family problems, the sick and disabled, the aged, etc. Local and central government encourage their cooperation with the statutory sector and also give grants.

The main coordinating body in England, which aims to provide central links between voluntary welfare organisations and official bodies, is the National Council for Voluntary Organisations. (The Scottish Council for Community and Voluntary Organisations, the Wales and the Northern Ireland Councils for Voluntary Action perform similar functions.) Coordination of government interests in the voluntary sector throughout Britain is the responsibility of the Home Office Voluntary Service Unit.

Among the large national organisations are the Family Welfare Association, the British Red Cross Society, the Women's Royal Voluntary Service, the Church of England Council for Social Aid, the Committee on Social Services of the Church of Scotland, the Salvation Army, to name only a few.

Deutsches Stichwortverzeichnis
Index of German Key Words

Mädchenarbeit
Management Committee
Mitarbeiter/Mitarbeiterinnen der Jugendhilfe

Partizipation Jugendlicher
Pflegekinderbereich/Pflegekinderwesen
Pflegschaft

Rechtsinstrumente
Rehabilitation Behinderter

Schwangerschaftsabbruch
Sozialarbeit/Sozialpädagogik
Sozialarbeiter/Sozialpädagoge
Soziale Sicherung/Soziale Sicherheit

Sozialer Wohnungsbau
Sozialhilfe
Strafaussetzung zur Bewährung
Subsidiaritätsprinzip

Tageseinrichtungen für Kinder
Träger der Jugendhilfe

Umweltschutz

Verein/Verband
Vormundschaft

Wandern
Wehrpflicht, allgemeine
Weiterbildung
Wohlfahrtsverbände, freie

Anmerkung
Dank der sprachlichen und fachlichen Unterstützung der Mitglieder der Redaktionsgruppe für das Glossar konnten, soweit sinnvoll, deutsche Institutionen, Gremien und Rechtsbegriffe in die englische Sprache übersetzt werden. Von einer Übersetzung entsprechender britischer Bezeichnungen wurde in vielen Fällen abgesehen, da dies die Möglichkeiten der Arbeitsgruppe überstieg und deutscherseits amtliche Übersetzungen kaum zu ermitteln waren.

Note
Through the linguistic and substantive assistance of the committee who helped compile this Glossary and Handbook, the names of German institutions and bodies as well as legal terms were translated into English wherever this seemed helpful. In many cases, however, it was decided to refrain from translating the British phrases into German, as this exceeded the committee's technical capacity and official translations were difficult, if not impossible, to obtain on the German side.

Englisches Register
English Index

Britische Bezeichnungen ohne genaue Entsprechung in der Bundesrepublik
Deutschland (Teil III)
British terminology for which there is no exact equivalent in the FRG (Part III)

A-levels
→ *Bildungswesen, UK*

Act of Parliament
→ *Rechtsinstrumente, UK*

advanced course
→ *Ausbildungsförderung, UK*
→ *Bildungswesen, UK*
→ *Weiterbildung, UK*

Albemarle Report, 1960
→ *Jugendforschung, UK*

associaton
→ *Verein/Verband, UK*

Bachelor of Arts (BA)
→ *Bildungswesen, UK*
→ *Mitarbeiter der Jugendhilfe, UK*

Bachelor of Science (BSc)
→ *Bildungswesen, UK*

borstal
→ *Jugendstrafrecht, Maßnahmen des,
UK*

British Youth Council
→ *Jugendringe, UK*

care and control
→ *Elterliche Sorge, UK*

care order
→ *Jugendstrafrecht, Maßnahmen des,
UK*
→ *Strafaussetzung zur Bewährung, UK*

care proceedings
→ *Jugendstrafrecht, Maßnahmen des,
UK*

careers centre
→ *Berufsfindung/Berufsvorbereitung,
UK*

careers teacher
→ *Berufsfindung/Berufsvorbereitung,
UK*

Central Council for Education and
Training in Social Work (CCETSW)
→ *Sozialarbeiter/Sozialpädagoge, UK*

central institution
→ *Bildungswesen, UK*

Certificate of Qualification in Social
Work (CQSW)
→ *Mitarbeiter der Jugendhilfe, UK*
→ *Sozialarbeiter/Sozialpädagoge, UK*

Children Act, 1989
→ *Jugendgesetze, UK*

Children and Young Persons Acts
→ *Jugendgesetze, UK*

circular
→ *Rechtsinstrumente, UK*

club
→ *Verein/Verband, UK*

club-based youth organisations
→ *Jugendverbände, UK*

code of practice
→ *Rechtsinstrumente, UK*

collective agreement
→ *Rechtsinstrumente, UK*

education committee
→ *Jugendamt, UK*

Education Reform Act, 1988
→ *Jugendarbeit, UK*

Employment Department Group
→ *Bundesanstalt für Arbeit, UK*
→ *Jugendarbeitslosigkeit, UK*

Employment Training
→ *Bundesanstalt für Arbeit, UK*

Enterprise Allowance Scheme
→ *Jugendarbeitslosigkeit, UK*

extra-mural department
→ *Bildungswesen, UK*
→ *Weiterbildung, UK*

family credit
→ *Sozialhilfe, UK*

first degree
→ *Bildungswesen, UK*

further education college
→ *Bildungswesen, UK*
→ *Weiterbildung, UK*

General Certificate of Education (G.C.E.)
→ *Bildungswesen, UK*

General Certificate of Secondary Education (G.C.S.E.)
→ *Bildungswesen, UK*

graduate apprentice
→ *Berufsbildung, UK*

graduate course
→ *Sozialarbeiter/Sozialpädagoge, UK*

grammar school
→ *Bildungswesen, UK*

guardian *ad litem*
→ *Jugendstrafrecht, Maßnahmen des, UK*

higher education
→ *Bildungswesen, UK*

independent school
→ *Bildungswesen, UK*

infant classes
→ *Bildungswesen, UK*
→ *Tageseinrichtungen für Kinder, UK*

infant department
→ *Bildungswesen, UK*
→ *Tageseinrichtungen für Kinder, UK*

infant school
→ *Bildungswesen, UK*
→ *Tageseinrichtungen für Kinder, UK*

interim care order
→ *Jugendschutz, UK*

intermediate treatment centre
→ *Jugendstrafrecht, Maßnahmen des, UK*

Intermediate Treatment Programme
→ *Jugendfürsorge/Jugendpflege, UK*

jobclubs
→ *Bundesanstalt für Arbeit, UK*

junior attendance centre
→ *Jugendstrafrecht, Maßnahmen des, UK*

junior department
→ *Bildungswesen, UK*

junior school
→ *Bildungswesen, UK*

leader of the council
→ *Kommunale Selbstverwaltung, UK*

Licensing Act, 1964
→ *Jugendgesetze, UK*
→ *Jugendschutz, UK*

Magistrates Juvenile Court
→ *Jugendstrafrecht, Maßnahmen des, UK*

management committee
→ *Verein/Verband, UK*

Master of Arts (MA)
→ *Bildungswesen, UK*

Regionalisation
→ *IJAB, Youth Exchange Centre*

regulations
→ *Rechtsinstrumente, UK*

remand home
→ *Jugendstrafrecht, Maßnahmen des, UK*

Restart
→ *Jugendarbeitslosigkeit, UK*

rules
→ *Rechtsinstrumente, UK*

Scottish Certificate of Education (S.C.E.)
→ *Bildungswesen, UK*

Scottish Community Education Council (SCEC)
→ *Sozialarbeiter/Sozialpädagoge, UK*

second degree
→ *Bildungswesen, UK*
→ *Mitarbeiter der Jugendhilfe, UK*

secondary modern school
→ *Bildungswesen, UK*

secretary (of an association/club)
→ *Verein/Verband, UK*

secure accommodation order
→ *Jugendstrafrecht, Maßnahmen des, UK*

shop steward
→ *Betriebsrat, UK*

social worker
→ *Erzieher, UK*
→ *Mitarbeiter der Jugendhilfe, UK*
→ *Sozialarbeiter, UK*

society
→ *Verein/Verband, UK*

standards
→ *Bildungswesen, UK*

statute
→ *Rechtsinstrumente, UK*

supervision order
→ *Jugendstrafrecht, Maßnahmen des, UK*
→ *Strafaussetzung zur Bewährung, UK*

Thompson Report (Experience and Participation, 1982)
→ *Jugendarbeit, UK*
→ *Jugendforschung, UK*

Training Agency
→ *Berufsbildung, UK*
→ *Bundesanstalt für Arbeit, UK*
→ *Jugendarbeitslosigkeit, UK*

Training and Enterprise Councils (TECs)
→ *Bundesanstalt für Arbeit, UK*

undergraduate course
→ *Sozialarbeiter/Sozialpädagoge, UK*

uniformed (youth) organisations
→ *Jugendverbände, UK*

warden
→ *Jugendfreizeitstätten, UK*

YES
→ *Beratungsdienste, UK*

YIPLINKS
→ *Beratungsdienste, UK*

Young Scientists of the Year
→ *Jugendforschung, UK*

youth and community work
→ *Jugendarbeit, UK*
→ *Mitarbeiter der Jugendhilfe, UK*
→ *Sozialarbeiter/Sozialpädagoge, UK*

youth and community worker
→ *Sozialarbeiter/Sozialpädagoge, UK*

youth club
→ *Jugendfreizeitstätten, UK*

youth committee
→ *Jugendamt, UK*

youth custody
→ *Jugendstrafrecht, Maßnahmen des, UK*

Anhang

Appendices

Diagramm zum Bildungswesen der Bundesrepublik Deutschland

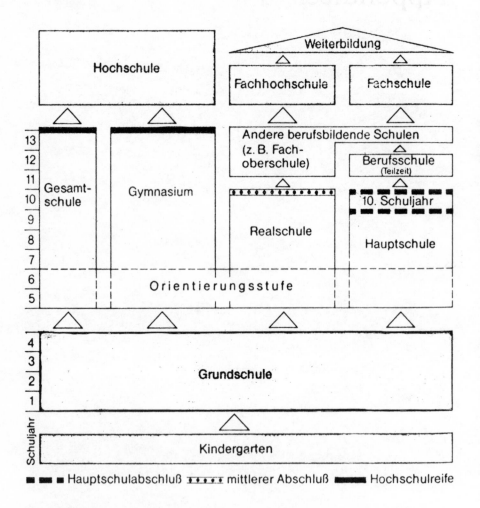

Quelle/Source:
Tatsachen über Deutschland, hg. vom Lexikon-Institut Bertelsmann, 6., neubearb. Aufl. 1989

Diagram of the Educational System in the United Kingdom

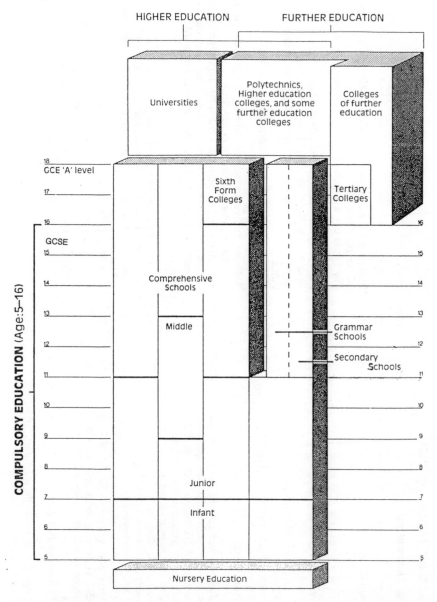

Quelle/Source:
Descriptions of the Vocational Training Systems (England and Wales), CEDEFOP 1984

Altersgrenzen im Jugendbereich

Bundesrepublik Deutschland	Alter	Alter	Vereinigtes Königreich
Beginn der Schulpflicht	6	5	Beginn der Unterrichtspflicht (Vollzeit-Unterricht in der Schule oder privat)
		U	Für Filme der Kategorie U (*Universal*) bestehen keine Einschränkungen
Besuch der jeweils für die Altersgruppe freigegebenen Filme	6,12	PG	Für Filme der Kategorie PG (*Parental Guidance*) ist der Besuch dem Gutdünken der Eltern überlassen.
Besuch der jeweils für die Altersgruppe freigegebenen Filme	16,18	15,18	Besuch der jeweils für die Altersgruppe freigegebenen Filme
Aktives und passives Wahlrecht für die Jugendvertretung im Betrieb	14	–	Keine Jugendvertretung in britischen Betrieben
Bedingte Strafmündigkeit	14	10	Bedingte strafrechtlicheVerantwortlichkeit je nach Fähigkeit, das begangene Unrecht einzusehen
Straftaten von Jugendlichen (14-18) werden in jedem Fall vor Jugendgerichten verhandelt; dies gilt auch für Heranwachsende (18-21), die zur Zeit der Tat nach ihrer sittlichen und geistigen Entwicklung noch einem Jugendlichen gleichstanden.	14-20	14-17	Straftaten von 14-17jährigen werden vor Jugendgerichten verhandelt, außer bei Tötungsdelikten oder wenn die Tat zusammen mit einem Erwachsenen begangen wurde.
Uneingeschränkte Strafmündigkeit	21	17	Uneingeschränkte Strafmündigkeit
Recht zum Erwerb des Führerscheins für:			Recht zum Erwerb eines vorläufigen Führerscheins für:
– Mofas bis 25 km Geschwindigkeit	15	16	– Mopeds, Behindertenfahrzeuge und einige Traktorentypen
– Mopeds bis 50 km und Leichtkrafträder bis 80 km	16	17	– Motorräder und PKW
– PKW (Kl. 3) und Motorräder bis 20 kW (Kl. 1a)	18	18	– LKW und Kleinbusse bis 16 Personen
– Motorräder (Kl. 1), vorausgesetzt, man besitzt den Führerschein 1a seit mindestens 2 Jahren	20		
– LKW (Kl. 2)	21	21	– Schwerlaster und Busse über 16 Personen
Erlaubnis zur Vollzeitbeschäftigung	15*/16	16	Erlaubnis zur Vollzeitbeschäftigung

* abhängig von der Dauer der Vollzeitschulpflicht in den einzelnen Ländern

Age Limits Relevant to Young People

Federal Republic of Germany	Age	Age	United Kingdom
Compulsory education (school attendance) begins.	6	5	Compulsory education begins (full-time education at school or elsewhere).
		U films	Universal films: Admittance to all ages
May see films released for this age group	6,12	PG films	Parental guidance: Children do not have to to be accompanied by an adult, viewing is left to the parents' discretion
May see films released for this age group	16,18	15,18	Admittance only to persons above the respective age group
May vote and stand for election to the youth representation in the works council	14	–	No youth representation in UK
Limited criminal responsibility	14	10-14	Limited criminal responsibility depending upon awareness of the seriousness of the offence
14-18-year-olds are tried in juvenile courts only; 18-21-year-olds likewise if their moral and intellectual development was that of a young person at the time of the offence.	14-20	14-17	14-17-year-olds are tried in juvenile courts unless charged with homicide or when jointly charged whith a person aged over 17.
May obtain a licence to drive:			May obtain a provisional licence to drive:
– Mofas (motor-driven bicycles) up to a speed limit of 25 km/ph	15	16	– mopeds, invalid carriages and certain types of tractors
– mopeds up to a speed limit of 50 km/ph and light motorbikes up to a speed limit of 80 km/ph	16	17	– motorbikes and cars
– cars and motorbikes up to 20 kw	18	18	– public service vehicles and buses seating a maximum of 16 persons
– motorbikes (provided one has had a licence for a 20 kw bike for at least 2 years)	20	21	– lorries and buses with more than 16 seats
– lorries	21	16	May begin full-time work
May begin full-time work	15*		

* depending on the age at which compulsory full-time education (differs from one *Land* to the other) ended

Altersgrenzen im Jugendbereich

Bundesrepublik Deutschland	Alter	Alter	Vereinigtes Königreich
Nachtschichten erlaubt	18	16	Nachtschichten erlaubt
Rauchen in der Öffentlichkeit gestattet	16	16	Kauf von Tabakwaren und Rauchen in der Öffentlichkeit erlaubt
Abgabe alkoholischer Getränke, außer Branntwein, an Jugendliche ab 16 Jahren gestattet	16	18	Barbesuch und Konsum von Alkohol erlaubt
Erlaubnis zur Anwesenheit bei öffentlichen Tanzveranstaltungen bis 24.00 Uhr	16	–	
Heirat mit Zustimmung des Vormundschaftsgerichtes ist möglich, wenn der künftige Gatte volljährig ist.	16	16	Befugnis zur Heirat mit Zustimmung der Eltern oder des zuständigen Sozialgerichts
Pflicht zum Besitz eines Personalausweises	16	16	Ende der Eintragung im Paß der Eltern (Im UK besteht keine Pflicht zum Besitz eines Personalausweises.)
Jungen dürfen sich mit Einwilligung der Eltern zum Grundwehrdienst melden.	17	16	Jungen dürfen mit Einwilligung der Eltern Mitglied der Streitkräfte werden
Kein Wehrdienst für Mädchen und Frauen	–	17	Mädchen dürfen mit Einwilligung der Eltern Mitglied der Streitkräfte werden
Beginn der Wehrpflicht für Männer	18	18	Jungen und Mädchen können ohne Erlaubnis der Eltern Mitglied der Streitkräfte werden (keine Wehrpflicht im UK).
Sexuelle Mündigkeit: keine feste Altersgrenze Strafbar ist für Erwachsene: 1. sexuelle Handlungen an einem Kind vorzunehmen oder durch ein Kind an sich vornehmen zu lassen; 2. Verführung von Mädchen unter 16 Jahren zum Beischlaf; 3. sexueller Mißbrauch von Schutzbefohlenen unter 18 Jahren.		16	Sexuelle Mündigkeit für beide Geschlechter. Jeder, der sexuelle Handlungen mit Minderjährigen unter 16 Jahren vornimmt, kann wegen Unzucht angeklagt werden.
Recht, einer Gewerkschaft beizutreten * sobald eine Lehre oder ein Arbeitsverhältnis begonnen wurde (15 oder 16)	*	16	Recht, einer Gewerkschaft beizutreten

Age Limits Relevant to Young People

Federal Republic of Germany	Age	Age	United Kingdom
May work at nights	18	16	May work at nights
May smoke in public	16	16	May buy tobacco and smoke in public
Permission to sell alcoholic drinks (except for spirits) to young persons aged 16 and over	16	18	May enter a bar and buy alcoholic drinks
May attend public dances until 24.00 hrs	16	–	
May marry with the consent of the guardianship court, provided the partner is of age	16	16	May marry with the consent of parents or of the civil court
Must hold an identity card	16	16	Can no longer be included on parents' passport (In the UK there is no liability to hold an identity card.)
Boys may join the Armed Forces with their parents' consent.	17	16	Boys may join the Armed Forces with their parents' permission.
No military service for girls and women		17	Girls may join the Armed Forces with their parents' permission.
Men are liable for military service.	18	18	Boys and girls may join the Armed Forces without parental permission (no liability for military service in the UK).
Age of sexual consent: No fixed age limit It is punishable by law for an adult to 1) perform a sexual act on a child or to make a child perform a sexual act on himself 2) induce girls under 16 to have sexual intercourse 3) to involve persons below 18 under one's custody in a sexual activity.		16	Age of sexual consent for both sexes; anyone involved in sexual activity with a person under 16 can be charged with indecent assault.
May join a trade union * as soon as one begins an apprenticeship training or starts work	*	16	May join a trade union

Altersgrenzen im Jugendbereich

Bundesrepublik Deutschland	Alter	Alter	Vereinigtes Königreich
Ende der Schulpflicht	18	16	Ende der Unterrichtspflicht
Volljährigkeit	18	18	Volljährigkeit
Aktives und passives Wahlrecht	18	18	Aktives Wahlrecht
		21	Passives Wahlrecht
Ende der Strafbarkeit für Homosexualität zwischen Männern	18	21	Ende der Strafbarkeit für Homosexualität zwischen Männern
Fähigkeit zum Dienst als ehrenamtlicher Richter oder als Schöffe	25	21	Fähigkeit zum Dienst als Schöffe

Altersgruppen im Sinne des Kinder- und Jugendhilfegesetzes

Kind	— wer noch nicht 14 Jahre alt ist
Jugendlicher	— wer 14, aber noch nicht 18 Jahre alt ist
junger Volljähriger	— wer 18, aber noch nicht 27 Jahre alt ist
junger Mensch	— wer noch nicht 27 Jahre alt ist

Age Limits Relevant to Young People

Federal Republic of Germany	Age	Age	United Kingdom
End of compulsory attendance at school	18	16	End of compulsory education
Age of majority	18	18	Age of majority
May vote and stand for election to local, *Land* and Federal parliaments	18	18	May vote
		21	May stand for election to local government and Parliament
Homosexual activity between men is no longer illegal.	18	21	Homosexual activity in private, between consenting men, is no longer illegal.
May be called for jury service and serve as a lay magistrate	25	21	May be called for jury service

The Child and Youth Services Act provides for the following age groups:

Kind	—	child (person under 14 years of age)
Jugendlicher	—	young person (person 14 and over, but not yet 18 years old)
junger Volljähriger	—	young adult (person 18 and over, but not yet 27 years old)
junger Mensch	—	person not yet 27 years old, youth population

Literatur
Bibliography

Aktuell — Das Lexikon der Gegenwart. Dortmund: Chronik Verlag in der Harenberg Kommunkation Verlags- und Mediengesellschaft, 1984.

Bellebaum, A.: Soziologie der modernen Gesellschaft. Hamburg, 1978.

Böhm, Winfried: Wörterbuch der Pädagogik. 12., neuverf. Auflage. Stuttgart: Kröner, 1982.

BP Kursbuch Deutschland 85/86. München: Goldmann, 1985.

The British Council (Hg.): The British Council Report 1986/87. London, 1987.

Bundesanstalt für Arbeit (Hg.): Beruf Aktuell. Für Schulabgänger. Ausgaben 1984 u. 1986. Nürnberg: werbestudio form + graphik.

Bundesanstalt für Arbeit (Hg.): Die Bundesanstalt für Arbeit stellt sich vor. Nürnberg, 1979.

Der Bundesminister für Jugend, Familie, Frauen und Gesundheit (Hg.): Sechster Jahresbericht 1984. Verbesserung der Chancengleichheit von Mädchen in der Bundesrepublik Deutschland. Deutscher Bundestag. 10. Wahlperiode. Drucksache 10/1007. Bonn, 1984.

Der Bundesminster für Jugend, Familie, Frauen und Gesundheit (Hg.): Siebter Jugendbericht 1986. Jugendhilfe und Familie — die Entwicklung familienunterstützender Leistungen der Jugendhilfe und ihre Perspektiven. Deutscher Bundestag. 10. Wahlperiode. Drucksache 10/6730. Bonn, 1986.

Der Bundesminister für Jugend, Familie, Frauen und Gesundheit (Hg.): Achter Jugendbericht 1990. Bericht über Bestrebungen und Leistungen der Jugendhilfe. Deutscher Bundestag. 11. Wahlperiode. Drucksache 11/6576. Bonn, 1990.

Der Bundesminister für Jugend, Familie, Frauen und Gesundheit. Richtlinien für den Bundesjugendplan (Erlaß v. 6.11.85). In: Gemeinsames Ministerialblatt, hg. v. Bundesminister des Innern, 36. Jg., Nr. 32 v. 11. Dez. 1985.

Bundesministerium für Arbeit und Sozialordnung (Hg.): Behinderte und Rehabilitation. 1984.

Central Council for Education and Training in Social Work (CCETSW) (Hg.): Care for Tomorrow. The Case for Reform of Education and Training for Social Workers and Other Care Staff. October 1987.

Central Council for Education and Training in Social Work (CCETSW) (Hg.): How to qualify for Social Work. CCETSW Handbook 9.3. London, 1990.

Central Office of Information (Hg.): Carnegy-Report. Training for Change. Edinburgh: SCEC, 1984.

Central Office of Information (Hg.): Britain 1984. An Official Handbook. London, 1984.

Central Office of Information (Hg.): Action for jobs. Pamphlet No. PL 782. London, 1982.

Central Office of Information (Hg.): Local Government in Britain. Pamphlet No. 12/RP/84. London, 1984.

Central Office of Information (Hg.): Social Welfare in Britain. Pamphlet No. 70/85. London, 1985.

Central Office of Information (Hg.): The Youth Service in Britain. Pamphlet No. 271/86. London, 1986.

Coote, Anna and Tess Gill: Women's Rights. A Practical Guide. Third education. Penguin, 1981.

Council for Education and Training in Youth and Community Work (CETYCW) (Hg.): Initial Training Courses in Youth and Community Work. Leicester, 1989.

Creifelds, Carl (Hg.): Rechtswörterbuch, 6., neubearb. Auflage. München: Beck, 1981.

Department of Education and Science (Hg.): Grants to Students. A Brief Guide 1988/ 89. London, 1988.

Department of Education and Science and Welsh Office (Hg.): Drug Misuse and the Young. A Guide for Teachers and Youth Workers. 1985.

Deutscher Verein für öffentliche und private Fürsorge (Hg.): Fachlexikon der sozialen Arbeit. 2. Auflage. Stuttgart, Berlin, Köln, Mainz: Kohlhammer, 1986.

Deutsch-Französisches Jugendwerk (Hg.): Lexique pour les Rencontres des Jeunes. Allemand — Français. L'Environnement Social des Jeunes. Neuwied, Darmstadt: Luchterhand, 1979.

Education in Britain 1986. COOJ No. 15/85 sowie neuere Ausgaben.

Employment Department, OECD (Hg.): Industry Committee Annual Review of Industrial Policies. 17. Jan. 1989.

Experience and Participation. Report of the Review Group on the Youth Service in England. London: HMSO, 1982.

Eyferth, H./Otto, H.-U./Thiersch, H. (Hg.): Handbuch zur Sozialarbeit/Sozialpädagogik. Neuwied, Darmstadt, 1984.

Family Welfare Association (Hg.): Guide to the Social Services. 1989.

Flamm, Franz: Sozialwesen und soziale Arbeit in der Bundesrepublik Deutschland. 3., neubearb. und erw. Auflage. Frankfurt/Main: Eigenverlag des Deutschen Vereins für öffentliche und private Fürsorge, 1980.

Haack, F.-W.: Die neuen Jugendreligionen. München, 1977.

Halsbury's Laws of England. Fourth edition. London: Butterworth Law Publishers Ltd., ersch. fortlfd.

Hohm, Hartmut: Rehabilitation. In: Wörterbuch Soziale Arbeit, hg. v. Dieter Kreft u. Ingrid Mielenz. 2. Auflage. Weinheim, Basel: Beltz, 1983.

Institute for the Study of Drug Dependence (Hg.): Drug Abuse Briefing. 1987.

Internationaler Jugendaustausch- und Besucherdienst der Bundesrepublik Deutschland (Hg.): Verbände und Institutionen der Jugendarbeit in der Bundesrepublik Deutschland. Ein Überblick. München: Juventa, 1980.

Inter Nationes (Hg.): Das Schulwesen in der Bundesrepublik Deutschland. BW 1984, Nr. 10/11.

Klafki, W.: Erziehungsstile. In: Funkkolleg Erziehungswissenschaft. Bd. 1. Frankfurt, 1975.

Kreft, Dieter/Ingrid Mielenz (Hg.): Wörterbuch Soziale Arbeit. Aufgaben, Praxisfelder, Begriffe und Methoden der Sozialarbeit und Sozialpädagogik. 2. Auflage. Weinheim, Basel: Beltz, 1983.

Der Kultusminister des Landes Nordrhein-Westfalen (Hg.): Der Kultusminister informiert. Die Schulreformen in der Sekundarstufe I. Hauptschule. Realschule. Gymnasium. Gesamtschule. (In englischer Sprache). Bochum: Kamp, 1986.

Landesarbeitsamt Nordrhein-Westfalen (Hg.): Förderungsmöglichkeiten für Berufsanfänger. 1984.

Landeszentrale für Politische Bildung Baden-Württemberg (Hg.): Jugend — Jugendprobleme — Jugendprotest. Stuttgart, 1982.

Ministerium für Soziales, Gesundheit und Sport (Hg.): Jugendliche in destruktiven religiösen Gruppen. Bericht der Landesregierung Rheinland-Pfalz über die sogenannten neuen Jugendreligionen. Mainz, 1979.

Morley & Whitey's Law Dictionnary. Ninth edition by John B. Saunders. London: Butterworth, 1977.

Mühlum, A.: Sozialpädagogik und Sozialarbeit. Frankfurt: Deutscher Verein, 1981.

National Association of Youth and Community Education Officers (NAYCEO). Policy Statement. 1987.

National Youth Bureau (Hg.): Detached Youth Work. 1981.

Opaschowski, H. (Hg.): Freizeit als gesellschaftliche Aufgabe. Düsseldorf, 1976.

Runde, P.: Rehabilitation. In: Eyferth, H./Otto, H.-U./Thiersch, H. (Hg.): Handbuch zur Sozialarbeit/Sozialpädagogik. Neuwied, Darmstadt, 1984.

Scholz, G.: Führungstil. In: Fachlexikon der sozialen Abeit, hg. v. Deutschen Verein für öffentliche und private Fürsorge. 2. Auflage. Stuttgart, Berlin, Köln, Mainz: Kohlhammer, 1986.

The Scottish Office, Department of Education and Science (Hg.): Education in Britain. COI 15/85, S. 155 – 171.

Seibel, Friedrich Wilhelm: Ausbildung für soziale Berufe. Ein Ländervergleich. In: Bellebaum, A., u.a. (Hg.): Helfen und helfende Berufe als soziale Kontrolle. Opladen: Westdeutscher Verlag, 1985, S. 211 – 235.

Specht, W.: Mobile Jugendarbeit. In: Eyferth, H./Otto, H.-U./Thiersch, H. (Hg.): Handbuch zur Sozialarbeit/Sozialpädagogik. Neuwied, Darmstadt, 1984, S. 549 – 557.

Tatsachen über Deutschland. Die Bundesrepublik Deutschland. Hg. v. Lexikon-Institut Bertelsmann. 6., neubearb. Auflage. Gütersloh, 1989.

Wissmann, Matthias/R. Hauck (Hg.): Jugendprotest im demokratischen Staat. Enquête-Kommission des Deutschen Bundestages. Stuttgart, 1983.

Wulf, Christoph (Hg.): Wörterbuch der Erziehung. 6. Auflage. München: Piper, 1984.

Youth Exchange Centre (Hg.): Youth Exchange Centre. A Brief Summary. London, o. J.